2016
青岛统计年鉴

QINGDAO STATISTICAL YEARBOOK

（总 第37期 VOL.37）

青 岛 市 统 计 局
国家统计局青岛调查队 编
QINGDAO MUNICIPAL STATISTICS BUREAU
NBS SURVEY OFFICE IN QINGDAO

中国统计出版社
China Statistics Press

图书在版编目(CIP)数据

青岛统计年鉴. 2016 / 青岛市统计局, 国家统计局青岛调查队编. -- 北京 : 中国统计出版社, 2016.8
ISBN 978-7-5037-7851-3

Ⅰ. ①青… Ⅱ. ①青… ②国… Ⅲ. ①统计资料－青岛市－2016－年鉴 Ⅳ. ①C832.523-54

中国版本图书馆CIP数据核字(2016)第161731号

青岛统计年鉴-2016

作　　者/ 青岛市统计局 国家统计局青岛调查队
责任编辑/ 陈越月
装帧设计/ 青岛天之韵广告文化传播有限公司
出版发行/ 中国统计出版社
地　　址/ 北京市丰台区西三环南路甲6号　邮政编码/ 100073
电　　话/ 邮购（010）63376909　书店（010）68783171
网　　址/ http://csp.stats.gov.cn
印　　刷/ 青岛国彩印刷有限公司
经　　销/ 新华书店
开　　本/ 890mmx1240mm 1/16
字　　数/ 1100千字
印　　张/ 25.25
版　　别/ 2016年8月第 1 版
版　　次/ 2016年8月第 1 次印刷
定　　价/ 280.00元

如有印装差错，由本社发行部调换。

全市生产总值构成（%）

Composition Of Gross Domestic Product（%）

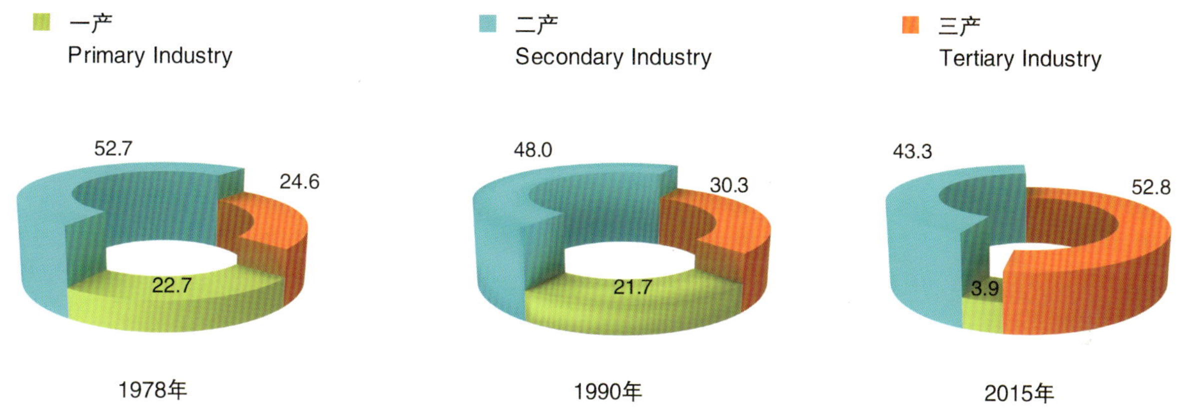

全市生产总值（亿元）

Gross Domestic Product (100 million yuan)

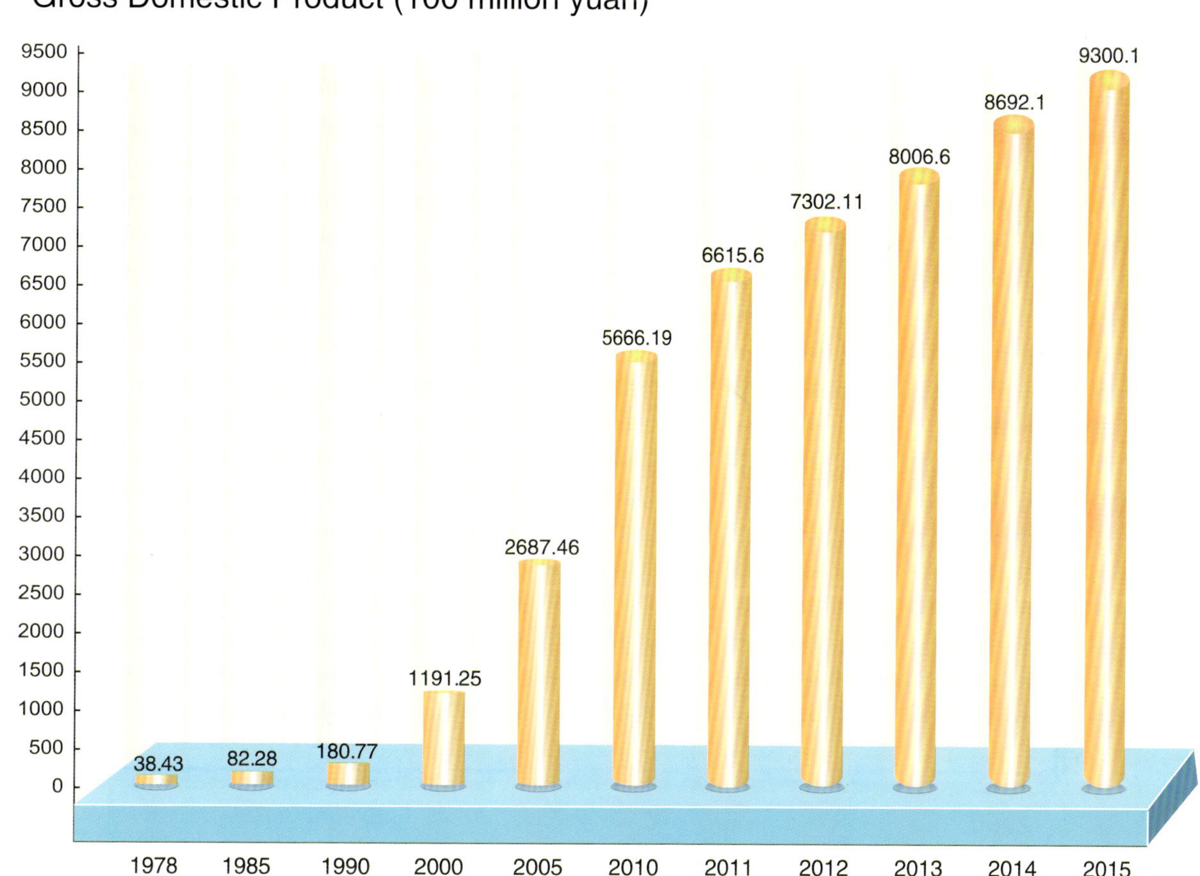

农林牧渔业总产值（亿元）
Gross Output Value Of Agriculture (100 million yuan)

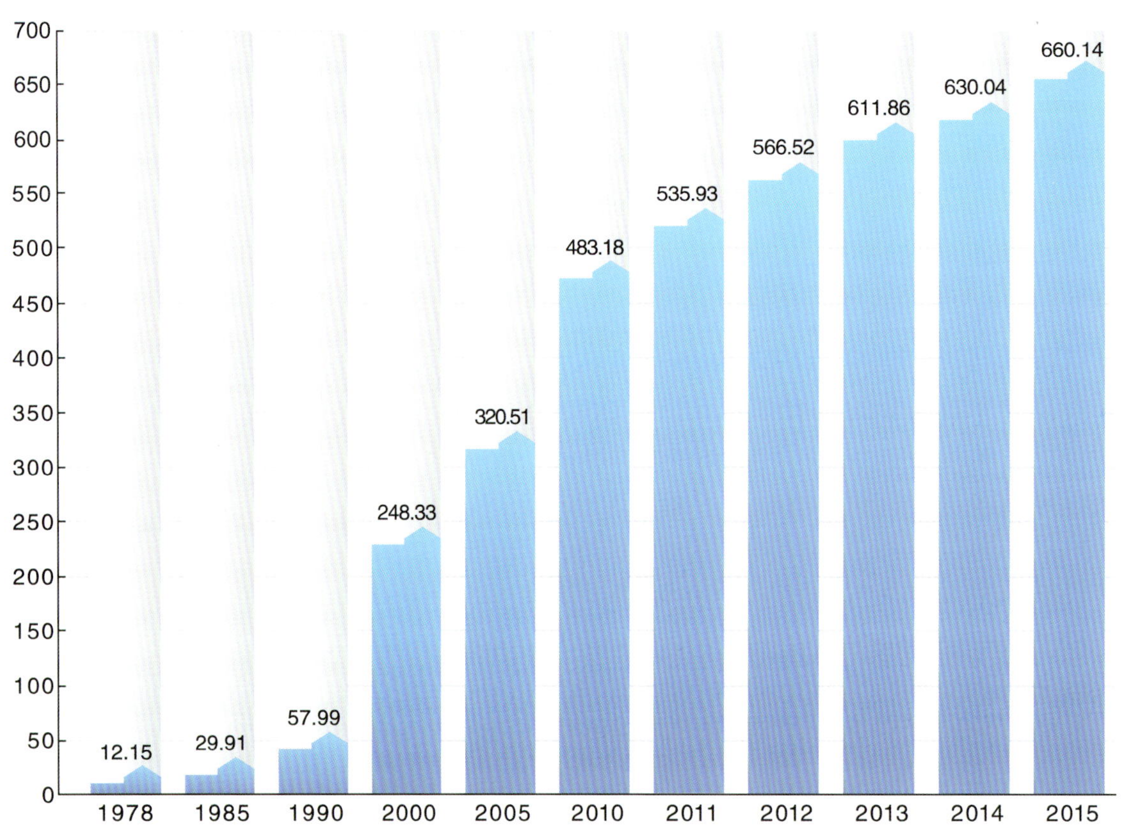

主要农产品产量（万吨）
Output Of Farm Products (10000 tons)

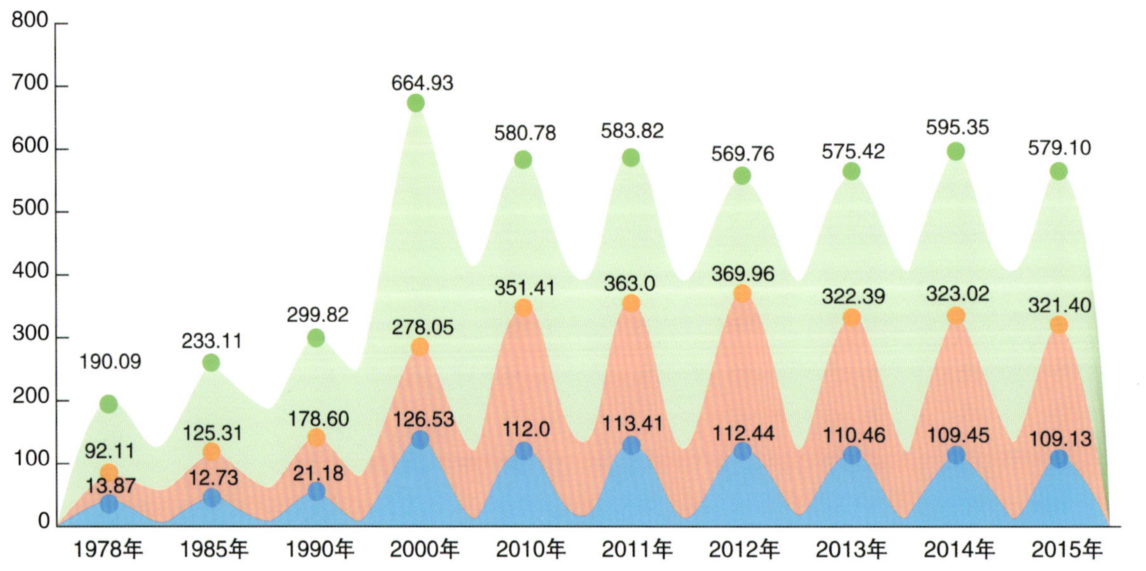

工业总产值（亿元）

Gross Industrial Output Value (100 million yuan)

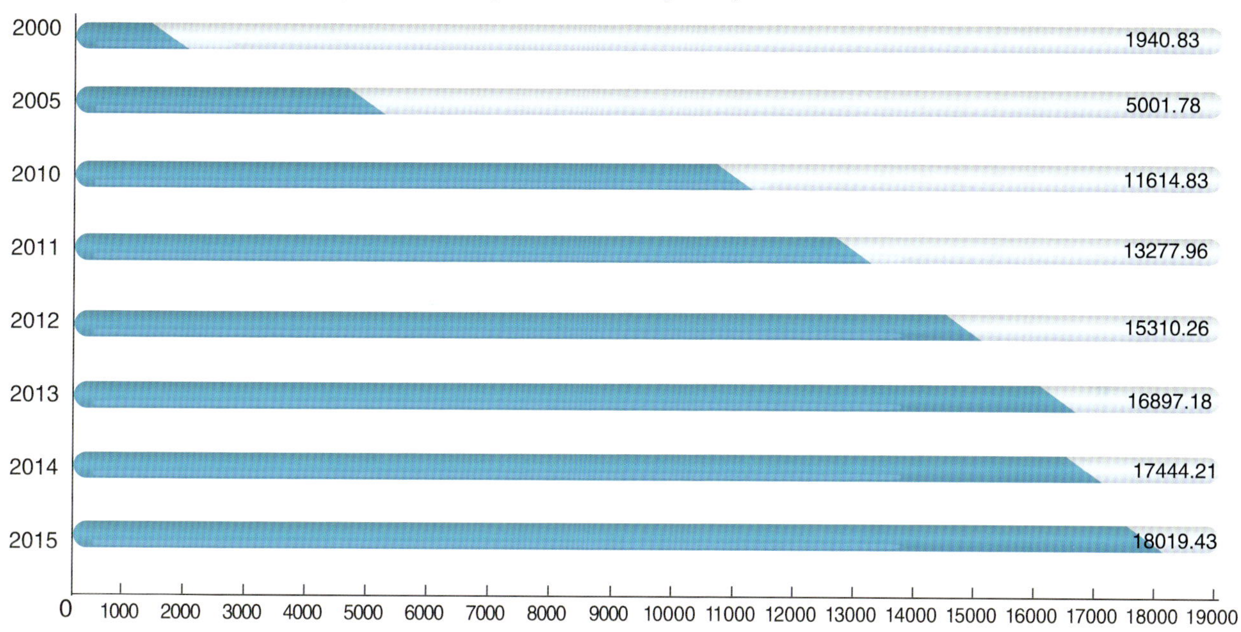

规模以上工业实现利润总额（亿元）

The Total Profits Made By The Industries Above The Designated Size (100 million yuan)

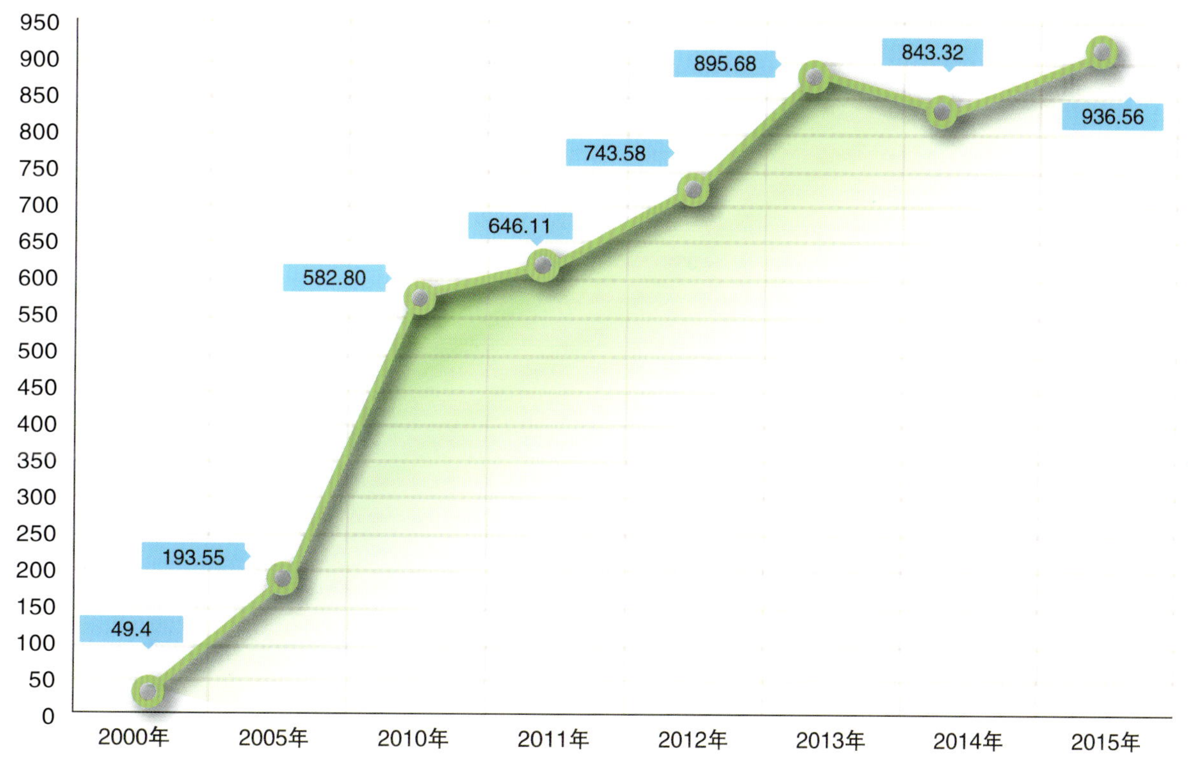

固定资产投资（亿元）

Investment In Fixed Assets (100 million yuan)

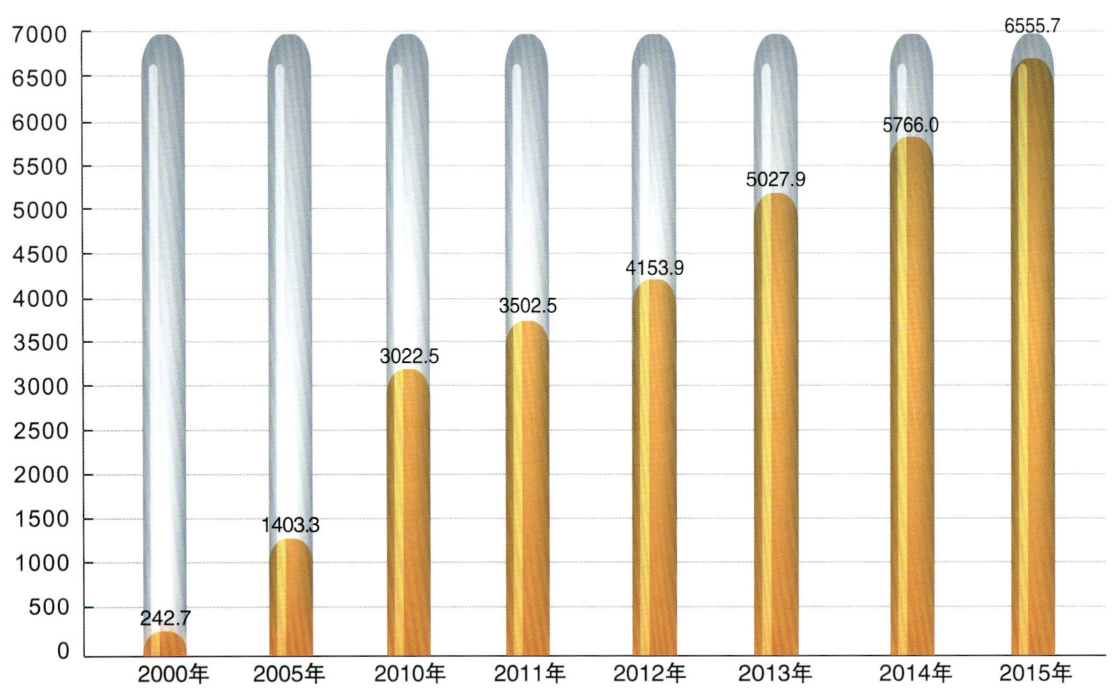

房地产开发投资（亿元）、房屋销售面积（万平方米）

Investment In Real Estate Development (100 million yuan)，Floor Space Of Commercial Buildings Sold (10000 sq.m)

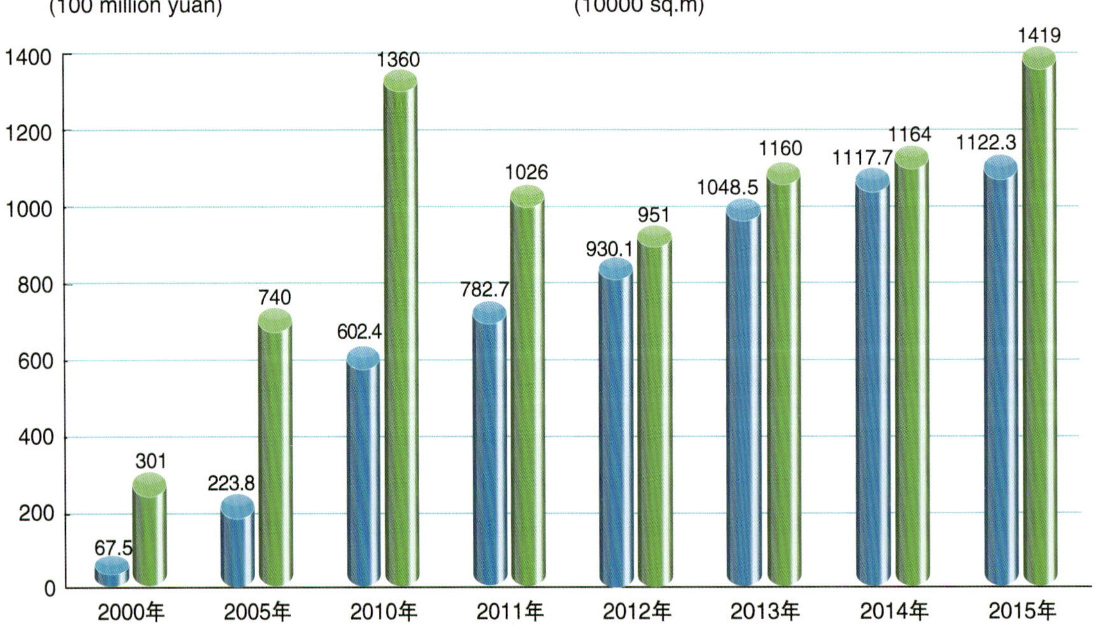

消费构成（%）(2015年)
2015 Composition Of Consumption (%)

社会消费品零售总额（亿元）
Total Retail Sales Of Consumer Goods(100 million yuan)

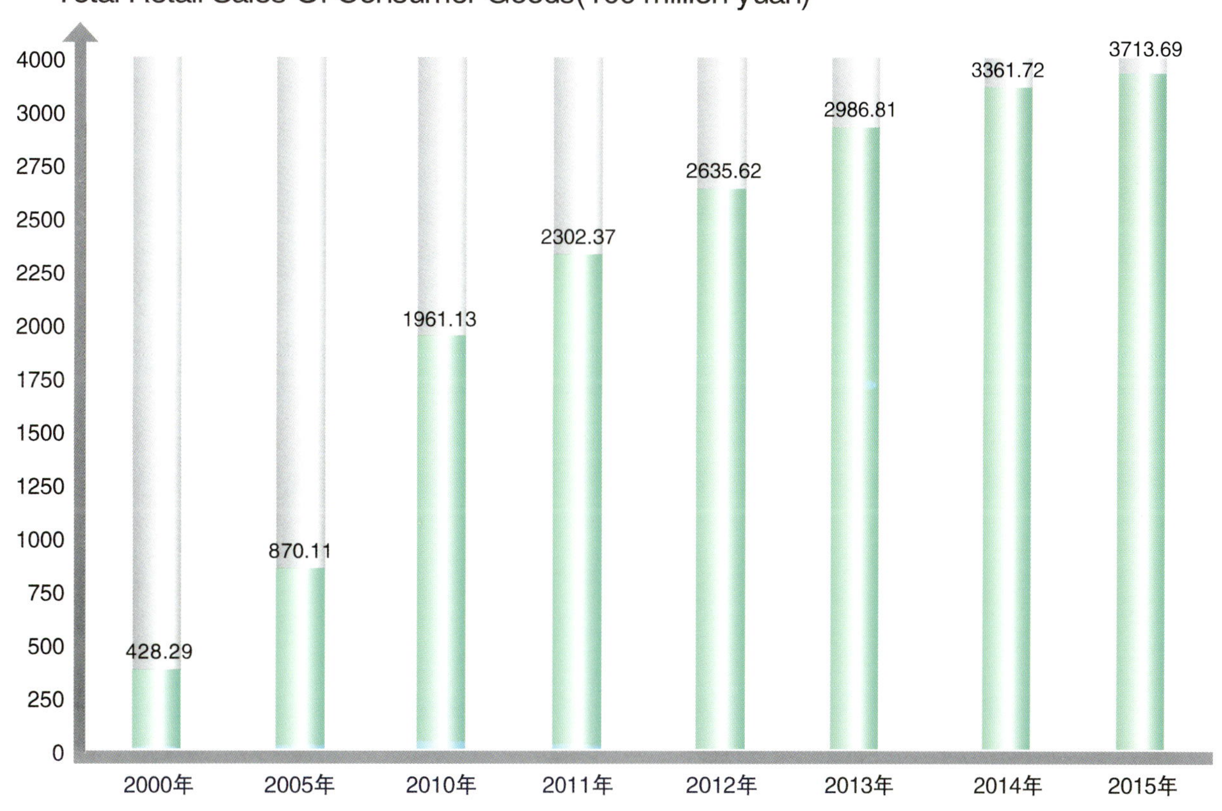

进出口总额（亿美元）
Total Imports And Exports (100 million USD)

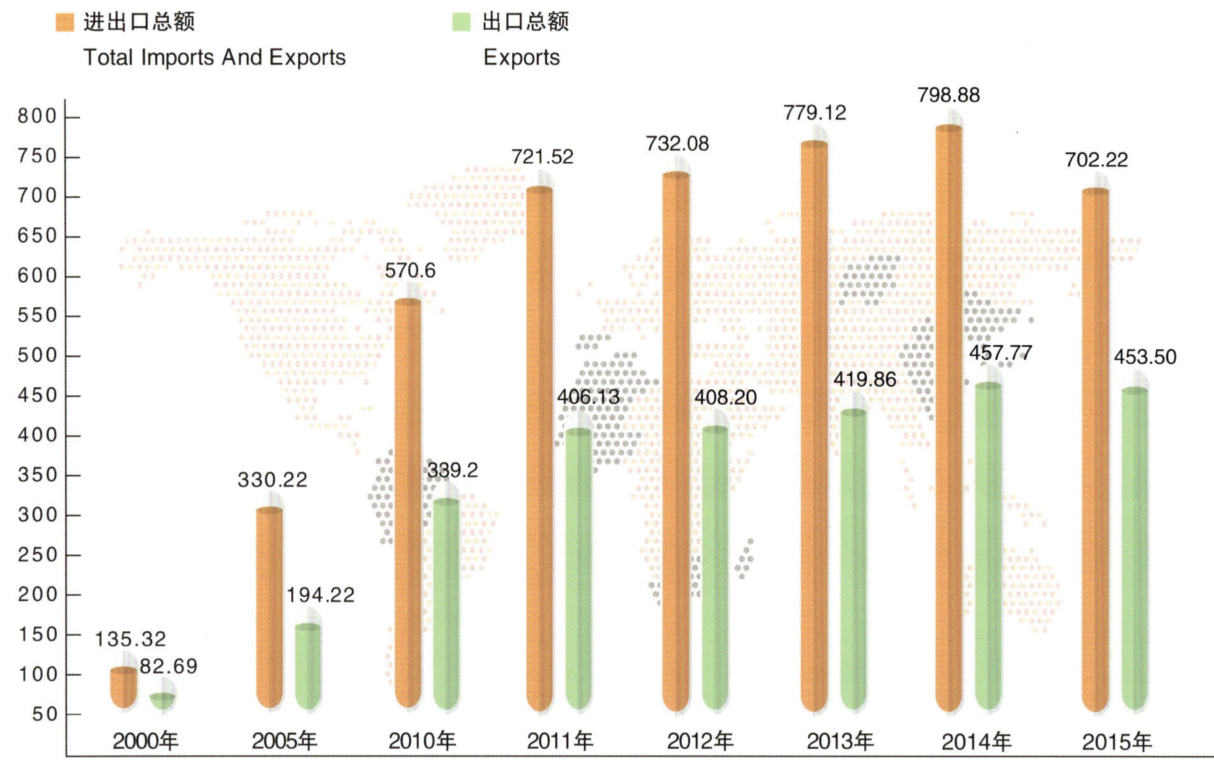

旅游总人数（万人次）
Number Of Tourists (10000 person-times)

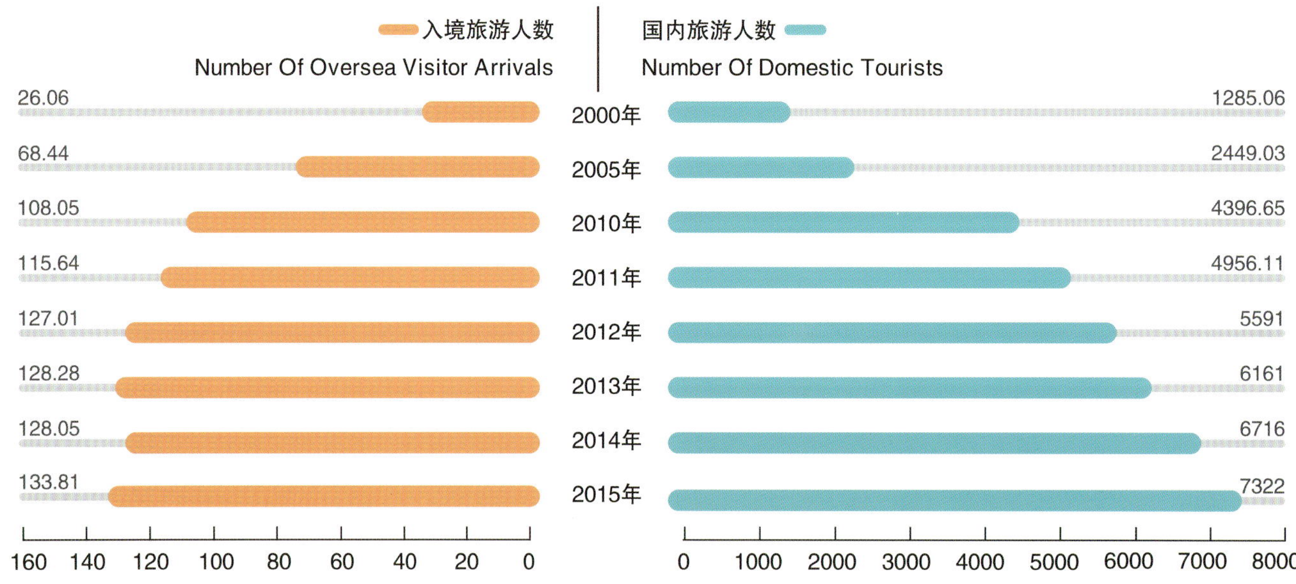

地方财政收入（亿元）

Revenue Of Local Government Finance (100 million yuan)

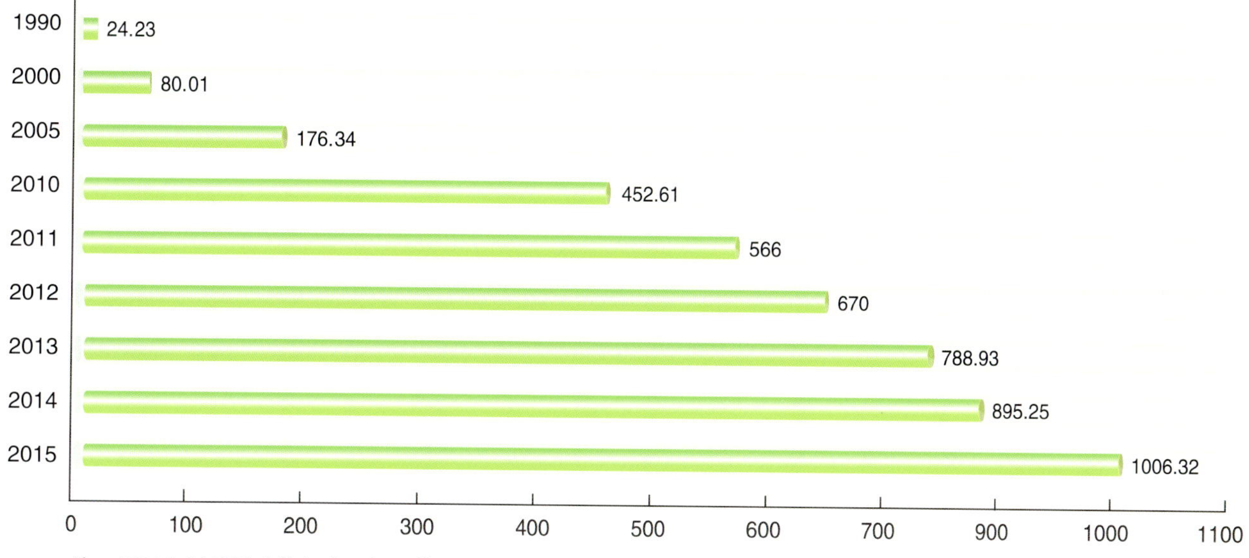

注：2002年以后财政收入为一般预算收入数。

Note:Since 2002,revenue of government finance refers to general budgetary revenue.

金融机构年末人民币存贷款余额（亿元）

Year-end Savings Deposits And Loans Of Financial Institution(RMB) (100 million yuan)

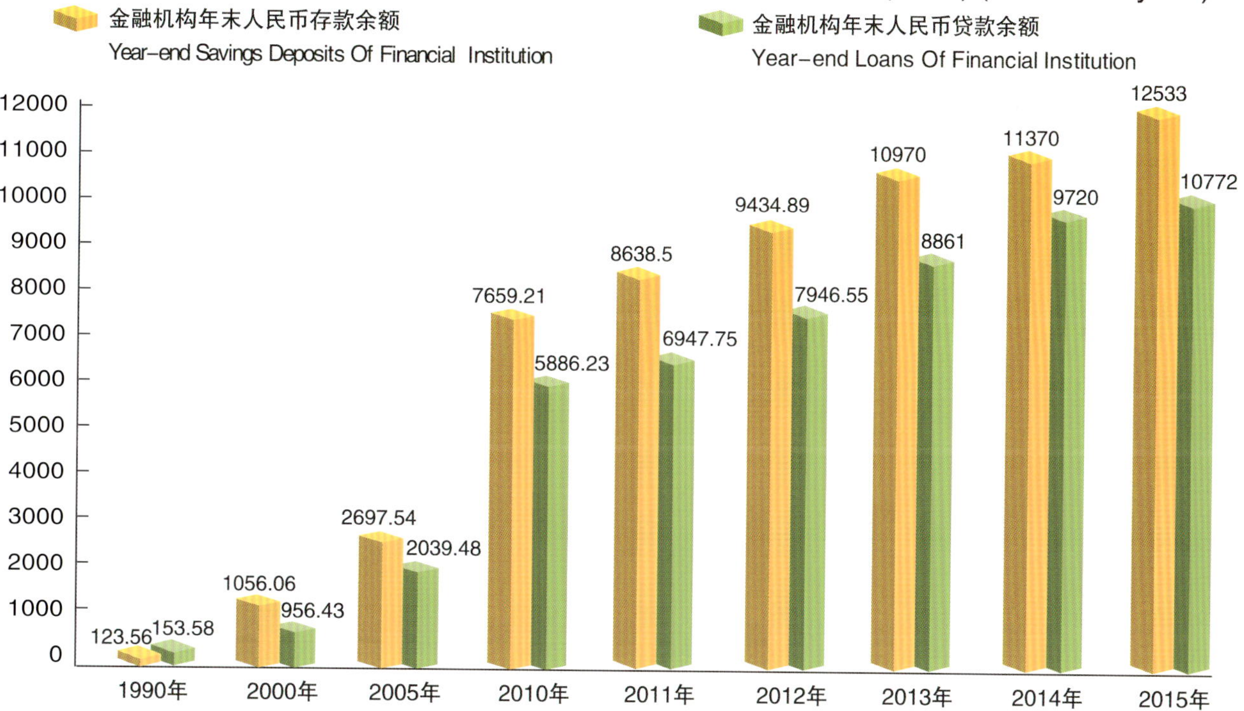

社会从业人数(万人)

Social Employment(10000 persons)

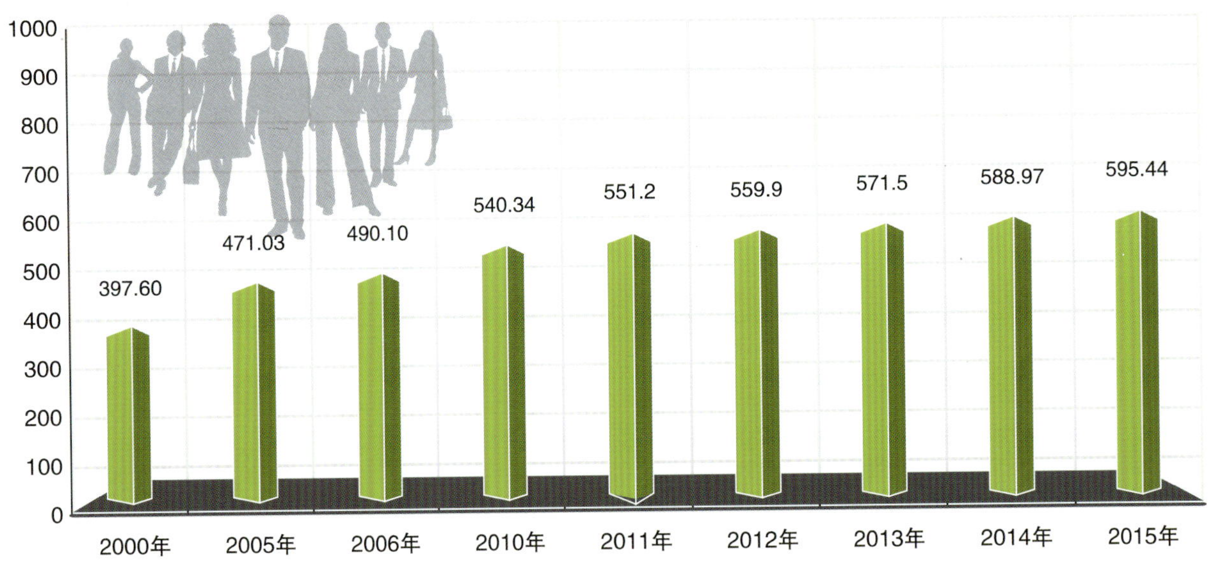

在岗职工平均工资(元)

Average Wage Of Employed Staff And Workers(yuan)

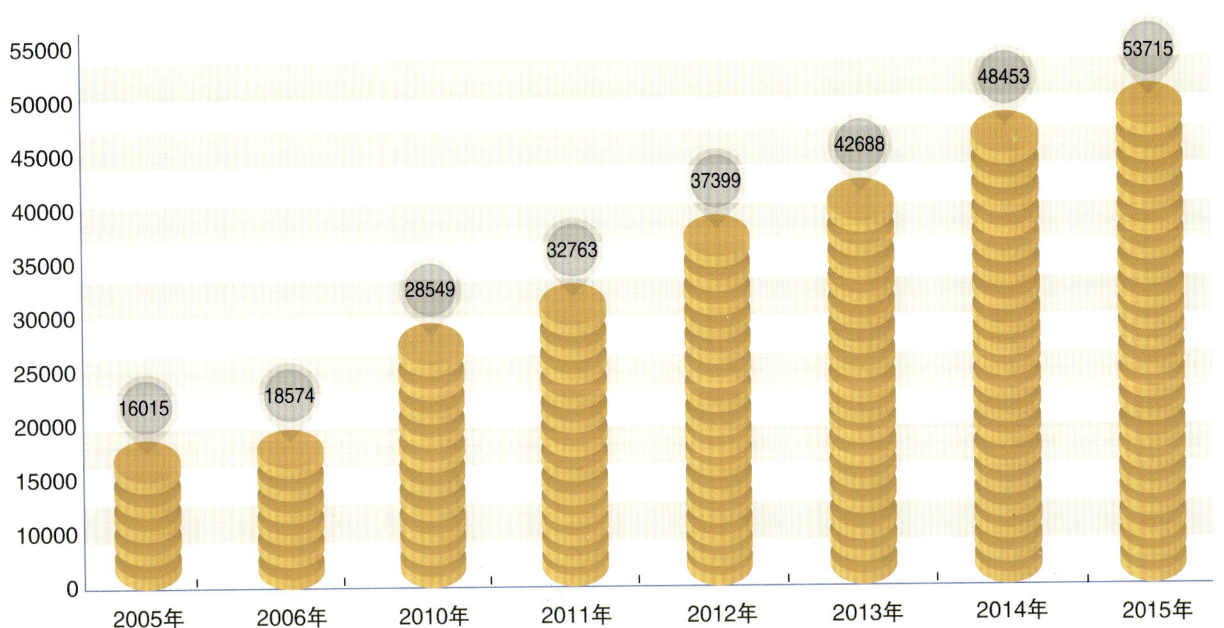

居民消费价格指数(上年=100)

Consumer Price Indices(preceding year=100)

商品零售价格指数(上年=100)

Retail Price Indices(preceding year=100)

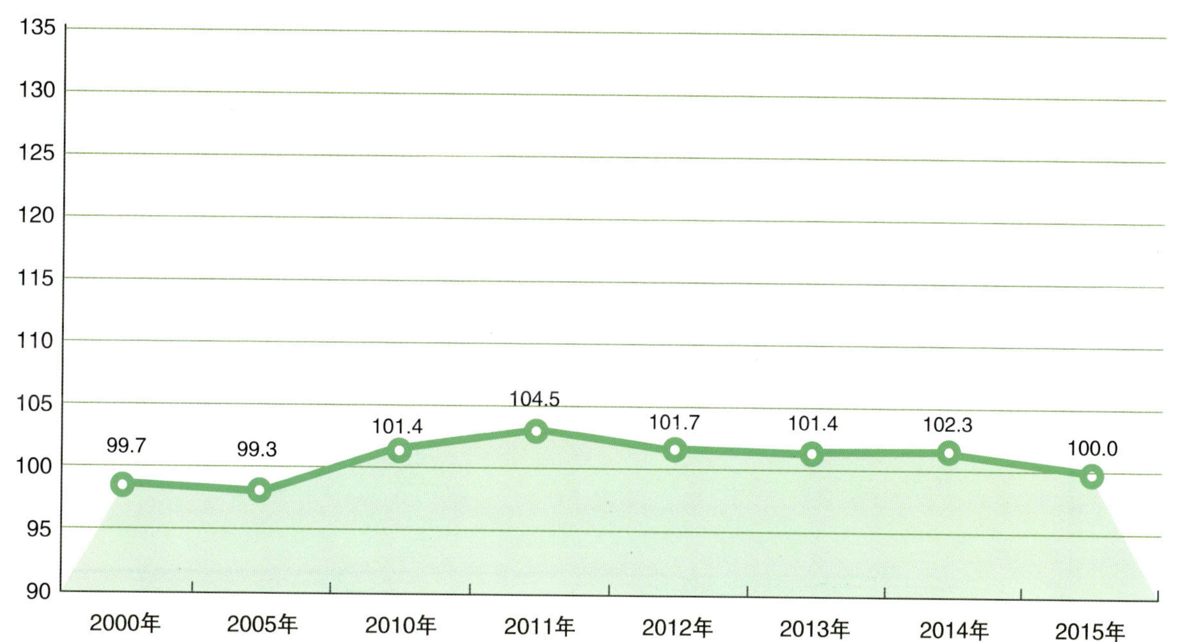

城市建成区面积、铺装道路面积

Developed Area Of the City And Area Of Roads

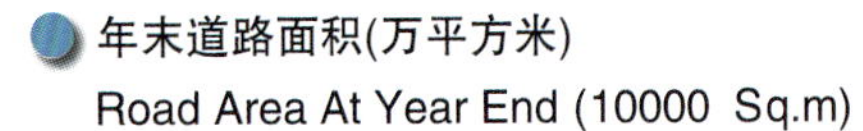

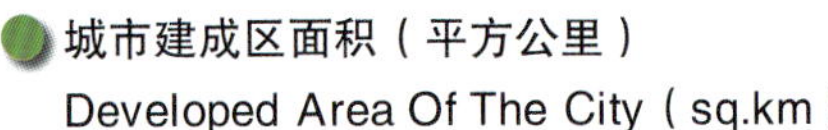

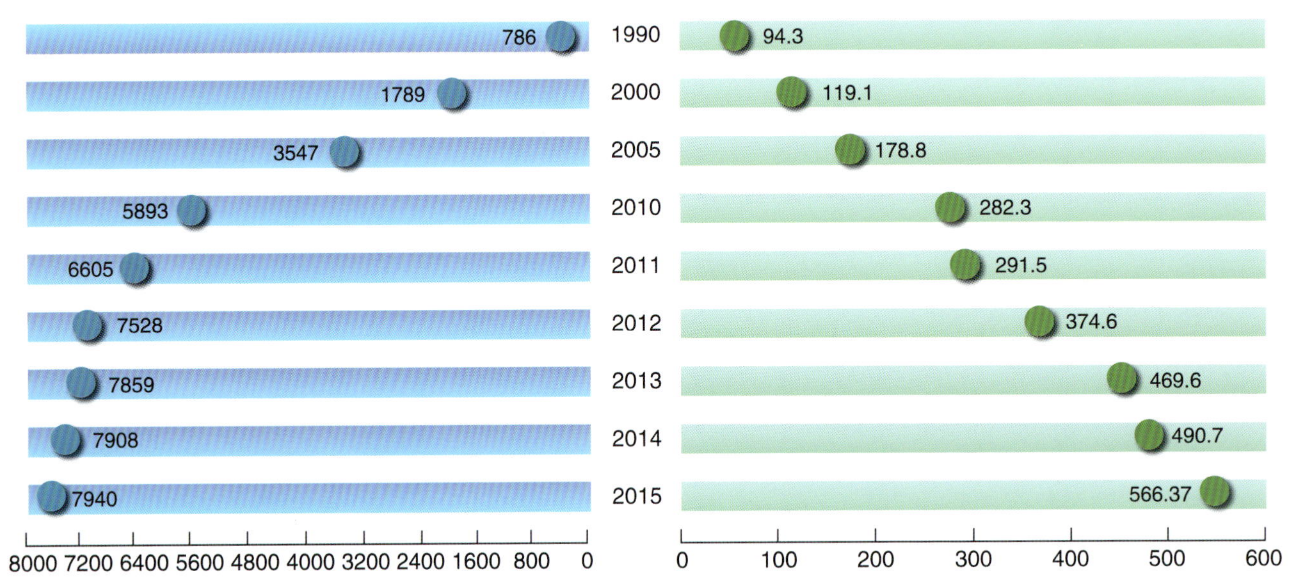

建成区绿化覆盖率（%）

Green Coverage Rate Of Developed Area(%)

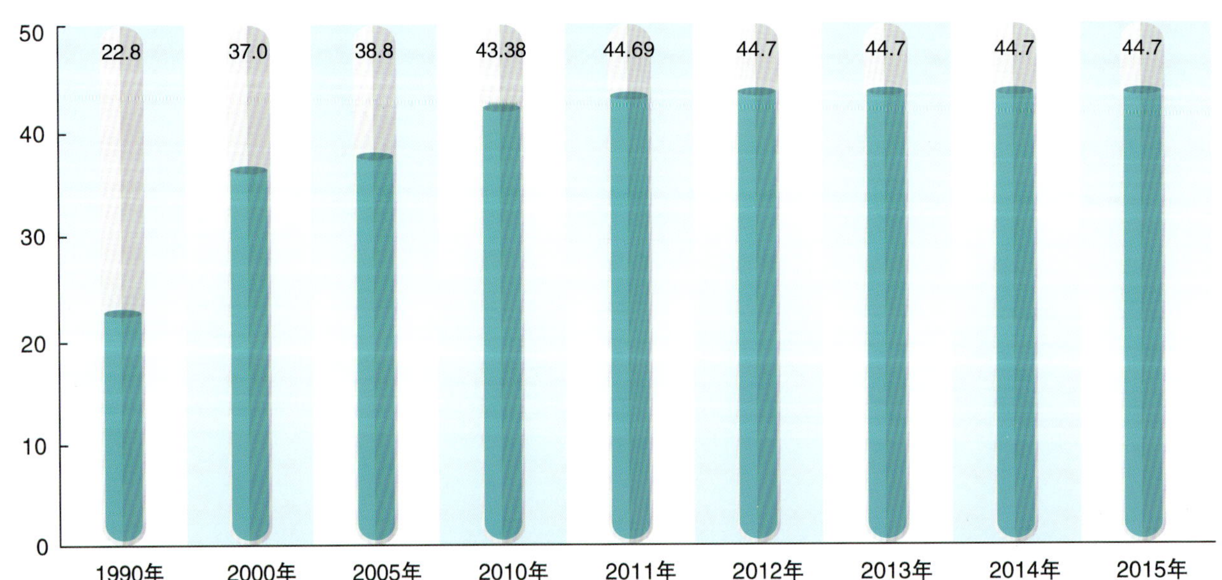

医疗卫生机构（个）Health Care Institutions(unit)

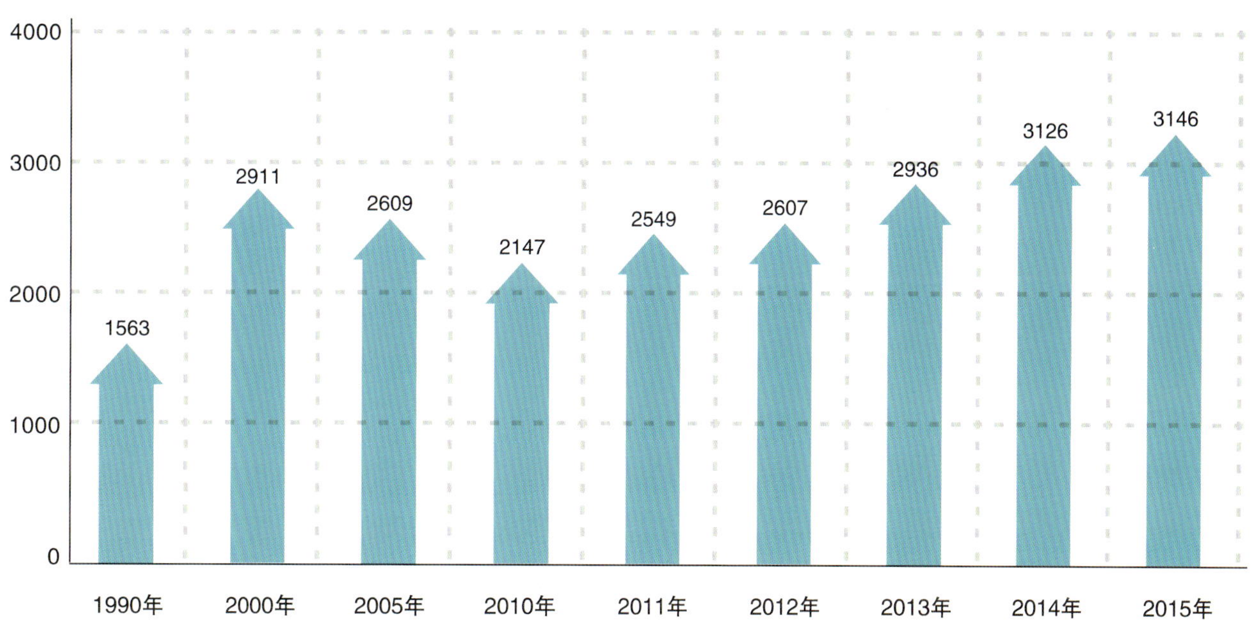

普通高校在校人数（万人）

Students Enrollment Of Regular Institutions Of Higher Education(10000 persons)

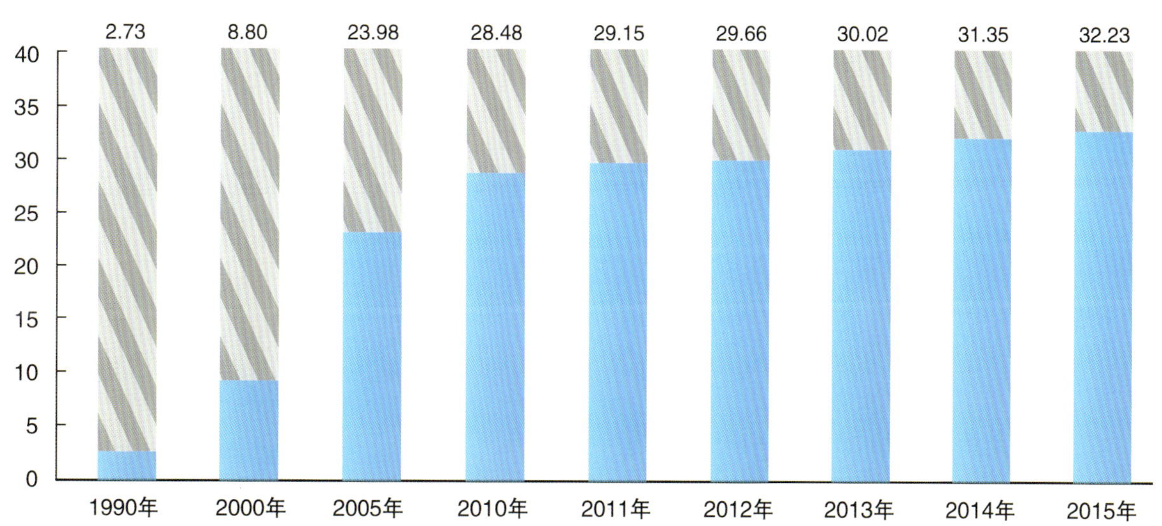

编辑委员会

EDITORIAL BOARD

编者说明

一、《青岛统计年鉴 -2016》是一部全面反映青岛市国民经济和社会发展情况、信息高度密集的资料工具书。

二、《青岛统计年鉴 -2016》共包括发展成果图、统计公报、统计表、附录四大部分。

统计表部分收录了 2015 年青岛市经济和社会等各方面的统计数据，以及建国以来重要年份和改革开放以来的主要统计数据，包括：综合，人口，从业人员及职工工资，固定资产投资，对外经济贸易，城市建设、环境保护，能源消耗，财政金融和保险业，价格指数，人民生活，农业，工业，建筑业，运输、邮电，批发和零售业，住宿、餐饮业和旅游，教育、科技和文化，体育、卫生和民政、司法。

为方便读者正确地使用年鉴资料，各篇章前设有《简要说明》，概括介绍各篇主要内容和资料来源；篇末还附有《主要统计指标解释》。

三、本《年鉴》部分历史数据已根据经济普查数据进行了调整，在此之前公布的数据凡与本年鉴数字不符的一律以本年鉴为准。

四、本年鉴中的符号说明：年鉴各表中的“空格”表示该项统计指标数据不足本表最小单位数、数据不详或无该项数据；"#" 表示其中的主要项。

五、《青岛统计年鉴》自公开出版以来，受到社会各界的关心和支持，对于年鉴的内容和编辑工作提出了许多宝贵的意见，对此我们深表谢意。限于我们的水平，欢迎读者继续对年鉴的不足之处给予批评和指正，帮助我们进一步改进年鉴编辑工作，以期更好地为广大读者服务。

《青岛统计年鉴》编委会

2016年8月

Editor's Note

Ⅰ. *Qingdao Statistical Yearbook 2016* is a very important reference book, which reflects various aspects of Qingdao's social and economic development and contains High-density information.

Ⅱ. The yearbook contains the following four parts: achievement graphs, statistic gazette, statistics and appendixes.

Statistics contains all kinds of data on Qingdao's social and economic development in 2015, and data in significant year or data since the beginning of reform and opening up, including: General Survey; Population; Employment and Wages; Investment in Fixed Assets; Foreign Trade; City Construction and Environment Protection; Consumption of Energy; Government Finance ,Financial Intermediation and Insurance; Price; People's Living Conditions; Agriculture; Industry; Construction; Transport, Postal and Telecommunication Services; Wholesale and Retail Trades; Hotels, Catering Services and Tourism; Education, Science and Culture; Sports, Public Health and Civil Affairs, Judicial Affairs; Enterprises Survey.

In brief introduction at the beginning of each chapter, main coverage, data sources and statistical coverage are concerned. Meanwhile explanatory notes on major statistical indicators have been attached for readers to use the data correctly.

Ⅲ. All of the data in the book are in accordance with new administrative division.

Some of the data have been adjusted on the basis of statistics of economic census. In any case the data of this book shall be deemed as the authentic ones.

Ⅳ. Marks in this book:

"(blank)" indicates that the figure is not large enough to be measured with the smallest unit in the table, or the data is not available;

"#" indicates the major items of the total.

Ⅴ. Previous editions of *Qingdao Statistical Yearbook* have won wide acclaim among the readers. We will continue to improve our work. Any comments and suggestions will be appreciated.

Editorial Board
August, 2016

目　　录
CONTENTS

2015 年青岛市国民经济和社会发展统计公报 …… (1)
Statistics Communique Qingdao' s Economic And Social Development During 2015

一、综　　合
Chapter 1. GENERAL SURVEY

简要说明
Brief Introduction
1—1 行政区划(2015 年底) …… (31)
Administrative Division(End of 2015)
1—2 气象情况(2015 年) …… (32)
Meteorology(2015)
1—3 市区分月气象情况(2015 年) …… (32)
Monthly Meteorology of Urban Area(2015)
1—4 各部门机构数(2015 年底) …… (33)
Grass-Roots Units in Various Sectors(End of 2015)
1—5 按行业分法人单位数 …… (35)
Number of Corporate Units by Sector
1—6 国民经济主要平均指标 …… (36)
Average Indicators on National Economy
1—7 主要年份社会经济主要指标 …… (38)
Major Year' s Indicators on Society and Economy
1—8 国民经济主要结构指标 …… (44)
Composition Indicators on National Economy
1—9 平均每天主要社会经济活动 …… (46)
Selected Indicators on Average Daily Social and Economic Activities
1—10 主要指标占全国全省比重(2015 年) …… (48)
Percentage of Main Indicators to China and Shandong(2015)
1—11 主要年份全市生产总值(按当年价格计算) …… (50)
Major Year' s Gross Domestic Product(At Current Price)
1—12 主要年份全市生产总值构成(以全市生产总值为 100) …… (52)
Composition of Major Year' s Gross Domestic Product(Gross Domestic Product = 100)
1—13 主要年份全市生产总值增长速度(以上年为 100) …… (53)
Growth Rate of Major Year' s Gross Domestic Product(Preceding Year = 100)
1—14 分市、区生产总值(2015 年) …… (55)
Gross Domestic Product by Region(2015)
1—15 按支出法计算的全市生产总值(2015 年) …… (56)
Gross Domestic Product by Expenditure Approach(2015)
1—16 全市生产总值构成(2015 年) …… (57)

Composition of Gross Domestic Product(2015)
主要统计指标解释 …… (58)
Explanatory Notes on Main Statistical Indicators

二、人　口

Chapter 2. POPULATION

简要说明
Brief Introduction
2—1 主要年份全市户籍人口数 …… (65)
Major Year's Total Registered Population
2—2 主要年份全市户数、人口数、人口密度(户籍) …… (66)
Major Year's Households, Population and Density of Population(With Permanent Residence)
2—3 主要年份全市常住人口数 …… (67)
Major Year's Total Resident Population
2—4 青岛市常住人口(2015 年底) …… (67)
Total Resident Population(End of 2015)
2—5 分市、区土地面积(2012 年底) …… (68)
Land Area(End of 2012)
2—6 第一、二、三、四、五、六次人口普查主要数据 …… (69)
Main Data From the Six National Population Censuses
2—7 计划生育情况(1978—2015 年) …… (70)
Family Planning Situation(1978—2015)
2—8 分市、区计划生育情况(2015 年) …… (71)
Family Planning Situation by Region(2015)
主要统计指标解释 …… (72)
Explanatory Notes on Main Statistical Indicators

三、从业人员及职工工资

Chapter 3. EMPLOYMENT AND WAGES

简要说明
Brief Introduction
3—1 社会从业人数(1978—2015 年) …… (75)
Social Employment(1978—2015)
3—2 主要年份全市单位从业人员人数 …… (76)
Major Year's Number of Employed Persons in All Units of the City
3—3 全市单位国民经济各行业从业人员人数(2015 年) …… (77)
Number of Employed Persons in All Units of the City by Sector(2015)
3—4 全市单位分市、区国民经济各行业从业人员人数(2015 年) …… (78)
Number of Employed Persons in All Units of the City by Region and Sector (2015)
3—5 全市单位分市、区全部从业人员人数(2015 年底) …… (82)
Number of Employed Persons in All Units of the City by Region(End of 2015)
3—6 全市在岗职工工资总额、平均工资(1978—2015 年) …… (83)

Total Wage Bill and Average Wage of Employed Staff and Workers(1978—2015)
3—7 全市在岗职工工资总额、平均工资指数(1978—2015 年) …… (84)
Indexes of Total Wage Bill and Average Wage of Employed Staff and Workers(1978—2015)
3—8 分行业在岗职工平均工资(2015 年) …… (85)
Average Wage of Employed Staff and Workers by Sector(2015)
3—9 分市、区在岗职工工资总额(2015 年) …… (86)
Total Wage Bill of Employed Staff and Workers by Region(2015)
3—10 分市、区在岗职工平均工资(2015 年) …… (87)
Average Wage of Employed Staff and Workers by Region(2015)
主要统计指标解释 …… (88)
Explanatory Notes on Main Statistical Indicators

四、固定资产投资

Chapter 4. INVESTMENT IN FIXED ASSETS

简要说明
Brief Introduction
4—1 主要年份固定资产投资 …… (93)
Major Year's Investment in Fixed Assets
4—2 主要年份固定资产投资构成(以投资总额为 100) …… (97)
Composition of Major Year's Investment in Fixed Assets(Total Investment = 100)
4—3 按三次产业分规模以上固定资产投资(2015 年) …… (101)
Investment in Fixed Assets Above Designated Size by Three Strata of Industry(2015)
4—4 分市、区固定资产投资额(2015 年) …… (101)
Investment in Fixed Assets by Region(2015)
4—5 规模以上固定资产投资(2015 年) …… (102)
Investment in Fixed Assets Above Designated Size(2015)
4—6 主要年份房地产开发投资 …… (107)
Major Year's Investment in Real Estate Development
4—7 房地产开发投资情况(2015 年) …… (108)
Investment in Real Estate Development(2015)
4—8 房地产施工、竣工面积及竣工价值(2015 年) …… (109)
Floor Space Under Construction and Completed and Completed Value of Real Estate(2015)
4—9 商品房屋销售情况(2015 年) …… (109)
Basic Statistics on Sales of Commercialized Buildings(2015)
主要统计指标解释 …… (110)
Explanatory Notes on Main Statistical Indicators

五、对外经济贸易

Chapter 5. FOREIGN TRADE

简要说明
Brief Introduction
5—1 青岛口岸进出口总额(1985—2015 年) …… (115)

Total Value of Imports and Exports of Qingdao Port(1985—2015)
5—2 进出口总额(1988—2015 年) …… (116)
Total Value of Imports and Exports(1988—2015)
5—3 分国别外贸出口总额 …… (117)
Totla Value of Exports by Countries or Regions
5—4 外贸出口商品分类 …… (118)
Export Commodities by Category
5—5 外贸进口商品分类 …… (119)
Import Commodities by Category
5—6 二十大出口商品出口情况 …… (120)
Information on the Exportation of Top 20 Products
5—7 二十大进口商品进口情况 …… (121)
Information on the Importation of Top 20 Products
5—8 利用外资情况(2000—2015 年) …… (122)
Utilization of Foreign Capital(2000—2015)
5—9 当年外商直接投资项目数和投资额(2015 年) …… (124)
Number of Projects and Total Amount of Foreign Direct Investment(2015)
5—10 对外投资与经济合作 …… (125)
Outbound Investment and International Economic Cooperation
5—11 对外投资分国别(地区)情况表(2015 年) …… (125)
Information on Outbound Investment by Country/Region For(2015)
主要统计指标解释 …… (127)
Explanatory Notes on Main Statistical Indicators

六、城市建设、环境保护

Chapter 6. CITY CONSTRUCTION AND ENVIRONMENT PROTECTION

简要说明
Brief Introduction
6—1 主要年份城市建设和公用事业 …… (131)
Major Year's City Construction and Public Utilities
6—2 全年供电(2015 年) …… (135)
Annual Electricity Supply(2015)
6—3 分行业用电(2015 年) …… (136)
Electricity Consumption by Sector(2015)
6—4 城市供水(2015 年) …… (137)
Urban Water Supply(2015)
6—5 城市公共交通(2015 年) …… (138)
Urban Public Traffic(2015)
6—6 城市供气(2015 年) …… (139)
Urban Gas Supply(2015)
6—7 城市环境卫生(2015 年) …… (140)
Urban Environmental Sanitation(2015)
6—8 城市道路、下水道及绿化(2015 年) …… (141)
Urban Road,Sewage and Green(2015)

6—9 环境保护基本情况(2015 年) …… (142)
Basic Conditions of Environmental Protection(2015)
6—10 环境质量状况(2015 年) …… (142)
Environment Condition(2015)
6—11 工业“三废”排放情况(2015 年) …… (143)
Discharge Conditions of Industrial Waste Water,Waste Gas and Solid Waste(2015)
主要统计指标解释 …… (144)
Explanatory Notes on Main Statistical Indicators

七、能源消耗

Chapter 7. CONSUMPTION OF ENERGY

简要说明
Brief Introduction
7—1 规模以上工业主要能源消费与库存(2015 年) …… (149)
Consumption and Stock of Major Energy of Industry Above Designated Size(2015)
7—2 规模以上工业主要能源分行业消费量(2015 年) …… (150)
Major Energy Consumption of Industry Above Designated Size by Sector (2015)
7—3 重点耗能工业企业能源加工转换(2015 年) …… (151)
Energy Conversion of Major Energy-Consuming Industrial Enterprises(2015)
7—4 规模以上工业主要能源工业消费量(2015 年) …… (152)
Major Energy Consumption of Industry Above Designated Size(2015)
主要统计指标解释 …… (160)
Explanatory Notes on Main Statistical Indicators

八、财政、金融和保险业

Chapter 8. GOVERNMENT FINANCE,FINANCIAL INTERMEDIATION AND INSURANCE

简要说明
Brief Introduction
8—1 主要年份地方财政收支 …… (163)
Major Year's Revenue and Expenditure of Local Government Finance
8—2 分市、区公共财政预算收入(2015 年) …… (164)
General Public Budget Revenue by City and District(2015)
8—3 分市、区公共财政预算支出(2015 年) …… (166)
General Public Budget Expenditure by City and District(2015)
8—4 主要年份金融系统人民币存贷款(年末余额) …… (168)
Major Year's Deposits and Loans of Financial Institutions(Year-End Balance)
8—5 金融系统人民币存贷款(年末余额) …… (169)
Deposits and Loans of Financial Institutions(Year-End Balance)
8—6 国内保险业务(2000—2015 年) …… (170)
Domestic Insurance Business(2000—2015)
主要统计指标解释 …… (172)
Explanatory Notes on Main Statistical Indicators

九、价格指数

Chapter 9. PRICE INDEXES

简要说明

Brief Introduction

9—1 主要年份居民消费和商品零售价格指数 …… (177)

Major Year's Consumer and Retail Price Indexes

9—2 主要年份居民消费和商品零售价格指数(以 1950 年价格为 100) …… (178)

Major Year's Consumer and Retail Price Indexes (1950 = 100)

9—3 主要年份生产投资价格指数 …… (179)

Major Year's Price Indexes for Production and Investment

9—4 工业生产者出厂价格指数 …… (180)

Producer Price Indexes for Industrial Producers

9—5 工业生产者购进价格指数 …… (182)

Purchasing Price Indexes for Industrial Producers

9—6 按工业行业分工业生产者出厂价格指数 …… (184)

Producer Price Indexes for Industrial Producers by Sector

9—7 固定资产投资价格指数 …… (186)

Price Indexes for Investment in Fixed Assets

9—8 住宅销售价格指数(2015 年) …… (186)

Sales Price Indexes for Residence(2015)

9—9 居民消费价格分类指数(2015 年) …… (187)

Consumer Price Indexes by Category(2015)

9—10 商品零售价格分类指数(2015 年) …… (189)

Retail Price Indexes by Category(2015)

主要统计指标解释 …… (191)

Explanatory Notes on Main Statistical Indicators

十、人民生活

Chapter 10. PEOPLE'S LIVING CONDITIONS

简要说明

Brief Introduction

10—1 城市居民收支(1978—2014 年) …… (195)

Income and Expenditure of Urban Residents(1978—2014)

10—2 农村居民收支(1978—2014 年) …… (196)

Income and Expenditure of Rural Residents (1978—2014)

10—3 城乡居民住房面积(1990—2014 年) …… (197)

Housing Area of Urban and Rural Residents (1990—2014)

10—4 全体居民家庭基本情况(2015 年) …… (198)

Basic Information on all Households (2015)

10—5 城镇居民家庭基本情况 (2015 年) …… (199)

Basic Conditions of Urban Households(2015)

10—6 农村居民家庭基本情况(2015 年) …… (200)
Basic Conditions of Rural Households(2015)
10—7 全体居民家庭消费构成 …… (201)
Household Consumption Structure
10—8 城镇居民家庭消费构成 …… (202)
Composition of Urban Households Consumption
10—9 农村居民家庭消费构成 …… (203)
Composition of Rural Households Consumption
10—10 城市住户每百户家庭主要耐用品拥有量 (1980—2015 年) …… (204)
Ownership of Major Durable Consumer Goods Per 100 Urban Households(1980—2015)
10—11 农村住户每百户家庭主要耐用品拥有量(1985—2015 年) …… (205)
Ownership of Major Durable Consumer Goods Per 100 Rural Households(1985—2015)
主要统计指标解释 …… (206)
Explanatory Notes on Main Statistical Indicators

十一、农 业

Chapter 11. AGRICULTURE

简要说明
Brief Introduction
11—1 农村基本情况(2000—2015 年) …… (209)
Basic Statistics on Rural Area(2000—2015)
11—2 农村劳动力(1985—2015 年) …… (211)
Rural Labor Force(1985—2015)
11—3 分市、区乡村户数、人口、劳动力(2015 年) …… (213)
Rural Households, Population and Labor Force by Region(2015)
11—4 主要年份农、林、牧、渔业总产值(按现价计算) …… (214)
Major Year's Gross Output Value of Farming, Forestry, Animal Husbandry and Fishery(Current Price)
11—5 分市、区农、林、牧、渔业总产值(2015 年,现价) …… (215)
Gross Output Value of Farming, Forestry, Animal Husbandry and Fishery by Region(2015, Current Price)
11—6 农、林、牧、渔业总产值、增加值(2015 年) …… (216)
Value-Added of Farming, Forestry, Animal Husbandry and Fishery(2015)
11—7 分市、区农、林、牧、渔业增加值(2015 年) …… (216)
Value-Added of Farming, Forestry, Animal Husbandry Fishery by Region(2015)
11—8 主要年份耕地面积与播种面积 …… (217)
Major Year's Cultivated and Sown Area
11—9 分市、区耕地面积(2015 年) …… (218)
Area of Cultivated Land by Region(2015)
11—10 分市、区农作物播种面积(2015 年) …… (219)
Sown Area of Farm Crops by Region(2015)
11—11 分市、区部分农作物产量(2015 年) …… (220)
Output of Farm Crops by Region(2015)
11—12 分市、区部分农作物播公顷单产量(2015 年) …… (221)
Output of Farm Crops Per Hectare by Region(2015)
11—13 主要年份农作物总产量 …… (222)

Major Year's Output of Farm Crops
11—14 分市、区部分蔬菜产量(2015年) ······ (223)
Production of Some Vegetables by City and District(2015)
11—15 分市、区牛头数(2015年) ······ (224)
The Number of Cattle by City and District (2015)
11—16 分市、区猪、羊及家禽存养量(2015年) ······ (224)
Hogs, Sheep, Goats and Poultry in Stock by Region(2015)
11—17 分市、区肉、蛋、奶产量(2015年) ······ (225)
Output of Meat, Eggs and Milk by Region(2015)
11—18 分市、区渔业养殖面积 ······ (225)
Aquaculture Area by Region
11—19 分市、区水产品总产量(2015年) ······ (226)
Output of Aquatic Products by Region(2015)
11—20 分市、区植树及造林面积(2015年) ······ (226)
Area of Forestation and Afforestation by Region(2015)
11—21 分市、区果园面积、水果总产量(2015年) ······ (227)
Area of Orchards and Output of Fruits by Region(2015)
11—22 分市、区果园、茶园面积和茶叶产量(2015年) ······ (228)
Area of Orchard and Tea Garden and Production of Tea and Cocoon by City and District(2015)
11—23 主要年份主要农业机械拥有量 ······ (229)
Major Year's Ownership of Agricultural Machinery
11—24 主要年份农业机械化、用电量、化肥施用量 ······ (230)
Major Year's Mechanization, Electricity and Chemical Fertilizer Consumption
11—25 分市、区农业机械化和电气化(2015年) ······ (231)
Mechanization and Electrification in Agriculture by Region(2015)
11—26 分市、区农用化肥施用量(2015年) ······ (232)
Consumption of Chemical Fertilizers by Region(2015)
11—27 分市、区农田水利(2015年) ······ (232)
Farmland Water Conservancy by Region(2015)
11—28 分市、区主要农业机械拥有量(2015年) ······ (233)
Ownership of Major Agricultural Machinery by Region(2015)
主要统计指标解释 ······ (236)
Explanatory Notes on Main Statistical Indicators

十二、工　业

Chapter 12. INDUSTRY

简要说明
Brief Introduction
12—1 规模以上工业企业单位数 ······ (241)
Number of Industrial Enterprises Above Designateo Size
12—2 分市、区全部工业企业单位数(2015年) ······ (247)
Number of All Industrial Enterprises by Region(2015)
12—3 历年全部工业总产值 ······ (248)
Gross Industrial Output Value Over the Years

12—4 分市、区全部工业总产值(2015 年) …… (251)
Gross Industrial Output Value by Region(2015)
12—5 分市、区规模以上工业总产值(2015 年) …… (252)
Gross Industrial Output Value Above Designated Size by Region(2015)
12—6 规模以上工业企业主要指标(2015 年) …… (256)
Main Indicators of Industrial Enterprises Above Designated Size(2015)
12—7 按行业分国有及国有控股工业企业主要指标(2015 年) …… (264)
Main Indicators of State-Owned and State-Holding Industrial Enterprises by Industrial Sector(2015)
12—8 按行业分规模以上外商投资和港澳台商投资工业企业主要指标(2015 年) …… (268)
Main Indicators of Foreign Funded Enterprises and Enterprises With Funds From Hong Kong,Macao and Taiwan Above Designated Size by Industrial Sector(2015)
12—9 按行业分大中型工业企业主要指标(2015 年) …… (272)
Main Indicators of Large and Medium-Sized Industrial Enterprises by Industrial Sector(2015)
12—10 按行业分规模以上工业企业主要经济效益指标(2015 年) …… (276)
Main Indicators on Economic Benefit of Industrial Enterprises Above Designated Size by Industrial Sector(2015)
12—11 按行业分国有控股工业企业主要经济效益指标(2015 年) …… (278)
Main Indicators on Economic Benefit of State Owned and State Holding Industrial Enterprises by Industrial Sector(2015)
12—12 按行业分规模以上外商及港澳台商投资工业企业主要经济效益指标(2015 年) …… (280)
Main Indicators on Economic Benefit of Foreign Funded Enterprises and Enterprises With Funds From Hong Kong,Macao and Taiwan Above Designated Size by Industrial Sector(2015)
12—13 按行业分大中型工业企业主要经济效益指标(2015 年) …… (282)
Main Indicators on Economic Benefit of Large and Medium-Sized Industrial Enterprises by Industrial Sector(2015)
12—14 主要年份主要工业产品产量 …… (284)
Major Year's Products Output of Industry Above Designated Size
12—15 规模以上工业主要产品产量 …… (290)
Output of Major Industrial Products of Industry Above Designated Size
12—16 规模以上工业主要产品生产能力 …… (293)
Production Capacity of Major Products of Industry Above Designated Size
主要统计指标解释 …… (294)
Explanatory Notes on Main Statistical Indicators

十三、建 筑 业
Chapter 13. CONSTRUCTION

简要说明
Brief Introduction
13—1 建筑业企业生产情况(2015 年) …… (297)
Production Situation of Construction Enterprises(2015)
13—2 建筑业企业财务状况(2015 年) …… (298)
Financial Situation of Construction Enterprises(2015)
13—3 建筑业企业主要经济效益指标(2015 年) …… (300)
Main Indicators on Economic Benefit of Construction Enterprises
13—4 建筑业增加值(2015 年) …… (301)
Value Added of Construction(2015)
13—5 重点建筑企业一览表(2015 年) …… (302)

List of Key Construction Enterprises(2015)
主要统计指标解释 …… (305)
Explanatory Notes on Main Statistical Indicators

十四、运输、邮电

Chapter 14. TRANSPORT,POSTAL AND TELECOMMUNICATION SERVICES

简要说明
Brief Introduction
14—1 主要年份客货运输及港口吞吐量 …… (309)
Major Year' s Passenger & Freight Traffic and Handling Capacity of the Ports
14—2 民用车辆拥有量(2015 年底) …… (310)
Possession of Civil Motor Vehicles(End of 2015)
14—3 客货运输及港口吞吐量(2015 年) …… (311)
Passenger & Freight Traffic and Handling Capacity of the Ports(2015)
14—4 独立核算运输邮电单位主要财务指标(2015 年) …… (311)
Main Financial Indicators of Independent Accounting Units of Transport,Postal and Telecommunication Services(2015)
14—5 邮电通讯基本情况(2015 年) …… (312)
Basic Conditions of Postal and Telecommunication Services(2015)
主要统计指标解释 …… (315)
Explanatory Notes on Main Statistical Indicators

十五、批发和零售业

Chapter 15. WHOLESALE AND RETAIL TRADES

简要说明
Brief Introduction
15—1 社会消费品零售总额(1985—2015 年) …… (319)
Total Retail Sales of Consumer Goods(1985—2015)
15—2 分市、区社会消费品零售总额(2015 年) …… (320)
Total Retail Sales of Consumer Goods by Region(2015)
15—3 限额以上批发和零售业商品购销存总额(2015 年) …… (321)
Total Purchases,Sales and Stock of Enterprises Above Designated Size of Wholesale and Retail Trades(2015)
15—4 限额以上批发和零售业商品分类销售额(2015 年) …… (322)
Sales Value of Enterprises Above Designated Size of Wholesale and Retail Trades by Category of Commodities(2015)
15—5 限额以上批发业财务状况(2015 年) …… (323)
Financial Position of Enterprises Above Designated Size of Wholesale Trade(2015)
15—6 限额以上零售业财务状况(2015 年) …… (324)
Financial Position of Enterprises Above Designated Size of Retail Trade(2015)
15—7 分市、区城乡亿元商品交易市场分布情况(2015 年) …… (325)
Basic Statistics on Commodity Exchange Markets of Transaction Value Over 100 Million Yuan by Region(2015)
15—8 批发和零售业企业网点数(2015 年底) …… (326)
Enterprises Outlets of Wholesale and Retail Trades(End of 2015)
15—9 批发和零售业企业从业人员(2015 年底) …… (327)

Enterprises Employment of Wholesale and Retail Trades(End of 2015)
15—10 批发和零售业个体网点数(2015 年底) …… (328)
Individual Outlets of Wholesale and Retail Trades(End of 2015)
15—11 批发和零售业个体从业人员(2015 年底) …… (329)
Individual Employment of Wholesale and Retail Trades(End of 2015)
主要统计指标解释 …… (330)
Explanatory Notes on Main Statistical Indicators

十六、住宿、餐饮业和旅游

Chapter 16. HOTELS, CATERING SERVICES AND TOURISM

简要说明
Brief Introduction
16—1 限额以上住宿和餐饮业法人企业经营情况(2015 年) …… (333)
Business Conditions of Enterprises of Hotels and Catering Services Above Designated Size(2015)
16—2 限额以上住宿业财务状况(2015 年) …… (334)
Financial Situation of Hotels Above Designated Size(2015)
16—3 限额以上餐饮业财务状况(2015 年) …… (335)
Financial Situation of Catering Services Above Designated Size(2015)
16—4 住宿和餐饮业企业网点数(2015 年底) …… (336)
Enterprises Outlets of Hotels and Catering Services(End of 2015)
16—5 住宿和餐饮业企业从业人员(2015 年底) …… (337)
Enterprisesl Employment of Hotels and Catering Services(End of 2015)
16—6 住宿和餐饮业个体网点数(2015 年底) …… (338)
Individual Outlets of Hotels and Catering Services(End of 2015)
16—7 住宿和餐饮业个体从业人员(2015 年底) …… (339)
Individual Employment of Hotels and Catering Services(End of 2015)
16—8 入境旅游人数(2000—2015 年) …… (340)
Number of Oversea Visitor Arrivals (2000—2015)
16—9 入境旅游收入(2000—2015 年) …… (340)
Earnings From International Tourism(2000—2015)
16—10 国内旅游人数及收入(2015 年) …… (342)
Number of Domestic Tourism Income(2015)
主要统计指标解释 …… (343)
Explanatory Notes on Main Statistical Indicators

十七、教育、科技和文化

Chapter 17. EDUCATION, SCIENCE & TECHNOLOGY AND CULTURE

简要说明
Brief Introduction
17—1 各级各类学校基本情况(2015 年) …… (347)
Basic Statistics on Schools by Level and Type of School(2015)
17—2 主要年份各级各类学校在校学生数 …… (348)

Major Year's Students Enrollment of Schools by Level and Type of School
17—3 主要年份普通高等学校基本情况 ………………………………………………… (349)
Major Year's Basic Statistics on Regular Institutions of Higher Education
17—4 各类成人教育基本情况(2015 年) ………………………………………………… (350)
Basic Statistics on Adult Education(2015)
17—5 分市、区普通中学情况(2015 年) ………………………………………………… (351)
Basic Statistics on Regular Secondary Schools by Region(2015)
17—6 分市、区职业中学、小学情况(2015 年) ………………………………………… (352)
Basic Statistics on Vocational Secondary Schools and Primary Schools by Region(2015)
17—7 分市、区中小学教职工情况(2015 年) ………………………………………… (353)
Basic Statistics on Teachers and Staff in Secondary and Primary Schools by Region(2015)
17—8 分市、区幼儿园基本情况(2015 年) ………………………………………… (354)
Basic Statistics on Kindergartens by Region(2015)
17—9 科研机构基本情况(1978—2015 年) ………………………………………… (355)
Basic Statistics on Scientific Research Institutions(1978—2015)
17—10 独立科学研究机构情况(2015 年) ………………………………………… (356)
Basic Statistics on Independent Institutions of Scientific Research(2015)
17—11 科学技术奖励情况(2015 年) ………………………………………… (356)
Award Statistics on Science and Technology(2015)
17—12 大中型工业企业技术开发主要相对指标(1995—2015 年) ……………………… (357)
Major Indicators of Technology Development of Large and Medium Size Industrial Enterprises(1995—2015)
17—13 主要年份文化机构数 ………………………………………… (358)
Major Year's Institutions of Culture
17—14 文化事业机构、人员数(2015 年) ………………………………………… (359)
Number of Institutions and Personnel in Culture (2015)
17—15 分市、区艺术表演、电影发行及放映机构数(2015 年) ……………………… (360)
Number of Institutions of Art Performance,Films Distribution and Projection by Region(2015)
17—16 艺术表演、电影放映情况(2015 年) ………………………………………… (360)
Statistics on Art Performance and Films Projection(2015)
17—17 文化部门艺术剧团情况(2015 年) ………………………………………… (361)
Statistics on Art Troupes of Cultural Department(2015)
17—18 图书馆、文化馆情况 ………………………………………… (361)
Statistics on Libraries and Cultural Centers
主要统计指标解释 ………………………………………… (362)
Explanatory Notes on Main Statistical Indicators

十八、体育、卫生和民政、司法

Chapter 18. SPORTS,PUBLIC HEALTH AND CIVIL AFFAIRS,JUDICIAL AFFAIRS

简要说明
Brief Introduction
18—1 体育事业情况(2000—2015 年) ………………………………………… (365)
Statistics on Sports(2000—2015)
18—2 主要年份卫生事业基本情况 ………………………………………… (367)
Major Year's Basic Statistics on Public Health

18—3 各类卫生机构、床位、人员数(2015 年底) …… (368)
Number of Health Institutions, Beds and Employed Persons(End of 2015)
18—4 分市、区各类卫生机构、床位、人员数(2015 年底) …… (370)
Number of Health Institutions, Beds and Employed Persons by Region(End of 2015)
18—5 收养性社会福利单位情况(2015 年) …… (374)
Basic Statictics on Social Welfare Institutions(2015)
18—6 社会救济情况(2015 年) …… (374)
Basic Statistics on Social Relief(2015)
18—7 分市、区婚姻登记情况(2015 年) …… (376)
Basic Statistics on Marriage Registration by Region(2015)
18—8 律师、公证、调解、社会治安基本情况(2000—2015 年) …… (378)
Basic Statistics on Lawyers, Notarization, Mediation and Social Order (2000—2015)
18—9 分区、市殡葬服务情况(2015 年) …… (380)
Basic Statistics on Funeral Services(2015)
主要统计指标解释 …… (382)
Explanatory Notes on Main Statistical Indicators

附 录

APPENDIX

2015 年省内各市主要经济指标对比情况 …… (384)
Major Economic Indicators on Cities of the Province(2015)
2015 年十五个副省级城市主要经济指标对比情况 …… (386)
Major Economic Indicators on Cities Under Provincial Levels(2015)
2015 年副省级城市之外部分城市主要经济指标情况 …… (388)
The Main Economic Indicators of Some Other Cities Than the Sub-Provincial City for(2015)

2015 年
青岛市国民经济和社会发展
统 计 公 报

青岛市统计局

国家统计局青岛调查队

（2016年3月17日）

2015 年，面对错综复杂的国内外环境，全市深入贯彻落实中央宏观调控各项措施，主动适应新常态，深入推进蓝色引领、全域统筹、创新驱动发展战略，全市经济运行总体平稳，稳中有进，稳中向好，民生保障持续加强，生态环境继续改善，社会事业全面发展，宜居幸福的现代化国际城市建设有序推进。

一、综 合

年末全市常住总人口为 909.70 万人，增长 0.56%；其中，市区常住人口 490.22 万人，增长 0.54%。

表 1：2015 年全市常住人口分布情况

区 市	数量(万人)
总 计	909.70
市南区	57.16
市北区	107.27
李沧区	54.38
崂山区	42.99
黄岛区	149.36
城阳区	69.17
即墨市	120.20
胶州市	87.60
平度市	136.21
莱西市	75.47
高新区	9.89

初步核算，2015 年全市生产总值 9300.07 亿元，按可比价格计算，增长 8.1%。其中，第一产业增加值 363.98 亿元，增长 3.2%；第二产业增加值 4026.46 亿元，增长 7.1%；第三产业增加值 4909.63 亿元，增长 9.4%。三次产业比例为 3.9:43.3:52.8。人均 GDP 达到 102519 元。

图 1："十二五"时期全市 GDP 总量及速度

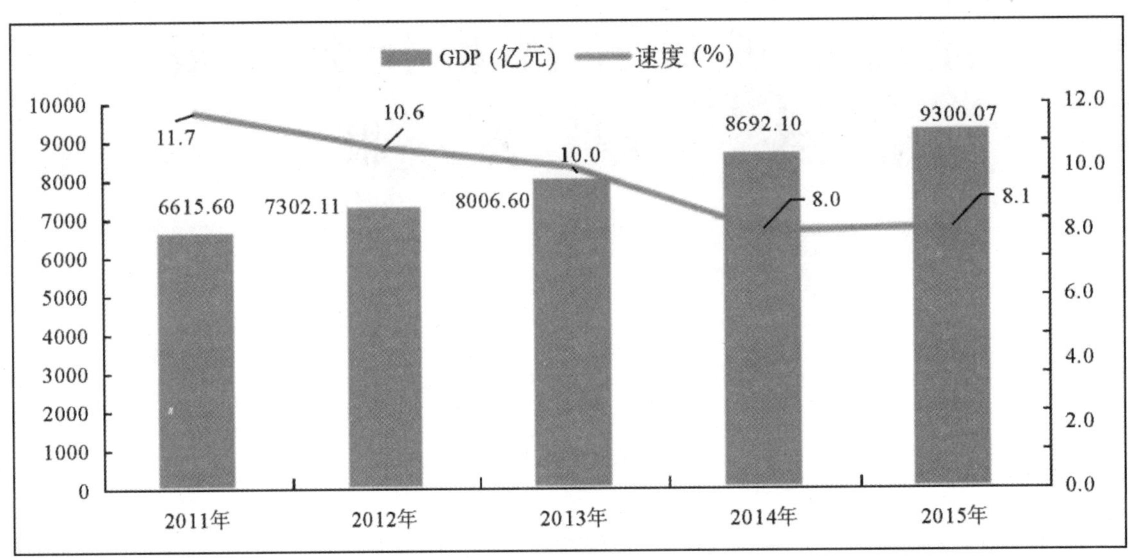

据初步测算，全年实现海洋生产总值 2093.4 亿元，增长 15.1%（现价），占 GDP 比重为 22.5%；现代服务业增加值 2589.8 亿元，增长 16.1%(现价)，占 GDP 比重为 27.8%，占服务业比重为 52.8%。

表 2：2015 年青岛市分行业增加值

行　业	总量（亿元）	增速(%)
全市生产总值	9300.07	8.1
农林牧渔业	379.06	3.6
工业	3547.60	6.9
建筑业	486.83	8.9
批发和零售业	1167.98	8.0
交通运输、仓储和邮政业	654.72	6.7
住宿和餐饮业	194.02	1.8
金融业	588.28	12.9
房地产业	479.93	11.1
其他服务业	1801.65	10.5

全年财政总收入实现2713.7亿元，下降4.3%；一般公共预算收入1006.3亿元，增长12.39%；一般公共预算支出1222.9亿元，增长13.8%。全年国税系统组织税收收入(含海关代征) 1200.1亿元，下降10.4%；其中，国内税收722.6亿元，增长4.5%。地税税收收入674.3亿元，增长12.6%。

全年全市居民消费价格比上年上涨1.2%，涨幅为"十二五"期间最低；工业生产者出厂价格下降3.0%，工业生产者购进价格下降5.8%。12月份市区新建住宅价格同比下降2.2%；二手住宅价格同比下降0.3%。

表 3：2015 年全市居民消费价格指数

指标名称	累计（上年同期=100）
居民消费价格总指数	101.2
非食品价格指数	101.0
服务项目价格指数	101.3
消费品价格指数	101.2
一、食品	101.7
#粮食	101.5
猪肉	110.9
蛋	90.1
鲜菜	109.4
二、烟酒	102.3
三、衣着	102.8
四、家庭设备用品及维修服务	100.6
五、医疗保健和个人用品	103.8
六、交通和通信	97.2
七、娱乐教育文化用品及服务	101.2
八、居住	100.3

图 2："十二五"时期全市 CPI 年度同比上涨幅度

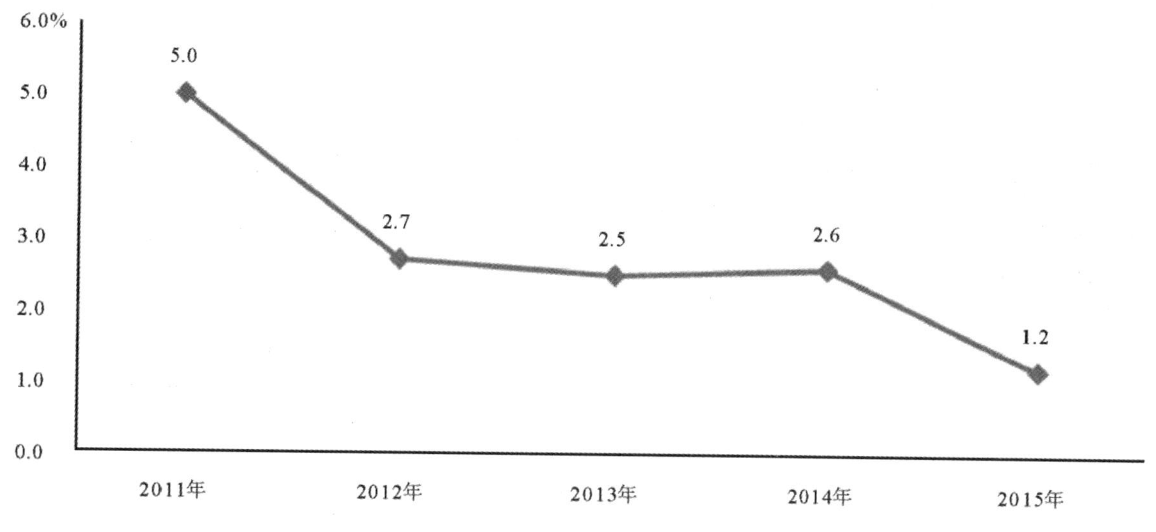

二、农 业

全年粮食播种面积49.3万公顷，比上年减少0.2万公顷；蔬菜播种面积10.5万公顷，减少331公顷；花生播种面积8.2万公顷，减少0.7万公顷。粮食总产量321.4万吨，比上年下降0.5%；蔬菜及食用菌总产量579.1万吨，下降2.7%；花生总产量34.6万吨，下降13.2%；水果（含果用瓜）总产量118.7万吨，与上年持平。现代农业园区695个，新增100个；"三品一标"（无公害农产品、绿色食品、有机农产品和农产品地理标志）产品805个，新增182个；农产品质量追溯体系覆盖全市标准化园区及“三品一标”基地比重达到85%。

图 3：“十二五”时期全市蔬菜、粮食、水产品产量

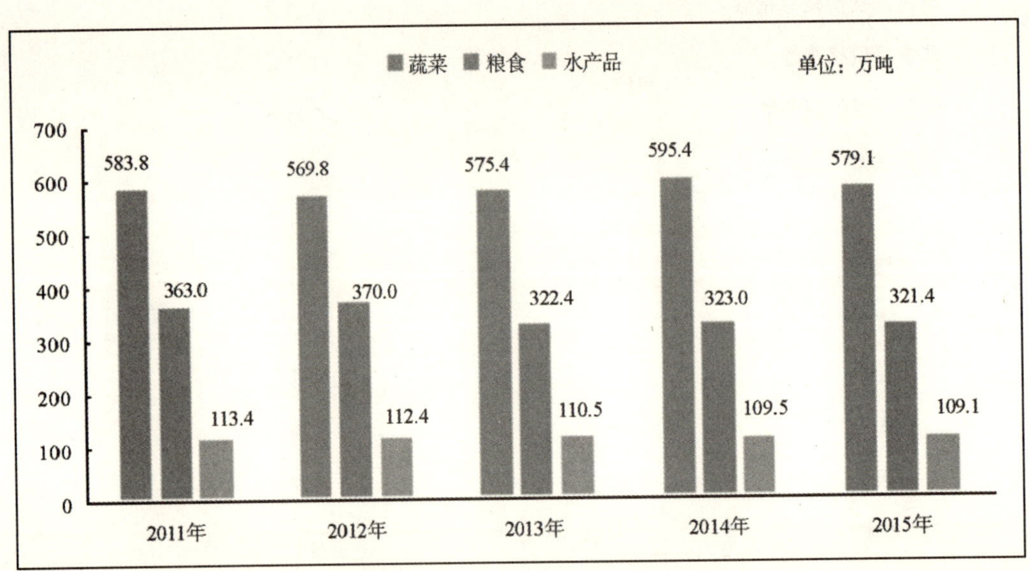

全年新增造林面积1万公顷。林木绿化率40%。

全年肉类总产量54.7万吨，下降8.2%；禽蛋产量18.3万吨，下降4.3%；奶类产量35.4万吨，下降5.7%。

全年水产品产量（不包括远洋捕捞）109.1万吨，下降0.3%。海、淡水养殖面积4.9万公顷，下降2.1%。远洋捕捞量13.6万吨，增长94.6%。

农机总动力854万千瓦，增加27万千瓦。农作物生产综合机械化水平达到90.2%。农田有效灌溉面积31.9万公顷，其中，节水灌溉面积14万公顷。

三、工业与建筑业

全年规模以上工业增加值增长7.5%。分行业看，金属制品业增加值增长12.3%，电气机械和器材制造业增长8.9%，农副食品加工业增长8.3%，铁路、船舶、航空航天和其他运输设备制造业增长10.6%，通用设备制造业增长7.6%，专用设备制造业增长9.3%，橡胶和塑料制品业增长11.0%；六大高耗能行业增加值比上年增长3.7%，其中，非金属矿物制品业增长8.9%，化学原料和化学制品制造业增长14.4%，有色金属冶炼和压延加工业增长9.9%，黑色金属冶炼和压延加工业下降2.3%，电力、热力生产和供应业下降0.5%，石油加工、炼焦和核燃料加工业下降3.8%。装备制造业增加值增长8.7%，占规模以上工业增加值的比重为44.2%。

表4：2015年规模以上工业增加值增速

指标	比上年增长(%)
规模以上工业总计	7.5
其中：轻工业	7.5
重工业	7.5
其中：国有企业	–0.3
集体企业	–0.4
股份合作企业	–6.6
股份制企业	8.4
外商及港澳台商投资企业	6.8
其他经济类型企业	12.8

全年规模以上工业企业完成工业总产值17349.8亿元，增长7.8%。其中，高新技术产业产值增长9.4%，占比为41.0%，较年初提高0.27个百分点；十条工业千亿级产业链产值增长7.8%，占比为75.0%；规模以上工业战略性新兴产业产值增长15.2%。

表5：2015年规模以上工业主要产品产量及增长速度

产品名称	单位	产量	比上年增长(%)
彩色电视机	万台	1736.2	1.2
其中：液晶电视机	万台	1736.2	1.2
家用电冰箱	万台	872.1	12.8
家用洗衣机	万台	595.1	0.7
房间空气调节器	万台	623.2	-9.1
卷烟	亿支	557.4	-0.5
啤酒	万千升	156.0	-4.1
碳酸钠（纯碱）	万吨	68.9	1.6
橡胶轮胎外胎	万条	5179.5	6.2
平板玻璃	万重量箱	535.0	-12.6
粗钢	万吨	154.6	-27.9
汽车	万辆	86.1	11.8
动车组	辆	2070	7.7
金属集装箱	万立方米	2140.3	15.5
原油加工量	万吨	1288.1	-16.6
发电量	亿千瓦时	173.5	-2.0

规模以上工业实现主营业务收入16715.2亿元，增长6.8%。实现利税1754.9亿元，增长15.0%。实现利润937.3亿元，增长15.3%，其中，国有及国有控股企业143.3亿元，增长32.8%；集体企业86.6亿元，增长13.1%，股份制企业577.8亿元，增长16.9%，外商及港澳台商投资企业249.7亿元，增长12.6%。

全年建筑业实现增加值486.8亿元，增长8.9%。实现利税总额83.4亿元，增长7.1%。

四、固定资产投资

全市固定资产投资(包括城镇、农村500万元以上投资项目)6555.7亿元，增长14.2%。其中，第一产业投资115亿元，增长9.8%；第二产业投资3253.5亿元，增长16.5%；第三产业投资3187.2亿元，增长12.1%。

表6：2015年分行业固定资产投资（不含农户）及增速

行　业	投资额（亿元）	比上年增长(%)
总　计	6555.7	14.2
农、林、牧、渔业	115	9.8
采矿业	12.1	–9.8
制造业	3059.4	15.8
电力、热力、燃气及水的生产和供应业	74.3	55.2
建筑业	107.7	21.2
批发和零售业	287	19.9
交通运输、仓储和邮政业	484.7	54.4
住宿和餐饮业	58.8	7.3
信息传输、软件和信息技术服务业	38.6	15.2
金融业	4.5	–51.2
房地产业	1347.1	0
租赁和商务服务业	196.2	9.2
科学研究和技术服务业	108.7	68
水利、环境和公共设施管理业	354	39
居民服务和其他服务业	13.9	–5.3
教育	77.7	5.6
卫生和社会工作	21.4	70.9
文化、体育和娱乐业	126.1	–35
公共管理和社会组织	68.5	31.4

全年固定资产投资施工项目6894个，新开工项目6120个，竣工项目5074个；在建项目计划总投资规模（含房地产）15951.9亿元。全年新增固定资产4524亿元，项目建成投产率73.6%，固定资产交付使用率69%。

全年房地产开发完成投资1122.3亿元，增长0.4%；其中，住宅投资756.9亿元，增长3.5%。商品房销售面积1418.6万平方米，增长21.9%；其中，住宅销售1239万平方米，增长21.2%。

图4："十二五"时期全市商品房销售情况

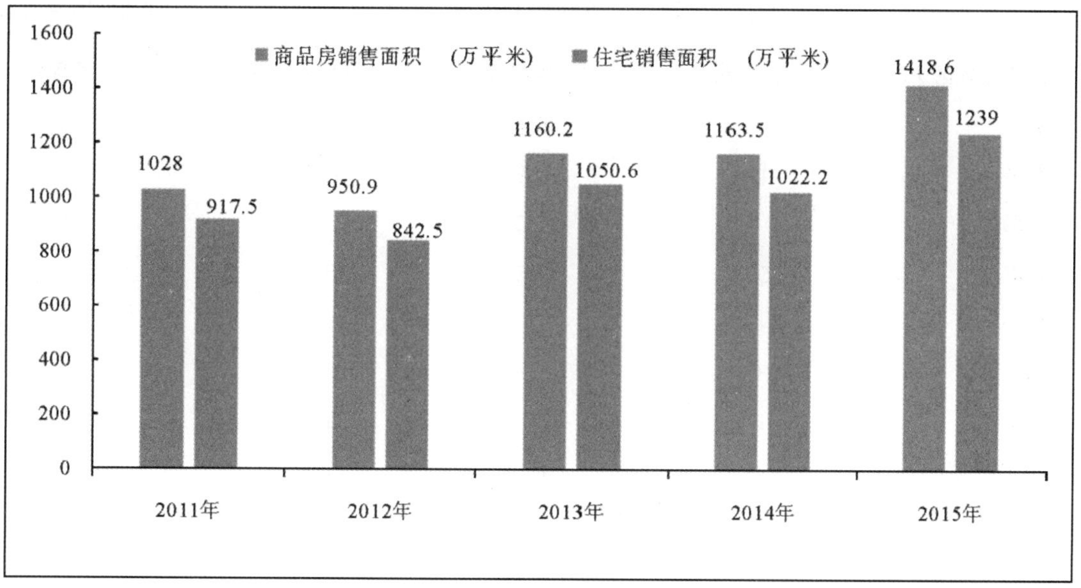

全年全市计划总投资亿元及以上的新开工项目（含房地产项目）545个，减少172个。从区域分布看，市区新开工项目266个，四市新开工项目248个，红岛经济区新开工项目31个。重点基础设施项目：青荣城际铁路引入青岛枢纽相关工程项目计划总投资33.4亿元，本年完成投资33.4亿元；青岛–海阳城际（蓝色硅谷段）项目计划总投资194.7亿元，本年完成投资55.6亿元；红岛–胶南城际轨道交通工程项目计划总投资135.5亿元，本年完成投资34.6亿元。重点板块建设：2015年西海岸经济新区完成投资1714.7亿元，增长15.8%；蓝色硅谷区域共有在建产业类项目（房地产开发类除外）210个，比上年增加12个，完成投资346.3亿元，增长15.8%，其中：核心区在建项目57个，比上年增加17个，完成投资211.2亿元，增长37.3%。

五、国内贸易

全年实现社会消费品零售额3713.7亿元，增长10.5%。分地域看，城镇市场实现零售额3109.1亿元，增长10.7%；乡村市场实现零售额604.6亿元，增长9.4%。分行业看，批发和零售业实现零售额3246.0亿元，增长10.3%；住宿和餐饮业实现零售额467.7亿元，增长11.9%。

全年限额以上法人企业实现消费品零售额1205.6亿元，增长9.6%。限额以上法人企业汽车类零售额308.7亿元，增长6.9%；石油及制品类零售额153.1亿元，下降10.9%；粮油、食品、饮料、烟酒类零售额158.4亿元，增长17.7%；日用品类零售额32.4亿元，增长0.1%；化妆品类零售额21.8亿元，增长5.4%。

六、对外经济

全市实现外贸进出口总额4361.3亿元，下降11.1%。其中，出口额2818.2亿元，增长0.3%，进口额1543.1亿元，下降26.3%。

表7：2015年全市主要商品进出口情况

单位：亿元、%

项　目	进出口		出　口		进　口	
	金额	增长	金额	增长	金额	增长
纺织服装	470.4	–10.0	431.9	–8.8	38.5	–21.1
农产品	603.8	–10.5	310.0	–2.9	293.8	–17.3
机电产品	1606.6	2.4	1195.9	8.6	410.7	–12.1
高新技术产品	474.3	–0.1	271.9	16.3	202.4	–16.0

表8：2015年对主要国家和地区货物进出口额及增速

单位：亿美元、%

国别（地区）	出口额	比上年增长	进口额	比上年增长
亚洲	190.5	–5.4	126.5	–22.8
香港	18.8	30.2	0.7	–37.7
台湾	4.6	–12.3	10.9	–23.1
日本	52.9	–11.6	18.7	–11.9
韩国	41.4	–13.2	36.5	–13.9
东盟	37.4	0.2	38.2	–8.6
南亚	11.8	–10.4	3.5	–55.1
中东	22.1	0.3	11.8	–58.5
非洲	19.2	–21.7	10.6	–57.2
南非	3.4	–5.6	2.5	–55.0
欧洲	90.6	–3.5	31.0	–20.5
欧盟	81.0	–1.4	20.7	–16.4
英国	14.3	0.2	1.7	14.4
德国	16.7	3.1	6.6	–26.2
法国	8.8	–1.7	2.6	13.7
意大利	6.3	–4.4	2.4	–23.9
独联体及东欧	6.6	–27.5	8.0	–28.8
俄罗斯	4.9	–28.6	7.1	–23.5
南美洲	30.0	–5.3	30.4	–27.1
巴西	3.9	–34.4	17.7	–28.6
北美洲	107.2	15.0	27.2	–9.1
美国	98.0	17.4	23.3	–3.4
加拿大	8.6	–1.5	3.6	–36.3
大洋洲	15.8	21.8	21.8	–41.1
澳大利亚	14.0	24.9	18.3	–46.0

注：本表非全口径。

据青岛海关统计，青岛口岸对外贸易进出口总额8972.6亿元，下降11.1%。其中，出口额5451.1亿元，增长1.6%；进口额3521.6亿元，下降26.3%。

实际到账外资金额66.9亿美元，增长10.0%。引进青岛市以外国内资金1516.2亿元，增长9.8%。

全年对外承包工程业务新签合同金额36.6亿美元，增长60.6%；完成营业额36.4亿美元，增长1.3%；对外劳务合作派出各类劳务人员17047人次，增长28.1%。

七、交通运输、邮电和旅游业

全市港口吞吐量5.0亿吨，增长4.3%；外贸吞吐量3.3亿吨，增长3.7%；集装箱吞吐量1743万标准箱，增长5.1%。

表9：2015年各种运输方式完成的运输量及增速

运输方式	运输量(单位)	比上年增长(%)
客运周转量	151.7亿人公里	4.3
铁路	73.9亿人公里	5.2
公路	77.6亿人公里	3.5
水运	0.3亿人公里	-10.0
货运周转量	1166.3亿吨公里	12.4
铁路	166.8亿吨公里	-1.4
公路	443.8亿吨公里	0.5
水运	555.7亿吨公里	30.2

年末拥有国内航线120条，国际航线19条，港澳台地区航线5条，全年航空旅客吞吐量达到1820.2万人次，增长10.9%；航空货邮吞吐量20.8万吨，增长1.8%。全年完成邮电业务总量218.0亿元，增长23.6%。其中，邮政业务总量41.6亿元，增长34.7%；电信业务总量176.4亿元，增长21.2%。快递业务量1.6亿件，增长53.3%。固定宽带互联网用户累计达249.3万户，增长9.7%。年末固定电话用户达到213.8万户；全市移动电话发展到1335.6万户。

全年全市接待游客总人数7455.8万人次，增长8.9%；实现旅游消费总额1270.0亿元，增长14.1%。其中，接待入境游客人数133.8万人次，增长4.5%；入境游客消费91797.9万美元，增长11.6%。接待国内游客人数7322.0万人次，增长9.0%；国内游客消费1132.5亿元，增长13.8%。年末拥有A级旅游景区113 处，其中，5A级旅游景区1处，4A级旅游景区24处,3A级旅游景区65处；拥有星级酒店124个，其中，5星级酒店9个，4星级酒店30个，3星级酒店75个；拥有旅行社460个，其中，经营出境旅游业务旅行社38个，经营入境和国内旅游业务旅行社422个。

八、金融业

年末金融机构本外币存款余额13155.7亿元，比年初增加1275.1亿元；人民币存款余额12533.0亿元，比年初增加1191.3亿元，其中，住户存款5023.6亿元，比年初增加381.6亿元。本外币贷款余额11576.8亿元，比年初增加1046.2亿元；人民币贷款余额10771.9亿元，比年初增加1051.8亿元。

全年全市承保金额83650.0亿元，增长36.3%，实现保费收入244.1亿元，增长20.2%。其中：财产险保费收入93.2亿元，增长5.8%；人身险保费收入150.9亿元，增长31.2%。赔款支出金额88.0亿元，增长14.7%；其中财产险赔付金额50.2亿元，人身险赔付金额37.8亿元。

全年辖区证券经营机构累计代理交易额69394.1亿元，增长215.8%。

九、科学技术和教育

初步统计，全年全市共取得重要科技成果639项。获得国家级科技奖励13项，其中，技术发明奖1项，科技进步奖12项；获得省级科技奖励31项，其中，自然科学奖1项，技术发明奖8项，科技进步奖22项。

全年共成交技术合同项目5206项，成交额89.54亿元。全年发明专利申请44962件，发明专利授权5170件。

教育事业较快发展。年末全市共有各类大专院校(含民办高校)23所，其中普通高校20所，全年研究生招生1.1万人，在学研究生3.1万人，毕业生0.9万人。普通本专科招生9.2万人，在校生32.2万人，毕业生8.0万人。中等职业教育招生4.1万人，在校生11.9万人，毕业生4.4万人。接受中等职业教育的学生占高中阶段在校生的50.5%。普通高中招生3.8万人，在校生11.7万人，毕业生4.1万人。初中招生7.3万人，在校生23.9万人，毕业生7.7万人。普通小学招生9.2万人，在校生53.6万人，毕业生7.4万人。特殊教育招生0.03万人，在校生0.2万人，毕业生0.04万人。幼儿园在园幼儿23.3万人。

十、文化、卫生和体育

年末全市文化系统共有影剧院47处，文化馆(站)152处，博物馆53处，公共图书馆13处，艺术表演团体8个，广播电台8座、13套节目，电视台10座、15套节目，全市有线电视用户达到217.54万户。全市共有档案馆12处。

年末全市共有卫生机构(含诊所)3146处，其中，医院、卫生院308处，疾病预防控制中心27处，妇幼保健机构11处，门诊部(所)、卫生保健所、医务室2368处。年末各类卫生技术人员6.6万人，其中，医生2.7万人。全市拥有医疗床位4.9万张，其中，医院、卫生院床位4.5万张。

全市运动员在各项比赛中共获得金牌228枚，银牌179枚，铜牌189枚。全市共有体育专业队1个，队员17人。重点体校2所，学员1032人，业余体校10所，学员1568人。

十一、城市建设

年末全市常住人口城镇化率达到69.99%,比上年提高1.58个百分点。全市建成区面积570平方公里，增长16.1%。城市平均每天供水量119万吨，增长2.6%。城市全年实际用水量3.8亿吨，增长4.4%，其中生产用水和生活用水分别为1.3亿吨和2.5亿吨。

城市使用液化气、煤制气、天然气的总户数达到161.6万户，全年供应液化气总量3.3万吨，供应天然气总量7.9亿立方米。城市气化率达到100%。

全年新增供热面积560万平方米，年末供热面积达到1.2亿平方米。

年末市区公共汽、电车线路417条，增长7.5%。共有营运的公交汽、电车6748辆。共有出租汽车10019辆。

年末城市道路总长度4601公里，城市下水道总长度6992公里。

据抽样调查，年末城镇居民人均现住房建筑面积31.5平方米，农村居民人均现住房建筑面积32.4平方米。

十二、能源、环境和安全生产

初步统计，全年全市规模以上工业综合能源消费量1484万吨标准煤，增长0.3%。其中，原煤消费量1283万吨，下降8.6%，原油消费量1292万吨，下降16.6%，天然气消费量4.7亿立方米，增长1.3%。全社会用电量342亿千瓦时，增长1.3%。其中，工业用电201亿千瓦时，下降1.7%；城乡居民生活用电65亿千瓦时，增长7.9%。

图5：“十二五”时期全市规模以上工业综合能源消费情况

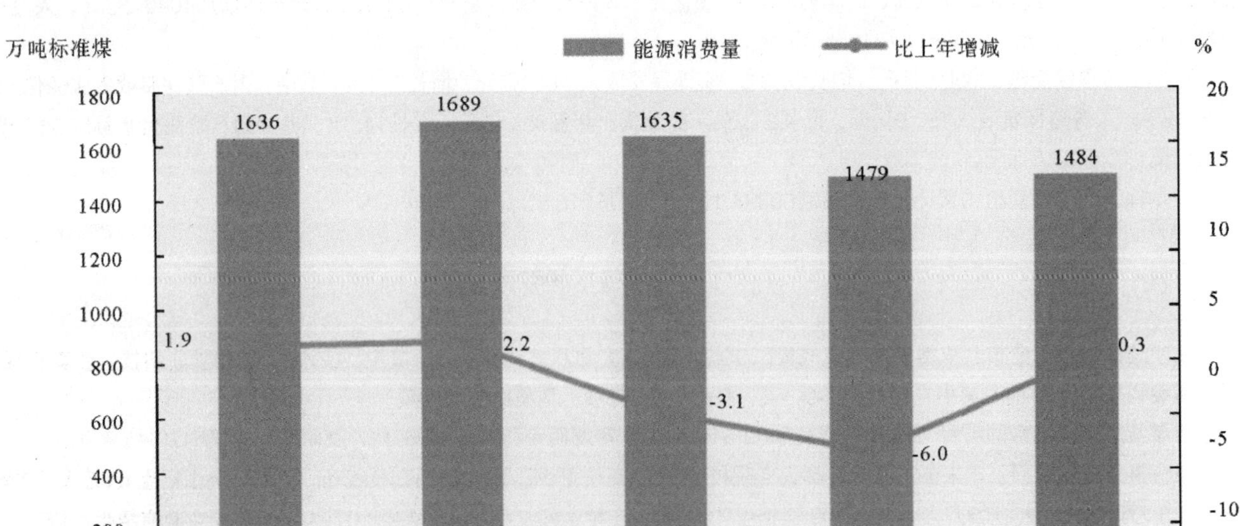

全年全市能源生产量2308万吨标准煤，下降14.6%。其中，原油加工量1288万吨，下降16.6%，汽油生产量363万吨，下降18.8%，柴油生产量366万吨，下降21.5%，火力发电量161亿千瓦时，下降4.4%，风力发电量12亿千瓦时，增长28.7%。

图6：“十二五”时期全市能源生产情况

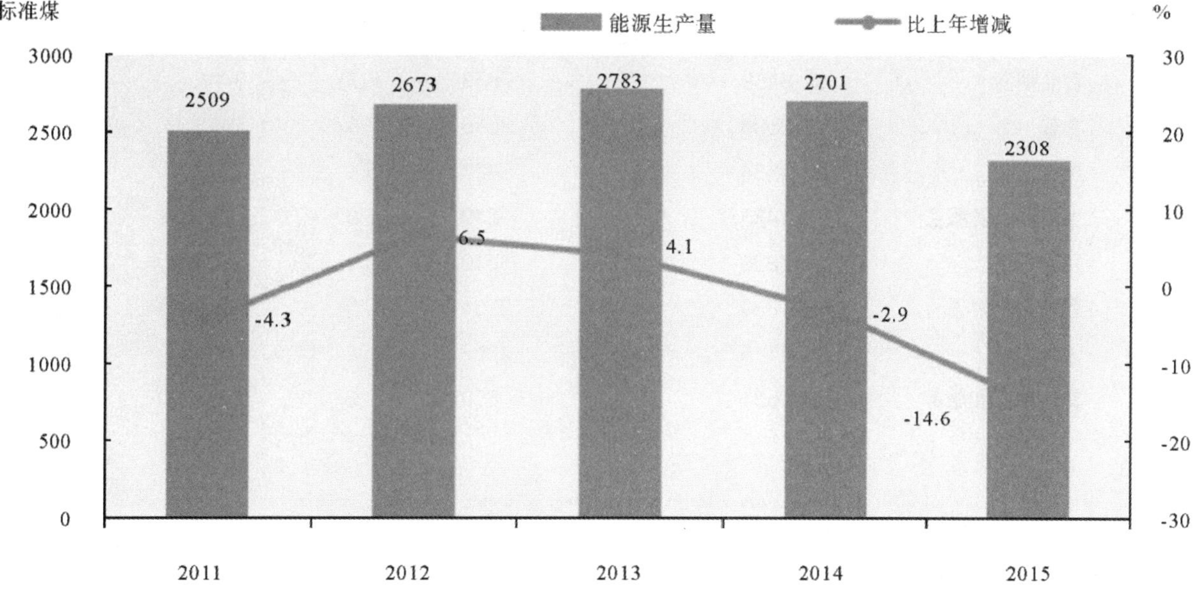

全市年平均气温13.7℃，平均年降水量为450.5毫米，年平均日照总时数为2261.9小时。市区空气质量优良天数达到293天，优良率80.3%。主要污染物可吸入颗粒物（PM2.5）、二氧化硫、二氧化氮年均值分别为0.051、0.028、0.033毫克/立方米，与上年相比,PM2.5下降13.6%,二氧化硫下降24.3%，二氧化氮下降23.3%。全市近岸海域水质达到或好于二类海水水质标准的点位数占81.3%,近岸海域功能区水质达标率为84.4%。全市重点考核断面主要污染物化学需氧量和氨氮浓度同比分别下降15.5%和11.2%。市区区域环境噪声平均值56.7分贝，市区交通干线噪声平均值68.4分贝。人均公园绿地面积14.6平方米。全市现有公园、动物园108个。

全市七个行业(领域)发生各类生产安全事故335起，死亡175人，事故起数比上年下降14.5%，死亡人数比上年下降16.7%。道路交通事故万车死亡1.43人，下降9.5%。

十三、人民生活和社会保障

全市居民人均可支配收入32885元，增长8.6%；全市居民人均消费支出21326元，增长8.5%。城镇居民人均可支配收入40370元，增长8.1%；城镇居民人均消费支出26052元，增长8.0%。农村居民人均可支配收入16730元，增长8.4%；农村居民人均消费支出11127元，增长8.3%。

表 10： 2015 年居民人均可支配收入情况

指标名称	全体居民		城镇居民		农村居民	
	绝对值（元）	增长（%）	绝对值（元）	增长（%）	绝对值（元）	增长（%）
可支配收入	32885	8.6	40370	8.1	16730	8.4
工资性收入	20068	9.4	25040	8.7	9337	9.6
经营净收入	6480	7.4	6277	7.9	6919	6.6
财产净收入	2522	5.2	3580	4.2	236	9.3
转移净收入	3815	9.2	5473	8.2	238	12.4

表 11：2015 年居民人均消费支出情况

指标名称	全体居民		城镇居民		农村居民	
	绝对值（元）	增长（%）	绝对值（元）	增长（%）	绝对值（元）	增长（%）
消费支出	21326	8.5	26052	8.0	11127	8.3
食品烟酒	6459	8.2	7856	7.7	3442	8.0
衣着	2096	7.8	2685	7.5	826	5.3
居住	4584	6.2	5607	5.8	2377	5.8
生活用品及服务	1485	8.1	1819	7.9	765	6.2
交通通信	3226	11.0	3810	10.3	1965	12.2
教育文化娱乐	1830	10.6	2264	10.0	895	10.6
医疗保健	1115	11.2	1352	10.2	604	13.5
其他用品和服务	531	8.8	659	9.3	253	3.3

表 12：2015 年每百户居民家庭主要耐用消费品拥有量

指标名称	单位	数量		
		全体居民	城镇居民	农村居民
家用汽车	辆	47	50	41
摩托车	辆	36	16	83
电冰箱（柜）	台	97	94	105
洗衣机	台	91	91	92
热水器	台	90	91	86
空调	台	81	91	54
彩色电视机	台	104	101	110
摄像机	台	14	18	3
照相机	台	47	57	21
计算机	台	70	80	46
中高档乐器	架	7	9	2
固定电话	部	45	47	41
移动电话	部	216	215	219

年末全市城镇职工基本养老保险参保缴费人数为247.75万人，参加失业保险人数为189.8万人，全年累计领取失业保险金的人数为7.66万人。年末全市城镇登记失业率为3%。

全市各类社会福利院床位达5.0万张，收养28123人。

注：

1、公报中统计数据均为初步统计数。

2、全市GDP及各产业增加值绝对数按现价计算，增长速度按可比价计算。根据《三次产业划分规定》（国统字〔2012〕108号），2015年将农林牧渔业中的农林牧渔服务业，工业中的开采辅助活动以及金属制品、机械和设备修理业等三个行业划入第三产业。根据新的三次产业划分规定和第三次经济普查数据，对2014年数据进行了修正。

3、规模以上工业企业为年主营业务收入2000万元及以上企业；限额以上贸易企业为批发业年主营业务收入在2000万元及以上、零售业500万元及以上、住宿和餐饮业200万元及以上的单位；固定资产投资项目统计的起点标准为计划总投资额500万元。

4、战略性新兴产业根据国家规划，现阶段主要包括节能环保、新一代信息技术、生物、高端装备制造、新能源、新材料、新能源汽车等七个产业领域。

5、常住人口包括：①住本户、户口在本乡镇街道的人（含户口在本户，外出不满半年的人）；②住本户半年以上，户口在外乡镇街道的人；③住本户不满半年，户口在外乡镇街道，离开户口登记地半年以上的人；④住本户，户口待定的人。

6、各类生产安全事故起数、死亡人数统计范围包括生产经营性道路交通、水上交通、铁路交通、民航飞行、农业机械、渔业船舶和工矿商贸七个行业（领域）发生的事故，不再包括森林火灾、火灾事故和非生产经营性道路交通。

7、自2015年开始，全市城乡住户调查统一使用一体化改革后的数据，与原数据相比，城乡居民收支指标的调查范围和口径均存较大变化。原“城市居民人均可支配收入”调整为“城镇居民人均可支配收入”；原“农民人均纯收入”调整为“农村居民人均可支配收入”。

8、资料来源：本公报中财政数据来自市财政局；登记失业率、社会保障数据来自市人力资源社会保障局；银行数据来自人民银行青岛市中心支行；证券数据来自青岛证监局；保险数据来自青岛保监局；水产品数据来自市海洋与渔业局；林业数据来自市林业局；“三品一标”、农机等数据来自市农委；灌溉面积数据来自市水利局；交通运输数据来自市交通运输委；邮政数据来自市邮政管理局；固定电话、宽带、移动电话等数据来自市通信管理局；建成区面积、供水、供气、供热、绿地面积、道路、下水道、公园、动物园等数据来自市城乡建设委；进出口、外资、对外承包工程、对外劳务合作等数据来自市商务局；旅游数据来自市旅游局；教育数据来自市教育局；科技、专利数据来自市科技局；文化、媒体等数据来自市文广新局；体育数据来自市体育局；卫生数据来自市卫生计生委；环境数据来自市环保局；气象数据来自市气象局；安全生产数据来自市安全监管局；居民收支、价格、城乡居民住房面积等数据来自国家统计局青岛调查队；其他数据来自市统计局。

STATISTICS COMMUNIQUE QINGDAO'S ECONOMIC AND SOCIAL DEVELOPMENT DURING 2015

Qingdao Statistics Bureau

NBS Qingdao Survey Office

March 17, 2016

In 2015, under difficult and international economic conditions, Qingdao saw steady economic growth in general. The local government has been resolutely implementing the Central Government's macroeconomic regulations and has taken the initiative to adapt itself to the new norm of the Chinese economy by further promoting the Blue Economy, regional planning and an innovation-driven development strategy. The people's livelihood, social security and ecological environment in Qingdao continue to improve. The city also witnessed, as planned, overall progress in social programs and advancement on building it into a livable, happy modern international city.

I. General

The total number of permanent residents in Qingdao was 9,097,000 by the end of 2015, an increase of 0.56% on 2014; of which 4,902,200 were registered permanent residents in urban areas, up 0.54%.

Table 1: Distribution of permanent resident population in Qingdao city

Region	Amount (10000 persons)
Total	909.70
Shinan District	57.16
Shibei District	107.27
Licang District	54.38
Laoshan District	42.99
Huangdao District	149.36
Chengyang District	69.17
Jimo	120.20
Jiaozhou	87.60
Pingdu	136.21
Laixi	75.47
High-tech Zone	9.89

Preliminary statistics showed a gross domestic product (GDP) of RMB 930.007 billion, up 8.1% year-on-year. Of the total, primary industries contributed RMB 36.398 billion in added value, up 3.2%, secondary industries contributed RMB 402.646 billion in added value, up 7.1%, and tertiary industries contributed RMB 490.963 billion in added value, up 9.4%. The ratio of primary, secondary and tertiary industries was 3.9, 43.3 and 52.8, and the per capita GDP reached RMB 102,519.

Fig. 1 Qingdao's GDP and Growth Rate during the 12th Five Year Plan Period

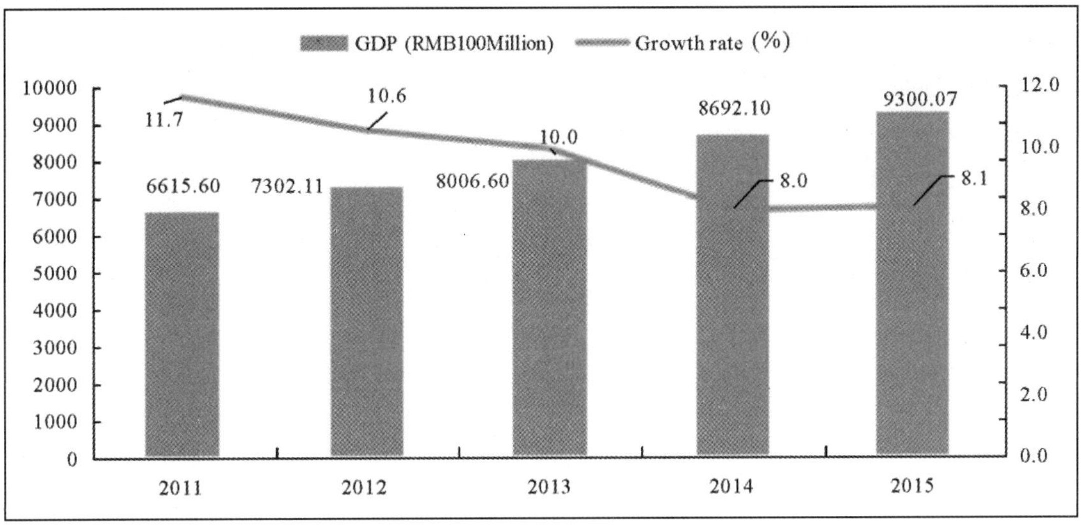

Preliminary statistics showed that the gross marine production was RMB 209.34 billion for the whole year, up 15.1% (based on current prices), accounting for 22.5% of GDP. Modern service industry generated a total of RMB 258.98 billion in added value, up 16.1% (based on current prices), accounting for 27.8% of GDP or 52.8% of the total of service industry.

Table 2: The added value of Qingdao by sector in 2015

Sector	Total Amount (100 million yuan)	Growth Rate (%)
GDP	9300.07	8.1
Farming,Forestry,Animal Husbandry and Fishery	379.06	3.6
Industry	3547.60	6.9
Construction	486.83	8.9
Wholesale and Retail Trade	1167.98	8.0
Transport, Storage and Post	654.72	6.7
Hotels and Catering Services	194.02	1.8
Financial Intermediation	588.28	12.9
Real Estate	479.93	11.1
Other Services	1801.65	10.5

Qingdao realized RMB 271.37 billion in the local government's total revenue, down 4.3%; RMB 100.63 billion in the public budget revenue, up 12.39%; and RMB 122.29 billion in the public budget expenditure, up 13.8%. The national tax revenue (including those collected by customs) fell 10.4% to RMB 120.01 billion. Of the total, internal revenue increased by 4.5% to RMB 72.26 billion and local tax revenue rose 12.6% to RMB 67.43 billion.

The total consumer price index (CPI) increased by 1.2% over the previous year, the lowest during the 12th Five Year Plan Period. The Producer Price Index for Industrial Products (PPI) fell 3.0%. The producer purchase price index decreased by 5.8%. In December, urban newly-built residential housing prices fell 2.2% while second-hand residential housing prices declined 0.3% year-on-year.

Table 3: Consumer price index of the city in 2015

Name	Total (the same period of last ear=100)
Consumer Price Index	101.2
Non-Food Price Index	101.0
Price Index of Services	101.3
Consumer Price Index	101.2
1、Food	101.7
# Grain	101.5
Pork	110.9
Egg	90.1
Vegetables	109.4
2、Tobacco and Liquor	102.3
3、Clothing	102.8
4、Household Facilities,Articles and Services	100.6
5、Medical Care and Personal Products	103.8
6、Transportation and Communication	97.2
7、Education,Cultural and Recreation Services	101.2
8、Residence	100.3

Fig. 2 The percentage of CPI going up in this city year-on-year during China's Twelfth Five-year Plan

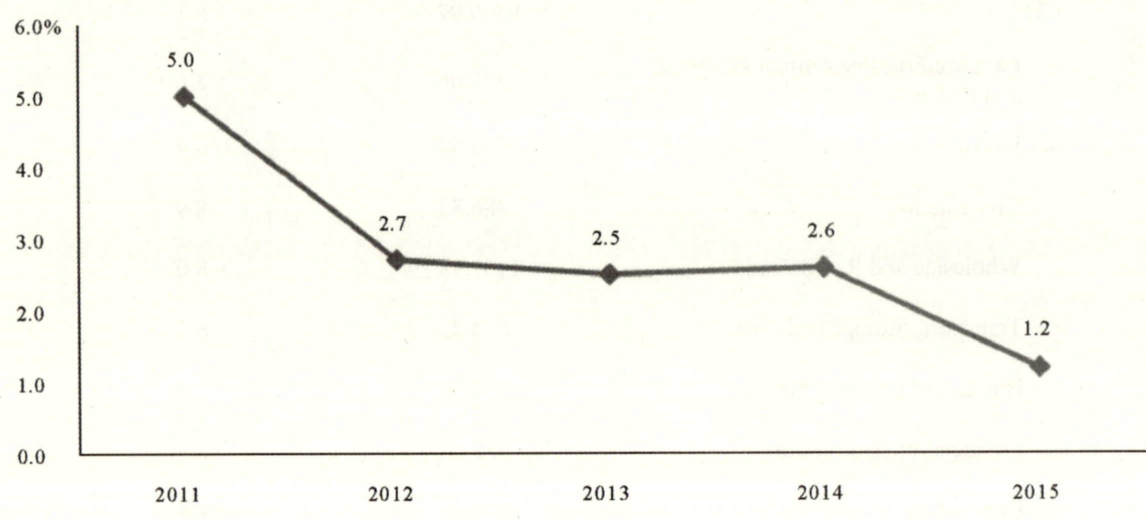

II. Agriculture

The sown area for crops totaled 493,000 hectares, a decrease of 2,000 hectares from the previous year;the sown area for vegetables totaled 105,000 hectares, a decrease of 331 hectares; the sown area for peanuts totaled 82,000 hectares, a decrease of 7,000 hectares. The total grain output decreased by 0.5% to 3,214,000 tons year-on-year; the total output of vegetables and edible fungi decreased by 2.7% to 5,791,000 tons; the total output of peanuts decreased by 13.2% to 346,000 tons; the total output of fruits including melons used as fruit was 1,187,000 tons, which was equal to that of the previous year. In Qingdao, there are 695 modern agricultural parks, 100 of them are new ones; and 805 pollution-free, green, organic and geographical indication-labeled agricultural products, an increase of 182 on 2014. The agricultural product quality traceability system covers 85% of its standardized parks and green food bases.

Fig. 3 Production of vegetables, grains and aquatic products during the 12th Five Year Plan period

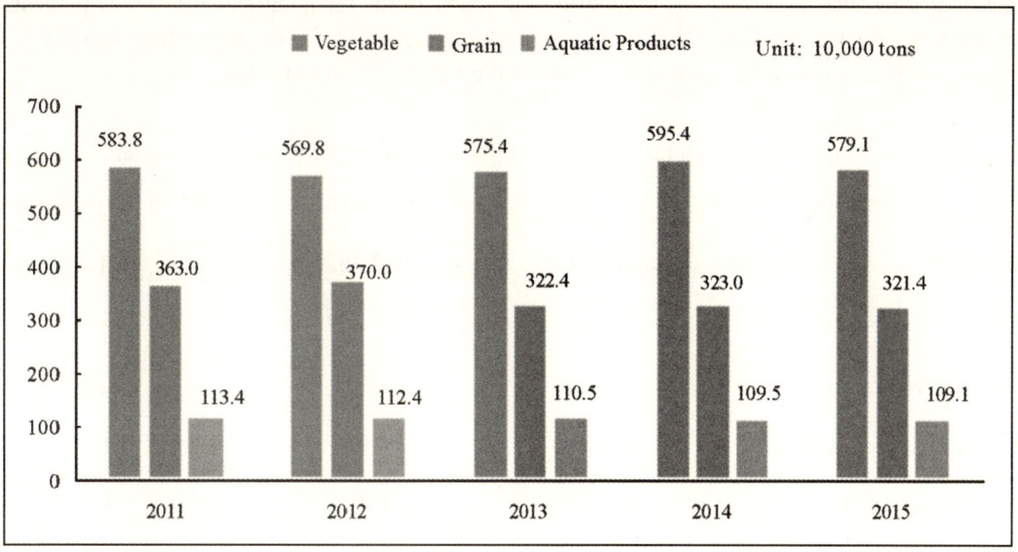

Vegetable Grain Aquatic Products Unit: 10,000 tons

2011: 583.8, 363.0, 113.4
2012: 569.8, 370.0, 112.4
2013: 575.4, 322.4, 110.5
2014: 595.4, 323.0, 109.5
2015: 579.1, 321.4, 109.1

10,000 hectares of trees were planted in the year. Forest coverage reached 40%.

Total meat output reached 547,000 tons, down 8.2 percent year-on-year. Egg output totaled 183,000 tons, down 4.3 percent. The total output of milk was 354,000 tons, down 5.7 percent.

The total output of aquatic products, excluding distant fishing, reached 1,091,000 tons, down 0.3%. The combined seawater and freshwater farming area was 49,000 hectares, down 2.1%. The total ocean catch was 136,000 tons, up 94.6%.

The power of agricultural machinery totals 8,540,000 kilowatts, an increase of 270,000 kilowatts. Integrated mechanization level of crop production reaches 90.2%. The effective irrigated area of farmland amounts to 319,000 hectares, of which water-saving irrigated area reaches 140,000 hectares.

III. Industry and Construction

In 2015, industries above designated size added value increased by 7.5%. By industry, the medal products industry's added value rose 12.3%; electrical machinery and equipment manufacturing industry up 8.9%; the agricultural and food processing industry increased by 8.3%; railroads, ships, aerospace and other transportation equipment manufacturing industries up 10.6%; general equipment manufacturing industry up 7.6%; special equipment manufacturing industry up 9.3.%; rubber and plastic products industry up 11.0%; the six energy-consuming industries added value rose 3.7% over the previous year, of which, non-metallic mineral products industry up 8.9%; chemistry raw materials and chemistry product industry up 14.4%; non-ferrous metal smelting and rolling processing industry up 9.9%; ferrous metal smelting and rolling processing industry down 2.3%; power, heat production and supply industry down 0.5%, petroleum processing, coking and nucleus fuel processing industry down 3.8%; and equipment manufacturing industries added value up 8.7%, accounting for 44.2% of added value of industries above designated size.

Table 4: Growth rate of added value of industries above designated size in 2015

Description of indicators	+/-% on the previous year
Total	7.5
Of which: Light industry	7.5
Heavy industry	7.5
Of which: State-owned enterprises	-0.3
Collective businesses	-0.4
Joint-stock cooperative businesses	-6.6
Shareholder businesses	8.4
Businesses invested by foreign business people and by compatriots from Hong Kong, Macao and Taiwan	6.8
Other types of business	12.8

The Industrial Enterprises above Designated Size finished a total output of RMB 1,734.98 billion, up 7.8%, of which, Hi-tech Industries increased by 9.4%, accounting for 41.0% of the total, an increase of 0.27 percentage from the beginning of the year; the ten-hundred-billion industry chains increased by 7.8%, accounting for 75.0% of the total; strategic emerging industries above Designated Size increased by 15.2% in output value.

Table 5: The output and growth rate of the main products of industries above designated size in 2015

Description	Unit	Output	+/-% on the previous year
Color TV sets	1,000 sets	17,362	1.2
Of which: LCD TV sets	1,000 sets	17,362	1.2
Household refrigerators	1,000 sets	8,721	12.8
Household washing machine	1,000 sets	5,951	0.7
Room air conditioners	1,000 sets	6,232	-9.1
Cigarettes	billion pieces	55.74	-0.5
Beer	1,000 kiloliters	1,560	-4.1
Sodium carbonate (soda ash)	1,000 tons	689	1.6
Tire casings	1,000 pieces	51,795	6.2
Sheet glass	1,000 weight cases	5,350	-12.6
Raw steel	1,000 tons	1,546	-27.9
Automobile	1,000 units	861	11.8
Motor train units or electric Multiple Unit (EMU)	units	2,070	7.7
Medal shipping containers	1,000 m^3	21,403	15.5
Crude oil processed	1,000 tons	12,881	-16.6
Power output	billion KWh	17.35	-2.0

Industries above designated size realized total operating income of RMB 1,671.52 billion, up 6.8%, total pre-tax profit of RMB 175.49 billion, up 15.0%, after-tax profit of RMB 93.73 billion, up 15.3%, of which, state-owned and controlled enterprises totaled 14.33 billion, an increase of 32.8 percent; collective enterprises totaled 8.66 billion, up 13.1 percent; joint-stock enterprises totaled 57.78 billion, up 16.9 percent; foreign invested enterprises including Hong Kong, Macao and Taiwan invested enterprises totaled 24.97 billion, up 12.6 percent.

The construction industries generated RMB 48.68 billion in added value, up 8.9% and RMB 8.34 billion in pre-tax profit, up 7.1%.

IV. Fixed Assets Investment

The fixed asset investment (including the projects with investment over RMB 5,000,000 in townships and rural areas) totaled RMB 655.57 billion, up 14.2%. Of the total, RMB 11.5 billion was invested in primary industries, up 9.8%, RMB 325.35 billion in secondary industries, up 16.5% and RMB 318.72 billion in tertiary industries, up 12.1%.

Table 6: Investment in the fixed assets (excluding farmers) by sector in 2015 and its growth

Sector	Investment (100 million yuan)	+/-% on the Previous year
Total	6555.7	14.2
Agriculture Forestry Animal Husbandry and Fishery	115	9.8
Mining	12.1	-9.8
Manufacturing	3059.4	15.8
Production and Supply of Electricity Gas and Water	74.3	55.2
Construction	107.7	21.2
Wholesale and Retail Trades	287	19.9
Transport Storage and Post	484.7	54.4
Hotels and Catering Services	58.8	7.3
Information Transmission Computer Services and Software	38.6	15.2
Financial Intermediation	4.5	-51.2
Real Estate	1347.1	0
Leasing and Business Services	196.2	9.2
Scientific Research and Technical Services	108.7	68
Management of Water Conservancy Environment and Public Facilities	354	39
Services to Households and Other Services	13.9	-5.3
Education	77.7	5.6
Health Social Security and Social Welfare	21.4	70.9
Culture Sports and Entertainment	126.1	-35
Public Management and Social Organizations	68.5	31.4

The fixed assets investment construction projects number 6,894. New start-up projects number 6,120 and completed projects number 5,074. The amount of investment in projects in progress (including real estate) was RMB 1,595.19 billion. Additional RMB 452.4 billion was invested in fixed assets for the whole year. The project completion ratio was 73.6% and the fixed asset delivery ratio was 69%.

Finished investment in real estate development for the whole year reached RMB 112.23 billion, up 0.4%, of which housing investment totaled 75.69 billion, up 3.5%. The total sold housing area was 14,186,000 square meters, up 21.9%, of which apartments sales totaled 12,390,000 square meters, up 21.2%.

Fig. 4 Commodity housing sales in the city during the Twelfth Five-year Plan Period

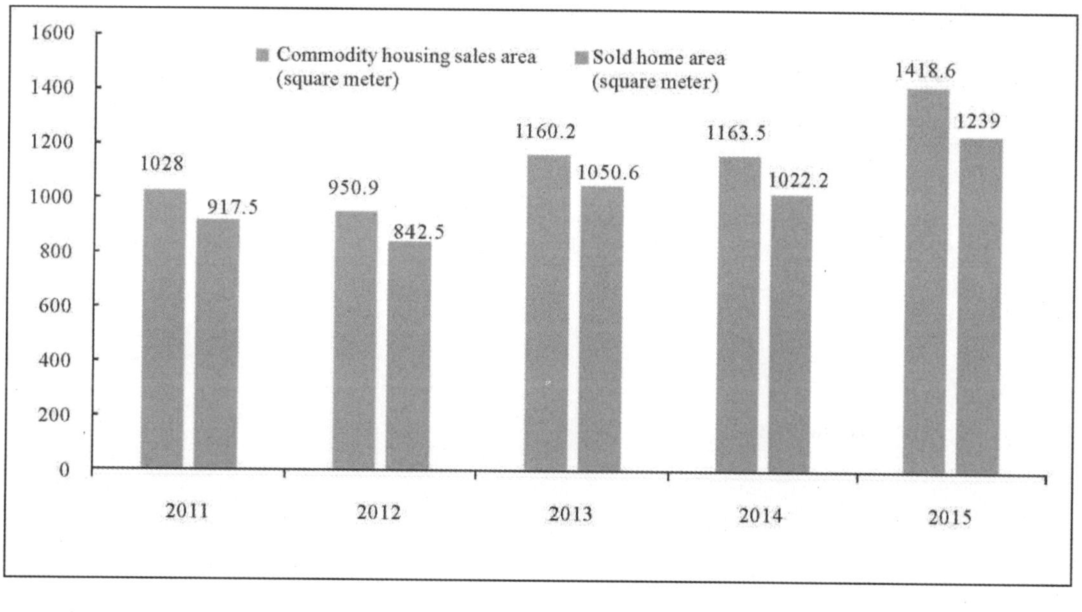

The new construction projects each with a planned total investment of RMB 100,000,000 or more (including real estate projects) numbered 545, a decrease of 172. By district, there were 266 new construction projects in urban areas, including 248 in the four cities and 31 in the Hongdao Economic Zone. Key infrastructure projects include the Qingdao-Rongcheng intercity railway, which is intergrated into the transporation hub and related projects in Qingdao with a total planned investment of RMB 3.34 billion, of which RMB 3.34 billion was invested in the year; Qingdao-Haiyang intercity railway (the Blue Silicon Valley sector) with a total planned investment of RMB 19.47 billion, of which RMB 5.56 billion was invested in the year; and Hongdao-Jiaonan intercity rail transit project with a total planned investment of RMB 13.55 billion, of which RMB 3.46 billion was invested in the year. Major construction projects include West-coast Economic New District with finished investment of RMB 171.47 billion in 2015, up 15.8%; industrial projects (excluding real estate development) under construction in the Blue Silicon Valley numbered 210, 12 more than the previous year, which have used investment of RMB 34.63 billion, up 15.8%, of which 57 projects under construction were in core areas, 17 more than the previous year, which have used investment of RMB 21.12 billion, up 37.3%.

V. Domestic Trade

In 2015, total retail sales of consumer goods rose 10.5% to RMB 371.37 billion. Geographically, RMB 310.91 billion was generated by urban markets, up 10.7% and RMB 60.46 billion by rural markets, up 9.4%. By industry, wholesale and retail industries realized sales of RMB 324.60 billion, up 10.3%, while the lodging and catering industries generated RMB 46.77 billion, up 11.9%.

In 2015, the retail sales of consumer goods of legal entities (businesses) above the limited value amounted to RMB 120.56 billion, up 9.6%. The retail sales of motor vehicles above the limited value reached RMB 30.87 billion, up 6.9%; that of petroleum and petroleum products totaled RMB 15.31 billion, down 10.9%; that of grains and oil, food, beverages, cigarettes and alcohols amounted to RMB 15.84 billion, up 17.7%; that of daily necessities added up to RMB 3.24 billion, up 0.1%; and that of cosmetics totaled RMB 2.18 billion, up 5.4%.

VI. Foreign Trade

Qingdao's import and export volume was RMB 436.13 billion, down 11.1%, with exports amounting to RMB 281.82 billion, up 0.3% and imports amounting to RMB 154.31 billion, down 26.3%.

Table 7: Import & export of main commodities to/from Qingdao

Unit: Billion, %

Category	Import & Export		Export		Import	
	Amount	Growth Rate %	Amount	Growth Rate %	Amount	Growth Rate %
Textiles and garments	47.04	-10.0	43.19	-8.8	3.85	-21.1
Agricultural products	60.38	-10.5	31.00	-2.9	29.38	-17.3
Electrical and mechanical products	160.66	2.4	119.59	8.6	41.07	-12.1
High-tech products	47.43	-0.1	27.19	16.3	20.24	-16.0

Note: This table is not full measurement.

Table 8: Import from and export to major countries and regions in 2015 and growth rates

Unit: 100 million USD, %

Country/Region	Export Amount (billion USD)	+/-% over the previous year	Import Amount (billion USD)	+/-% over the previous year
Asia	190.5	-5.4	126.5	-22.8
Hong Kong	18.8	30.2	0.7	-37.7
Taiwan	4.6	-12.3	10.9	-23.1
Japan	52.9	-11.6	18.7	-11.9
Korea	41.4	-13.2	36.5	-13.9
ASEAN	37.4	0.2	38.2	-8.6
South Asia	11.8	-10.4	3.5	-55.1
Middle East	22.1	0.3	11.8	-58.5
Africa	19.2	-21.7	10.6	-57.2
South Africa	3.4	-5.6	2.5	-55.0
Europe	90.6	-3.5	31.0	-20.5
EU	81.0	-1.4	20.7	-16.4
U.K.	14.3	0.2	1.7	14.4
Germany	16.7	3.1	6.6	-26.2
France	8.8	-1.7	2.6	13.7
Italy	6.3	-4.4	2.4	-23.9
CIS and Eastern Europe	6.6	-27.5	8.0	-28.8
Russia	4.9	-28.6	7.1	-23.5
South America	30.0	-5.3	30.4	-27.1
Brazil	3.9	-34.4	17.7	-28.6
North America	107.2	15.0	27.2	-9.1
U.S.A.	98.0	17.4	23.3	-3.4
Canada	8.6	-1.5	3.6	-36.3
Oceania	15.8	21.8	21.8	-41.1
Australia	14.0	24.9	18.3	-46.0

Note: This table is not full measurement.

According to Qingdao Customs' statistics, imports and exports registered at Qingdao ports totaled RMB 897.26 billion, down 11.1%. Of the total, RMB 545.11 billion were exports, up 1.6% and RMB 352.16 billion were imports, down 26.3%.

In 2015, direct foreign investment reached USD 6.69 billion, up 10.0% while domestic investment from outside investors totaled RMB151.62 billion, up 9.8%.

Total contracted value of overseas contractor projects and services was USD 3.66 billion, up 60.6%. Turnover amounted to USD 3.64 billion, up 1.3%; the number of personnel sent overseas reached 17,047, up 28.1%.

VII. Transportation, Post, Telecommunications and Tourism

Port throughput totaled 0.5 billion tons for the whole year, up 4.3%, with 0.33 billion tons handled for foreign trade, up 3.7%. Container throughput reached 17,430,000 TEUs, up 5.1%.

Table 9: Volume completed by various transportation means and increase/decrease

Transportation means	Volume (Unit)	+/-% on the previous year
Passenger volume	15.17 billion person-km	4.3
Railways	7.39 billion person-km	5.2
Highways	7.76 billion person-km	3.5
Waterways	0.03 billion person-km	-10.0
Cargo volumes	116.63 billion ton-km	12.4
Railways	16.68 billion ton-km	-1.4
Highways	44.38 billion ton-km	0.5
Waterways	55.57 billion ton-km	30.2

By the end of the year, there were 120 domestic airlines, 19 international airlines and 5 airlines to/from Hong Kong, Macao and Taiwan. The airport passenger throughput for the whole year reached 18,202,000 person-times, up 10.9%. Air cargo and mail throughput was 208,000 tons, up 1.8%. Postal and telecommunication service business transactions in 2015 totaled RMB 21.8 billion, up 23.6%. Of the total, RMB 4.16 billion was from the postal service, up 34.7%, and RMB 17.64 billion from the telecommunication service, up 21.2%. The total number of express deliveries was 160 million, up 53.3%. Internet users number 2,493,000 in 2015, up 9.7%. At the end of the year, fixed-line telephone users number 2,138,000. Mobile phone users number 13,356,000.

Tourists to Qingdao during the year totaled 74,558,000 person-times, up 8.9%. Tourism income for the year totaled RMB 127 billion, up 14.1%. Of the total, international tourists totaled 1,338,000 person-times, up 4.5%; Tourism income of international tourists totaled USD 917,979,000, up 11.6%. Domestic tourists totaled 73,220,000 person-times, up 9.0%; Tourism income of domestic tourists totaled RMB 113.25 billion, up 13.8%. By the end of the year, there were 113 A-rated tourist attractions, of which one is 5A-rated, 24 are 4A-rated and 65 are 3A-rated; there were 124 star-rated hotels, of which 9 are five-star hotels, 30 four-star hotels, 75 three-star hotels; there were 460 travel agencies, of which, 38 operate outbound travel services and 422 are engaged in inbound and domestic tourists services.

VIII. Finance

At year-end, the balance of local and foreign currencies on the deposit accounts with financial institutions in Qingdao stood at RMB 1,315.57 billion, an increase of RMB 127.51 billion from the beginning of the year. The balance of deposits in local currency (RMB) was RMB 1,253.3 billion, an increase of RMB 119.13 billion from the beginning of the year. Of the total, the balance of residents' savings was RMB 502.36 billion, an increase of RMB 38.16 billion from the beginning of the year. The loan balance in local and foreign currencies reached RMB 1,157.68 billion, an increase of RMB 104.62 billion from the beginning of the year. The loan balance in local currency (RMB) was RMB 1,077.19 billion, an increase of RMB 105.18 billion from the beginning of the year.

The insured amount was RMB 8,365 billion, up 36.3%. The insurance premium totaled RMB 24.41 billion, up 20.2%. Of the total, RMB 9.32 billion was for property insurance, up 5.8%; and RMB 15.09 billion for personal insurance, up 31.2%. Expenses for claims amounted to RMB 8.8 billion, up 14.7%. Of the total, RMB 5.02 billion was for property claims and RMB 3.78 billion for personal claims.

The trading amount of the securities institutions for the whole year reached RMB 6,939.41 billion, up 215.8%.

IX. Science, Technology and Education

Preliminary statistics show that Qingdao achieved 639 key scientific and technological results in 2015 and received 13 national scientific and technological prizes. Of the total, 1 was for technological inventions and 12 were for scientific and technological progress; it also received 31 provincial-level scientific and technological prizes. Of them, 1 was for natural science, 8 were for technological inventions, and 22 were for scientific and technological progress.

In 2015, there were a total of 5,206 technology transfer contracts completed with a value of RMB 8.954 billion;

44,962 patents were pending and 5,170 were granted with patent certificates.

The education sector develops rapidly. By the end of 2015, there were 23 higher education schools (including private schools) with 20 regular colleges and universities. 11,000 new postgraduate students were enrolled last year, 31,000 postgraduate students were in school and 9,000 of them graduated. Regular colleges and universities enrolled 92,000 new students, 322,000 students were in school and 80,000 of them graduated. Technical secondary schools and vocational schools enrolled 41,000 new students, 119,000 students were in school, and 44,000 of them graduated. The number of students in vocational secondary schools accounted for 50.5% of the number of senior high school students. 38,000 new students were enrolled by regular high schools, 117,000 students were in school, 41,000 of them graduated. 73,000 new students were enrolled by junior high schools, 239,000 students were in school, 77,000 of them graduated. Primary schools enrolled 92,000 new students, 536,000 students were in school, 74,000 of them graduated. Special education schools enrolled 300 new students, 2,000 students were in school and 400 of them graduated. 233,000 children were in kindergartens.

X. Culture, Public Health Services and Sports

At year-end, cultural institutions in Qingdao includes 47 cinemas and theaters, 152 cultural centers (stations), 53 museums, 13 public libraries, 8 performing arts troupes, 8 radio and broadcasting stations with 13 programs and 10 TV stations with 15 programs. Cable TV users number 2,175,400. There were 12 archives in Qingdao.

At the end of the year, there were 3,146 public health institutions (including clinics). Of the total, there were 308 hospitals, 27 epidemic prevention institutions, 11 children and women's health care centers and 2,368 clinical and medical health locations. There were 66,000 medical professionals, including 27,000 doctors. Medical beds number 49,000, with 45,000 beds in hospitals and clinics.

Qingdao athletes won 228 gold medals, 179 silver medals and 189 bronze medals in various games. There was 1 professional sport team with 17 members. Key sports schools number 2, enrolling 1,032 students. Part-time sports schools number 10, enrolling 1,568 students.

XI. Urban Construction

At the end of the year, the urbanization rate accounts for 69.99% of the city, up 1.58%. Built-up area reached 570 square kilometers, up 16.1%. Urban water supply averaged 1,190,000 tons per day, up 2.6%. The actual urban water consumption for the year totaled 0.38 billion tons, up 4.4%, including 0.13 billion tons for production use and 0.25 billion tons for residential use.

Liquefied petroleum fuel, coal gas and natural gas users number 1,616,000. The total supply for liquefied petroleum fuel for the year was 33,000 tons, and for natural gas was 0.79 billion cubic meters. The urban gas coverage was 100%.

Total heating space increased by 5,600,000 square meters to 0.12 billion square meters by the end of the year.

At the end of the year, there were 417 public bus and trolley lines operating in urban areas, up 7.5%. 6,748 public buses and trolleys were in operation. Taxicabs number 10,019.

Distance covered by roads in urban areas totaled 4,601 km. The total length of underground sewers was 6,992 km.

A survey showed that the per capita average floor space in urban areas was 31.5 square meters at the end of the year, and the per capita average floor space for rural residents was 32.4 square meters.

XII. Energy, Environment and Work Safety

Preliminary statistics showed that the total energy consumption of industrial enterprises above the designated size in Qingdao in 2015 was 14,840,000 tons of standard coal, up 0.3% from the previous year. Of the total, consumption of raw coal was 12,830,000 tons, down 8.6%; consumption of crude oil was 12,920,000 tons, down 16.6%; and consumption of natural gas was 0.47 billion cubic meters, up 1.3%. The total power consumption was 34.2 billion kilowatt-hours, up 1.3%. Of the total, industrial power consumption was 20.1 billion kilowatt-hours, down 1.7%; rural and urban residents' power consumption was 6.5 billion kilowatt-hours, up 7.9%.

Fig. 5 Comprehensive energy consumption of industrial enterprises above designed size in the city during the Twelfth Five-year Plan Period

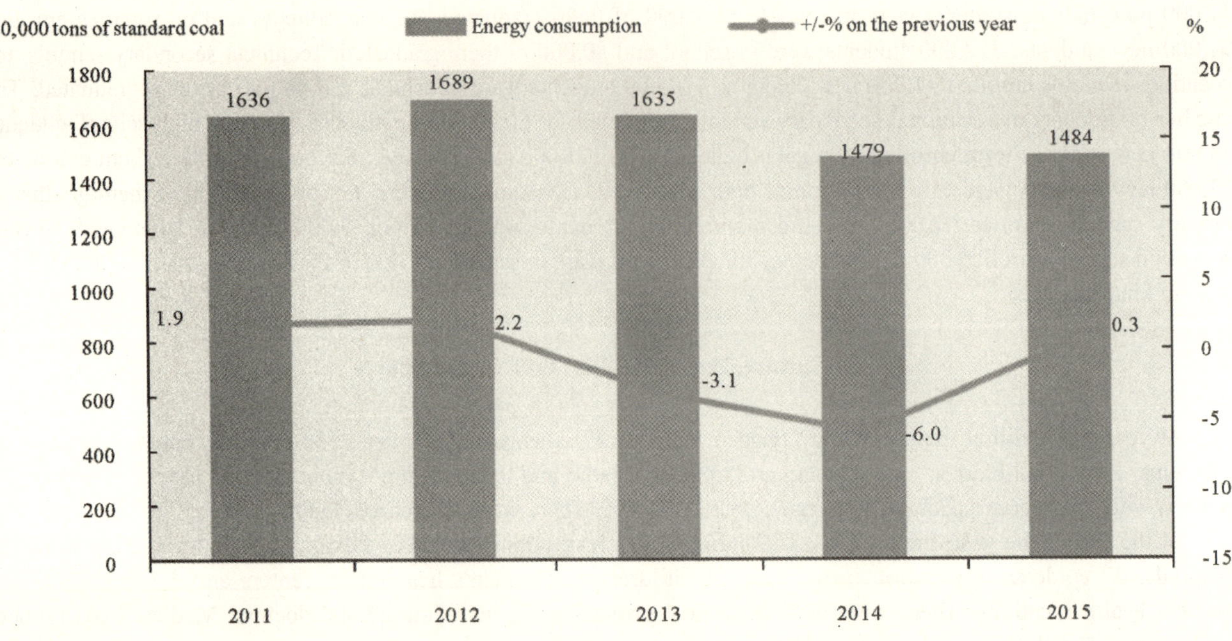

The total power output in Qingdao in 2015 was 23,080,000 tons of standard coal, down 14.6% from the previous year. Of the total, the amount of crude oil processed was 12,880,000 tons, down 16.6%, the output of gasoline was 3,630,000 tons, down 18.8%, and the output of diesel oil was 3,660,000 tons, down 21.5%. The total thermal power output was 16.1 billion kilowatt-hour, down 4.4%; while the amount of wind power generation was 1.2 billion kilowatt-hour, up 28.7%.

Fig. 6 Energy production during the 12th Five Year Plan period

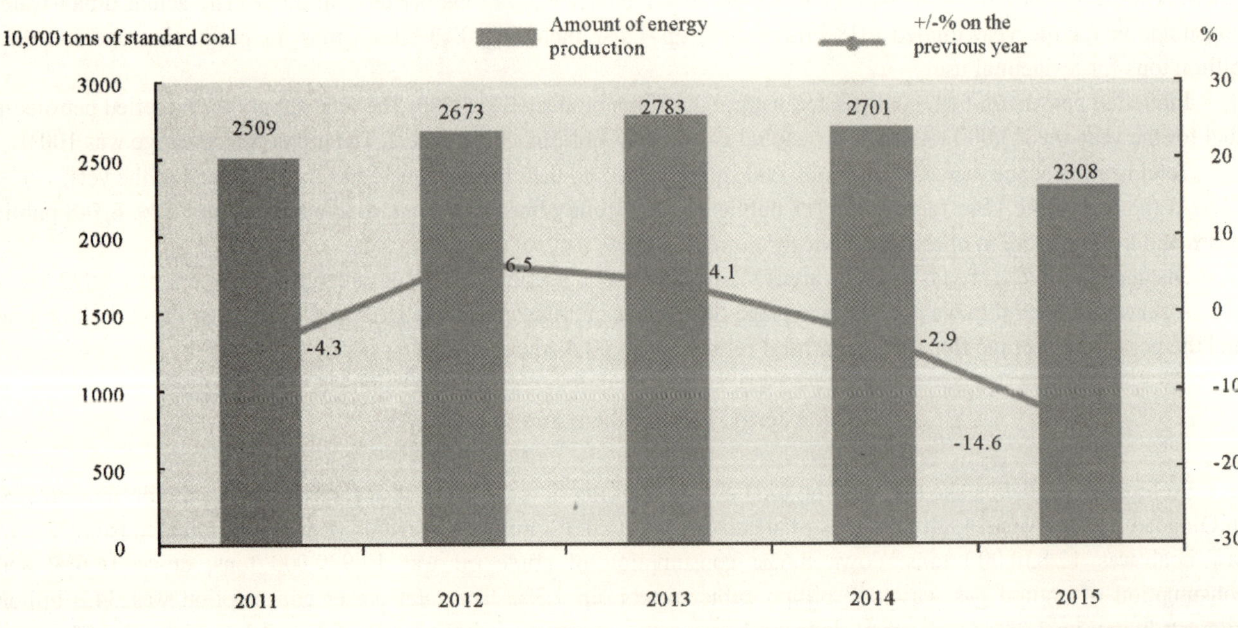

The average temperature was 13.7℃ for the whole year, the average amount of precipitation was 450.5 millimeters and annual average sunshine time reached 2,261.9 hours. Acceptable air quality percentages in urban areas reached 293 days, accounting for 80.3% of the whole year. Major pollutants inhalable particulate matter (PM2.5), sulfur dioxide and nitrogen dioxide averaged 0.051, 0.028 and 0.033 milligram/cubic meter respectively. Compared to the previous year, the amount of PM2.5 decreased by 13.6%, sulfur dioxide dropped 24.3%, and nitrogen dioxide decreased by 23.3%. The area of the city's coastal water up to or better than the second class of sea water quality standard was 81.3% of the total. The compliance rate of water in the inshore functional areas was 84.4%. COD (Chemical Oxygen Demand) and ammonia nitrogen concentration of major pollutants in key rivers being monitored by the city government fell 15.5% and 11.2% respectively. Environmental noise pollution in urban areas averaged 56.7 dB. Noise pollution at traffic trunk lines in urban areas averaged 68.4 dB. Per capita "green area" was 14.6 square meters. There are 108 parks and zoos in Qingdao.

There were 335 accidents happened at work of 7 industries (sectors), down 14.5%, with 175 people died, down 16.7%. The road traffic death toll per 10 thousand vehicles was 1.43 persons, a decrease of 9.5%.

XIII. Living Conditions and Social Security

The per capita disposable income of residents in Qingdao was RMB 32,885, up 8.6%. The per capita consumption expense of all residents was RMB 21,326, up 8.5%. The per capita disposable income of urban residents was RMB 40,370, up 8.1%. The per capita consumption expense of urban residents was RMB 26,052, up 8.0%. The per capita disposable income of rural residents was RMB 16,730, up 8.4%. The per capita consumption expense of rural residents was RMB 11,127, up 8.3%.

Table 10：Per capita disposable income in 2015

Description of indicators	Residents		Urban Residents		Rural Residents	
	Absolute Value (RMB)	Growth Rate %	Absolute Value (RMB)	Growth Rate %	Absolute Value (RMB)	Growth Rate %
Disposable income	32,885	8.6	40,370	8.1	16,730	8.4
Salary income	20,068	9.4	25,040	8.7	9,337	9.6
Operating net income	6,480	7.4	6,277	7.9	6,919	6.6
Property net income	2,522	5.2	3,580	4.2	236	9.3
Transfer net income	3,815	9.2	5,473	8.2	238	12.4

Table 11：Per capita consumption expense in 2015

Description of indicators	Residents		Urban Residents		Rural Residents	
	Absolute Value (RMB)	Growth Rate %	Absolute Value (RMB)	Growth Rate %	Absolute Value (RMB)	Growth Rate %
Consumption expense	21,326	8.5	26,052	8.0	11,127	8.3
Food, tobacco and liquor	6,459	8.2	7,856	7.7	3,442	8.0
Clothing	2,096	7.8	2,685	7.5	826	5.3
Housing	4,584	6.2	5,607	5.8	2,377	5.8
Living product and services	1,485	8.1	1,819	7.9	765	6.2
Transportation and communication	3,226	11.0	3,810	10.3	1,965	12.2
Education, culture and entertainment	1,830	10.6	2,264	10.0	8950	10.6
Medical and health care	1,115	11.2	1,352	10.2	604	13.5
Other product and services	531	8.8	659	9.3	253	3.3

Table 12: Amount of major durable consumer goods owned by every 100 rural households

Description of indicators	Unit	Quantity		
		Residents	Urban Residents	Rural Residents
Household automobile	unit	47	50	41
Motorcycles	unit	36	16	83
Refrigerators	set	97	94	105
Washing machines	set	91	91	92
Water heaters	set	90	91	86
Air-conditioners	set	81	91	54
Color TV sets	set	104	101	110
Video cameras	set	14	18	3
Cameras	set	47	57	21
Computers	set	70	80	46
High-end musical instruments	unit	7	9	2
Fixed-line telephones	set	45	47	41
Mobile telephones	set	216	215	219

At the end of 2015, the number of people covered under the basic pension program was 2,477,500, people who participated in the unemployment insurance program number 1,898,000, and people who received payment from the unemployment insurance program number 76,600. At year-end, the registered urban unemployment rate was 3%.

Nursing homes registered 50,000 beds with 28,123 residents.

Notes:

1. Figures reported herein are preliminary statistics.
2. The GDP and the absolute added value of industries in Qingdao were calculated at current prices and growth rates were calculated at comparable prices. According to the *Regulation on Classification of the Three Industries (NBS No. (2012) 108)*, in 2015, three sectors, such as the service sector of farming, forestry, animal husbandry and fishery, mining support activities of industry, metal products, machinery and equipment repair industry were classified into the tertiary industry. In line with the new *Regulation* and the data of the third economic census, corrections have been made to the numbers for 2014.
3. The statistics starting point for industries above the designated size is RMB 20,000,000 in terms of annual operating revenue. The statistics starting point for trading companies above limited value is RMB 20,000,000 in terms of annual operating revenue in wholesale industry, for retail industry is RMB 5,000,000, for hotels and catering industry is RMB 2,000,000; The statistics starting point for fixed asset investment projects is RMB 5,000,000 in terms of total planned investment amount.
4. According to the national planning, the strategic emerging industries refer to the seven industries or sectors including energy conservation and environmental protection, the new generation of information technology, biology, high-end equipment manufacturing, new energy, new materials and new energy vehicles.
5. Permanent residents including: ① the people who have maintained residency in the local and registered in the household register with a local township or sub-district (including those who are registered in the household register and have left home for less than half a year); ② those who have maintained residency in the local for more than half a year and registered in the household register with other township or sub-district; ③ those who have maintained residency in the local for less than half a year, registered in the household register with other township or sub-district and have left his/her place of household registration for more than half a year; ④ those who have maintained residency in the local, but his/her permanent residence is yet to be registered.
6. The statistics of various accidents happened at workplace and death toll cover that happened in 7 industries or sectors, including productive or operative road traffic, waterway, railway, civil aviation flight, agricultural machinery, fishing boats and industrial and mining business and trade, excluding forest fire, fire accident and non-productive or operative road traffic.
7. From 2015 on, the data used are statistics of the integrated survey of residents in urban and rural areas. Compared with previous data, there is a significant change in statistic coverage and gauge for indicators of urban and rural residents' income and expenditure. The 'per capita disposable income of residents' in cities was changed to 'per capita disposable income of urban residents'; the 'per capita net income of farmers' was changed to 'per capita disposable income of rural residents'.
8. Sources: The financial data in this Communique was from Qingdao Finance Bureau; the registered unemployment rate and social security data were from Qingdao Human Resources and Social Security Bureau; banking data from Qingdao Central Branch of the People's Bank of China; securities data from Qingdao Office of CSRC; insurance data from Qingdao Insurance Regulatory Bureau; aquatic products data from Qingdao Marine and Fishery Bureau; forestry data from Qingdao Forestry Bureau; the 'green food', farming machinery and other data from Qingdao Agricultural Commission; irrigated areas data from Qingdao Water Conservancy Bureau; transportation data from Qingdao Transportation Committee; postal data from Qingdao Postal Administration; fixed-line, broadband, mobile phones and other data from Qingdao Communication Administration; data in respect of the built-up area, water supply, gas supply, heating, green area, roads, drains and sewers, parks, zoos, etc. were provided by Qingdao Rural and Urban Construction Commission; data of import and export, foreign investment, foreign contracted projects, foreign labor cooperation, etc. from Qingdao Commerce Bureau; travel data from Qingdao Tourism Bureau; educational statistics from Qingdao Education Bureau; scientific and technological and patent data from the Qingdao Science and Technology Bureau; data of culture, media, etc. from Qingdao Administration for Culture, Radio, TV, News and Publishing; sports data from Qingdao Sports Bureau; health data from Qingdao Health and Family Planning Commission; environmental data from Qingdao Environmental Protection Bureau; meteorological data was provided by Qingdao Meteorological Bureau; safety work data provided by Qingdao Safety Supervision Bureau; residents' income and expenditure, prices, housing area of urban and rural residents and other data provided by National Bureau of Statistics (NBS) Qingdao Survey Office; other data from Qingdao Statistics Bureau.

1 综合 GENERAL SURVEY

简要说明

一、本篇资料的主要内容

本篇资料是对我市行政区划、气象情况、分行业法人单位数、各部门机构数和国民经济、社会发展的综合反映，主要包括行政区划、气象情况、分行业法人单位数、各部门机构数、国民经济主要比例关系、国民经济和社会发展主要指标占全国全省比重、国民经济和社会发展主要指标及其增长速度等资料。

二、本篇资料的来源

1、“行政区划”主要包括2015年底各区(市)街道办事处(乡镇)、社区居委会(村民委员会)区划资料，数据来源于市民政局。

2、“气象情况”包括分区市、市区分月气象资料，数据来源于市气象局。

3、“全市生产总值”来源于国民经济核算统计报表，由市统计局国民经济核算处整理提供。

4、国民经济和社会发展综合部分来源于本年鉴各篇章中的资料，由市统计局国民经济综合统计处加工整理。

Brief Introduction

I. Main Content

Data in this chapter cover the main indicators on divisions of administrative areas, meteorology, corporate units, number of grass-roots units and national economy and social development, including divisions of administrative areas, meteorology, number of corporate units, number of grass-roots units, average daily social and economic activities, ratio, and percentage of main indicators of Qingdao to the whole nation and the whole province and growth rate of main indicators.

II. Source of Data

(1) Data on divisions of administrative areas are mainly including the information on sub-district offices (villages and towns) and community neighborhood committees (villagers residents' committees) at the end of 2015.The data are provided by Qingdao Municipal Bureau of Civil Affairs.

(2)Data on meteorology are provided by Qingdao Municipal Meteorological Bureau.

(3)Data on gross national product are prepared according to the data of national accounts and compiled by the Division of National Accounts of Qingdao Municipal Bureau of Statistics.

(4)Data on general survey of economy and society are based on those of different chapters and compiled by the Division of Comprehensive Statistics of Qingdao Municipal Bureau of Statistics.

1-1 行政区划(2015 年底)
ADMINISTRATIVE DIVISION(END OF 2015)

单位:个(unit)

市、区名称	Region	街道办事处 Subdistrict Offices	社区居委会 Community Residents' Committees	镇 Town	村民委员会 Villagers' Committees
		小计 Sub-total		小计 Sub-total	
全　市	**Whole Municipality**	**102**	**1 153**	**43**	**5 445**
市南区	Shinan District	14	65		
市北区	Shibei District	31	135		
李沧区	Licang District	11	1116		
崂山区	Laoshan District	4	157		
黄岛区	Huangdao District	12	259	10	962
城阳区	Chengyang District	8	245		1
即墨市	Jimo	8	54	7	1 028
胶州市	Jiaozhou	6	51	6	811
平度市	Pingdu	5	42	12	1 782
莱西市	Laixi	3	29	8	861

1 –2 气象情况(2015 年)
METEOROLOGY(2015)

市、区名称	Region	平均气温（摄氏度）Average Temperature（℃）	极端气温 Extreme Temperature(centigrade)		降水量（毫米/年）Precipitation（millimeter/year）	日照时数（小时/年）Sunshine Hours（hour/year）	平均气压（百帕）Average Atmospheric Pressure(100 pa)
			最高(摄氏度) Maximum(℃)	最低(摄氏度) Minimum(℃)			
市　区	Urban Area	13.7	34.8	-6.5	421.2	2 117.9	1 008.3
崂山区	Laoshan District	14.6	35.7	-7.2	389.2	2 279.3	1 012.3
黄岛区	Huangdao District	13.9	35.7	-9.5	510.3	2 268.9	1 016.2
即墨市	Jimo	13.7	35.5	-10.2	391.2	2 230.7	1 011.6
胶州市	Jiaozhou	13.6	36.5	-9.2	485.4	2 170.5	1 007.5
平度市	Pingdu	13.3	36.4	-11.3	428.0	2 348.5	1 009.9
莱西市	Laixi	12.8	35.6	-11.6	528.4	2 429.8	1 008.1

注:以上为 7 个国家基准站或基本站。
Note:These are 7 national reference or base stations.

1 –3 市区分月气象情况(2015 年)
MONTHLY METEOROLOGY OF URBAN AREA(2015)

月　份	Month	平均气温（摄氏度）Average Temperature（℃）	降水量（毫　米）Precipitation（millimeter）	日照时数（小　时）Sunshine Hours（hour）
一月	Jan.	1.9	2.9	152
二月	Feb.	2.6	10.4	155.6
三月	Mar.	7.0	2.7	217.4
四月	Apr.	12.0	46.6	211.4
五月	May	17.0	32.7	220.3
六月	June	20.9	46.3	164.6
七月	July	24.6	41.7	173.8
八月	Aug.	26.2	38.2	209.3
九月	Sept.	22.4	70.6	212.6
十月	Oct.	17.5	42.6	192.8
十一月	Nov.	8.8	79.2	76.2
十二月	Dec.	3.7	7.3	131.9
全年	Annual Total	13.7	421.2	2 117.9

1 –4 各部门机构数(2015 年底)

GRASS-ROOTS UNITS IN VARIOUS SECTORS(END OF 2015)

项　目	Item	单位	Unit	机构数 Grass-roots Units
农村基层单位	**Rural Grass-roots Units**			
镇政府	Town Governments	个	unit	43
乡村户数	Number of Rural Households	万户	10 000 households	155.4
工业企业单位	**Industrial Enterprises**	**个**	**unit**	**24 896**
规模以上工业	Above Designated Size	个	unit	4 876
#国有企业	State-owned Enterprises	个	unit	141
集体企业	Collective-owned Enterprises	个	unit	15
外商及港澳台商投资企业	Enterprises with Funds from Hong Kong, Macao, Taiwan and Foreign Countries	个	unit	1 361
规模以下工业	Under Designated Size	个	unit	20 110
交通运输业	**Transportation**			
铁路	Railway	个	unit	
公路	Highway	个	unit	96
水运	Waterway	个	unit	22
邮电业	**Postal and Telecommunication Services**			
邮电局所	Post Offices	处	unit	651
建筑业企业	**Construction Enterprises**	**个**	**unit**	**562**
国有企业	State-owned Enterprises	个	unit	23
集体企业	Collective-owned Enterprises	个	unit	14
其他	Others	个	unit	525
批发和零售业、住宿和餐饮业	**Wholesale & Retail Trades, Hotels and Catering Services**			
限额以上批发业	Wholesale Trade above Designated Size	个	unit	1 069
限额以上零售业	Retail Trade above Designated Size	个	unit	648
限额以上住宿业	Hotel above Designated Size	个	unit	164
限额以上餐饮业	Catering Service above Designated Size	个	unit	170

1 -4 续表
continued

项　目	Item	单位	Unit	机构数 Grass-roots Units
教育事业	**Education**			
普通高等学校	Regular Institutions of Higher Education	所	unit	24
中等专业学校	Specialized Secondary Schools	所	unit	6
普通中学	Regular Secondary Schools	所	unit	293
普通小学	Regular Primary Schools	所	unit	772
幼儿园	Kindergartens	所	unit	2 221
科研机构	**Science and Technology Institutions**	**个**	**unit**	
中央属	Central Level	个	unit	19
地方属	Local	个	unit	35
文化及相关产业	**Culture and Related Industry**			
文化事业机构	Cultural Institutions	个	unit	480
公共图书馆	Public Libraries	个	unit	12
影剧院	Cinemas	个	unit	47
广播、电视台	**Radio and Television Broadcasting Stations**			
广播电台	Radio Stations	个	unit	8
电视台	Television Stations	个	unit	10
卫生事业	**Public Health**	**个**	**unit**	
#医院	Hospitals	个	unit	308
民政行政单位	**Civil Affairs Departments**			
#社会福利事业机构	Institutions of Social Welfare	个	unit	209

1 -5 按行业分法人单位数
NUMBER OF CORPORATE UNITS BY SECTOR

单位：个(unit)

行 业	Sector	2015
总 计	**Total**	**232 828**
农、林、牧、渔业	Agriculture Forestry Animal Husbandry and Fishery	4 452
采矿业	Mining	140
制造业	Manufacturing	44 272
电力、燃气及水的生产和供应业	Production and Supply of Electricity Gas and Water	332
建筑业	Construction	12 344
批发和零售业	Wholesale and Retail Trades	86 486
交通运输、仓储和邮政业	Transport Storage and Post	8 855
住宿和餐饮业	Hotels and Catering Services	2 752
信息传输、软件和信息技术服务业	Information Transmission Computer Services and Software	6 460
金融业	Financial Intermediation	1 380
房地产业	Real Estate	5 143
租赁和商务服务业	Leasing and Business Services	25 463
科学研究和技术服务业	Scientific Research and Technical Services	10 250
水利、环境和公共设施管理业	Management of Water Conservancy Environment and Public Facilities	1 240
居民服务、修理和其他服务业	Services to Households and Other Services	4 878
教 育	Education	3 646
卫生和社会工作	Health Social Security and Social Welfare	1 520
文化、体育和娱乐业	Culture Sports and Entertainment	2 716
公共管理、社会保障和社会组织	Public Management and Social Organizations	10 499
国际组织	International Organization	

1 -6 国民经济主要平均指标
AVERAGE INDICATORS ON NATIONAL ECONOMY

指　　标	Indicator	单　位	Unit	2000	2005
人口密度	Density of Population	人/平方公里	person/sq. km	664	695
每户年平均人口	Average Household Size	人	person	3.14	3.12
城镇非私营单位在岗职工年平均工资	The Average Annual Wage of Staff and Workers in the Post in Non-Private Units in Towns and Cities	元	yuan	10 072	19 086
城市居民人均年可支配收入	Annual Per Capita Disposable Income of Urban Households	元	yuan	8 016	12 920
农民人均年纯收入	Annual Per Capita Net Income of Rural Households	元	yuan	3 637	5 806
每一播亩平均粮食产量	Output of Grain Per Mu of Sowing Area	千克	kg	411	421
每亩蔬菜平均产量	Average Output of Vegetables Per Mu	千克	kg	2 735	2 985
每亩茶叶平均产量	Average Output of Tea Per Mu	千克	kg	8.1	16.5
每亩花生平均产量	Average Output of Peanut Per Mu	千克	kg	298	327
每亩棉花平均产量	Average Output of Cotton Per Mu	千克	kg	83	74
每台拖拉机负担耕地面积	Cultivated Area Ploughed by Per Tractor	亩/台	mu/unit	56	39
每亩耕地施用化肥量(折纯)	Chemical Fertilizer Consumption Per Mu(convert to pure amount)	千克	kg	45	52
每人平均消费品零售额	Per Capita Retail Sales of Consumer Goods	元	yuan	6 077	11 822
城市每天平均生活用水量	Daily Residential Consumption of Water	万吨	10 000 tons	33.33	34.35
城市每人平均公园绿地面积	Per Capita Public Green Areas	平方米	sq. m	8.50	11.82
每万人拥有医疗床位	Number of Hospital Beds per 10000 Population	张	bed	34.5	41.3
每万人拥有医生数	Number of Doctors per 10000 Population	人	person	21.0	20.3
每万人中高等学校学生数	Students Enrollment of Institutions of Higher Education per 10 000 Population	人	person	65	324
每万人中中等学校学生数	Students Enrollment of Secondary Schools per 10 000 Population	人	person	704	768
每万人中小学学生数	Students Enrollment of Primary Schools per 10000 Population	人	person	757	648

注:自 2015 年开始,全市城乡住户调查统一使用一体化改革后的数据,与原数据相比,城乡居民收支指标的调查范围和口径均存较大变化。原"城市居民人均可支配收入"调整为"城镇居民人均可支配收入";原"农民人均纯收入"调整为"农村居民人均可支配收入"。

Note:From 2015 on, the data used are statistics of the integrated survey of residents in urban and rural areas across Qingdao. Compared with previous data, there is a significant change in statistic coverage and gauge for indicators of urban and rural residents' income and expenditure. The 'per capita disposable income of residents in cities was changed to 'per capita disposable income of urban residents'; the 'per capita net income of farmers' was changed to 'per capita disposable income of rural residents.

2006	2007	2008	2009	2010	2011	2012	2013	2014	2015
703	711	715	676	677	679	682			
3.13	3.14	3.13	3.12	3.1	3.09	3.09			
22 575	26 201	29 404	32 507	37 501	43 077	49 052	55 363	62 104	69 465
15 328	17 856	20 464	22 368	24 998	28 567	32 145	35 227	38 294	40 370
6 546	7 477	8 509	9 249	10 550	12 370	13 990	15 731	17 461	16 730
407	422	436	446	437	444	456	430	435	435
3 078	3 166	3 511	3 562	3 606	3 759	3 756	3 802	3 786	3 694
18.0	21.0	28.0	28	30	30	33	29	30	32
309	312	315	312	303	313	321	309	299	281
76	75	78	79	78	87	105	100	111	104
36	36	36	35	32	31			38	38
52	55	50	48	47	47			37	36
13 640	16 137	19 640	22 699	25 694	30 043	34 248	38 606	43 064	47 423
29.27	31.25	30.96	33.56	34.31	27.53	33.21	32.50	40.60	42.10
11.80	13.30	14.53	14.50	14.58	14.58	14.60	14.60	14.60	14.60
38.3	39.7	42.5	43.0	47.2	52.2	61.4	58.0	60.3	62.0
20.6	19.8	21.4	21.9	23.2	23.9	28.1	31.2	32.0	33.5
347	349	354	361	373	380	386	388	402	411
740	737	765	740	701	659	635	626	614	596
646	640	627	610	606	626	630	642	662	685

1－7 主要年份社会经济主要指标
MAJOR YEAR'S INDICATORS ON SOCIETY AND ECONOMY

指　　标	Indicator	单　位	Unit	2000	2005
人口	**Population**				
总人口(年末)	Population at Year-end	万人	10 000 persons	706.65	740.91
男性人口	Male	万人	10 000 persons	357.74	374.03
女性人口	Female	万人	10 000 persons	348.91	366.87
市区人口	Urban Area	万人	10 000 persons	234.60	265.43
就业	**Employment**				
社会从业人员	Employment	万人	10 000 persons	397.6	471.0
#单位从业人员	Employed Persons in Units	万人	10 000 persons	118.3	224.3
经济总量	**Gross Economic Amount**				
全市生产总值(当年价)	GDP(at current price)	亿元	100 million yuan	1 191.25	2 687.46
第一产业增加值	Primary Industry	亿元	100 million yuan	140.85	178.33
第二产业增加值	Secondary Industry	亿元	100 million yuan	555.21	1 392.02
第三产业增加值	Tertiary Industry	亿元	100 million yuan	495.19	1 117.10
人均生产总值	Per Capita GDP	元	yuan	16 009	33 085
农林牧渔业总产值(当年价)	Gross Output Value of Farming, Forestry, Animal Husbandry and Fishery (at current price)	亿元	100 million yuan	248.33	320.51
工业总产值(当年价)	Gross Industrial Output Value (at current price)	亿元	100 million yuan	1 940.83	5 001.78

注:1. 单位从业人员 2004 年以前为职工人数(不含私营企业)。
　2. 规模以上固定资产投资数据 2003 年以前为城镇以上统计范围。
　3. 2002 年以前地方财政一般公共预算收支数据为地方财政收支口径。

Note:1. Before 2004, the data of employed persons in units refers to the number of staff and workers(excluding private enterprises).
　2. Before 2003, the data of investment in fixed assets above designated size refers to urban investment.
　3. Before 2002, the data of general budgetaty revenue and expenditure of local government finance refers to revenue and expenditure of local government finance.

2006	2007	2008	2009	2010	2011	2012	2013	2014	2015
749.38	757.99	761.56	762.92	763.64	766.36	769.56			
377.99	381.66	382.46	382.35	381.92	382.69	383.82			
371.39	376.33	379.10	380.56	381.72	383.67	385.74			
270.99	275.55	276.25	275.47	275.50	277.09	279.57			
490.1	505.8	513.8	525.7	540.3	551.2	559.9	571.5	589.0	595.4
243.2	249.8	254.1	260.5	269.4	275.9	283.2	293.7	303.0	309.2
3 183.18	3 750.16	4 401.56	4 853.87	5 666.19	6 615.60	7 302.11	8 006.56	8 692.10	9 300.07
183.95	203.59	223.40	230.25	276.99	306.38	324.41	340.50	349.62	363.98
1 666.96	1 934.52	2 234.83	2 420.14	2 758.62	3 150.72	3 402.23	3 651.39	3 890.41	4 026.46
1 332.28	1 612.05	1 943.33	2 203.48	2 630.58	3 158.50	3 575.47	4 014.67	4 452.07	4 909.63
38 608	44 964	52 266	57 251	65 827	75 563	82 680	89 797	96 524	102 519
339.61	342.99	400.85	408.61	483.18	535.93	566.52	611.86	630.04	660.14
5 918.81	7 430.64	8 946.73	10 255.62	11 614.83	13 277.96	15 306.32	16 897.18	17 444.21	18 019.43

1 -7 续表 1
continued

指　标	Indicator	单　位	Unit	2000	2005
财政	**Government Finance**				
公共财政预算收入	Public Budget Revenue	亿元	100 million yuan	80.01	176.34
公共财政预算支出	Public Budget Expenditure	亿元	100 million yuan	87.87	203.06
规模以上固定资产投资额	**Investment in Fixed Assets above Designated Size**	**亿元**	**100 million yuan**	**242.68**	**1 403.30**
社会消费品零售额	**Total Retail Sales of Consumer Goods**	**亿元**	**100 million yuan**	**428.29**	**870.11**
港口吞吐量	**Volume of Freight Handled in Ports**	**万吨**	**10 000 tons**	**8 661**	**18 727**
集装箱吞吐量	**Volume of Containers Handled**	**万标箱**	**Ten Thousand TEUs**	**212.0**	**630.7**
民航货邮吞吐量	**Volume of Freight and Mail Handled in Civil Aviation**	**万吨**	**10 000 tons**	**4.84**	**8.91**
对外贸易	**Foreign Trade**				
外贸进出口总额	Imports and Exports (excluding central and provincial companies)	亿美元	100 million USD	108.31	304.55
#出口总额	Exports	亿美元	100 million USD	61.14	175.88
教育、卫生、文化	**Education Public Health, Culture**				
小学在校学生数	Students Enrollment in Primary Schools	万人	10 000 persons	53.49	47.98
普通中学在校学生	Students Enrollment in Regular Secorndary Schools	万人	10 000 persons	39.85	39.11

2006	2007	2008	2009	2010	2011	2012	2013	2014	2015
225.77	292.58	342.44	376.99	452.61	566.14	670.18	788.93	895.25	1 006.26
236.79	321.18	369.41	433.58	532.39	658.06	765.98	1 014.23	1 074.71	1 222.87
1 485.69	**1 635.36**	**2 019.01**	**2 458.89**	**3 022.48**	**3 502.54**	**4 153.91**	**5 027.86**	**5 766.03**	**6 555.70**
1 016.35	**1 216.22**	**1 492.22**	**1 730.22**	**1 961.13**	**2 302.37**	**2 635.62**	**2 986.81**	**3 361.72**	**3 713.69**
22 438	**26 507**	**30 029**	**31 668**	**35 012**	**37 971**	**41 465**	**45 782**	**47 701**	**49 749**
770.0	**946.6**	**1 037.7**	**1 027.7**	**1 201**	**1 302**	**1 450**	**1 552**	**1 658**	**1 743**
10.10	**11.57**	**13.05**	**13.54**	**16.37**	**16.65**	**17.19**	**18.62**	**20.44**	**20.80**
365.57	436.05	521.59	439.86	561.49	712.63	732.08	779.12	798.88	702.22
216.45	267.76	314.62	269.22	333.51	400.56	408.20	419.86	457.77	453.50
48.39	48.48	47.72	46.50	46.27	47.95	49.50	49.63	51.65	53.65
36.52	36.04	37.39	37.74	38.00	37.32	36.96	36.51	36.26	35.54

1－7 续表 2
continued

指　　标	Indicator	单　位	Unit	2000	2005
高等学校在校学生	Students Enrollment in Institutions of Higher Education	万人	10 000 persons	4.61	23.98
小学专任教师	Full-time Teachers in Primary Schools	万人	10 000 persons	3.17	3.17
普通中学专任教师	Full-time Teachers in Regular Secorndary Schools	万人	10 000 persons	2.63	2.97
影剧院	Cinemas	个	unit	45	39
医生总数	Doctors	万人	10 000 persons	1.49	1.50
医院床位数	Hospital Beds	万张	10 000 beds	2.01	2.86
人民生活	**People's Living Conditions**				
在岗职工工资总额	Total Wage Bill of Employed Staff and Workers	亿元	100 million yuan	120.40	359.5
城市居民人均可支配收入	Per Capita Disposable Income of Urban Households	元	yuan	8 016	12 920
农民人均纯收入	Per Capita Net Income of Rural Households	元	yuan	3 637	5 806
城乡人民币储蓄存款余额	Savings Deposit of Urban and Rural Households	亿元	100 million yuan	535.32	1 343.10
物价指数	**Price Indexes**				
商品零售价格指数（以1950年价格为100）	Retail Price Index(1950 = 100)	%	%	520.5	495.0
居民消费价格指数（以1950年价格为100）	Consumer Price Index(1950 = 100)	%	%	711.9	753.1
#食品价格指数（以1950年价格为100）	Food Price Index(1950 = 100)	%	%	800.1	871.8

注：1. 在岗职工工资总额2005年前统计范围为全部职工不含私营企业。
2. 2015年“城乡人民币储蓄存款余额”改为“住户存款”。

Note: 1. Before 2005, the statistics range of total wage bill of employed staff and workers is all the staff and workers except those in private enterprises.
2. In 2015, “balance of RMB deposits in urban and rural areas” changed to “household deposits.”

2006	2007	2008	2009	2010	2011	2012	2013	2014	2015
26.03	26.49	26.93	27.52	28.49	29.15	29.66	30.02	31.35	32.23
3.22	3.26	3.24	3.22	3.2	3.16	3.17	3.28	3.22	3.45
2.92	2.96	2.99	3.06	3.08	3.14	3.20	3.18	3.2	3.29
40	40	40	40	40	40	36	40	43	47
1.55	1.50	1.63	1.67	1.77	1.83	2.16	2.41	2.5	2.63
2.67	2.81	2.99	3.05	3.34	3.56	4.12	3.97	4.3	4.51
445.6	518.1	578.7	638.1	738.0	877.5	1 044.3	1 251.7	1 456.0	1 644.4
15 328	17 856	20 464	22 368	24 998	28 567	32 145	35 227	38 294	40 370
6 546	7 477	8 509	9 249	10 550	12 370	13 990	15 731	17 461	16 730
1 567.62	1 702.04	2 123.36	2 527.88	2 912.33	3 198.51	3 757.60	4 141	4 436	5 024
493.5	506.8	526.6	519.2	526.5	550.2	559.6	567.4	580.5	580.5
759.9	794.1	831.4	835.6	854.0	896.7	920.9	943.9	968.4	980.0
886.6	989.5	1 105.3	1 123.0	1 194.9	1 327.5	1 384.6	1 458.0	1 522.2	1 548.1

1-8 国民经济主要结构指标
COMPOSITION INDICATORS ON NATIONAL ECONOMY

指　　标	Indicator	2000	2005	2006
社会从业人员	**Employment**			
产业结构	Industrial Composition			
第一产业	Primary Industry	36.4	22.2	21.0
第二产业	Secondary Industry	33.9	41.8	42.8
第三产业	Tertiary Industry	29.7	36.0	36.2
全市生产总值	**GDP**			
产业结构	Industrial Composition			
第一产业	Primary Industry	11.8	6.6	5.8
第二产业	Secondary Industry	46.6	51.8	52.4
第三产业	Tertiary Industry	41.6	41.6	41.8
农业	**Agriculture**			
农林牧渔业产值结构	Composition of Farming, Forestry, Animal Husbandry and Fishery			
#农业	Farming	45.0	39.5	40.1
林业	Forestry	0.8	0.8	0.7
牧业	Animal Husbandry	27.9	33.4	31.7
渔业	Fishery	26.4	26.3	25.2
工业	**Industy**			
轻重工业产值结构	Composition of Output Value of Light and Heavy Industry			
轻工业	Light Industry	64.1	49.4	48.5
重工业	Heavy Industry	35.9	50.6	51.5
固定资产投资	**Investment in Fixed Assets**			
投资结构	Composition of Investment			
生产性	Productive	54.0	65.4	62.0
非生产性	Non-productive	46.0	34.6	38.0

单位:%

2007	2008	2009	2010	2011	2012	2013	2014	2015
20.2	19.9	20.1	19.5	19.2	18.8	18.8	18.4	18.1
43.1	43.0	41.9	41.4	41.2	41.0	40.6	39.0	38.6
36.7	37.1	38.0	39.1	39.6	40.2	40.6	42.6	43.3
5.4	5.1	4.7	4.9	4.6	4.4	4.3	4.0	3.9
51.6	50.8	49.9	48.7	47.6	46.6	45.6	44.8	43.3
43.0	44.1	45.4	46.4	47.8	49.0	50.1	51.2	52.8
43.3	44.4	45.4	48.4	44.1	44.0	46.4	47.6	51.1
0.6	0.6	0.5	0.4	0.4	0.4	0.4	0.4	0.4
28.4	30.3	28.4	26.2	29.1	27.9	26.8	26.3	24.6
24.2	21.4	22.0	21.8	23.0	24.2	22.8	21.8	19.7
45.0	42.3	41.7	38.7	38.3	39.5	39.5	38.8	39.5
55.0	57.7	58.3	61.3	61.7	60.5	60.5	61.2	60.5
62.6	61.6	56.3	53.6	53.2	58.4	61.65	57.08	63.16
37.4	38.4	43.7	46.4	46.8	41.6	38.35	42.92	36.84

1-9 平均每天主要社会经济活动
SELECTED INDICATORS ON AVERAGE DAILY SOCIAL AND ECONOMIC ACTIVITIES

指　标	Indicator	单位	Unit	2000	2005
全市生产总值	GDP	万元	10 000 yuan	32 637	73 629
工业总产值	Gross Industrial Output Value	万元	10 000 yuan	53 174	137 035
农林牧渔业总产值	Gross Output Value of Farming, Forestry, Animal Husbandry and Fishery	万元	10 000 yuan	6 803	8 781
主要工业产品产量	Output of Major Industrial Products				
发电量	Electricity	万千瓦时	10 000 kW·h	2 489	2 701
钢材	Rolled-steel	吨	ton	2 558	9 049
纱	Yarn	吨	ton	191	198
布	Cloth	万米	10 000 m	114	141
家用电冰箱	Refrigerator	台	unit	8 523	24 899
彩色电视机	Color TV set	台	unit	10 395	36 282
社会消费品零售总额	Total Retail Sales of Consumer Goods	万元	10 000 yuan	11 734	23 839
固定资产投资	Investment in Fixed Assets above Designated Size	万元	10 000 yuan	6 649	38 446
外贸进出口总额	Imports and Exports	万美元	10 000 USD	3 707	9 047
港口吞吐量	Volume of Freight Handled in Ports	万吨	10 000 tons	23.73	51.31

注:固定资产投资包括城镇、农村500万元以上投资项目。

Note: Investment in fixed assets includes construction projects involving an urban or rural investment of 5,000,000 yuan and over.

2006	2007	2008	2009	2010	2011	2012	2013	2014	2015
87 210	102 744	120 591	132 983	155 238	181 249	200 058	219 359	238 140	254 796
162 159	203 579	245 116	280 976	318 215	363 780	419 351	462 936	477 924	493 683
9 304	9 397	10 982	11 195	13 238	14 683	15 521	16 763	17 261	18 086
3 412	4 255	4 509	4 730	4 984	4 759	4 787	4 935	4 885	4 754
10 288	10 015	9 593	9 579	9 136	9 101	7 525	6 312	5 830	3 853
154	131	118	106	97	53	53	92	89	76
151	121	133	85	48	120	134	141	122	77
35 342	22 173	19 813	22 663	21 951	19 686	15 754	14 366	16 714	23 893
33 030	23 989	22 922	29 170	30 444	31 622	39 452	41 426	46 984	37 704
27 845	33 321	40 883	47 403	52 130	63 079	72 209	81 831	92 102	101 745
40 704	44 804	55 315	67 367	82 808	95 960	113 806	137 751	157 973	179 608
12 527	12 527	14 695	12 288	15 633	19 768	20 057	21 346	21 887	19 239
61.47	72.62	82.27	86.76	96	104	114	125	131	136

1－10 主要指标占全国全省比重(2015 年)
PERCENTAGE OF MAIN INDICATORS TO CHINA AND SHANDONG(2015)

指　标	Indicator	单位	Unit
一、生产总值	GDP	亿元	100 million yuan
第一产业	Primary Industry	亿元	100 million yuan
第二产业	Secondary Industry	亿元	100 million yuan
第三产业	Tertiary Industry	亿元	100 million yuan
二、年末总人口(常住人口)	The Total Population (Resident Population) at the End of the Year	万人	
三、主要工业产品产量	Output of Major Industrial Products		
纱	Yarn	万吨	10 000 tons
布	Cloth	亿米	100 million m
家用电冰箱	Refrigerator	万台	10 000 units
彩色电视机	Color TV Set	万台	10 000 units
发电量	Electricity	亿千瓦时	100 million kW · h
钢材	Rolled-steel	万吨	10 000 tons
水泥	Cement	万吨	10 000 tons
四、主要农产品产量	Output of Major Farm Products		
粮食	Grain	万吨	10 000 tons
油料	Oil Plants	万吨	10 000 tons
棉花	Cotton	万吨	10 000 tons
肉类产量	Meat	万吨	10 000 tons
水产品	Aquatic Products	万吨	10 000 tons
五、固定资产投资额	Investment in Fixed Assets	亿元	100 million yuan
六、社会消费品零售总额	Total Retail Sales of Consumer Goods	亿元	100 million yuan
七、高等学校在校学生	Students Enrollment of Institutions of Higher Education	万人	10 000 persons

注:1. 本表全国、全省均为公报数。
2. 青岛市主要工业产品产量数据为本地口径。

Note:1. The number of the country and the province in the table are obtained from the statistical report.
2. The output of main industrial products of qingdao are at local calibre.

全国 China	全省 Shandong	青岛市 Qingdao	青岛市占全国 比重(%) Qingdao/China	青岛市占全省 比重(%) Qingdao/Shandong
676 708	63 002.3	9 300.07	1.37	14.76
60 863	4 979.1	363.98	0.60	7.31
274 278	29 485.9	4 026.46	1.47	13.66
341 567	28 537.4	4 909.63	1.44	17.20
137 462	9 847.16	909.70	0.66	9.24
3 538	892.9	2.8	0.08	0.31
893	115.9	2.8	0.31	2.42
7 993	872.1	872.1	10.91	100.00
14 476	1 766.9	1 736.20	11.99	98.26
58 106	4 651.4	173.5	0.30	3.73
112 350	9 003.2	140.6	0.13	1.56
236 000	15 173.9	532.4	0.23	3.51
62 144	4 712.7	321.4	0.52	6.82
3 547	324.1	34.6	0.98	10.68
561	53.7	0.16	0.03	0.30
8 625	762.0	54.7	0.63	7.18
6 690	884.3	109.1	1.63	12.34
551 590	47 381.5	6 555.7	1.19	13.84
300 931	27 761.4	3 713.7	1.23	13.38
2 625	190.1	32.22	1.23	16.95

1-11 主要年份全市生产总值(按当年价格计算)
MAJOR YEAR'S GROSS DOMESTIC PRODUCT(AT CURRENT PRICE)

单位:亿元 (100 million yuan)

年 份 Year	全市生产总值 GDP	第一产业 Primary Industry	第二产业 Secondary Industry	#工 业 Industry	第三产业 Tertiary Industry	人均生产总值(元) Per Capita GDP (yuan)
1949	2.87	1.19	1.10	-	0.58	71
1952	6.74	1.76	3.25	2.95	1.73	163
1957	10.82	2.00	5.76	5.39	3.06	239
1962	9.69	1.11	4.68	4.27	3.90	205
1965	15.50	1.80	9.36	8.48	4.74	325
1970	23.23	3.15	14.46	13.86	5.62	451
1975	29.07	6.93	15.39	14.67	6.75	522
1978	38.43	8.73	20.25	19.15	9.45	663
1980	48.65	10.19	26.27	24.28	12.19	819
1985	82.28	21.29	37.55	34.03	23.44	1 311
1988	142.87	32.72	70.32	63.42	39.83	2 199
1989	159.68	30.79	82.03	74.33	46.86	2 426
1990	180.77	39.26	86.76	79.34	54.75	2 714
1991	205.65	43.04	98.94	89.64	63.67	3 053
1992	261.35	43.92	130.27	117.61	87.16	3 856
1993	371.90	62.20	183.35	164.35	126.35	5 455
1994	510.81	85.12	244.30	218.87	181.39	7 436
1995	631.45	112.53	294.43	263.98	224.49	9 089
1996	713.60	133.27	322.33	289.87	258.00	10 130
1997	802.59	117.47	378.25	342.80	306.87	11 235
1998	901.19	140.66	409.60	369.89	350.93	12 443

1 -11 续表
continued

年 份 Year	全市生产总值 GDP	第一产业 Primary Industry	第二产业 Secondary Industry	#工 业 Industry	第三产业 Tertiary Industry	人均生产总值(元) Per Capita GDP (yuan)
1999	1 018.97	138.19	468.67	424.15	412.11	13 884
2000	1 191.25	140.85	555.21	504.44	495.19	16 009
2001	1 368.55	144.35	643.44	582.99	580.76	18 128
2002	1 583.51	147.21	758.33	686.55	677.97	20 655
2003	1 869.44	148.92	923.76	832.31	796.76	23 986
2004	2 270.16	163.49	1 149.94	1 032.50	956.73	28 540
2005	2 687.46	178.33	1 392.02	1 259.06	1 117.10	33 085
2006	3 183.18	183.95	1 666.96	1 517.28	1 332.28	38 608
2007	3 750.16	203.59	1 934.52	1 766.28	1 612.05	44 964
2008	4 401.56	223.40	2 234.83	2 034.25	1 943.33	52 266
2009	4 853.87	230.25	2 420.14	2 174.43	2 203.48	57 251
2010	5 666.19	276.99	2 758.62	2 454.19	2 630.58	65 827
2011	6 615.60	306.38	3 150.72	2 794.56	3 158.50	75 563
2012	7 302.11	324.41	3 402.23	3 041.31	3 575.47	82 680
2013	8 006.56	340.50	3 651.39	3 234.56	4 014.67	89 797
2014	8 692.10	349.62	3 890.41	3 434.97	4 452.07	96 524
2015	9 300.07	363.98	4 026.46	3 547.60	4 909.63	102 519

注:1. 人均生产总值按常住人口计算 。

2. 自 2005 年起三次产业分类采用《国民经济行业分类》(GB/T4754-2002)标准,自 2013 年起,根据《国民经济行业分类》(GB/T4754 - 2011)和《三次产业划分规定》(国统字[2012]108 号),将农林牧渔业中的农林牧渔服务业以及工业中的开采辅助活动和金属制品、机械和设备修理业归入第三产业。

Note:1. Per capita GDP are calculated at permanent population.

2. Three Industries are grouped by "Classification and Code of the Sectors of the National Economy" (GB / T4754-2002) since 2005, from 2013 on, According to the Industrial Classification for National Economic Activities (GB/T4754-2011) and the Rules for Classification of Three Industries (NBS No. [2012]108), the service industries of Agriculture, Forestry, Animal Husbandry and Fishery and mining auxiliary activities and metal products, machinery and equipment repair industries in the Industry are classified into the tertiary industry.

1－12 主要年份全市生产总值构成(以全市生产总值为100)

COMPOSITION OF MAJOR YEAR'S GROSS DOMESTIC PRODUCT(GROSS DOMESTIC PRODUCT＝100)

单位:%

年　份 Year	全市生产总值 GDP	第一产业 Primary Industry	第二产业 Secondary Industry	#工　业 Industry	第三产业 Tertiary Industry
1952	100	26.1	48.2	43.8	25.7
1957	100	18.5	53.3	49.8	28.2
1962	100	11.4	48.3	44.1	40.3
1965	100	11.6	57.8	54.7	30.6
1970	100	13.6	62.2	59.7	24.2
1975	100	23.9	52.9	50.5	23.2
1978	100	22.7	52.7	49.8	24.6
1980	100	21.0	54.0	49.9	25.1
1985	100	25.9	45.6	41.4	28.5
1988	100	22.9	49.2	44.4	27.9
1989	100	19.3	51.4	46.6	29.3
1990	100	21.7	48.0	43.7	30.3
1991	100	20.9	48.1	43.6	31.0
1992	100	16.8	49.8	45.0	33.4
1993	100	16.7	49.3	44.2	34.0
1994	100	16.7	47.8	42.8	35.5
1995	100	17.8	46.6	41.8	35.6
1996	100	18.7	45.2	40.6	36.2
1997	100	14.6	47.1	42.7	38.2
1998	100	15.6	45.5	41.0	38.9
1999	100	13.6	46.0	41.6	40.4
2000	100	11.8	46.6	42.3	41.6
2001	100	10.5	47.0	42.6	42.4
2002	100	9.3	47.9	43.4	42.8
2003	100	8.0	49.4	44.5	42.6
2004	100	7.2	50.7	45.5	42.1
2005	100	6.6	51.8	46.8	41.6
2006	100	5.8	52.4	47.7	41.8
2007	100	5.4	51.6	47.1	43.0
2008	100	5.1	50.8	46.2	44.1
2009	100	4.7	49.9	44.8	45.4
2010	100	4.9	48.7	43.3	46.4
2011	100	4.6	47.6	41.5	47.8
2012	100	4.4	46.6	41.6	49.0
2013	100	4.3	45.6	40.4	50.1
2014	100	4.0	44.8	39.5	51.2
2015	100	3.9	43.3	38.1	52.8

1-13 主要年份全市生产总值增长速度(以上年为100)

GROWTH RATE OF MAJOR YEAR'S GROSS DOMESTIC PRODUCT(PRECEDING YEAR=100)

单位:%

年份 Year	全市生产总值 GDP	第一产业 Primary Industry	第二产业 Secondary Industry	第三产业 Tertiary Industry	人均生产总值 Per Capita GDP
1979	12.0	10.6	12.9	11.4	10.4
1980	10.4	4.3	13.1	10.3	9.4
1981	-2.0	-9.1	-2.4	4.7	-3.2
1982	4.1	5.5	-0.2	11.9	2.6
1983	16.9	42.8	9.3	12.7	15.3
1984	13.0	18.9	11.5	10.3	12.0
1985	9.9	5.4	5.8	21.3	9.3
1986	9.2	2.6	12.1	10.0	8.3
1987	12.0	3.6	16.0	12.0	10.6
1988	13.8	-0.3	21.5	11.2	12.1
1989	5.1	-0.8	4.6	9.9	3.8
1990	9.3	9.8	7.3	12.2	8.0
1991	10.6	9.9	11.0	10.5	9.4
1992	18.1	2.7	23.5	20.7	17.4
1993	22.4	20.5	21.1	25.6	21.7
1994	14.4	3.6	14.7	20.2	13.5
1995	12.0	10.9	12.1	12.4	10.8
1996	7.2	7.7	7.6	6.4	5.7
1997	11.5	-10.6	16.8	14.6	9.9
1998	12.9	17.6	11.3	13.4	11.3
1999	13.9	4.1	15.5	15.3	12.4
2000	15.2	6.5	16.4	16.4	13.6

1－13 续表
continued

单位:%

年份 Year	全市生产总值 GDP	第一产业 Primary Industry	第二产业 Secondary Industry	第三产业 Tertiary Industry	人均生产总值 Per Capita GDP
2001	13.7	2.3	16.3	14.2	12.1
2002	14.5	3.2	16.9	14.6	12.7
2003	16.3	2.5	20.1	14.9	14.4
2004	16.7	2.7	20.3	15.2	14.3
2005	16.6	0.4	19.6	15.7	14.1
2006	15.3	0.9	16.8	15.8	13.6
2007	15.5	－2.6	15.3	18.3	14.2
2008	13.2	1.4	11.1	17.1	12.1
2009	12.2	3.0	12.8	12.5	11.4
2010	12.9	1.4	12.6	14.4	11.2
2011	11.7	5.0	11.6	12.4	9.8
2012	10.6	3.2	11.5	10.5	9.7
2013	10.0	2.0	10.1	10.6	9.0
2014	8.0	3.8	8.5	7.9	6.9
2015	8.1	3.2	7.1	9.4	7.3
1978－2010 平均每年增长 1978－2010 Average Increase Rate	12.4	5.3	13.1	13.9	11.0
1991－2010 平均每年增长 1991－2010 Average Increase Rate	14.2	4.2	15.5	15.3	12.8
1996－2010 平均每年增长 1996－2010 Average Increase Rate	13.8	2.5	15.2	14.5	13.0
2001－2010 平均每年增长 2001－2010 Average Increase Rate	14.7	1.5	16.1	15.2	13.0
2006－2010 平均每年增长 2006－2010 Average Increase Rate	13.8	0.8	13.7	15.6	12.5
2010－2015 平均每年增长 2010－2015Average Increase Rate	9.7	2.8	9.7	10.3	8.5

1－14 分市、区生产总值(2015 年)
GROSS DOMESTIC PRODUCT BY REGION(2015)

单位:亿元(100 million yuan)

市、区名称	Region	地区生产总值 GDP	第一产业 Primary Industry	第二产业 Secondary Industry	第三产业 Tertiary Industry
市南区	Shinan District	945.22		79.57	865.65
市北区	Shibei District	640.17		126.78	513.39
李沧区	Licang District	324.61		114.05	210.56
崂山区	Laoshan District	509.80	5.77	244.62	259.41
黄岛区	Huangdao District	2 500.35	61.70	1 227.22	1 211.43
保税港区	Qingdao Free Trade Port Area of China	94.38		21.04	73.34
城阳区	Chengyang District	882.11	3.41	475.79	402.91
即墨市	Jimo	1 100.89	60.19	598.04	442.66
胶州市	Jiaozhou	981.15	53.14	517.81	410.20
平度市	Pingdu	779.25	106.22	408.85	264.18
莱西市	Laixi	526.02	63.36	254.74	207.92
红岛经济区	Qingdao National High-tech Industrial Development Zone	80.46	12.35	39.41	28.70

1 -15 按支出法计算的全市生产总值(2015 年)

GROSS DOMESTIC PRODUCT BY EXPENDITURE APPROACH(2015)

单位:亿元(100 million yuan)

项　目	Item	2015	2014	2015 年为 2014 年% 2015/2014(%)
支出法计算的全市生产总值	**Gross Domestic Product by Expenditure Approach**	**9 300.07**	**8 692.10**	**108.1**
(一)最终消费	Final Consumption Expenditures	3 281.55	3 009.94	108.9
1. 居民消费	Household Consumption Expenditures	2 404.89	2 221.66	108.0
农村居民	Rural Household	420.47	386.77	108.3
城镇居民	Urban Household	1 984.42	1 834.89	108.0
2. 政府消费	Government Consumption Expenditures	876.66	788.28	111.4
(二)资本形成总额	Gross Capital Formation	5 763.06	5 323.52	115.9
1. 固定资本形成总额	Gross Fixed Capital Formation	5 542.16	5 196.23	114.1
2. 存货增加	Change in Inventories	220.89	127.30	185.5
(三)货物和服务净流出	Net Exports of Goods and Services	255.47	358.64	45.9

注:绝对额按当年价格计算,速度按可比价格计算。

Note: The absolute numbers are calculated at current price, their growth are calculated at constant price.

1 –16 全市生产总值构成(2015 年)

COMPOSITION OF GROSS DOMESTIC PRODUCT(2015)

指　标	Indicator	增加值(亿元) Added Value (100 million yuan)	2015 年为 2014 年% 2015/2014(%)
地区生产总值	**GDP**	**9 300.07**	**108.1**
农、林、牧、渔业	Farming, Forestry, A nimal Husbandry and Fishery	379.06	103.6
农、林、牧、渔服务业	Agriculture, Forestry, Animal Husbandry and Fishery Service Industry	15.08	114.5
工业	Industry	3 547.60	106.9
#开采辅助活动	# Mining Auxiliary Activities		
#金属制品、机械和设备修理业	#Metal Products, Machinery and Equipment Repair Industries	7.97	115.7
建筑业	Construction	486.83	108.9
批发和零售业	Wholesale and Retail Trade	1 147.76	107.4
交通运输、仓储和邮政业	Transport, Storage and Post	662.49	107.7
住宿和餐饮业	Hotels and Catering Services	188.09	98.0
信息传输、软件和信息技术服务业	Information Transmission Computer Services and Software	183.90	113.8
金融业	Financial Intermediation	588.28	113.3
房地产业	Real Estate	463.49	108.0
租赁和商务服务业	Leasing and Business Services	347.67	120.0
科学研究和技术服务业	Scientific Research and Technical Services	154.68	104.3
水利、环境和公共设施管理业	Management of Water Conservancy Environment and Public Facilities	54.85	90.9
居民服务、修理和其他服务业	Services to Households and Other Services	176.67	105.9
教育	Education	339.97	122.4
卫生和社会工作	Health Social Security and Social Welfare	186.33	123.7
文化、体育和娱乐业	Culture Sports and Entertainment	71.74	102.6
公共管理、社会保障和社会组织	Public Management and Social Organizations	320.66	99.2
第一产业	Primary Industry	363.98	103.2
第二产业	Secondary Industry	4 026.46	107.1
第三产业	Tertiary Industry	4 909.63	109.4

主要统计指标解释

国内生产总值(GDP)　指按市场价格计算的一个国家(或地区)所有常住单位在一定时期内生产活动的最终成果。国内生产总值有三种表现形态,即价值形态、收入形态和产品形态。从价值形态看,它是所有常住单位在一定时期内生产的全部货物和服务价值超过同期中间投入的全部非固定资产货物和服务价值的差额,即所有常住单位的增加值之和;从收入形态看,它是所有常住单位在一定时期内创造并分配给常住单位和非常住单位的初次收入分配之和;从产品形态看,它是所有常住单位在一定时期内最终使用的货物和服务价值与货物和服务净出口价值之和。在实际核算中,国内生产总值有三种计算方法,即生产法、收入法和支出法。三种方法分别从不同的方面反映国内生产总值及其构成。对于一个地区来说,称为地区生产总值或地区 GDP。

人均 GDP　人均 GDP 是一定时期内 GDP 与同期人口平均数的比值。按照国际标准,人口平均数应该是同期平均常住人口。我国在核算制度中也规定,无论是国家还是地区,人口数都采用常住人口。国家统计局规定从 2004 年开始,过去采用户籍人口计算人均 GDP 的地区,作为过渡性措施,可在两年内同时计算两种口径的人均 GDP(数据后面必须注明是什么口径),两年后取消按户籍人口计算的人均 GDP。我市采用常住人口计算人均 GDP。

三次产业　是根据社会生产活动历史发展的顺序对产业结构的划分,产品直接取自自然界的部门称为第一产业,对初级产品进行再加工的部门称为第二产业,为生产和消费提供各种服务的部门称为第三产业。它是世界上通用的产业结构分类,但各国的划分不尽一致。我国的三次产业划分是:

第一产业:是指农业、林业、畜牧业、渔业和农林牧渔服务业。

第二产业:是指采矿业,制造业,电力、燃气及水的生产和供应业;建筑业。

第三产业:除第一、第二产业以外的其他行业。

支出法国内生产总值　是从最终使用角度反映一个国家(或地区)一定时期内生产活动最终成果的一种方法,包括最终消费支出,资本形成总额及货物和服务净出口三部分。对于地区,名称为“支出法地区生产总值”。

最终消费　指常住单位为满足物质、文化和精神生活的需要,从本国经济领土和国外购买的货物和服务的支出;不包括非常住单位在本国经济领土内的消费支出。最终消费分为居民消费和政府消费。

居民消费　指常住住户在一定时期内对货物和服务的全部最终消费支出。居民消费支出除了直接以货币形式购买货物和服务的消费之外,还包括以其他方式获得的货物和服务的消费支出,即所谓的虚拟消费支出。居民虚拟消费支出包括以下几种类型:单位以实物报酬及实物转移的形式提供给劳动者的货物和服务;住户生产并由本住户消费了的货物和服务,其中的服务仅指住户的自有住房服务和付酬的家庭雇员提供的家庭和个人服务;金融机构提供的金融媒介服务。

政府消费　指政府部门为全社会提供公共服务的消费支出和免费或以较低价格向居民住户提供的货物和服务的净支出。前者等于政府服务的产出价值减去政府单位所获得的经营收入的价值;后者等于政府部门免费或以较低价格向居民住户提供的货物和服务的市场价值减去向住户收取的价值。

资本形成总额　指常住单位在一定时期内获得的减去处置的固定资产和存货的净额,包括固定资本形成总额和存货增加。

固定资本形成总额　指常住单位在一定时期内获得的固定资产减处置的固定资产的价值总额。固定资产是通过生产活动生产出来的,且使用年限在一年以上、单位价值在规定标准以上的资产,不包括自然资产。分有形固定资产形成总额和无形固定资产形成总额。有形固定资产形成总额包括一定时期内完成的建筑工程、安装工程和设备工器具购置(减处置)价值,以及土地改良、新增役、种、奶、毛、娱乐用牲畜和新增经济林木价值。无形固定资产形成总额包括矿藏的勘探、计算机软件等获得减处置。

存货增加　指常住单位在一定时期内存货实物量变动的市场价值,即期末价值减期初价值的差额,再扣除当期由于价格变动而产生的持有收益。存货增加可以是正值,也可以是负值;正值表示存货上升,负值表示存货下降。它包括生产单位购进的原材料、燃料和储备物资等存货,以及生产单位生产的产成品、在制品和半成品等存货。

货物和服务净出口　指货物和服务出口减货物和服务进口的差额。出口包括常住单位向非常住单位出售或无偿转让的各种货物和服务的价值;进口包括常住单位从非常住单位购买或无偿得到的各种货物和服务的价值。由于服务活动的提供与使用同时发生,一般把常住单位从国外得到的服务作为进口,非常住单位从本国得到的服务作为出口。货物的出口和进口都按离岸价格计算。

气候　指地球与大气之间长期能量交换与质量交换所形成的一种自然环境状态,它是多种因素综合作用的结果。气候既是人类生活和生产的环境要素之一,又是供给人类生活和生产的重要资源。气温、降水、湿度等气象要素的多年平均值是用来描述一个地区气候状况的主要参数,而各种气象要素某年、某月的平均值(或总量)则可以反映出该时期天气气候状况的重要特征。

气温　指空气的温度,我国一般以摄氏度(℃)为单位表示。气象观测的温度表是放在离地面约 1.5 米处通风良好的百叶箱里测量的,因此,通常说的气温指的是离地面 1.5 米处百叶箱中的温度。其统计计算方法为:月平均气温是将全月各日的平均气温相加,除以该月的天数而得。

年平均气温　是将 12 个月的月平均气温累加后除以 12 而得。

降水量　指从天空降落到地面的液态或固态(经融化后)水,未经蒸发、渗透、流失而在地面上积聚的深度。其统计计算方法为:月降水量是将全月各日的降水量累加而得。年降水量是将 12 个月的月降水量累加而得。

Explanatory Notes on Main Statistical Indicators

Gross Domestic Product(GDP)　refers to the final products at market prices producted by all resident units in a country(or a region)during a certain period of time. Gross domestic product is expressed in three different persperctives, namely value, income, and products respectively. GDP in its value perspective refers to the total value of all goods and services produced by all resident units during a certain period of time, minus the total value of input of goods and services of the nature of non-fixed assets; in other words, it is the sum of the value-added of all resident units. GDP from the perspective of products refers to the value of all goods and services for final consumption by all resident units minus the net exports of goods and services during a given period of time. In the practice of national accounting, gross domestic product is calculated from three approaches, namely production approach, income approach and expenditure approach, which reflect gross domestic product and its composition from different angles. For a certain region, it refers region gross product or region GDP.

Per Capita GDP　refers to the ratio of GDP in a certain term and average population in the same term. According to the international standard, average population should be average permanent population in the same term. In the account regulation, population of both the country and the region should be permanent population. In the after two yers since 2004, per capita GDP can be calculated at two coverage. i. e. at permanent population and household registered population(the note of coverage should follow the data.)The per capita GDP calculated with household registered population will be abolished after two years. Per capita GDP of Qingdao is calculated at permanent population.

Three Strata of Industries　has been classfied according to the historical sequence of development. Primary industry refers to extraction of natural resources; secondary industry involves processing of primary products; and tertiary industry provides services of various kinds for production and consumption. The above classification is universal although it varies to some extent form country to country. In China economic activities are categorized into the following three strata of industry:

Primary industry refers to farming, forestry, animal husbandryand fishery and services in support of these industries.

Secondary industry refers to mining and quarrying, manufacturing, production and supply of electricity, water and gas, and construction.

Tertiary industry refers to all other economic activities not included in primary or secondary industries.

GDP by Expenditure Approach　refers to the method of measuring the final results of production activities of a country (region) during a given period from the perspective of final use. It includes final consumption, total capital formation and net export of goods and services. It reflects use and composition of gross domestic product. For a certain region, it refers region gross product by expenditure approach.

Final Consumption refers to the total expenditure of resident units for purchases of goods and services from both the domestic economic territory and abroad to meet the needs of material, cultural and spiritual life. It does not include the expenditure of non-resident units on consumption in the economic territory of the country. The final consumption is broken down into household consumption and government consumption.

Household Consumption refers to the total expenditure of resident households on the final consumption of goods and services. In addition to the consumption of goods and services bought by the households directly with money, the household consumption also includes expenditure on goods and services obtained by the households in other ways, i. e. the so-called imputed consumption, which includes the following: (a) the goods and services provided to households by employers in the form of payment in kind and transfer in kind; (b) goods and services produced and consumed by the households themselves, in which the services refer to the owner-occupied housing and services offered by payed family employees; (c) financial intermediate services provided by financial institution.

Government Consumption refers to the consumption expenditure spent for the provision of public services provided by the government to the whole country and the net expenditure on the goods and services provided by the government to households free of charge or at reduced prices. The former equals to the output value of the government services minus the value of operating income obtained by the government departments. The latter equals to the market value of the goods and services provided by the government free of charge or at reduced prices to the households minus the value received by the government from the households.

Gross Capital Formation refers to the fixed assets acquired less disposal and the net value of inventory, thus including the gross fixed capital formation and charges in inventories.

Gross Fixed Capital Formation refers to the value of acquisitions less those disposals of fixed assets during a given period. Fixed assets are the assets produced through production activities with unit value above a specified amount and which could be used for over one year. Natural assets are not included. Gross fixed capital formation can be categorized into total tangible fixed capital formation and total intangible fixed capital formation. Total tangible fixed capital formation includes the value of the construction projects and installation projects completed and the equipment, apparatus and instruments purchased (less those disposed) as well as the value of land improved, the value of draught animals, breeding stock and animals for milk, for wool and for recreational purposes and the newly increased forest with economic value. Total intangible fixed capital formation includes the prospecting of minerals and the acquisition of computer software minus the disposal of them.

Charges in Inventories refers to the market value of the change in the physical volume of inventory of resident units during a given period, i. e. the difference between the values at the beginning and at the end of the period minus the gains due to the change in prices. The changes in inventories can have a positive or a negative value. A positive value indicates an increase in inventory while a negative value indicates a decrease in inventory. The inventory includes raw materials, fuels and reserve materials purchased by the production units as well as the inventory of finished products, semi-finished products and work-in-progress.

Net Export of Goods and Services refers to the exports of goods and services subtracting the imports of goods and services. Exports include the value of various goods and services sold or gratuitously transferred by resident units to non-resident units. Imports include the value of various goods and services purchased or gratuitously acquired resident units from non-resident units. Because the provision of services and the use of them happen simultaneously, the acquisition of services by resident units from abroad is usually treated as import while the acquisition of services by non-resident units in this country is usually treated as export. The exports and imports of goods are calculated at FOB.

Climate refers to the natural environmental status formed by the long-term exchange of energy and mass between the earth and the air, and is the results of interaction of many factors. Climate is both one of the environment factors and the important resources for the living and production activities of the human being. The average values across several years of meteorological factors such as temperature, rainfall and humidity are used as important parameters to describe the climate of a region, while the average values (or total values) of a given year or month of meteorological factors reflect the key characteristics of climate for that period of time.

Temperature refers to the air temperature. China uses centigrade as the unit. The thermometry used for weather observation is put in a breezy shutter, which is 1.5 meters high from the ground. Therefore, the commonly used temperature refers to the temperature in the breezy shutter 1.5 meters away from the ground. The calculation method is as follows:

Monthly average temperature is the summation of average daily temperature of one month divided by the actual days of that particular month.

Annual average temperature is the summation of monthly average of a year divided by 12 months.

Volume of Precipitation refers to the deepness of liquid state or solid state (thawed) water falling from the sky to the ground that has not been evaporated, infiltrated or run off. The calculation method is as follows:

Monthly precipitation is the summation of daily precipitation of a month.

Annual precipitation is the summation of 12 months precipitation of a year.

2 人　口

POPULATION

简 要 说 明

一、本篇资料的主要内容

本篇资料主要反映了全市人口方面的基本情况，包括全市主要年份和区(市)的户数、人口数、人口密度、土地面积数据、人口出生率、死亡率、自然增长率、计划生育等数据。另外还对建国以来开展的六次人口普查主要数据进行了比较。

二、本篇资料的来源

本篇资料分别来源于国家开展的人口普查、人口抽样调查和市公安局的户籍登记资料，由市统计局人口和社会科技统计处整理提供。

Brief Introduction

I. Main Content

Data in this chapter show the basic condition of population, such as the basic condition of districts and county-level cities, household, population, density of population, birth rate, death rate, natural growth rate and family planning situation. Furthermore, relevant figures obtained from the six national population censuses have been compared.

II. Source of Data

Data in this chapter are from national population censuses, national sample survey. Some are derived from household registration provided by Qingdao Municipal Bureau of Public Security. The data are compiled by the Division of Population and Science & Technology of Qingdao Municipal Bureau of Statistics.

2-1 主要年份全市户籍人口数
MAJOR YEAR'S TOTAL REGISTERED POPULATION

单位：人(person)

年 份 Year	总人口 Total Population	按性别分 Grouped by Sex 男 Male	女 Female	平均人口 Average Population
1949	4 056 550	1 997 293	2 059 257	4 054 431
1952	4 233 586	2 125 392	2 108 194	4 203 428
1957	4 822 756	2 424 729	2 398 027	4 773 862
1962	4 627 432	2 319 658	2 307 774	4 578 313
1965	4 901 670	2 461 629	2 440 041	4 859 712
1970	5 391 852	2 720 633	2 671 219	5 337 282
1975	5 742 206	2 904 347	2 837 859	5 717 456
1978	5 853 321	2 959 800	2 893 521	5 841 638
1980	5 961 129	3 015 357	2 945 772	5 937 187
1985	6 267 223	3 185 409	3 081 814	6 253 157
1988	6 516 920	3 319 534	3 197 386	6 474 541
1989	6 571 597	3 348 454	3 223 143	6 544 259
1990	6 666 482	3 392 253	3 274 229	6 619 040
1991	6 709 277	3 411 776	3 297 501	6 687 880
1992	6 731 072	3 420 886	3 310 186	6 720 175
1993	6 753 497	3 431 149	3 322 348	6 742 285
1994	6 785 291	3 446 019	3 339 272	6 769 394
1995	6 846 346	3 476 300	3 370 046	6 815 819
1996	6 902 677	3 502 600	3 400 077	6 874 512
1997	6 954 391	3 527 588	3 426 803	6 928 534
1998	6 995 666	3 545 403	3 450 263	6 975 029
1999	7 029 707	3 561 061	3 468 646	7 012 687
2000	7 066 481	3 577 367	3 489 114	7 048 094
2001	7 104 875	3 595 652	3 509 223	7 085 678
2002	7 156 537	3 619 778	3 536 759	7 130 706
2003	7 206 806	3 644 032	3 562 774	7 181 672
2004	7 311 228	3 692 991	3 618 237	7 259 017
2005	7 409 052	3 740 309	3 668 743	7 360 140
2006	7 493 812	3 779 891	3 713 921	7 451 432
2007	7 579 910	3 816 620	3 763 290	7 536 861
2008	7 615 647	3 824 665	3 790 982	7 597 779
2009	7 629 161	3 823 534	3 805 627	7 622 404
2010	7 636 392	3 819 240	3 817 152	7 632 777
2011	7 663 612	3 826 931	3 836 681	7 650 002
2012	7 695 585	3 838 205	3 857 380	7 679 599

注：截止出书前，未获得公安部门青岛市 2013 年—2015 年户籍人口信息。

Note: Data come from the Qingdao Nunicipal Public Security Bureau, and the Data of 2013— 2015 are absent.

2－2 主要年份全市户数、人口数、人口密度(户籍)

MAJOR YEAR'S HOUSEHOLDS, POPULATION AND DENSITY OF POPULATION(WITH PERMANENT RESIDENCE)

年份 Year	总户数(万户) Total Households (10000 households)		总人口(万人) Total Population (10000 persons)		平均每户人口(人) Average Persons Per Household(person)		人口密度(人/平方公里) Density of Population (person/sq. km)	
	全市 Whole Municipality	市区 Urban Area	全市 Whole Municipality	市区 Urban Area	全市 Whole Municipality	市区 Urban Area	全市 Whole Municipality	市区 Urban Area
1949	90.64	21.68	405.66	103.69	4.48	4.78	381	941
1952	93.96	22.70	423.36	107.62	4.51	4.74	397	977
1957	102.56	27.41	482.28	134.76	4.70	4.92	453	1 223
1962	106.11	29.29	462.74	137.86	4.36	4.71	434	1 251
1965	105.31	29.64	490.17	146.74	4.65	4.95	460	1 332
1970	113.07	32.14	539.19	150.81	4.77	4.69	506	1 369
1975	123.18	36.56	574.22	161.13	4.66	4.41	539	1 462
1978	131.27	40.08	585.33	168.00	4.46	4.19	549	1 525
1980	138.44	43.03	596.11	175.27	4.31	4.07	560	1 591
1985	157.06	53.43	626.72	190.87	3.99	3.57	588	1 732
1988	169.72	58.95	651.69	201.38	3.84	3.42	612	1 827
1989	177.47	61.57	657.16	203.63	3.70	3.31	617	1 848
1990	186.79	63.94	666.65	205.78	3.57	3.22	626	1 867
1991	192.46	67.15	670.93	207.22	3.49	3.09	630	1 880
1992	199.08	68.94	673.11	209.28	3.38	3.04	632	1 899
1993	201.36	70.13	675.35	212.06	3.35	3.02	634	1 924
1994	204.05	71.24	678.53	214.97	3.33	3.02	637	1 951
1995	208.13	72.53	684.63	218.38	3.29	3.01	643	1 982
1996	212.40	75.11	690.27	223.86	3.25	2.98	648	2 032
1997	215.12	76.39	695.44	227.22	3.23	2.97	653	2 062
1998	218.59	77.90	699.57	229.58	3.20	2.95	657	2 084
1999	222.61	79.27	702.97	231.94	3.16	2.93	660	2 105
2000	224.73	80.46	706.65	234.60	3.14	2.92	664	2 129
2001	227.43	81.41	710.49	237.60	3.12	2.92	667	2 156
2002	229.67	82.85	715.65	241.74	3.12	2.92	672	2 194
2003	232.26	84.15	720.68	246.77	3.10	2.93	677	2 240
2004	235.29	86.93	731.12	258.40	3.11	2.97	686	2 229
2005	237.35	87.99	740.91	265.43	3.12	3.02	695	2 290
2006	239.33	89.12	749.38	271.00	3.13	3.04	703	2 338
2007	241.55	90.21	757.99	275.55	3.14	3.05	711	2 377
2008	243.18	91.22	761.56	276.25	3.13	3.03	715	2 384
2009	244.74	92.15	762.92	275.47	3.12	2.99	676	1 873
2010	246.11	93.30	763.64	275.50	3.10	2.95	677	1 873
2011	247.94	94.69	766.36	277.09	3.09	2.93	679	1 884
2012	249.27	95.87	769.56	279.57	3.09	2.92	682	1 901

2－3 主要年份全市常住人口数
MAJOR YEAR'S TOTAL RESIDENT POPULATION

单位：万人(10000 persons)

年份 Year	总人口 Total Population
2005	819.55
2006	829.42
2007	838.67
2008	845.61
2009	850.03
2010	871.51
2011	879.51
2012	886.85
2013	896.41
2014	904.62
2015	909.70

2－4 青岛市常住人口(2015 年底)
TOTAL RESIDENT POPULATION(END OF 2015)

市、区名称	Region	2015	2014	2015 年比 2014 年±% 2015/2014(±%)
全市	**Whole Municipality**	**909.70**	**904.62**	**0.56**
市南区	Shinan District	57.16	56.74	0.74
市北区	Shibei District	107.27	106.90	0.35
李沧区	Licang District	54.38	54.14	0.44
崂山区	Laoshan District	42.99	42.75	0.56
黄岛区	Huangdao District	149.36	148.42	0.63
城阳区	Chengyang District	69.17	68.80	0.54
即墨市	Jimo	120.20	119.42	0.65
胶州市	Jiaozhou	87.60	87.10	0.57
平度市	Pingdu	136.21	135.44	0.57
莱西市	Laixi	75.47	75.07	0.53
红岛经济区	Qingdao National High-tech Industrial Development Zone	9.89	9.84	0.51

2-5 分市、区土地面积(2012 年底)
LAND AREA(END OF 2012)

市、区名称	Region	土地面积 Land Area	
		面积(平方公里) Area(sq. km)	比重(%) Percentage(%)
总　计	**Total**	**11 282**	**100.00**
市　区	Urban Area	1 471	13.03
即 墨 市	Jimo	1 921	17.03
胶 州 市	Jiaozhou	1 324	11.74
原胶南市	Original Jiaonan	1 822	16.15
平 度 市	Pingdu	3 176	28.15
莱 西 市	Laixi	1 568	13.90

注:土地面积为第二次全国土地调查数据。
Note:Data on land area are based on the data of the Second China Land Census.

2-6 第一、二、三、四、五、六次人口普查主要数据
MAIN DATA FROM THE SIX NATIONAL POPULATION CENSUSES

项 目	Item	第一次人口普查 1st National Population Census	第二次人口普查 2nd National Population Census	第三次人口普查 3rd National Population Census	第四次人口普查 4th National Population Census	第五次人口普查 5th National Population Census	第六次人口普查 6th National Population Census
一、总人口（万人）	**Total Population (10000 persons)**	**91.68**	**138.34**	**422.76**	**666.40**	**749.42**	**871.51**
按性别分	By Sex						
男（万人）	Male(10000 persons)	48.44	69.64	214.09	338.86	375.74	439.18
女（万人）	Female(10000 persons)	43.24	68.71	208.67	327.54	373.68	432.33
二、总户数（万户）	**Total Household (10000 households)**	**19.27**	**28.01**	**101.41**	**186.61**	**241.62**	**296.64**
家庭户（万户）	Family Household (10000 households)			101.09	185.56	232.70	282.43
平均家庭户规模(人)	Average Family Household Size(person)			4.07	3.49	2.97	2.79
三、民 族	**Ethnicity**						
民族个数（个）	Number of Ethnic Groups (unit)	14	16	25	41	51	53
汉族人口（万人）	Population of Han (10000 persons)	91.33	137.76	422.09	665.58	746.12	863.84
少数民族人口（万人）	Populaiton of Ethnic Minorities(10000 persons)	0.36	0.58	0.67	0.82	3.3	7.67
四、各种文化程度人口	**Poption with Various Education Attainments**						
大 学（万人）	College(10000 persons)		1.51	3.62	12.39	41.64	129.54
高 中（万人）	Senior Secondary School (10000 persons)		4.86	34.82	68.42	111.40	150.82
初 中（万人）	Junior Secondary School (10000 persons)		13.72	102.28	195.10	281.91	334.22
小 学（万人）	Primary School (10000 persons)		51.25	144.52	236.34	206.91	170.77

2-7 计划生育情况(1978-2015年)
FAMILY PLANNING SITUATION(1978-2015)

年份 Year	已婚有生育能力的人数(人) Married and Fertile Persons(person)	节育人数(人) Persons under Birth Control(person)	节育率(%) Contraceptive Prevalence Rate(%)	四项手术人数(人) Persons Performed Four-operation(person)	#放环人数 Persons Set Rings
1978	694 292	571 077	82.25	125 913	68 475
1980	763 226	673 069	88.19	180 979	70 927
1985	1 017 649	929 284	91.32	146 742	67 234
1990	1 258 232	1 165 216	92.61	149 327	70 964
1991	1 319 722	1 219 795	92.43	153 970	77 406
1992	1 348 503	1 256 271	93.16	90 107	56 226
1993	1 380 717	1 271 884	92.12	76 783	45 492
1994	1 400 425	1 268 378	90.57	73 169	41 482
1995	1 427 442	1 285 264	90.04	84 099	52 716
1996	1 459 465	1 316 516	90.21	84 370	57 648
1997	1 482 204	1 340 399	90.43	76 579	55 285
1998	1 505 499	1 367 648	90.84	74 199	50 526
1999	1 523 471	1 378 131	90.46	73 663	44 976
2000	1 521 331	1 371 447	90.15	74 285	45 999
2001	1 514 274	1 360 543	89.85	70 205	43 601
2002	1 541 855	1 400 145	90.81	50 575	45 453
2003	1 518 448	1 354 917	89.23	57 458	47 953
2004	1 540 706	1 357 703	88.04	52 934	42 859
2005	1 590 476	1 417 755	89.14	58 097	49 716
2006	1 604 665	1 427 785	88.98	51 864	42 457
2007	1 595 390	1 426 787	89.43	50 074	41 198
2008	1 587 344	1 410 426	88.85	120 539	93 291
2009	1 623 969	1 418 178	87.33	111 084	100 193
2010	1 591 103	1 377 726	86.59	78 721	51 794
2011	1 581 231	1 355 808	85.74	70 823	48 210
2012	1 575 996	1 349 572	85.63	62 880	43 021
2013	1 527 731	1 293 810	84.69	53 252	30 851
2014	1 506 274	1 275 142	84.66	34 008	12 827
2015	1 475 887	1 226 439	83.10	34 879	9 108

2-8 分市、区计划生育情况(2015年)
FAMILY PLANNING SITUATION BY REGION(2015)

市、区名称	Region	计划生育率(%) Fertility Rate (%)	计划内出生(人) Birth within the Plan(person)		计划外出生(人) Birth without the Plan(person)		多胎(人) Third Birth and Above (person)
			一胎 First Birth	二胎 Second Birth	一胎 First Birth	二胎 Second Birth	
全市	**Whole Municipality**	**95.56**	**34 453**	**25 646**	**167**	**2050**	**586**
市南区	Shinan District	97.09	3 241	1 421	3	123	17
市北区	Shibei District	97.15	4 580	1 862	18	156	16
李沧区	Licang District	96.89	1 286	828	4	56	10
崂山区	Laoshan District	96.38	1 776	965	3	90	10
黄岛区	Huangdao District	97.42	2 276	1 694	5	84	16
城阳区	Chengyang District	94.09	6 047	4 804	31	560	93
即墨市	Jimo	95.61	3 312	3 526	18	208	88
胶州市	Jiaozhou	93.82	3 704	3 659	28	341	119
平度市	Pingdu	95.15	5 426	4 758	28	332	160
莱西市	Laixi	96.37	2 805	2 129	29	100	57

主要统计指标解释

人口数 指一定时点、一定地区范围内有生命的个人总和。

出生率(又称粗出生率) 指在一定时期内(通常为一年)一定地区的出生人数与同期内平均人数(或期中人数)之比,用千分率表示。本资料中的出生率指年出生率,其计算公式为:

$$出生率 = \frac{年出生人数}{年平均人数} \times 1000‰$$

式中:出生人数指活产婴儿,即胎儿脱离母体时(不管怀孕月数),有过呼吸或其他生命现象。

死亡率(又称粗死亡率) 指在一定时期内(通常为一年)一定地区的死亡人数与同期内平均人数(或期中人数)之比,用千分率表示。本资料中的死亡率指年死亡率,其计算公式为:

$$死亡率 = \frac{年死亡人数}{年平均人数} \times 1000‰$$

人口自然增长率 指在一定时期内(通常为一年)人口自然增加数(出生人数减死亡人数)与该时期内平均人数(或期中人数)之比,用千分率表示。计算公式为:

$$人口自然增长率 = \frac{本年出生人数 - 本年死亡人数}{年平均人数} \times 1000‰$$
$$= 人口出生率 - 人口死亡率$$

Explanatory Notes on Main Statistical Indicators

Total Population refers to the total number of people alive at a certain point of time within a given area.

Birth Rate (or Crude Birth Rate) refers to the ratio of the number of births to the average population (or mid-period population) during a certain period of time (usually a year), expressed in ‰. Birth rate in the chapter refers to annual birth rate. The following formula is used:

Birth Rate = (Number of Births/Average Number of Population) × 1000‰

Number of births in the formula refers to live births, i. e. when a baby has breathed or showed any vital phenomena regardless of the length of pregnancy.

Annual average number of population is the average of the number of population at the beginning of the year and that at the end of the year. Sometimes it is substituted by the mid-year population.

Death Rate (or Crude Death Rate) refers to the ratio of the number of deaths to the average population (or mid-period population) during a certain period of time (usually a year), expressed in ‰. Death rate in the chapter refers to annual death rate. The following formula is used:

Death Rate = (Number of Deaths/Annual Average Number of Population) × 1000‰

Natural Growth Rate of Population refers to the ratio of natural increase in population (number of births minus number of deaths) in a certain period of time (usually a year) to the average population (or mid-period population) of the same period, expressed in ‰. The following formula is applied:

Natural Growth Rate of Population = [(Number of Births-Number of Deaths)/Average Number of Population] × 1000‰

Natural Growth Rate of Population = Birth Rate-Death Rate

3 从业人员及职工工资
EMPLOYMENT AND WAGES

简要说明

一、本篇资料的主要内容

本篇资料主要反映了全市从业人员和职工工资方面的基本情况，主要包括全市社会从业人数及各区（市）单位从业人数、在岗职工工资总额和平均工资等方面的资料。

二、本篇资料的来源

单位从业人员和职工工资来源于劳动统计年报，全市从业人员根据劳动统计年报、农村年报和市工商行政管理局、市人力资源和社会保障局、市交通委相关资料测算。由市统计局人口和社会科技统计处整理提供。

Brief Introduction

I. Main Content

Data in this chapter show the basic conditions of Qingdao's employment and wages, including the main data on labor statistics of employment, number of employment of the whole city and 10 district and county-level cities, total wage bill and average wage of staff and workers, etc.

II. Source of Data

Data on employment and wages are prepared according to the annual reports of labor statistics.Data on social employment are measured according to the annual reports of labor statistics,countryside statistics and related information from Industry & Commerce Administration Bureau,Human Resources & Social Security Bureau and Transportation Commision.

Data in this chapter are compiled by the Division of Population and Science & Technology of Qingdao Municipal Bureau of Statistics.

3-1 社会从业人数(1978-2015年)
SOCIAL EMPLOYMENT(1978-2015)

单位:万人(10 000 persons)

年份 Year	合计 Total	第一产业 Primary Industry	第二产业 Secondary Industry	第三产业 Tertiary Industry
1978	256.70	157.40	65.60	33.70
1979	265.60	156.10	72.20	37.30
1980	270.10	153.60	82.10	43.20
1981	278.90	153.60	82.10	43.20
1982	282.70	151.10	86.20	45.40
1983	289.60	156.40	85.00	48.10
1984	304.20	149.20	97.70	57.40
1985	315.30	149.20	104.50	61.70
1986	326.40	149.90	112.10	64.60
1987	334.80	149.90	120.20	64.70
1988	336.50	147.60	123.20	65.70
1989	344.20	152.50	122.10	69.60
1990	352.80	156.50	123.30	73.10
1991	361.20	161.90	124.30	74.90
1992	370.30	161.70	127.80	80.80
1993	365.70	160.50	128.80	76.40
1994	367.60	157.10	129.40	81.20
1995	374.20	155.40	132.40	86.40
1996	381.50	152.20	137.10	92.20
1997	388.70	155.20	138.10	95.30
1998	393.10	154.80	138.60	99.70
1999	396.10	150.30	142.00	103.80
2000	397.60	144.70	134.91	117.99
2001	400.50	133.90	142.30	124.30
2002	413.31	121.38	153.85	138.08
2003	438.96	119.91	163.93	155.12
2004	458.81	113.98	180.63	164.20
2005	471.03	104.48	196.80	169.75
2006	490.10	102.97	209.83	177.30
2007	505.80	102.30	217.80	185.70
2008	513.80	102.40	220.80	190.60
2009	525.71	105.65	220.33	199.73
2010	540.34	105.16	223.85	211.33
2011	551.18	106.02	227.08	218.08
2012	559.88	104.95	229.79	225.14
2013	571.47	107.59	232.17	231.71
2014	588.97	108.45	229.91	250.61
2015	595.44	107.92	229.51	258.01

3－2 主要年份全市单位从业人员人数

MAJOR YEAR'S NUMBER OF EMPLOYED PERSONS IN ALL UNITS OF THE CITY

单位:万人(10 000 persons)

年 份 Year	合 计 Total	#市 区 Urban Area	#国有单位 State-owned Units	#集体单位 Collective-owned Units	其他所有制单位 Other Ownership Units
1949	14.8	13.4	9.3	5.5	
1952	23.4	20.1	18.3	5.1	
1957	29.7	24.5	24.1	5.6	
1962	32.3	26.8	24.5	7.8	
1965	36.7	30.6	26.8	9.9	
1970	45.6	37.4	32.2	13.4	
1975	53.4	43.5	38.0	15.4	
1978	70.7	54.5	49.2	21.5	
1980	79.2	61.5	55.0	24.2	
1985	88.8	66.7	59.8	28.9	0.1
1988	98.2	70.0	66.7	31.2	0.3
1989	99.2	70.4	67.7	31.0	0.5
1990	103.2	70.6	69.5	32.9	0.8
1991	105.4	78.4	71.5	32.5	1.4
1992	108.2	80.4	73.6	32.8	1.8
1993	109.4	80.8	75.3	29.5	4.6
1994	110.1	80.2	72.4	28.3	9.4
1995	111.6	80.2	72.4	27.5	11.7
1996	118.4	81.1	71.6	26.0	20.8
1997	117.1	78.1	69.0	22.6	25.5
1998	116.2	75.6	64.2	19.0	33.0
1999	119.0	78.3	60.4	16.6	42.0
2000	118.3	76.6	57.6	14.2	46.5
2001	117.5	75.1	53.2	12.2	52.1
2002	119.1	75.2	49.5	10.3	59.3
2003	118.0	74.3	47.2	8.9	61.9
2004	207.1	111.1	43.7	18.0	145.4
2005	224.3	122.3	43.9	18.2	162.2
2006	243.2	133.7	41.7	16.2	185.3
2007	249.8	137.3	45.1	17.9	186.8
2008	254.1	140.9	44.4	15.4	194.3
2009	260.5	145.6	44.4	14.6	201.5
2010	269.4	151.1	44.6	15.1	209.7
2011	275.9	156.5	44.3	14.7	216.9
2012	283.2	162.1	44.0	13.8	225.4
2013	293.7	184.1	37.8	5.4	250.5
2014	303.0	191.4	36.7	4.9	261.4
2015	309.2	192.4	35.8	4.6	268.8

注:1.2004 年以前为城镇单位职工人数。

2.2013 年统计口径变化,国有单位、集体单位数据与上年不可比。

Note:1. Before 2004, the data refer to number of staff and workers in urban units.

2. Because of the adjustment about the statistics system, the data of State-owned Units and Collective-owned Units since 2013 are not fully comparable with historical statistics.

3-3 全市单位国民经济各行业从业人员人数(2015年)

NUMBER OF EMPLOYED PERSONS IN ALL UNITS OF THE CITY BY SECTOR(2015)

单位:万人(10 000 persons)

		2015		2014	
		合计 Total	女性 Female	合计 Total	女性 Female
总计	**Total**	**309.2**	**120.6**	**303.0**	**122.1**
1. 农、林、牧、渔业	Farming, Forestry, Animal Husbandry and Fishery	1.4	0.5	1.3	0.6
2. 采矿业	Mining	0.3		0.2	
3. 制造业	Manufacturing	146.8	57.6	146.3	61.7
4. 电力、热力、燃气及水生产和供应业	The Electricity, Heat, Gas and Water Production and Supply Industry	3.0	0.7	2.9	0.7
5. 建筑业	Construction	25.8	4.0	25.2	3.5
6. 批发和零售业	Wholesale and Retail Trade	42.5	19.6	40.8	18.7
7. 交通运输、仓储和邮政业	Transport, Storage and Post	12.7	3.5	13.0	3.9
8. 住宿和餐饮业	Hotels and Catering Services	5.7	2.8	5.7	3.2
9. 信息传输、软件和信息技术服务业	Information Transmission Computer Services and Software	3.6	1.4	4.2	1.3
10. 金融业	Financial Intermediation	6.3	3.4	5.5	2.9
11. 房地产业	Real Estate	7.5	2.9	7.3	2.8
12. 租赁和商务服务业	Leasing and Business Services	11.0	4.3	10.5	3.8
13. 科学研究和技术服务业	Scientific Research and Technical Services	5.6	2.0	5.0	1.8
14. 水利、环境和公共设施管理业	Management of Water Conservancy, Environment and Public Facilities	3.1	1.1	2.9	1.0
15. 居民服务、修理和其他服务业	Residents Service, Repair and Other Services	2.5	0.9	2.1	1.1
16. 教育	Education	13.4	7.7	12.9	7.3
17. 卫生和社会工作	Health and Social Welfare	6.6	4.6	6.3	4.3
18. 文化、体育和娱乐业	Culture, Sports and Entertainment	1.5	0.6	1.5	0.7
19. 公共管理、社会保障和社会组织	Public Management, Social Security and Social Organization	9.9	3.0	9.4	2.8

3-4 全市单位分市、区国民经济各行业从业人员人数(2015年)

NUMBER OF EMPLOYED PERSONS IN ALL UNITS OF THE CITY BY REGION AND SECTOR (2015)

市、区名称	Region	合计 Total	农林牧渔业 Farming, Forestry, Animal Husbandry and Fishery	采矿业 Mining	制造业 Manufacturing	电力热力燃气及水生产和供应业 The Electricity, Heat, Gas and Water Production and Supply Industry
全市	**Whole Municipality**	**309.2**	**1.6**	**0.3**	**147.0**	**3.0**
市内三区	The Three Districts of Qingdao City	73.2			11.4	1.0
崂山区	Laoshan District	20.5			6.0	0.1
黄岛区	Huangdao District	59.3	0.50		27.0	0.6
城阳区	Chengyang District	33.6	0.10		22.6	0.1
即墨市	Jimo	41.6	0.10		28.5	0.3
胶州市	Jiaozhou	34.2			22.1	0.2
平度市	Pingdu	18.9	0.20	0.1	11.8	0.4
莱西市	Laixi	22.1	0.60	0.1	13.8	0.3
红岛经济区	Qingdao National High-tech Industrial Development Zone	3.9	0.10		2.8	
保税港区	Qingdao Free Trade Port Area of China	1.9			1.0	

单位:万人(10 000 persons)

建筑业 Construction	批发和零售业 Wholesale and Retail Trade	交通运输仓储及邮政业 Transport, Storage and Post	住宿和餐饮业 Hotels and Catering Services	信息传输软件和信息技术服务业 Information Transmission Computer Services and Software
25.7	**42.4**	**12.4**	**5.6**	**3.5**
5.4	17.5	5.9	2.6	2.1
3.6	2.9	0.7	0.4	0.8
7.0	8.2	3.2	1.0	0.6
1.3	3.1	1.4	0.5	
2.7	3.5	0.3	0.7	
3.0	3.5	0.4	0.1	
0.7	1.5	0.1	0.1	
1.8	1.5	0.2	0.1	
0.2	0.1		0.1	
	0.6	0.2		

3-4 续表
Continued

市、区名称	Region	金融业 Financial Intermediation	房地产业 Real Estate	租赁和商务服务业 Leasing and Business Services	科学研究和技术服务业 Scientific Research and Technical Services	水利环境和公共设施管理业 Management of Water Conservancy, Environment and Public Facilities
全市	**Whole Municipality**	**6.3**	**7.7**	**11.0**	**5.5**	**3.1**
市内三区	The Three Districts of Qingdao City	4.4	2.9	5.4	2.1	1.2
崂山区	Laoshan District	0.2	1.0	1.1	1.0	0.1
黄岛区	Huangdao District	0.3	1.3	2.1	1.3	0.4
城阳区	Chengyang District	0.5	0.4	1.0	0.2	0.2
即墨市	Jimo	0.3	0.4	0.7	0.1	0.8
胶州市	Jiaozhou	0.3	0.8	0.4	0.2	0.1
平度市	Pingdu	0.2	0.2		0.3	0.1
莱西市	Laixi	0.1	0.6		0.3	0.2
红岛经济区	Qingdao National High-tech Industrial Development Zone		0.1	0.3		
保税港区	Qingdao Free Trade Port Area of China					

单位:万人(10 000 persons)

居民服务其他服务业 Services to Households and Other Services	教育 Education	卫生和社会工作 Health and Social Welfare	文化体育和娱乐业 Culture, Sports and Entertainment	公共管理社会保障和社会组织 Public Management, Social Security and Social Organization	国际组织 International Organization
2.5	**13.5**	**6.7**	**1.5**	**9.9**	
0.4	3.9	3.4	0.6	3.0	
0.6	0.7	0.2	0.3	0.7	
0.7	2.5	0.7	0.3	1.6	
0.1	1.0	0.4	0.1	0.6	
0.2	1.3	0.5	0.1	1.1	
	1.4	0.6	0.1	1.0	
	1.8	0.5		0.8	
0.5	0.8	0.4	0.1	0.9	
	0.1		0.1	0.1	
				0.1	

3-5 全市单位分市、区全部从业人员人数(2015 年底)

NUMBER OF EMPLOYED PERSONS IN ALL UNITS OF THE CITY BY REGION(END OF 2015)

单位:万人(10 000 persons)

市、区名称	Region	年末人数 Year-end Population	国有单位 State-owned Units	集体单位 Collective-owned Units	其他经济类型单位 Units in Other Types of Economy
全市	**Whole Municipality**	**309.2**	**35.8**	**4.6**	**268.8**
市内三区	The Three Districts of Qingdao City	73.3	13.9	0.8	58.6
崂山区	Laoshan District	20.5	3.0	2.0	15.5
黄岛区	Huangdao District	59.3	5.7	0.4	53.2
城阳区	Chengyang District	33.6	1.9	0.1	31.6
即墨市	Jimo	41.6	2.5	0.7	38.4
胶州市	Jiaozhou	34.1	3.2	0.2	30.7
平度市	Pingdu	18.9	2.7	0.3	15.9
莱西市	Laixi	22.1	2.4	0.1	19.6
红岛经济区	Qingdao National High-tech Industrial Development Zone	3.9	0.4		3.5
保税港区	Qingdao Free Trade Port Area of Chin	1.9	0.1		1.8

3-6 全市在岗职工工资总额、平均工资(1978-2015年)
TOTAL WAGE BILL AND AVERAGE WAGE OF EMPLOYED STAFF AND WORKERS(1978-2015)

年 份 Year	工资总额(亿元) Total Wage Bill(100 million yuan)		平均工资(元) Average Wage(yuan)	
	全社会单位 All Units	其中:非私营单位 of which:Non-private Units	全社会单位 All Units	其中:非私营单位 of which:Non-private Units
1978		4.0		584
1979		4.8		662
1980		6.0		782
1981		6.3		778
1982		6.6		785
1983		6.9		809
1984		9.0		1 041
1985		9.6		1 103
1986		11.8		1 311
1987		14.2		1 519
1988		18.0		1 862
1989		20.7		2 120
1990		24.4		2 400
1991		26.4		2 553
1992		31.8		2 970
1993		40.4		3 694
1994		59.5		5 455
1995		68.3		6 164
1996		78.2		6 640
1997		82.5		7 030
1998		87.2		7 518
1999		100.1		8 405
2000		120.4		10 072
2001		135.8		11 426
2002		153.8		12 839
2003	225.6	160.3	12 597	15 335
2004	280.5	193.4	13 932	17 190
2005	359.5	242.8	16 015	20 022
2006	445.6	292.0	18 574	23 457
2007	518.1	338.6	21 419	27 083
2008	578.7	371.9	23 296	30 233
2009	638.1	393.2	25 396	33 258
2010	738.0	446.8	28 549	37 805
2011	877.5	522.0	32 763	43 077
2012	1 044.3	613.1	37 399	49 052
2013	1 251.7	785.7	42 688	55 363
2014	1 456.0	890.5	48 453	62 104
2015	1 644.4	993.0	53 715	69 465

注:2003 年以前为职工工资总额、平均工资。

Note:The data before 2003 refer to the total wage bill and average wage of staff and workers.

3-7 全市在岗职工工资总额、平均工资指数(1978-2015年)

INDEXES OF TOTAL WAGE BILL AND AVERAGE WAGE OF EMPLOYED STAFF AND WORKERS(1978-2015)

年份 Year	工资总额指数 Total Wage Bill Indexes		平均工资指数 Average Wage Indexes	
	全社会单位 All Units	其中:非私营单位 of which:Non-private Units	全社会单位 All Units	其中:非私营单位 of which:Non-private Units
1978		120.80		104.66
1979		119.53		113.36
1980		123.95		118.13
1981		106.71		99.49
1982		103.80		100.90
1983		104.14		103.06
1984		130.64		128.68
1985		107.11		105.96
1986		123.22		118.86
1987		120.10		115.87
1988		126.48		122.58
1989		115.29		113.86
1990		117.66		113.21
1991		108.28		106.38
1992		120.26		116.33
1993		127.09		124.38
1994		147.46		147.67
1995		114.76		113.00
1996		114.54		107.72
1997		105.50		105.87
1998		105.64		106.94
1999		114.81		111.80
2000		120.29		119.83
2001		112.77		113.44
2002		113.31		112.37
2003		108.84		110.30
2004	124.34	120.65	110.60	112.10
2005	128.16	125.54	114.95	116.47
2006	123.95	120.26	115.98	117.16
2007	116.27	115.96	115.32	115.46
2008	111.70	109.83	108.76	111.63
2009	110.26	105.73	109.01	110.01
2010	115.66	113.63	112.42	113.67
2011	118.90	116.83	114.76	113.95
2012	119.01	117.45	114.15	113.87
2013	119.86	128.15	114.14	112.87
2014	116.32	113.34	113.50	112.18
2015	112.94	111.51	110.86	111.85

注:2004年以前为职工工资总额、平均工资指数。

Note:The data before 2004 refer to the indexes of total wage bill and average wage of staff and workers.

3－8 分行业在岗职工平均工资(2015 年)

AVERAGE WAGE OF EMPLOYED STAFF AND WORKERS BY SECTOR(2015)

行　业	Sector	全部单位(元) All Units (yuan)	非私营单位(元) Non-private Units (yuan)	私营单位(元) Private Units (yuan)
总　计	**Total**	**53 715**	**69 465**	**41 737**
(一)农、林、牧、渔业	Farming, Forestry, Animal Husbandry and Fishery	47 046	50 059	46 791
(二)采矿业	Mining	46 203	46 071	46 283
(三)制造业	Manufacturing	47 878	54 361	42 304
(四)电力、热力、燃气及水生产和供应业	The Electricity, Heat, Gas and Water Production and Supply Industry	69 189	77 009	40 517
(五)建筑业	Construction	49 332	60 065	40 893
(六)批发和零售业	Wholesale and Retail Trade	41 599	50 753	39 380
(七)交通运输、仓储和邮政业	Transport, Storage and Post	64 488	76 942	44 657
(八)住宿和餐饮业	Hotels and Catering Services	40 005	46 256	36 009
(九)信息传输、软件和信息技术服务业	Information Transmission Computer Services and Software	71 940	101 298	53 809
(十)金融业	Financial Intermediation	142 743	152 521	49 058
(十一)房地产业	Real Estate	56 410	72 904	40 480
(十二)租赁和商务服务业	Leasing and Business Services	48 761	65 988	43 694
(十三)科学研究和技术服务业	Scientific Research and Technical Services	69 076	97 122	45 255
(十四)水利、环境和公共设施管理业	Management of Water Conservancy, Environment and Public Facilities	50 831	57 582	43 925
(十五)居民服务、修理和其他服务业	Residents Service, Repair and Other Services	43 658	49 858	40 144
(十六)教育	Education	96 220	100 825	28 002
(十七)卫生和社会工作	Health and Social Welfare	88 297	92 091	40 076
(十八)文化、体育和娱乐业	Culture, Sports and Entertainment	71 433	75 799	56 869
(十九)公共管理、社会保障和社会组织	Public Management, Social Security and Social Organization	99 751	99 822	

3-9 分市、区在岗职工工资总额(2015年)

TOTAL WAGE BILL OF EMPLOYED STAFF AND WORKERS BY REGION(2015)

单位:亿元(100 million yuan)

市、区名称	Region	合计 Total	国有单位 State-owned Units	集体单位 Collective-owned Units	其他所有制单位 Other Ownership Units
全市	**Whole Municipality**	**1 644.4**	**335.7**	**36.1**	**1 272.6**
市内三区	The Three Districts of Qingdao City	450.6	136.7	5.2	308.7
崂山区	Laoshan District	131.8	28.5	17.4	85.9
黄岛区	Huangdao District	313.6	50.7	0.5	262.4
城阳区	Chengyang District	182.0	19.9	1.2	160.9
即墨市	Jimo	188.6	24.0	7.6	157.0
胶州市	Jiaozhou	165.5	25.5	1.6	138.4
平度市	Pingdu	84.2	26.1	1.6	56.5
莱西市	Laixi	96.8	21.1	1.0	74.7
红岛经济区	Qingdao National High-tech Industrial Development Zone	21.4	2.7		18.7
保税港区	Qingdao Free Trade Port Area of China	9.9	0.5		9.4

3－10 分市、区在岗职工平均工资(2015 年)
AVERAGE WAGE OF EMPLOYED STAFF AND WORKERS BY REGION(2015)

单位:元/年(yuan/year)

市、区名称	Region	合计 Total	国有单位 State-owned Units	集体单位 Collective-owned Units	其他所有制单位 Other Ownership Units
全市	**Whole Municipality**	**53 715**	**96 932**	**81 146**	**48 958**
市内三区	The Three Districts of Qingdao City	64 223	102 421	61 995	55 173
崂山区	Laoshan District	68 118	98 659	84 497	59 658
黄岛区	Huangdao District	54 475	92 884	48 476	50 464
城阳区	Chengyang District	54 115	103 468	91 274	50 956
即墨市	Jimo	47 087	98 204	108 789	42 368
胶州市	Jiaozhou	49 388	82 213	75 605	45 829
平度市	Pingdu	46 521	93 185	71 339	37 983
莱西市	Laixi	46 297	90 873	89 360	40 440
红岛经济区	Qingdao National High-tech Industrial Development Zone	55 575	75 970	86 839	53 477
保税港区	Qingdao Free Trade Port Area of China	52 516	81 530		51 513

主要统计指标解释

单位从业人员　指报告期末最后一日24时在本单位中工作,并取得工资或其他形式劳动报酬的人员数。该指标为时点指标,不包括最后一日当天及以前已经与单位解除劳动合同关系的人员,是在岗职工、劳务派遣人员及其他就业人员之和。就业人员不包括:

(1)离开本单位仍保留劳动关系,并定期领取生活费的人员;

(2)利用课余时间打工的学生及在本单位实习的各类在校学生;

(3)本单位因劳务外包而使用的人员。

在岗职工　指在本单位工作且与本单位签订劳动合同,并由单位支付各项工资和社会保险、住房公积金的人员,以及上述人员中由于学习、病伤、产假等原因暂未工作仍由单位支付工资的人员。在岗职工还包括:

(1)应订立劳动合同而未订立劳动合同人员(如使用的农村户籍人员);

(2)处于试用期人员;

(3)编制外招用的人员;

(4)派往外单位工作,但工资仍由本单位发放的人员(如挂职锻炼、外派工作等情况)。

工资总额　指根据《关于工资总额组成的规定》(1990年1月1日国家统计局发布的一号令)进行修订,在报告期内(季度或年度)直接支付给本单位全部就业人员的劳动报酬总额。包括计时工资、计件工资、奖金、津贴和补贴、加班加点工资、特殊情况下支付的工资,是在岗职工工资总额、劳务派遣人员工资总额和其他就业人员工资总额之和。

工资总额是税前工资,包括单位从个人工资中直接为其代扣或代缴的房费、水费、电费、住房公积金和社会保险基金个人缴纳部分等。

工资总额不论是计入成本的还是不计入成本的,不论是以货币形式支付的还是以实物形式支付的,均应列入工资总额的计算范围。

平均工资　指单位就业人员在一定时期内平均每人所得的工资额。它表明一定时期工资收入的高低程度,是反映就业人员工资水平的主要指标。

Explanatory Notes on Main Statistical Indicators

Personnel employed by organization　refers to the number of personnel who are working in the organization within the 24 hours of the last day at the end of the reporting period and get salaries or other forms of labor remuneration. This indicator is a time-point indicator, excluding those who have terminated the labor contract relationship with the organization on the last day or earlier, and is the sum of staff and workers on the job, workers dispatched by labor service or other employees. The following are excluded:

(1) The personnel who have left the organization but still retain labor relation and receive living expenses on a regular basis;

(2) Students who use their spare time to work for money and the full-time students who are doing internship with the organization;

(3) Personnel who are used by the organization due to labor outsourcing.

Staff and workers in the post　refers to the personnel who have been working and entered into employment contract with the organization and paid salaries and social insurance and housing provident funds by the organization and those that are not working due to studying, getting sick or injured, maternity leave or other reasons but still paid salaries by the organization. Staff and workers in the post also include:

(1) The personnel who should enter into employment contract but have not yet done so (such as rural workers being used);

(2) Personnel in probation;

(3) Personnel recruited as non-staff;

(4) Personnel sent to work with other organization but whose salaries are still paid by the organization (such as on-the-job training, expatriate work and others).

Total payroll refers to the total amount of labor remuneration directly paid to all the employees of the organization within the reporting period (a quarter or year) revised in accordance with the Regulations on Composition of Payrolls (Order No. 1 issued by the National Bureau of Statistics on January 1, 1990, including hourly wage, piecework wage, bonus, allowances and subsidies, overtime pay, pay under special circumstances, the sum of payrolls of staff and workers in the post, personnel dispatched by labor service or other personnel in employment.

Total payroll is pre-tax wage, including charges for house, water, electricity as well as the part of housing provident funds and social insurance funds to be paid by individuals, which are directly deducted from personal wages or submitted by the organization on their behalf.

Total payroll whether counted in costs or not, paid in monetary form or in kind, should be included in its calculation range.

Average wage refers to the amount of wage earned by employees on average of an organization in a period of time. It indicates a level of wage income in a period of time and a main indicator indicating employees' wage level.

4 固定资产投资

INVESTMENT IN FIXED ASSETS

简要说明

一、本篇资料的主要内容

本篇资料主要反映了全市固定资产投资及房地产开发方面的情况，主要包括固定资产投资的规模、结构、资金来源和房地产开发投资、施竣工及销售情况等方面的资料。

二、本篇资料的来源

本篇资料来源于固定资产投资及房地产开发投资统计年报，由市统计局固定资产投资统计处整理提供。

Brief Introduction

I. Main Content

Data in this chapter show the basic conditions of investment in fixed assets and real estate development of the whole city, mainly including the total investment in fixed assets, the structure of investment, the resources of investment and investment in real estate development, construction, completion, sales, etc.

II. Source of Data

Data in this chapter are based on the annual report on investment in fixed assets and real estate development, and provided by the Division of Investment and Construction Statistics of Qingdao Municipal Bureau of Statistics.

4-1 主要年份固定资产投资
MAJOR YEAR'S INVESTMENT IN FIXED ASSETS

单位:万元(10 000 yuan)

年份 Year	规模以上固定资产投资总额 Investment in Fixed Assets above Designated Size	按用途分 Grouped by Use		
		生产性投资 Productive Investment	非生产性投资 Non- Productive Investment	#住宅投资 Investment in Residential Buildings
1949	16	12	4	3
1952	3 097	1 368	1 729	1 007
1957	5 923	3 947	1 976	1 151
1962	2 747	2 049	698	192
1965	5 481	4 155	1 326	375
1970	6 100	5 813	287	154
1975	15 839	13 548	2 381	1 064
1978	29 660	23 499	6 161	3 203
1980	47 499	33 865	13 634	9 335
1985	107 421	60 643	73 424	19 058
1989	262 214	190 950	71 264	26 592
1990	284 576	210 453	74 123	38 898
1991	349 031	256 633	92 398	51 898
1992	583 068	420 748	162 320	83 844
1993	953 274	511 684	441 590	162 419
1994	1 329 716	728 532	601 184	324 094
1995	1 648 281	925 194	723 087	390 206
1996	1 610 562	972 398	638 164	285 412
1997	1 611 902	932 207	679 695	278 951
1998	1 909 711	1 125 821	783 890	316 999

4 -1 续表 1
continued

单位:万元(10 000 yuan)

年份 Year	规模以上固定资产投资总额 Investment in Fixed Assets above Designated Size	按用途分 Grouped by Use		
		生产性投资 Productive Investment	非生产性投资 Non- Productive Investment	#住宅投资 Investment in Residential Buildings
1999	2 205 891	1 246 328	959 563	421 151
2000	2 426 820	1 311 538	1 115 282	470 963
2001	2 934 728	1 487 762	1 446 966	729 181
2002	3 683 623	1 962 588	1 721 035	765 030
2003	5 475 526	3 023 930	2 451 596	1 038 304
2004	9 845 646	6 336 279	3 509 367	1 608 738
2005	14 032 960	9 172 206	4 860 754	1 841 644
2006	14 856 894	9 214 578	5 642 316	2 222 733
2007	16 353 636	10 231 673	6 121 963	2 720 970
2008	20 190 098	12 443 179	7 746 919	3 315 538
2009	24 588 889	13 852 653	10 736 236	3 831 976
2010	30 224 785	16 207 885	14 016 900	5 609 189
2011	35 025 382	18 622 819	16 402 563	5 707 625
2012	41 539 146	24 246 803	17 292 343	6 689 114
2013	50 278 649	30 996 768	19 281 881	7 220 432
2014	57 660 308	32 913 906	24 746 402	7 311 090
2015	65 556 685	41 402 714	24 153 971	7 569 123

注:1. 规模以上固定资产投资数据 2003 年以前为城镇以上统计范围。
2. 因 2004 年以来数据有调整,故表中数据不可比。

Note:1. The data of investment above designated size refer to investment above city and town level before 2003.
2. The data since 2004 are not comparable with other data because of the adjustment.

4－1 续表2
continued

单位：万元(10 000 yuan)

年 份 Year	按构成分 Grouped by Composition of Funds			按资金来源分 Grouped by Sources of Funds			
	建筑安装工程 Construction and Installation	设备工器具购置 Purchase of Equipment and Instruments	其他费用 Others	国家投资 State Investment	国内贷款 Domestic Loans	利用外资 Foreign Investment	自筹及其他 Self-raising Fund and Others
1949	11	3	2	16			
1952	2 146	870	81	1 512			1 585
1957	2 853	2 773	297	3 816			2 107
1962	1 631	984	132	2 205			542
1965	3 346	1 859	276	4 451			1 030
1970	3 136	2 835	129	2 721			3 379
1975	7 489	8 133	217	9 378	1 362		5 099
1978	19 968	9 124	568	16 828	1 601		11 231
1980	30 993	15 541	965	10 371	12 925	1 420	22 783
1985	64 665	35 100	7 656	17 377	35 888	1 136	53 020
1989	141 821	95 333	17 269	38 747	79 999	25 081	114 939
1990	167 731	91 305	25 540	24 687	91 895	23 688	144 306
1991	196 212	108 929	43 890	22 615	131 676	38 325	156 415
1992	304 060	208 384	70 624	22 660	213 217	89 130	258 061
1993	600 011	225 555	127 708	23 736	208 672	94 469	626 397
1994	842 809	272 126	214 781	26 062	318 334	221 265	764 055
1995	1 020 484	385 934	241 863	25 683	379 198	328 124	915 276
1996	929 735	458 284	222 543	35 639	444 443	310 722	819 758

4－1 续表3
continued

单位:万元(10 000 yuan)

年份 Year	按构成分 Grouped by Composition of Funds			按资金来源分 Grouped by Sources of Funds			
	建筑安装工程 Construction and Installation	设备工器具购置 Purchase of Equipment and Instruments	其他费用 Others	国家投资 State Investment	国内贷款 Domestic Loans	利用外资 Foreign Investment	自筹及其他 Self-raising Fund and Others
1997	875 057	485 122	251 723	27 928	297 089	363 789	923 096
1998	1 034 500	574 852	300 359	67 762	491 812	170 709	1 179 428
1999	1 456 473	459 596	289 822	128 603	584 120	145 589	1 347 579
2000	1 476 397	652 640	297 783	75 978	489 697	164 175	1 806 238
2001	1 781 235	744 549	408 944	93 491	620 562	217 526	2 157 787
2002	2 328 492	796 685	558 446	78 775	719 677	411 704	2 831 288
2003	3 544 790	1 133 333	797 403	127 861	989 178	722 644	4 237 643
2004	6 413 046	2 312 139	1 120 461	85 549	1 100 297	1 016 145	8 245 272
2005	8 949 231	3 141 732	1 941 997	136 632	1 250 343	1 850 921	11 540 604
2006	8 818 614	3 668 191	2 370 089	391 315	2 126 523	1 662 897	11 856 506
2007	9 981 666	4 171 878	2 200 092	215 649	2 427 031	1 788 056	13 109 824
2008	11 795 435	5 907 195	2 487 468	322 484	3 309 471	1 951 468	15 855 082
2009	14 911 874	5 869 214	3 807 801	778 090	4 217 265	1 593 287	21 555 685
2010	18 725 922	6 362 880	5 135 983	1 305 737	5 881 886	2 135 736	27 898 294
2011	22 865 421	7 521 441	4 638 520	1 640 702	5 871 709	1 766 278	33 579 182
2012	26 080 239	8 601 282	6 857 625	1 324 159	5 484 459	1 561 597	37 356 847
2013	33 237 368	9 969 777	7 071 504	1 959 340	8 154 829	1 528 585	49 552 883
2014	39 006 113	11 640 126	3 764 630	1 404 667	7 452 983	1 181 541	55 024 776
2015	42 893 643	15 972 153	6 690 889	2 067 396	7 249 574	1 098 178	62 458 544

4-2 主要年份固定资产投资构成(以投资总额为100)

COMPOSITION OF MAJOR YEAR'S INVESTMENT IN FIXED ASSETS(TOTAL INVESTMENT = 100)

年份 Year	按用途分 Grouped by Use		
	生产性投资 Productive Investment	非生产性投资 Non-Productive Investment	#住宅投资占非生产性比重 Percentage of Investment in Residential Buildings to Non-Productive Investment
1949	75.00	25.00	75.00
1952	44.17	55.83	58.24
1957	66.64	33.36	58.25
1962	74.59	25.41	27.51
1965	75.81	24.19	28.28
1970	95.30	4.70	53.66
1975	84.97	15.03	44.69
1978	79.23	20.77	51.99
1980	71.30	28.70	68.47
1985	56.45	43.55	40.74
1989	72.82	27.18	37.30
1990	73.95	26.05	52.50
1991	73.53	26.47	56.17
1992	72.16	27.84	51.65
1993	53.68	46.32	36.78
1994	54.79	45.21	53.91
1995	56.10	43.90	54.00
1996	60.40	39.60	44.70

4-2 续表 1
continued

年份 Year	按用途分 Grouped by Use		
	生产性投资 Productive Investment	非生产性投资 Non-Productive Investment	#住宅投资占非生产性比重 Percentage of Investment in Residential Buildings to Non-Productive Investment
1997	57.80	42.20	41.00
1998	59.00	41.00	16.60
1999	56.50	43.50	19.10
2000	54.00	46.00	19.40
2001	50.70	49.30	50.40
2002	53.30	46.70	44.50
2003	55.20	44.80	42.40
2004	64.40	35.60	45.80
2005	65.40	34.60	37.90
2006	62.00	38.00	39.40
2007	62.60	37.40	44.40
2008	61.60	38.40	42.80
2009	56.30	43.70	35.70
2010	53.62	46.38	40.02
2011	53.17	46.83	34.80
2012	58.37	41.63	38.68
2013	61.65	38.35	37.45
2014	57.08	42.92	29.54
2015	63.16	36.84	31.34

4-2 续表2
continued

年 份 Year	按构成分 Grouped by Composition of Funds			按资金来源分 Grouped by Sources of Funds			
	建筑安装工程 Construction and Installation	设备工器具购置 Purchase of Equipment and Instruction	其他费用 Others	国家投资 State Investment	国内贷款 Domestic Loans	利用外资 Foreign Investment	自筹及其他 Self-raising Fund and Others
1949	68.75	18.75	12.5	100			
1952	69.29	28.09	2.62	48.82			51.18
1957	48.17	46.82	5.01	64.43			35.57
1962	59.37	35.82	4.81	80.27			19.73
1965	61.05	33.92	5.03	81.21			18.79
1970	51.41	46.48	2.11	44.61			55.39
1975	47.28	51.35	1.37	59.21	8.60		32.19
1978	67.32	30.76	1.92	56.74	5.40		37.86
1980	65.25	32.72	2.03	21.83	27.21	2.99	47.97
1985	60.20	32.68	7.12	16.18	33.41	1.06	49.35
1989	54.08	36.36	6.59	14.78	30.51	9.56	45.15
1990	58.94	32.08	8.98	8.68	32.29	8.32	50.71
1991	56.22	31.21	12.57	6.48	37.73	10.98	44.81
1992	52.15	35.74	12.11	3.89	36.56	15.29	44.26
1993	62.94	23.66	13.40	2.49	21.89	9.91	65.71
1994	63.38	20.46	16.16	1.96	23.94	16.64	57.46
1995	61.9	23.4	14.7	1.6	23.0	19.9	55.5
1996	57.7	28.5	13.8	2.2	27.6	19.3	50.9
1997	54.3	30.1	15.6	1.7	18.4	22.6	57.3

4-2 续表3
continued

年　份 Year	按构成分 Grouped by Composition of Funds			按资金来源分 Grouped by Sources of Funds			
	建筑安装工程 Construction and Installation	设备工器具购置 Purchase of Equipment and Instruction	其他费用 Others	国家投资 State Investment	国内贷款 Domestic Loans	利用外资 Foreign Investment	自筹及其他 Self-raising Fund and Others
1998	54.2	20.8	15.7	3.5	25.8	8.9	61.8
1999	66.0	20.8	13.2	5.8	26.5	6.6	61.1
2000	60.8	26.9	12.3	3.1	20.2	6.8	74.4
2001	60.7	25.4	13.9	3.0	20.1	7.0	69.9
2002	63.2	21.6	15.2	1.9	17.8	10.2	70.1
2003	64.7	20.7	14.6	2.1	16.3	11.9	69.7
2004	65.1	23.5	11.4	0.8	10.6	9.7	78.9
2005	63.8	22.4	13.8	0.9	8.5	12.5	78.1
2006	59.4	24.7	15.9	2.4	13.3	10.4	73.9
2007	61.0	25.5	13.5	1.2	13.8	10.2	74.8
2008	58.4	29.3	12.3	1.5	15.4	9.1	74.0
2009	60.6	23.9	15.5	2.8	15.0	5.6	76.6
2010	62.0	21.0	17.0	3.5	15.8	5.7	75.0
2011	65.3	21.5	13.2	3.8	13.7	4.1	78.4
2012	62.8	20.7	16.5	2.9	12.0	3.4	81.7
2013	66.1	19.8	14.1	3.2	13.3	2.5	81.0
2014	67.6	20.2	12.2	2.2	11.5	1.8	84.6
2015	65.4	24.4	10.2	2.8	10.0	1.5	85.7

4-3 按三次产业分规模以上固定资产投资(2015年)

INVESTMENT IN FIXED ASSETS ABOVE DESIGNATED SIZE BY THREE STRATA OF INDUSTRY(2015)

单位:万元(10 000 yuan)

指　标	Indicator	2015
总　计	**Total**	**65 556 685**
第一产业	Primary Industry	1 149 513
第二产业	Secondary Industry	32 535 645
#工业	Industry	31 458 278
第三产业	Tertiary Industry	31 871 527

4-4 分市、区固定资产投资额(2015年)

INVESTMENT IN FIXED ASSETS BY REGION(2015)

单位:万元(10 000 yuan)

市、区名称	Region	规模以上固定资产投资额 Investment in Fixed Assets above Designated Size	#房地产开发 Investment in Real Estate Development
全市	**Whole Municipality**	**65 556 685**	**11 223 458**
市南区	Shinan District	1 253 379	661 011
市北区	Shibei District	2 239 189	1 377 804
李沧区	Licang District	4 383 811	2 522 022
崂山区	Laoshan District	2 197 364	1 443 638
黄岛区	Huangdao District	17 101 586	2 331 560
保税港区	Qingdao Free Trade Port Area of China	44 972	2 960
城阳区	Chengyang District	6 114 144	1 187 943
即墨市	Jimo	9 076 627	518 925
胶州市	Jiaozhou	8 980 124	352 602
平度市	Pingdu	6 778 909	422 947
莱西市	Laixi	6 019 344	125 694
红岛经济区	Qingdao National High-tech Industrial Development Zone	1 367 236	276 352

4-5 规模以上固定资产投资(2015年)
INVESTMENT IN FIXED ASSETS ABOVE DESIGNATED SIZE(2015)

单位:万元(10 000 yuan)

项　　目	Item	合计 Total	#房地产开发 Investment in Real Estate Development
一、本年施工项目(个)	**Projects Under Construction This Year(unit)**	**6 894**	
#本年新开工(个)	of which:Newly Started(unit)	6 120	
二、本年建成投产项目(个)	**Projects Completed and Put into Use This Year(unit)**	**5 074**	
三、本年完成投资	**Investment Completed This Year**	**65 556 685**	**11 223 458**
1.按构成分	Grouped by Composition		
#建筑工程	Construction Projects	38 151 836	6 781 118
安装工程	Installation Projects	4 741 807	1 165 278
设备工器具购置	Purchase of Equipment and Instruments	15 972 153	158 262
#用于更新的设备	Equipment Used in Updates	4 039 739	
2.按建设性质分	Grouped by Type of Construction		
#新　建	New Construction	26 310 207	
扩　建	Expansion	12 607 584	
改　建	Reconstruction	12 457 934	
3.按隶属关系分	Grouped by Subordination Relation		
中央单位	Central Units	1 248 588	564 378
地方单位	Local Units	64 308 097	10 659 080
4.按国民经济行业分	Grouped by Economic Sector		
(1)农、林、牧、渔业	Farming,Forestry,Animal Husbandry and Fishery	1 149 513	
农　业	Farming	403 555	
林　业	Forestry	51 494	
畜牧业	Animal Husbandry	88 003	
渔　业	Fishery	479 838	
农、林、牧、渔服务业	Farming,Forestry,Animal Husbandry and Fishery Services	126 623	
(2)采矿业	Mining	121 435	
煤炭开采和洗选业	Mining and Washing of Coal		
石油和天然气开采业	Extraction of Petroleum and Natural Gas	9 600	
黑色金属矿采选业	Mining of Ferrous Metal Ores	28 245	
有色金属矿采选业	Mining of Non-ferrous Metal Ores	24 271	
非金属矿采选业	Mining and Processing of Nonmetal Ores	54 619	
开采辅助活动	Auxiliary Activities of Mining		
其他采矿业	Mining of Other Ores	4 700	

4－5 续表 1
continued

单位:万元(10 000 yuan)

项　　目	Item	合计 Total	#房地产开发 Investment in Real Estate Development
(3)制造业	Manufacturing	30 593 722	
农副食品加工业	Processing of Food from Agricultural Products	1 953 288	
食品制造业	Manufacture of Foods	697 385	
酒、饮料和精制茶制造业	Manufacture of Liquor, Beverage and Refind Tea	223 331	
烟草制品业	Manufacture of Tobacco	1 533	
纺织业	Manufacture of Textile	591 045	
纺织服装、服饰业	Manufacture of Textile Wearing Apparel	1 390 854	
皮革、毛皮、羽毛及其制品和制鞋业	Manufacture of Leather, Fur, Feather & Its Products Footwear	466 937	
木材加工和木、竹、藤、棕、草制品业	Processing of Timbers, Manufacture of Wood, Bamboo, Rattan, Palm and Straw Products	388 852	
家具制造业	Manufacture of Furniture	465 403	
造纸和纸制品业	Manufacture of Paper and Paper Products	393 943	
印刷和记录媒介复制业	Printing, Reproduction of Recording Media	685 273	
文教、工美、体育和娱乐用品制造业	Manufacture of Articles for Culture, Arts & Crafts, Sports and Entertainment	1 015 257	
石油加工、炼焦和核燃料加工业	Processing of Petroleum, Coking, Processing of Nucleus Fuel	357 800	
化学原料和化学制品制造业	Manufacture of Chemical Raw Material and Chemical Products	1 536 337	
医药制造业	Manufacture of Medicines	434 262	
化学纤维制造业	Manufacture of Chemical Fiber	65 316	
橡胶和塑料制品业	Manufacture of Rubber and Plastic	1 822 686	
非金属矿物制品业	Manufacture of Non-metallic Mineral Products	1 729 845	
黑色金属冶炼和压延加工业	Smelting and Pressing of Ferrous Metals	332 681	
有色金属冶炼和压延加工业	Smelting and Pressing of Non-ferrous Metals	214 116	
金属制品业	Manufacture of Metal Products	3 708 097	
通用设备制造业	Manufacture of General Purpose Machinery	3 653 232	
专用设备制造业	Manufacture of Special Purpose Machinery	2 897 793	
汽车制造业	Manufacture of Vehicle	1 557 822	
铁路、船舶、航空航天和其他运输设备制造业	Manufacture of Transport Equipment for Railway, Shipping, Aerospace and other uses	1 351 118	
电气机械和器材制造业	Manufacture of Electrical Machinery & Equipment	1 329 560	
计算机、通信和其他电子设备制造业	Manufacture of Computer, Communication Equipment and Other Electronic Equipment	907 901	
仪器仪表制造业	Manufacture of Measuring Instrument	205 818	
其他制造业	Manufacture of Other Products	149 310	
废弃资源综合利用业	Recycling and Disposal of Waste Resources	50 489	
金属制品、机械和设备修理业	Maintenance of Metal Products, Machinery and Equipment	16 438	

4 -5 续表 2
continued

单位:万元(10 000 yuan)

项　目	Item	合计 Total	#房地产开发 Investment in Real Estate Development
(4)电力、燃气及水的生产和供应业	Production and Supply of Electricity Gas and Water	743 121	
电力、热力的生产和供应业	Production and Supply of Electric Power and Heat Power	379 690	
燃气生产和供应业	Production and Supply of Gas	110 799	
水的生产和供应业	Production and Supply of Water	252 632	
(5)建筑业	Construction	1 077 367	
(6)交通运输、仓储及邮政业	Transport Storage and Post	4 847 540	
铁路运输业	Railway Transport	127 451	
道路运输业	Road Transport	3 492 651	
水上运输业	Water Transport	220 488	
航空运输业	Air Transport	11 242	
管道运输业	Pipeline Transport	25 836	
装卸搬运和运输代理业	Handing,Corrying and Transportation Agent	87 304	
仓储业	Ware houses and Storage	882 568	
邮政业	Post		
(7)信息传输、软件和信息技术服务业	Information Transmission Computer Services and Software	385 729	
(8)批发和零售业	Wholesale and Retail Trade	2 870 016	
(9)住宿和餐饮业	Hotels and Catering Services	587 602	
(10)金融业	Financial Intermediation	45 232	
(11)房地产业	Financial Intermediation	13 470 873	11 223 458

4 -5 续表3
continued

单位:万元(10 000 yuan)

项　目	Item	合计 Total	#房地产开发 Investment in Real Estate Development
(12)租赁和商务服务业	Leasing and Business Services	1 961 791	
(13)科学研究、技术服务和地质勘察业	Scientific Research, Technical Service and Geologic Prospecting	1 086 819	
(14)水利、环境和公共设施管理业	Management of Water Conservancy, Environment and Public Facilities	3 539 886	
水利管理业	Management of Water Conservancy	171 066	
环境管理业	Environmental Management	94 566	
公共设施管理业	Management of Public Facilities	3 274 254	
(15)居民服务和其他服务业	Services to Households and Other Services	138 733	
居民服务业	Services to Households	46 148	
机动车、电子产品和日用产品修理业	Maintenance of Vehicle, Electronic Products and Daily Articles	62 530	
其他服务业	Other Services	30 055	
(16)教育	Education	776 585	
(17)卫生和社会工作	Health and Social Work	214 401	
卫生	Health	181 759	
(18)文化、体育和娱乐业	Culture, Sports and Entertainment	1 260 919	
新闻出版业	Journalism and Publishing Activities	8 230	
广播、电视、体育和音像业	Broadcasting, Movies, Televisions and Audiovisual Activities	787 600	
文化艺术业	Cultural and Art Activities	316 275	
体育	Sports Activities	60 802	
娱乐业	Entertainment	88 012	
(19)公共管理、社会保障和社会组织	Public Management, Social Security and Social Organization	685 401	
中国共产党机关	Communist Party of China		
国家机构	Government Agencies	349 167	
人民政协、民主党派	People's Political Consultatioe Conference, Democratic Party		
社会保障	Social Security		
群众团体、社会团体和其他成员组织	Non-Governmental Institutions, Social Organizations and Other Organizations	7 700	
基层群众自治组织	Local People Self-government Organization	328 534	
(20)国际组织	International Organization		

4－5 续表4
continued

单位:万元(10 000 yuan)

项　目	Item	合计 Total	#房地产开发 Investment in Real Estate Development
四、本年新增固定资产	**Newly Increased Fixed Assets This Year**	**45 240 273**	**5 090 931**
(1)农、林、牧、渔业	Farming, Forestry, Animal Husbandry and Fishery	1 024 002	
(2)采矿业	Mining	116 202	
(3)制造业	Manufacturing	22 563 827	
(4)电力、燃气及水的生产和供应业	Production and Supply of Electricty, Gas and Water	466 051	
(5)建筑业	Construction	817 259	
(6)交通运输、仓储和邮政业	Transport, Storage and Post	1 842 151	
(7)信息传输、计算机服务和软件业	Information Transmission, Computer Services and Software	3 384 858	
(8)批发和零售业	Wholesale and Retail Trade	361 394	
(9)住宿和餐饮业	Hotels and Catering Services	91 411	
(10)金融业	Financial Intermediation	31 208	
(11)房地产业	Real Estate	6 666 129	5 090 931
(12)租赁和商务服务业	Leasing and Business Services	934 002	
(13)科学研究、技术服务	Scientific Research and Technical Services	592 508	
(14)水利、环境和公共设施管理业	Management of Water Conservancy, Environment and Public Facilities	4 643 047	
(15)居民服务、修理和其他服务业	Services to Households, Repair and Other Services	166 982	
(16)教育	Education	564 279	
(17)卫生和社会工作	Health and Social Work	127 029	
(18)文化、体育和娱乐业	Culture, Sports and Entertainment	281 587	
(19)公共管理、社会保障和社会组织	Public Management, Social Security and Social Organization	566 347	
(20)国际组织	International Organization		
五、本年资金来源合计	**Total Funds This Year**	**79 743 323**	**22 765 013**
上年末结余资金	Balance of Last Year	6 869 631	5 727 255
本年资金来源小计	Sub-total Funds This Year	72 873 692	17 037 758
国家预算内资金	State Budget	2 067 396	
国内贷款	Domestic Loans	7 249 574	3 399 550
债券	State Treasury Bond		
利用外资	Foreign Investment	1 098 178	2 070
自筹资金	Self-raising Funds	55 122 609	6 930 435
其他资金来源	Others	7 335 935	6 705 703

4-6 主要年份房地产开发投资
MAJOR YEAR'S INVESTMENT IN REAL ESTATE DEVELOPMENT

单位:万元、万平方米(10 000 yuan,10 000 sq. m)

年份 Year	房地产开发投资额 Investment in Real Estate Development	房屋施工面积 Floor Space Under Construction	房屋竣工面积 Floor Space Completed	房屋实际销售面积 Floor Space of Buildings Sold	房屋实际销售额 Sale of Buildings
1995	562 861	1 008	240	103	185 384
1996	455 765	748	203	80	125 150
1997	426 570	675	237	113	216 311
1998	438 059	742	259	178	351 805
1999	629 717	900	474	240	430 123
2000	675 142	1 047	352	301	550 401
2001	925 153	1 374	532	406	802 364
2002	1 036 476	1 417	537	427	933 031
2003	1 277 969	1 765	552	469	1 121 885
2004	1 626 965	2 101	635	516	1 530 964
2005	2 238 370	2 363	811	740	2 666 738
2006	2 683 631	2 751	654	719	3 054 907
2007	3 223 547	3 224	641	833	4 333 566
2008	3 805 652	3 773	672	770	3 924 175
2009	4 594 829	4 310	814	1 262	7 036 744
2010	6 024 387	5 058	1 020	1 360	8 952 942
2011	7 827 193	5 693	925	1 026	7 702 379
2012	9 301 099	6 474	1 212	951	7 660 684
2013	10 485 229	7 073	957	1 160	9 786 176
2014	11 177 297	8 171	1 136	1 164	9 708 984
2015	11 223 458	8 971	1 523	1 419	12 628 568

4 -7 房地产开发投资情况(2015 年)
INVESTMENT IN REAL ESTATE DEVELOPMENT(2015)

单位:万元(10 000 yuan)

指标名称	Indicator	合计 Total	按经济类型分 Grouped by Economic Types		
			国有经济 State-owned	集体经济 Collective-owned	其他经济 Others
本年完成投资额	**Investment Completed This Year**	**11 223 458**	**859 971**	**9 568**	**10 353 919**
1.住宅	Residential Buildings	7 569 123	471 088	8 445	7 089 590
2.办公楼	Office Buildings	807 305	108 728	417	698 160
3.商业营业用房	Houses for Business Use	1 712 610	143 485	310	1 568 815
4.其他	Others	1 134 420	136 670	396	997 354

4 -7 续表
continued

单位:万元(10 000 yuan)

指标名称	Indicator	按资质等级分 Grouped by Qualification Criteria					
		一级 First Grade	二级 Second Grade	三级 Third Grade	四级 Fourth Grade	暂定 Provisional	其他 Others
本年完成投资额	**Investment Completed This Year**	**252 358**	**818 061**	**495 286**	**209 231**	**8 653 209**	**795 313**
1.住宅	Residential Buildings	148 766	655 339	283 305	87 613	5 925 712	468 388
2.办公楼	Office Buildings	6 595	27 390	24 083	46 436	553 469	149 332
3.商业营业用房	Houses for Business Use	11 270	65 736	150 387	55 521	1 352 893	76 803
4.其他	Others	85 727	69 596	37 511	19 661	821 135	100 790

4-8 房地产施工、竣工面积及竣工价值(2015年)
FLOOR SPACE UNDER CONSTRUCTION AND COMPLETED AND COMPLETED VALUE OF REAL ESTATE(2015)

单位:万平方米(10 000 sq. m)

施工、竣工房屋面积及竣工价值	Indicator	施工面积 Floor Space Under Construction	#新开工 Newly Started	竣工面积 Floor Space Completed	竣工房屋价值(万元) Completed Value (10 000 yuan)
房屋建筑面积总计	**Floor Space of Buildings**	**8 971**	**1 962**	**1 523**	**3 978 828**
住　宅	Residential Buildings	5 875	1 369	1 047	2 717 626
办公楼	Office Buildings	620	119	79	228 026
商业营业用房	Houses for Business Use	1 090	152	169	435 912
其　他	Others	1 386	322	228	597 264

4-9 商品房屋销售情况(2015年)
BASIC STATISTICS ON SALES OF COMMERCIALIZED BUILDINGS(2015)

单位:万平方米(10 000 sq. m)

商品房屋销售情况	Sales and Rental of Commercialized Buildings	实际销售 Actual Sales	实际销售额(万元) Actual Sales Volume (10 000 yuan)	待售面积 Area for Sale
房屋面积总计	**Floor Space of Buildings**	**1 419**	**12 628 568**	**673**
住　宅	Residential Buildings	1 239	10 452 844	418
办公楼	Office Buildings	57	820 897	57
商业营业用房	Houses for Business Use	94	1 157 140	131
其　他	Others	29	197 687	67

主要统计指标解释

固定资产投资 是以货币形式表现的在一定时期内全社会建造和购置固定资产的工作量以及与此有关的费用的总称。该指标是反映固定资产投资规模、结构和发展速度的综合性指标,又是观察工程进度和考核投资效果的重要依据。全社会固定资产投资按登记注册类型可分为国有、集体、个体、联营、股份制、外商、港澳台商、其他等。

城镇固定资产投资 是指城镇各种登记注册类型的企业、事业、行政单位及个体户进行的计划总投资(或实际需要总投资)500 万元及 500 万元以上的建设项目投资、房地产开发投资、城镇和工矿区私人建房投资。县城及以上区域内发生的投资,县及县以上各级政府及主管部门直接领导、管理的建设项目和企业事业单位的投资均为城镇固定资产投资。

固定资产投资 包括城镇、农村 500 万元以上投资项目。

房地产开发投资 指各种登记注册类型的房地产开发公司、商品房建设公司及其他房地产开发法人单位和附属于其他法人单位实际从事房地产开发或经营活动的单位统一开发的包括统代建、拆迁还建的住宅、厂房、仓库、饭店、宾馆、度假村、写字楼、办公楼等房屋建筑物和配套的服务设施,土地开发工程(如道路、给水、排水、供电、供热、通讯、平整场地等基础设施工程)的投资;不包括单纯的土地交易活动。

固定资产投资的资金来源根 据固定资产投资的资金来源不同,分为国家预算内资金、国内贷款、利用外资、自筹资金和其他资金。

固定资产投资 按国民经济行业分根据建设项目建成投产后的主要产品或主要用途及社会经济活动性质来确定国民经济行业。一般情况下,一个建设项目或一个企业、事业单位只能属于一种国民经济行业。

固定资产投资 按建设性质分建设项目的性质一般分为新建、扩建、改建和技术改造、迁建、恢复。

固定资产投资 按构成分固定资产投资活动按其工作内容和实现方式分为建筑安装工程,设备、工具、器具购置,其他费用三个部分。

施工项目 指报告期内进行过建筑或安装施工活动的项目。凡是报告期内施过工的建设项目,不论施工时间长短,均作为施工项目统计。

新增生产能力(或工程效益) 指通过固定资产投资活动而增加的设计能力(或工程效益),它是以实物形态表现的固定资产投资成果。

新增生产能力(或工程效益) 一般有以下几种表现形式:
(1)以建设项目或单项工程建成后的年产能力表示,如煤炭开采,石油开采等。
(2)以建设项目或单项工程建成后处理原料的能力表示,如选矿工程的年处理矿石能力,城市污水处理能力等。
(3)以新增加的主要设备的数量或容量表示,如新增棉布织机、电机组容量等。
(4)用建筑物容积、容量、面积、长度表示,如新建公路、水库容量、学校学生席位等。

房屋施工面积 是指报告期内施工的全部房屋建筑面积。包括本期新开工的面积和上期开工跨入本期继续施工的房屋面积,以及上期已停缓建在本期恢复施工的房屋面积。本期竣工和本期施工后又停缓建的房屋,其建筑面积仍计入本期房屋施工面积中。

房屋竣工面积 是指在报告期内房屋建筑按照设计要求全部完工,达到住人和使用条件,经验收鉴定合格(或达到竣工验收标准),正式移交使用单位的各栋房屋建筑面积的总和。

新增固定资产又称交付使用的固定资产 是指已经完成建造和购置过程,并已交付生产或使用单位的固定资产价值。新增固定资产是表示固定资产投资成果的价值量指标,也是反映建设进度、计算固定资产投资效果的必要数据。

固定资产交付使用率 指一定时期新增固定资产与同期完成投资额的比率。该指标是反映固定资产动用速度,衡量建设过程中宏观投资效果的综合指标。由于新增固定资产是较长时期内形成的结果,而投资额则是当年完成的,因此,该指标一般适宜于反映较长时期内固定资产的动用情况。

Explanatory Notes on Main Statistical Indicators

Investment in Fixed Assets referss to the volume of activities in construction and purchases of fixed assets and related fees, expressed in monetary terms. It is a comprehensive indicator which shows the size, structure and growth of the investment in fixed assets, providing basis for observing the progress of construction projects and evaluating results of investment. Total investment in fixed assets in the whole country includes, by type of ownership, the investment by the state-owned units, collective units, individuals, joint ownership units, share-holding units, as well as investment by businessmen from foreign countries and from Hong Kong, Macau and Taiwan, and by other units.

Urban Investment in Fixed Assets refers to construction projects involving a total planned (or required) investment of 5,000,000 yuan and over by urban enterprises and institutions of various types of ownership, by administrative units and by individuals, investment in real estate development, and housing investment by individuals in urban areas and in industrial and mining areas. In other words, all investments that take place in county towns and urban areas, investment in construction projects under the direct leadership and management of government agencies at and above county levels and investments by enterprises and institutions at and above county levels are covered in urban investment in fixed assets.

Investment in Fixed Assets includes construction projects involving an urban or rural investment of 5,000,000 yuan and over.

Investment in Real Estate Development refers to the investment by the real estate development companies, commercial buildings construction companies and other real estate development units of various types of ownership in the construction of house buildings, such as residential buildings, factory buildings, warehouses, hotels, guesthouses, holiday villages, office buildings, and the complementary service facilities and land development projects, such as roads, water supply, water drainage, power supply, heating, telecommunications, land leveling and other projects of infrastructure. It excludes the activities in pure land transactions.

Sources of Funds for Investment in Fixed Assets include fund from state budget, domestic loans, foreign investment, self-raised funds, and others depending on the source of investment.

Investment in Fixed Assets by SectorThe classification of construction projects by sector is determined by the major products or the purpose of the projects when they are put into production or use, and by the nature of their social economic activities. In general, one project or one enterprise or institution can only be classified into one sector.

Investment in Fixed Assets by Type of ConstructionThe construction projects in general can be classified, by the type of construction, into new construction, expansion, reconstruction and technical transformation, moving and restoration. However, investment by type of construction is not applied to investment by real-estate development units, investment in rural areas and investment in housing by urban individuals.

Investment in Fixed Assets by StructureBy their contents, investment activities are classified into 3 categories, i. e. construction and installation, purchase of equipment and instrument, and other expenses.

Projects under Construction refer to projects with construction and installation activities undertaken in the reference period. All projects that have construction activities undertaken during the reference period are reported as projects under construction irrespective of the length of construction work.

Newly Increased Production Capacity (or Project Efficiency) refers to the increase of designed capacity (or project efficiency) through investment in fixed assets, which reflects the accomplishment of investment in fixed assets in kind.

The newly increased production capacity (project efficiency) are usually expressed in one of the following forms:

(1) output of products, i. e. the output that the project can produce during a given period (usually a year). For instance, the capacity in coal mining is expressed in 10,000 tons/year, the capacity in producing chemical pesticides expressed in ton/year, the capacity in producing tractors in tractor/year, etc. For some chemical products where the effective contents differ significantly, the production capacity is expressed as the designed effective content equivalent, such as in the case of sulphuric acid, soda ash, caustic soda, etc;

(2) raw materials processing capacity, i. e. the volume of raw materials that could be processed by the project per day (or per hour), such as tons of materials processed per day by a sugar refining project or edible vegetable oil project, or tons of urban sewage processed per day;

(3) number or capacity of major equipment increased, such as number of cotton or silk looms increased, wool spindles increased, or capacity (in kilowatts) of power generators increased;

(4) physical measures (volume, capacity, area, and length) of construction, which is typical for non-industrial projects, for instance, the length of railways put into operation, the length of highways, the capacity of reservoirs, the capacity of warehouses, the floor space of housing projects, capacity for new students in schools or beds in hospitals, areas under new irrigation project, etc.

Floor Space of Buildings under Construction refers to total floor space of all buildings under construction during the reference period, including floor space of newly started buildings during the reference period, floor space of construction extended from the previous period to the current period, and floor space of construction suspended during the previous period and resumed in the current period. Floor space of construction completed in the current period, and floor space of construction started and then suspended in the current period are also included in the floor space under construction of the current year.

Floor Space of Buildings Completed refers to the floor space of all buildings completed in the reference period, which have been appraised and accepted (or come up to the designed standards) and have been transferred to the owners for use.

Newly Increased Fixed Assets refer to the newly increased value of fixed assets constructed or purchased, that have been transferred to the investors. This is an indicator that demonstrates the results of investment in fixed assets in monetary terms, and an important indicator to reflect the speed of construction and to calculate the efficiency of investment.

Rate of Projects of Fixed Assets Completed and Put into Operation refers to the ratio of the newly increased fixed assets to the total investment made in the same period. This is a comprehensive indicator reflecting the speed of the employment of fixed assets and the investment efficiency at the macro-level. As the newly increase fixed assets is the result of a long period while the investment is completed in the current year, this indicator is expected to be used to reflect the employment of fixed assets over a long period of time.

5 对外经济贸易

FOREIGN TRADE

简要说明

一、本篇资料的主要内容

本篇资料主要反映了全市外经外贸和外资企业的基本情况，主要包括外贸进出口、利用外资、对外投资与经济合作情况等方面的资料。

二、本篇资料的来源

1、口岸进出口数据来源于青岛海关。

2、进出口、利用外资、对外投资与经济合作等资料来源于市商务局。

本篇资料由市统计局外经贸易统计处整理提供。

Brief Introduction

I. Main Content

Data in this chapter show the basic conditions of foreign trade and foreign-funded enterprises, mainly including imports and exports, utilization of foreign capitals, production and operation condition of foreign-funded enterprises, etc.

II. Source of Data

(1)Data on imports and exports of Qingdao port are provided by Office of Qingdao Port Administration.

(2)Data on imports & exports and utilization of foreign capitals are provided by Qingdao Municipal Commerce Bureau.

Data in this chapter are prepared and compiled by the Division of Trade and External Economic Relations Statistics of Qingdao Municipal Bureau of Statistics.

5-1 青岛口岸进出口总额(1985-2015年)

TOTAL VALUE OF IMPORTS AND EXPORTS OF QINGDAO PORT(1985-2015)

单位:万美元(10000 USD)

年份 Year	青岛口岸进出口总额 Total Value of Imports and Exports of Qingdao Port	#出口 Exports	进口 Imports
1985	414 448	234 652	179 796
1986	382 840	191 926	190 914
1987	445 090	259 458	185 632
1988	474 516	259 176	215 340
1989	506 152	268 397	237 755
1990	477 117	304 011	173 106
1991	519 273	332 949	186 324
1992	581 495	350 163	231 332
1993	678 013	360 297	317 716
1994	888 574	510 760	377 814
1995	1 307 508	705 245	602 263
1996	1 391 323	760 566	629 757
1997	1 542 284	936 142	609 142
1998	1 463 718	933 392	530 326
1999	1 696 514	1 063 768	632 746
2000	2 520 420	1 423 266	1 097 154
2001	2 797 085	1 636 888	1 160 197
2002	3 128 048	1 889 612	1 238 436
2003	4 088 096	2 366 046	1 722 050
2004	5 677 570	3 197 697	2 479 873
2005	6 932 944	3 959 947	2 972 997
2006	8 019 198	4 495 731	3 523 467
2007	9 257 099	5 263 539	3 993 560
2008	11 558 079	5 953 501	5 604 578
2009	9 049 699	4 694 832	4 354 867
2010	11 912 702	5 988 254	5 924 448
2011	15 095 088	7 294 226	7 800 862
2012	14 888 716	7 120 813	7 767 903
2013	15 662 732	7 696 141	7 966 591
2014	16 489 966	8 736 358	7 753 608
2015	14 448 349	8 776 286	5 672 063

5-2 进出口总额(1988-2015年)

TOTAL VALUE OF IMPORTS AND EXPORTS(1988-2015)

单位:万美元(10000 USD)

年 份 Year	进出口总额(含中央、省驻青公司) Total Value of Imports and Exports (including central and provincial companies)	#出口 Exports	进口 Imports	进出口总额(不含中央、省驻青公司) Total Value of Imports and Exports (excluding central and provincial companies)	#出口 Exports	进口 Imports
1988				28 097	21 731	6 366
1989				39 327	27 797	11 530
1990				41 649	33 529	8 120
1991				54 624	44 746	9 878
1992				88 600	66 291	22 309
1993	517 643	346 288	171 355	139 048	100 201	38 847
1994	633 213	434 102	199 111	234 978	164 135	70 843
1995	858 560	536 386	322 174	376 372	245 072	131 300
1996	863 521	516 317	347 204	461 950	287 123	174 827
1997	916 269	579 261	377 008	521 967	338 535	183 432
1998	882 042	573 020	309 022	595 826	382 657	213 169
1999	1 009 885	631 072	378 813	775 565	446 260	329 305
2000	1 353 222	826 891	526 331	1 083 133	611 426	471 707
2001	1 541 564	950 160	591 404	1 235 781	712 024	523 757
2002	1 692 567	1 057 141	635 426	1 409 598	850 420	559 178
2003	2 065 912	1 239 199	826 713	1 784 556	1 035 528	749 028
2004	2 698 781	1 578 167	1 120 614	2 433 188	1 391 171	1 042 017
2005	3 302 230	1 942 242	1 359 988	3 045 542	1 758 834	1 286 708
2006	3 911 543	2 346 552	1 564 991	3 655 737	2 164 541	1 491 196
2007	4 572 534	2 831 004	1 741 530	4 360 499	2 677 596	1 682 903
2008	5 363 659	3 262 476	2 101 183	5 215 886	3 146 246	2 069 640
2009	4 485 115	2 729 865	1 755 250	4 398 639	2 692 197	1 706 442
2010	5 705 963	3 391 560	2 314 403	5 614 928	3 335 141	2 279 787
2011	7 215 217	4 061 309	3 153 908	7 126 310	4 005 572	3 120 738
2012				7 320 781	4 081 968	3 238 813
2013				7 791 217	4 198 605	3 592 612
2014				7 988 833	4 577 696	3 411 137
2015				7 022 243	4 535 015	2 487 228

注:2012年起,中央、省驻青公司外贸统计划归青岛,取消含中央、省驻青公司统计口径。

Note:Since 2012,the statistical calibre including central and provincial companies has been cancled.

5-3 分国别外贸出口总额
TOTLA VALUE OF EXPORTS BY COUNTRIES OR REGIONS

单位:万美元(10000 USD)

国别(地区)	Country(Region)	2015	2015年比2014年±% 2015/2014(±%)	占比%
亚洲	Asia	1 904 881	-5.4	42.0
香港	Hong Kong	187 613	30.2	4.1
日本	Japan	528 984	-11.6	11.7
韩国	Korea	413 618	-13.2	9.1
台湾	Taiwan	45 955	-12.3	1.0
非洲	Africa	191 642	-21.7	4.2
南非	South Africa	34 018	-5.6	0.8
欧洲	Europe	905 663	-3.5	20.0
欧盟	EU	810 470	-1.4	17.9
南美洲	South America	300 342	-5.3	6.6
北美洲	North America	1 071 582	15.0	23.6
美国	United States	980 038	17.4	21.6
大洋洲	Oceanica	157 836	21.8	3.5
澳大利亚	Australia	139 505	24.9	3.1

5-4 外贸出口商品分类
EXPORT COMMODITIES BY CATEGORY

单位:万美元(10000 USD)

项　目	Item	2015	2015年比2014年±% 2015/2014(±%)	占比%
合　计	**Total**	**4 535 015**	**-0.9**	**100.0**
按企业性质划分	By Enterprises Nature			
国有企业	State-owned Enterprises	454 243	-10.4	10.0
外商投资企业	Foreign Funded Enterprises	1 623 573	-6.0	35.8
其他企业	Other Enterprises	2 457 199	4.9	54.2
按贸易方式划分	By Customs Regime			
一般贸易	Ordinary Trade	2 886 066	5.3	63.6
加工贸易	Processing Trade	1 494 557	-7.3	33.0
其他贸易	Others	154 392	-31.9	3.4
按大类商品划分	By Category of Commodities			
纺织服装	Textile Garments	695 060	-9.8	15.3
农产品	Agricultural Products	498 890	-3.9	11.0
机电产品	Mechanical and Electrical Products	1 924 418	7.3	42.5
高新技术产品	High-tech Products	437 535	15.0	9.7

5-5 外贸进口商品分类
IMPORT COMMODITIES BY CATEGORY

单位：万美元(10000 USD)

项　目	Item	2015	2015年比2014年±% 2015/2014(±%)	占比%
合　计	**Total**	**2 487 228**	**-27.1**	**100.0**
按企业性质划分	By Enterprises Nature			
国有企业	State-owned Enterprises	660 991	-47.7	26.6
外商投资企业	Foreign Funded Enterprises	839 826	-12.8	33.8
其他企业	Other Enterprises	986 411	-16.6	39.7
按贸易方式划分	By Customs Regime			
一般贸易	Ordinary Trade	1 401 187	-29.0	56.3
加工贸易	Processing Trade	567 778	-13.2	22.8
其他贸易	Others	518 263	-33.8	20.8
按大类商品划分	By Category of Commodities			
纺织服装	Textile Garments	62 021	-21.8	2.5
农产品	Agricultural Products	473 484	-17.9	19.0
机电产品	Mechanical and Electrical Products	661 955	-13.2	26.6
高新技术产品	High-tech Products	326 196	-16.8	13.1

5-6 二十大出口商品出口情况
INFORMATION ON THE EXPORTATION OF TOP 20 PRODUCTS

单位:万美元(10000 USD)

商品名称	Name	2015	2015年比2014年±% 2015/2014(±%)	占比%
合计	**Total**	**3 836 056**	**-0.6**	**100.0**
机械设备	Machinery and Equipment	602 732	3.0	15.7
电器及电子类产品	Electric Appliance and Electronic Products	472 845	-0.8	12.3
服装	Garments	458 953	-10.3	12.0
运输工具	Transport Tools	423 953	11.8	11.1
计算机与通信技术	Computer and Communication Technology	349 557	12.5	9.1
金属制品	Metal Products	262 772	6.9	6.9
纺织品	Textile Products	236 107	-8.9	6.2
轮胎	Tyre	148 093	-17.1	3.9
水海产品	Aquatic and Seawater Products	128 558	-10.0	3.4
电话机	Telephone Sets	116 497	0.9	3.0
家具及其零件	Furniture	109 802	6.1	2.9
鞋类	Shoes	101 695	-2.1	2.7
蔬菜	Vegetables	93 691	9.6	2.4
箱包	Luggage and Bags	85 207	-2.8	2.2
钢材	Rolled Steel	83 881	-21.1	2.2
塑料制品	Plastic Articles	82 999	3.0	2.2
汽车零件	Parts of Motor Vehicles	56 691	-3.0	1.5
空调	Air Conditioner	21 890	-15.6	0.6
游戏机	Game Console	112	-75.3	
铁合金	Ferroalloy	20	-62.1	

5-7 二十大进口商品进口情况
INFORMATION ON THE IMPORTATION OF TOP 20 PRODUCTS

单位:万美元(10000 USD)

商品名称	Name	2015	2015年比2014年±% 2015/2014(±%)	占比%
合计	**Total**	**1 671 366**	**-25.3**	**100.0**
电器及电子产品	Electric Appliance and Electronic Products	260 793	-12.4	15.6
机械设备	Machinery and Equipment	186 548	-15.0	11.2
铁矿砂	Iron Sand	183 389	-53.6	11.0
仪器仪表	Instruments and Meters	141 378	-15.9	8.5
粮食	Grain	139 641	-29.1	8.4
集成电路	Integrated Circuits	106 091	1.9	6.3
天然橡胶	Natural Rubber	96 534	-23.3	5.8
冻鱼	Frozen Fish	95 724	-12.2	5.7
塑料原料	Plastic Raw Materials	89 875	-17.5	5.4
液晶显示板	Liquid Crystal Display	84 117	-22.4	5.0
纺织品	Textile Products	59 503	-21.9	3.6
棉花	Cotton	50 498	-41.8	3.0
合成橡胶	Synthetic Rubber	43 520	13.1	2.6
钢材	Rolled Steel	39 897	-11.6	2.4
运输工具	Means of Conveyance	38 789	-1.9	2.3
成品油	Refined Petroleum Products	28 491	-52.2	1.7
塑料制品	Plastic Articles	11 317	-10.0	0.7
铝锭及铝材	Aluminum Ingots and Aluminum Products	7 460	-53.5	0.4
钻石	Diamonds	5 986	-36.3	0.4
氧化铝	Alumina	1 816	-90.0	0.1

5－8 利用外资情况(2000－2015 年)

UTILIZATION OF FOREIGN CAPITAL(2000－2015)

项　目	Item	单位	Unit	2000	2005
批准企业(项目)个数	**Number of Enterprises (Projects) Approved**	**个**	**unit**	**1 132**	**2 530**
一、外商直接投资	Foreign Direct Investments	个	unit	1 128	2 530
中外合资企业	Sino-foreign Joint Ventures	个	unit	303	274
中外合作企业	Sino-foreign Cooperative Enterprises	个	unit	57	18
外商独资企业	Foreign-owned Enterprises	个	unit	76	2 236
其它	Others	个	unit	1	2
二、外商其他投资	Other Foreign Investments	个	unit	4	
合同外资金额	**Total Amount of Contracted Foreign Investment**	**万美元**	**10000 USD**	**269 081**	**954 486**
一、外商直接投资	Foreign Direct Investments	万美元	10000 USD	266 221	954 486
中外合资企业	Sino-foreign Joint Ventures	万美元	10000 USD	69 889	112 777
中外合作企业	Sino-foreign Cooperative Enterprises	万美元	10000 USD	26 835	17 588
外商独资企业	Foreign-owned Enterprises	万美元	10000 USD	169 370	813 485
其它	Others	万美元	10000 USD	127	10 636
二、外商其他投资	Other Foreign Investments	万美元	10000 USD	2 860	
实际利用外资金额	**Total Amount of Foreign Investment Actually Utilized**	**万美元**	**10000 USD**	**128 171**	**365 625**
一、外商直接投资	Foreign Direct Investments	万美元	10000 USD	126 132	365 625
中外合资企业	Sino-foreign Joint Ventures	万美元	10000 USD	39 224	77 636
中外合作企业	Sino-foreign Cooperative Enterprises	万美元	10000 USD	3 886	5 654
外商独资企业	Foreign-owned Enterprises	万美元	10000 USD	82 992	280 130
其它	Others	万美元	10000 USD	30	2 205
二、外商其他投资	Other Foreign Investments	万美元	10000 USD	2 039	

单位:万美元(10000 USD)

2006	2007	2008	2009	2010	2011	2012	2013	2014	2015
1 397	**1 068**	**640**	**647**	**731**	**707**	**553**	**645**	**619**	**763**
1 397	1 068	640	647	731	707	553	645	619	763
267	165	99	99	153	158	113	165	140	162
13	11	4	2	4	4	2	2	1	2
1 117	892	537	545	574	544	438	478	475	597
			1		1			3	2
311 697	**382 500**	**304 505**	**271 504**	**475 723**	**528 501**	**600 231**	**758 063**	**638 637**	**827 357**
311 697	382 500	304 505	271 504	475 723	528 501	600 231	758 063	638 637	827 357
31 368	51 821	81 796	61 734	124 148	142 535	102 252	191 172	126 878	116 013
6 883	13 878	367	4 531	9 179	15 173	122	4 765	-849	1 731
273 446	316 187	221 759	204 187	341 977	369 425	490 764	562 208	506 271	706 172
	614	583	1 052	419	1 368	7 093	-82	6 337	3 441
365 815	**380 652**	**264 295**	**186 397**	**284 281**	**363 350**	**460 027**	**552 227**	**608 100**	**669 062**
365 815	380 652	264 295	186 397	284 281	363 350	460 027	552 227	608 100	669 062
49 240	46 370	43 810	46 856	84 920	100 699	169 469	159 424	172 180	135 671
7 123	15 490	2 945	3 971	3 567	2 759	6 262	2 355	128	1 570
309 452	318 578	217 540	135 026	194 500	255 763	275 579	390 210	435 102	531 544
	214		544	1 294	4 129	8 717	238	690	277

5-9 当年外商直接投资项目数和投资额(2015年)
NUMBER OF PROJECTS AND TOTAL AMOUNT OF FOREIGN DIRECT INVESTMENT(2015)

项　　目	Item	批准企业项目数(个) Number of Projects Approved (unit)	合同外资金额(万美元) Total Amount of Contracted Foreign Investment(10000 USD)	实际利用外资金额(万美元) Total Amount of Foreign Investment Actually Utilized(10000 USD)
外商直接投资	**Foreign Direct Investments**			
一、按投资方式分	**Grouped by Investment Form**			
#中外合资企业	Sino-foreign Joint Ventures	162	116 013	135 671
中外合作企业	Sino-foreign Cooperative Enterprises	2	1 731	1 570
外商独资企业	Foreign-owned Enterprises	597	706 172	531 544
二、按主要行业分	**Grouped by Sector**			
#农、林、牧、渔业	Farming, Forestry, Animal Husbandry and Fishery	8	32 605	9 892
制造业	Manufacturing	254	356 455	405 965
电力、燃气及水的生产和供应业	Production and Supply of Electricity, Gas and Water	5	9 454	4 360
建筑业	Construction	3	1 838	1 957
交通运输、仓储和邮政业	Transport, Storage and Post	6	21 417	50 270
批发和零售业	Wholesale and Retail Trades	295	97 630	37 471
住宿和餐饮业	Hotels and Catering Services	28	864	1 860
租赁和商务服务业	Leasing and Business Services	56	38 589	28 341
科学研究、技术服务和地质勘查业	Scientific Research, Technical Service and Geological Survey	43	97 994	39 662
三、按主要国别(地区)分	**Grouped by Countries(Regions)**			
#香港	Hong Kong	153	449 418	319 422
韩国	Korea	348	184 187	128 345
日本	Japan	29	11 028	42 309
新加坡	Singapore	11	9 296	41 878
台湾省	Taiwan	45	45 406	28 227
英属维尔京群岛	Virgin Islands(E)	5	10 051	16 719
美国	United States	41	58 069	11 860

5-10 对外投资与经济合作
OUTBOUND INVESTMENT AND INTERNATIONAL ECONOMIC COOPERATION

名 称	Name	计算单位	Unit	2015	2015年比2014年±% 2015/2014(±%)
对外投资项目数	Number of Outbound Investment Projects	个	unit	185	25.9
对外投资中方投资额	The Amount of Investment by Chinese Sides in Outbound Investment	万美元	10000 USD	329 597	124.2
对外承包工程新签合同额	The Amount of New Contracts for Foreign Contracted Projects	万美元	10000 USD	365 578	60.6
对外承包工程完成营业额	The Completed Turnover of Foreign Contracted Projects	万美元	10000 USD	363 814	1.3
对外劳务合作派出人数	Number of Persons Sent Overseas for International Labor Service Cooperation	人	person	17 047	30.1

5-11 对外投资分国别(地区)情况表(2015年)
INFORMATION ON OUTBOUND INVESTMENT BY COUNTRY/REGION FOR(2015)

国别(地区)	Country(Region)	项目数量(个) Number of Projects (unit)	2015年比2014年±% 2015/2014(±%)	中方投资额(万美元) Amount of Investment by Chinese Sides (10000 USD)	2015年比2014年±% 2015/2014(±%)
总 计	**Total**	**185**	**25.9**	**329 597**	**124.2**
亚洲	Asia	100	31.6	199 570	156.1
中国香港	Hong Kong	33	10.0	39 348	78.8
韩国	Korea	12		893	-70.2
柬埔寨	Cambodia	7	133.3	18 203	970.8
日本	Japan	7	75.0	476	44.2
越南	Vietnam	7	250.0	29 950	4 304.4
马来西亚	Malaysia	5	0.0	11 083	2.4
阿拉伯联合酋长国	The United Arab Emirates	5		527	
印度尼西亚	Indonesia	5		41 125	111.9
新加坡	Singapore	5	66.7	11 731	817.8
泰国	Thailand	4	33.3	17 011	98.9
菲律宾	The Philippines	2		20	
吉尔吉斯斯坦	Kyrgyz	2		11 390	
老挝	Laos	1		121	
哈萨克斯坦	Kazakhstan	1		3 025	
巴基斯坦	Pakistan	1		2 000	601.8
孟加拉	Bangladesh	1	0.0	11 808	

5-11 续表
continued

国别(地区)	Country(Region)	项目数量(个) Number of Projects (unit)	2015年比2014年 ±% 2015/2014(±%)	中方投资额(万美元) Amount of Investment by Chinese Sides (10000 USD)	2015年比2014年 ±% 2015/2014(±%)
缅甸	Myanmar	1		848	
乌兹别克斯坦	Uzbekistan	1		12	
非洲	Africa	16	45.5	24 356	-7.8
塞舌尔	Seychelles	3	200.0	12 990	26 529.5
津巴布韦	Zimbabwe	2	100.0	3 000	275.0
肯尼亚	Kenya	2		3 690	
马达加斯加	Madagascar	1		1 000	
加纳	Ghana	1		20	
赤道几内亚	Equatorial Guinea	1		1	
纳米比亚	Namibia	1		0	
南非	South Africa	1		10	-96.7
尼日利亚	Nigeria	1		320	-46.7
莫桑比克	Mozambique	1		25	
坦桑尼亚	Tanzania	1	0.0	3 000	4 900.0
毛里求斯	Mauritius	1	0.0	300	-96.9
欧洲	Europe	19	171.4	17 626	78.6
德国	Germany	8	166.7	4 007	-42.9
俄罗斯联邦	Russian Federation	6	200.0	4 185	234.8
英国	U. K.	2		395	
法国	France	1	0.0	8 736	8 454.7
瑞典	Sweden	1		36	
意大利	Italy	1		268	
拉丁美洲	Latin America	7	250.0	4 990	
墨西哥	Mexico	2		2 025	
开曼群岛	The Cayman Islands	1	0.0	500	
巴西	Brazil	1		15	
乌拉圭	Uruguay	1		2 000	
英属安圭拉	British Anguilla	1		100	
圣卢西亚	Saint Lucia	1		350	
北美洲	North America	36		79 448	476.5
美国	United States	29		14 789	98.5
加拿大	Canada	6	20.0	46 659	637.1
百慕大群岛	Bermuda	1		18 000	
大洋洲	Oceanica	7	16.7	3 607	-71.8
澳大利亚	Australia	6	0.0	3 563	-72.2
新西兰	New Zealand	1		43	

主要统计指标解释

批准企业(项目)个数 是指外商直接投资中批准设立的外商投资企业个数、批准的合作开发项目个数。

合同外资金额 是指批准外商投资企业的合同、章程中规定的外国投资者认缴的出资额和企业投资总额内的应由外方投资者以自己的境外自有资金直接向企业提供的贷款。包括新批准企业合同外资和原有企业的增资减资,增资减资不对企业(项目)个数进行调整。

实际使用外资金额 是指合同外资金额的实际执行金额。

外商直接投资 是指外国企业和经济组织或个人(包括华侨、港澳台胞以及我国在境外注册的企业)按我国有关政策、法规,用现汇、实物、技术等在我国境内开办外商独资企业、与我国境内的企业或经济组织共同举办中外合资经营企业、合作经营企业或合作开发资源的投资(包括外商投资收益的再投资)以及经政府有关部门批准的项目投资总额内,企业从境外借入的资金。

外商其它投资 是指除外商直接投资以外其他方式吸收的外资。

进出口总额 是指实际进出我国国境的货物总金额。包括对外贸易实际进出口货物,来料加工装配进出口货物,国家间、联合国及国际组织无偿援助物资和赠送品,华侨、港澳台同胞和外籍华人捐赠品,租赁期满归承租人所有的租赁货物,进料加工进出口货物,边境地方贸易及边境地区小额贸易进出口货物(边民互市贸易除外),中外合资企业、中外合作经营企业、外商独资经营企业进出口货物和公用物品,到、离岸价格在规定限额以上的进出口货样和广告品(无商业价值、无使用价值和免费提供出口的除外),从保税仓库提取在中国境内销售的进口货物,以及其他进口货物。

对外投资 是指在中华人民共和国境内依法设立的企业通过新设、并购及其他方式在境外拥有非金融企业或取得既有非金融企业所有权、控制权、经营管理权及其他权益的行为。

对外承包工程 是指中国的企业或其他单位承包境外建设工程的活动。

对外劳务合作 是指组织劳务人员赴其他国家或地区为国外的企业或机构工作的经营性活动。

Explanatory Notes on Main Statistical Indicators

Enterprises(Projects) Permitted refers to number of foreign invested enterprises and developed projects under cooperation through the permission.

Contracted Foreign Investment refers to expenditure promised by the foreign investor and loan stemed from broad innate fund of the foreign investor, according to the contract and regulation approved of enterprise invested by foreigner.

Actual Utilization of Foreign Investment refers to actual usage of contracted foreign investment, including cash, investment in kind and incorporeal agreed by the both sides as part of the investment, such as services and technology.

Foreign Direct Investment refers to the investments by foreign enterprises and economic organizations or individuals(including overseas Chinese, compatriots from Hong dong, Macao and Taiwan, and Chinese enterprises registered abroad), following the relevant policies and laws of China, for the establishment of ventures and cooperative enterprises or cooperative exploration of resources with enterprises or economic organizations in China, lt includes the reinvestment of the foreign entrepreneurs with the profits gained from the investment and the funds that enterprises borrow from aboard in the total investment of projects which are approved by the relevant department of the government.

Other Investment by Foreign Entrepreneurs refers to all forms of utilization of foreign capitals other than foreign direct investment.

Total Imports and Exports refers to the real value of commodities imported into and exported from the boundary of China. They include the actual imports and exports through foreign trade, imported and exported goods under the processing and assembling trades and materials, supplies and gifts as aid given gratis between governments and by the United Nations and other international organizations, and contributions donated by overseas Chinese, compatriots in Hong Kong and Macao and Chinese with foreign citizenship, leasing commodities owned by tenant at the expiration of leasing period, the imported and exported commodities processed with imported materials, commodities trading in border areas (excluding mutual exchange goods), the imported and exported commodities and articles for public use of the Sino-foreign joint ventures, cooperative enterprises and ventures exclusively with foreign own investment. Also included are import or export of samples and advertising goods for whose CIF or FOB value are beyond the permitted ceiling (excluding goods of no trading or use value and free commodities for export), imported goods sold in China from bonded warehouses and other imported or exported goods.

Outbound investment refers to such actions as to own a non-financial business or acquire the ownership, control or management of a established non-financial business and other rights and interests outside the People's Republic of China by incorporation, merger and acquisition and/or other means by an enterprise incorporated in the People's Republic of China by law.

Foreign engineering contracting refers to the activities of Chinese enterprises or other units involved in contracting construction projects outside the People's Republic of China.

Foreign labor service cooperation refers to the business activities of organizing and sending labor service personnel to other countries or regions to work for the businesses or institutions in foreign countries.

6 城市建设、环境保护

CITY CONSTRUCTION AND ENVIRONMENT PROTECTION

简要说明

一、本篇资料的主要内容

本篇资料主要反映了全市城市基础设施基本情况，包括市政设施、供水、供电、公共交通、园林绿化、燃气供热、城市环卫、环境保护及工业“三废”排放情况等方面的资料。

二、本篇资料的来源

1、本篇资料中市政设施、供水、公共交通、园林绿化、燃气供热、城市环卫相关资料来源于市建设委员会的城市建设统计年报，由市统计局固定资产投资统计处整理提供。

2、本篇资料中供电资料来源于青岛供电公司，由市统计局能源统计处整理提供。

3、本篇资料中环境保护、环境质量及工业“三废”排放情况来源于市环境保护局，由市统计局能源统计处整理提供。

Brief Introduction

I. Main Content

Data in this chapter show the basic conditions of public facilities of the whole city, including urban construction and infrastructure, water supply, electricity supply, public communications, urban greenery, gas and heating, urban sanitation, environmental protection and discharge conditions of industrial waste water, waste gas and solid waste, etc.

II. Source of Data

(1)Data on conditions of urban construction and infrastructure,watersupply,public communications, urban greenery, gas and heating, urban sanitation are based on the annual report of city construction provided by Qingdao Municipal Construction Commission, and compiled by the Division of Investment and Construction Statistics of Qingdao Municipal Bureau of Statistics.

(2)Data on electricity supply are provided by Qingdao Power Corporation, and compiled by the Division of Energy Statistics of Qingdao Municipal Bureau of Statistics.

(3)Data on environmental protection, environmental conditions and discharge conditions of industrial waste water, waste gas and solid waste are provided by Qingdao Municipal Bureau of Environmental Protection ,and compiled by the Division of Energy Statistics of Qingdao Municipal Bureau of Statistics.

6－1 主要年份城市建设和公用事业

MAJOR YEAR'S CITY CONSTRUCTION AND PUBLIC UTILITIES

年 份 Year	建成区面积 (平方公里) Developed Areas(sq. km)	年末道路长度 (公里) Length of Roads at Year-end(km)	年末道路面积 (万平方米) Area of Roads at Year-end (10000 sq. m)	公共汽车、电车线路 网长度(公里) Network Length of Bus and Trolley Bus(km)
1949	27	243	206	26.4
1952	29	245	213	124.4
1957	36	248	217	232.3
1962	55	266	235	252.8
1965	57	266	235	308.1
1970	59	374	346	358.5
1975	63	392	355	389.3
1978	66	408	368	422.1
1980	72	408	377	474.1
1985	79	462	464	611.3
1987	81	578	575	581
1989	92.5	541	583	661
1990	94.3	667	786	777
1991	94.7	673	826	922
1992	95.4	683	840	988
1993	99.9	764	944	1 094
1994	103.9	811	985	1 372
1995	106	936	1 177	1 101
1996	110	991	1 339	1 211
1997	112	1 047	1 436	1 492
1998	114	1 106	1 436	1 859
1999	116	1 171	1 698	2 339
2000	119.1	1 192	1 789	2 711
2001	123	1 248	2 169	2 521
2002	133	1 426	2 594	896
2003	145.9	1 595	2 816	973
2004	154.8	1 755	3 254	1 185
2005	178.8	1 862	3 547	1 159
2006	227.5	3 160	5 218	1 362
2007	250.7	3 288	5 411	1 480
2008	267.1	3 318	5 596	1 470
2009	272.9	3 402	5 763	1 216
2010	282.3	3 409	5 893	1 383
2011	291.5	3 705	6 605	1 719
2012	374.6	4 281	7 528	1 978
2013	469.6	4 334	7 859	2 002
2014	490.7	4 393	7 908	2 023
2015	566.4	4 375	7 940	2 106

注:1. 自 2002 年起人均公共绿地面积按辖区内全部人口计算。

2. 2005 年以前所用园林绿地面积;公共绿地面积;人均公共绿地面积;公园、动物园个数;公园、动物园面积指标分别改为现在的绿地面积;公共绿地面积;人均公园绿地面积;公园个数;公园面积。

3. 2012 年城市建设数据由建委提供,包括范围:市南区、市北区、李沧区、崂山区、黄岛区、城阳区。黄岛区包含开发区、保税区和原胶南划入的 6 个街道办事处的数据。与以前年度范围不同,数据不可比。

Note:1. Per capita public green areas is calculated at total population in the area under jurisdiction since 2002.

2. Before 2005, the corresponding indicators of greenbelt area, park greenbelt area, per capita park greenbelt area, coverage rate of greenbelt, number of parks and area of parks were greenland area , public greenbelt area , per capita public greenbelt area, coverage rate of green, number of parks and zoos, area of parks and zoos.

3. In 2012, the data on city construction are provided by Qingdao Urban and Rural Construction Commision, include: Shinan, Shibei, Licang, Laoshan, Huangdao, Chengyang. The statistics of Huangdao include Development Zone. Free Trade Zone and 6 sub-districts to be under the jurisdiction of original Jiaonan. The figures are not comparable with those over the years.

6－1 续表1
continued

年 份 Year	自来水供水管道长度（公里）Length of Tap Water Pipelines (km)	全年供水总量（万立方米）Annual Volume of Tap Water Supply (10000 cu. m)	#全年售水量（万立方米）Annual Volume of Tap Water Sale (10000 cu. m)	#居民家庭用水 of which: Consumption for Residential Use	用水普及率（%）Coverage Rate of Population with Access to Tap Water(%)	排水管道长度（公里）Length of Sewage Pipes(km)	全年用电量（亿千瓦时）Annual Volume of Electricity Supply (100 million kW·h)	#居民生活用电 of which: Consumption for Residential Use
1949	308	721	456	331	89.0	200	0.88	0.14
1952	341	778	612	310	90.0	227	1.85	0.14
1957	412	1 392	1 296	606	93.0	273	2.61	0.26
1962	483	2 700	2 512	937	98.0	290	3.77	0.57
1965	500	3 220	2 979	929	98.0	295	5.92	0.68
1970	521	4 503	4 106	1 085	99.0	350	9.83	1.02
1975	564	6 726	6 302	1 950	99.0	361	12.41	1.43
1978	572	5 334	4 975	1 314	99.0	382	16.34	1.62
1980	588	8 224	7 874	2 577	99.0	394	21.48	2.78
1985	685	7 557	7 038	2 628	99.9	505	26.39	2.87
1987	749	10 716	9 155	3 691	99.9	569	34.15	4.01
1989	853	10 349	8 606	3 666	97.0	620	38.36	3.38
1990	873	11 896	10 211	4 270	96.9	645	41.08	4.32
1991	908	13 865	11 760	4 990	96.6	649	44.51	5.34
1992	1 035	16 385	13 070	5 931	96.5	672	51.78	6.84
1993	1 123	16 137	14 027	6 124	99.1	734	55.02	7.66
1994	1 124	17 367	14 716	6 405	100	811	60.74	8.78
1995	1 046	22 513	15 810	7 050	100	990	67.23	10.16
1996	1 182	23 277	16 566	7 731	100	1 051	72.87	12.23
1997	1 266	24 130	17 215	8 787	100	1 167	77.82	13.73
1998	1 390	23 845	17 271	9 115	100	1 210	79.65	14.28
1999	1 471	23 849	18 558	10 032	100	1 301	88.12	15.31
2000	1 524	25 414	20 642	11 405	100	1 460	106.80	16.00
2001	1 665	22 225	18 556	10 555	100	1 539	116.10	17.62
2002	1 781	27 662	21 684	10 129	100	1 641	131.44	18.31
2003	2 060	27 594	21 483	10 142	100	1 884	147.68	19.88
2004	2 566	30 877	23 864	11 695	100	2 002	167.95	23.63
2005	2 876	33 265	25 874	12 536	100	2 309	193.81	33.76
2006	3 984	30 524	25 572	10 682	100	3 994	215.35	34.87
2007	4 187	31 533	26 454	11 408	100	4 079	236.42	37.40
2008	4 642	32 675	27 396	11 301	100	4 229	250.07	40.31
2009	4 767	33 490	28 274	12 250	100	4 555	259.42	43.29
2010	4 926	34 909	29 617	12 524	100	4 708	292.97	49.50
2011	5 121	34 109	28 837	10 049	100	5 187	313.44	50.13
2012	5 243	38 945	33 039	12 121	100	6 814	318.36	51.64
2013	5 522	38 331	32 418	11 851	100	6 536	339.27	57.52
2014	6 177	46 649	40 612	14 834	100	6 840	337.82	59.95
2015	6 142	46 203	40 202	15 381	100	6 993	342.29	64.71

6－1 续表 2
continued

年 份 Year	公共汽车、电车营运车辆(辆) Number of Bus and Trolley Bus under Operation(unit)	全年客运量(万人次) Annual Passenger Traffic(10000 person-times)	出租汽车(辆) Number of Taxi(unit)	使用液化气、煤气、天然气人数(万人) Population with Access to Gas(10000 persons)	液化气 Liquefied Petroleum	煤 气 Coal Gas	天然气 Natural Gas	液化气供气量(吨) Volume of Liquefied Petroleum Supply(ton)
1949	32	298						
1952	76	932						
1957	112	4 110						
1962	127	4 747						
1965	173	6 092						
1970	224	13 002						
1975	324	14 426		2	2			184.9
1978	409	27 351		17	17			3 246
1980	485	38 981	48	24	24			4 345
1985	621	48 852	219	42.1	42.1			10 619
1987	679	56 102	652	56.4	45.4	11.0		12 947
1989	751	63 212	782	62.5	47.5	15.0		14 503
1990	801	63 495	832	75.0	57.4	17.6		17 512
1991	1 372	67 552	1 070	76.2	57.4	18.8		17 963
1992	1 470	73 529	1 828	82.8	62.0	20.8		19 565
1993	1 875	72 427	4 874	88.4	64.6	23.8		22 224
1994	1 850	78 231	5 806	103.6	77.4	26.2		24 684
1995	1 891	71 867	5 887	116.2	82.9	33.3		32 443
1996	2 012	49 077	6 660	126.0	88.0	38.0		40 651
1997	2 148	55 642	6 861	133.6	92.9	40.7		38 717
1998	2 184	51 042	7 469	146.8	97.8	49.0		45 381
1999	2 470	55 414	7 839	154.9	98.3	56.6		40 537
2000	3 141	59 879	7 933	164.1	93.3	70.8		46 951
2001	3 453	60 167	8 110	168.8	87.5	81.3		45 295
2002	3 681	61 713	8 376	224.2	133.8	90.4		60 123
2003	3 648	58 792	8 109	246.7	138.3	93.1	15.3	67 803
2004	3 848	66 463	8 144	258.4	140.6	78.8	39.0	58 548
2005	4 039	68 776	8 121	265.0	132.6	45.7	86.7	78 000
2006	4 167	73 726	8 146	271.0	112.5	49.5	109.0	97 343
2007	4 524	78 702	8 221	275.6	104.1	12.1	159.4	79 715
2008	4 701	82 460	9 241	276.3	91.9	10.5	173.9	81 987
2009	4 288	81 768	9 316	276.1	59.8	12.3	204.0	96 721
2010	4 664	85 251	9 539	276.3	36.7	12.6	227.0	80 073
2011	5 419	89 614	9 683	277.1	25.8	12.6	238.7	79 812
2012	5 640	97 922	9 693	313.7	36.7	13.1	263.9	54 341
2013	6 179	101 108	9 826	318.9	33.0	无	285.9	41 302
2014	6 515	105 592	9 720	325.4	33.0	无	292.4	39 255
2015	6 748	102 402	10 033	338.3	28.9	无	309.4	35 255

注：1990 年以前公共营运车辆不包括系统外及个体。

Note: Vehicles not belonging to system and individual vehicles are not contained in public operating vehicles before 1990.

6-1 续表3
continued

年份 Year	煤气供气量（万立方米）Volume of Coal Gas Supply (10000 cu. m)	天然气供气量（万立方米）Volume of Natural Gas Supply (10000 cu. m)	燃气普及率（%）Coverage Rate of Population with Access to Gas (%)	绿地面积（公顷）Area of Green Areas (hectare)	公园绿地面积（公顷）Park Green Areas (hectare)	人均公园绿地面积（平方米）Per Capita Park Green Areas (sq. m)	建成区绿化覆盖率（%）Green Coverage Rate of Developed Areas (%)	公园（个）Number of Parks and Zoos (unit)	公园面积（公顷）Area of Parks and Zoos (hectare)
1949				133	42	0.7	4.9	3	43
1952				134	43	0.7	4.4	4	45
1957				245	132	1.7	6.9	10	122
1962				771	184	2.2	14.0	12	174
1965				777	184	2.1	13.7	12	174
1970				772	184	2.1	13.0	6	117
1975			2.3	465	162	1.8	7.6	5	134
1978			18.6	469	162	1.7	7.6	6	165
1980			24.5	625	206	2.1	10.4	6	152
1985			36.3	1 072	255	2.3	17.3	7	153
1987	491		47.0	1 790	427	3.6	21.8	20	372
1989	2 585		47.3	1 941	459	3.5	21.7	22	381
1990	3 073		56.2	2 120	492	3.7	22.8	26	404
1991	3 439		56.5	2 318	500	3.7	24.4	28	443
1992	3 824		60.0	2 471	515	3.7	25.9	28	417
1993	4 215		63.1	2 488	543	3.9	26.5	31	453
1994	4 116		63.1	2 866	572	4.0	27.9	31	463
1995	4 734		79.2	4 547	771	5.3	30.1	33	675
1996	5 447		83.9	4 679	836	5.6	30.4	33	675
1997	5 920		87.3	4 717	924	6.0	31.3	34	730
1998	5 959		92.5	6 812	1 047	6.6	35.0	35	775
1999	7 319		96.0	7 007	1 186	7.4	35.9	36	791
2000	9 567		98.0	7 439	1 423	8.5	37.0	37	790
2001	11 814		99.0	7 688	1 588	9.3	37.5	39	832
2002	13 500		99.5	7 967	1 791	8.1	36.4	43	926
2003	14 826	1 181	100	8 829	2 305	9.3	37.5	45	1 034
2004	15 503	2 710	100	10 047	2 842	11	38.0	48	1 421
2005	16 573	7 456	100	11 137	3 132	11.8	38.8	47	1 110
2006	9 821	13 876	100	11 756	3 198	11.8	39.2	47	1 188
2007	9 516	18 103	100	15 369	3 661	13.3	37.8	73	1 268
2008	8 691	21 780	100	15 630	4 014	14.5	41.5	77	1 815
2009	7 523	26 948	100	16 003	4 003	14.5	43.4	71	1 897
2010	9 153	35 681	100	16 619	4 027	14.6	43.38	72	1 917
2011	9 137	46 147	100	18 013	4 041	14.6	44.69	74	1 931
2012	8 148	68 397	100	21 471	4 573	14.6	44.7	78	2 112
2013	无	70 918	100	28 007	4 649	14.6	44.7	87	2 698
2014	无	74 823	100	28 805	4 741	14.6	44.7	91	2 988
2015	无	70 311	100	29 117	4 802	14.6	44.7	87	3 163

注：1. 自2002年起人均公共绿地面积按辖区内全部人口计算。
2. 2005年以前所用园林绿地面积；公共绿地面积；人均公共绿地面积；公园、动物园个数；公园、动物园面积指标分别改为现在的绿地面积；公共绿地面积；人均公园绿地面积；公园个数；公园面积。

Note: 1. Per capita public green areas is calculated at total population in the area under jurisdiction since 2002.
2. Before 2005, the corresponding indicators of greenbelt area, park greenbelt area, per capita park greenbelt area, coverage rate of greenbelt, number of parks and area of parks were greenland area, public greenbelt area, per capita public greenbelt area, coverage rate of green, number of parks and zoos, area of parks and zoos.

6-2 全年供电(2015 年)
ANNUAL ELECTRICITY SUPPLY(2015)

全年供电项目	Item	单位	Unit	2015
发电设备总容量	Total Capacity of Generation Equipment	万千瓦	10000 kW	425.97
#青岛电厂	Qingdao Power Plant	万千瓦	10000 kW	122.00
黄岛电厂	Huangdao Power Plant	万千瓦	10000 kW	156.50
全年发电量	Annual Electricity Generation	亿千瓦时	100 million kW · h	170.41
#青岛电厂	Qingdao Power Plant	亿千瓦时	100 million kW · h	62.13
黄岛电厂	Huangdao Power Plant	亿千瓦时	100 million kW · h	73.70
全年实际用电量	Annual Electricity Consumption	亿千瓦时	100 million kW · h	342.29
#工业	Industrial Consumption	亿千瓦时	100 million kW · h	201.34
农业	Agricultural Consumption	亿千瓦时	100 million kW · h	6.19
生活	Residential Consumption	亿千瓦时	100 million kW · h	64.71
平均每日用电量	Average Daily Consumption	万千瓦时	10000 kW · h	9 378

6－3 分行业用电(2015 年)
ELECTRICITY CONSUMPTION BY SECTOR(2015)

单位:万千瓦时(10 000 kW·h)

行业	Sector	2015	2015 年比 2014 年增长(%) Growth Rate in 2015 over 2014(%)
全社会用电总计	**Total Electricity Consumption**	**3 422 929**	**1.32**
一、农、林、牧、渔业	Farming, Forestry, Animal Husbandryand Fishery	61 933	14.33
二、工业	Industry	2 013 414	－1.72
三、建筑业	Construction	62 097	9.01
四、交通运输、仓储和邮政业	Transport, Storage and Post	105 916	4.28
五、信息传输、计算机服务和软件业	Information Transmission, Computer Services and Software	43 623	13.99
六、商业、住宿和餐饮业	Trade, Hotels and Catering Services	172 513	0.13
七、金融、房地产、商务及居民服务业	Financial Intermediation, Real Estate and Business Services	171 351	－2.23
八、公共事业及管理组织	Public Management and Social Organization	144 961	10.29
九、城乡居民生活用电	Household Consumption	647 121	7.94
城镇居民	Urban Area	358 003	7.70
乡村居民	Rural Area	289 118	8.25

6－4 城市供水(2015 年)
URBAN WATER SUPPLY(2015)

项　　目	Item	单位	Unit	2015
自来水供水管道长度	Length of Tap Water Pipelines	公里	km	6 142
综合生产能力	Synthesis Production Capacity	万立方米/日	10000 cu. m/day	183.8
全年供水总量	Annual Volume of Tap Water Supply	万立方米	10000 cu. m	46 203
#售水量	of which:Volume of Tap Water Sale	万立方米	10000 cu. m	40 201
#生产运营用水	of which:Consumption for Production Use	万立方米	10000 cu. m	14 400
公共服务用水	Consumption for Public Services Use	万立方米	10000 cu. m	9 367
居民家庭用水	Consumption for Residential Use	万立方米	10000 cu. m	15 381
其他用水	Consumption for Other Uses	万立方米	10000 cu. m	1 053
平均每日供水量	Daily Volume of Tap Water Supply	万立方米	10000 cu. m	110.1
#生产用	of which:Consumption for Production Use	万立方米	10000 cu. m	39.5
生活用	Consumption for Residential Use	万立方米	10000 cu. m	42.1
用水户数	Households with Access to Water	户	household	1 083 550
用水人口	Population with Access to water	万人	10000 persons	323
工业用水量重复利用率	Recycle Rate of Water for Industrial Use	%	%	87.51

6－5 城市公共交通(2015 年)
URBAN PUBLIC TRAFFIC(2015)

项　目	Item	单位	Unit	2015
公共汽车、电车线路网长度	Network Length of Bus and Trolley Bus	公里	km	2 106
公共汽车、电车营运车辆	Number of Bus and Trolley Bus under Operation	辆	unit	6 748
#汽车	Bus	辆	unit	5 782
电车	Trolley Bus	辆	unit	966
公共汽车、电车全年客运量	Annual Passenger Traffic of Bus and Trolley Bus	万人次	10000 person-times	102 402
公共汽车、电车平均每日客运量	Daily Passenger Traffic of Bus and Trolley Bus	万人	10000 persons	281
出租汽车数	Number of Taxi	辆	unit	10 033
轮渡运营船数	Number of Ferry Boat under Operation	艘	ship	2
轮渡客运总量	Passenger Traffic of Ferry Boat	万人次	10000 person-times	74
轮渡平均每日客运量	Daily Passenger Traffic of Ferry Boat	万人	10000 persons	0.2

6-6 城市供气(2015年)
URBAN GAS SUPPLY(2015)

项　目	Item	单位	Unit	2015
煤气供应总量	Volume of Coal Gas Supply	万立方米	10000 cu. m	0
#家庭用量	Household Consumption	万立方米	10000 cu. m	0
煤气用气户数	Households with Access to Coal Gas	户	household	0
#家庭用户	Household Users	户	household	0
液化石油气供应总量	Volume of Liquefied Petroleum Supply	吨	ton	35 255
#家庭用量	Household Consumption	吨	ton	16 384
液化石油气用气户数	Households with Access to Liquefied Petroleum	户	household	173 460
#家庭用户	Household Users	户	household	171 944
天然气供应总量	Volume of Natural Gas Supply	万立方米	10000 cu. m	70 311
#家庭用量	Household Consumption	万立方米	10000 cu. m	18 630
天然气用气户数	Households with Access to Natural Gas	户	household	1 464 222
#家庭用户	Household Users	户	household	1 456 332
燃气普及率	Coverage Rate of Population with Access to Gas	%	%	100

6－7 城市环境卫生(2015 年)
URBAN ENVIRONMENTAL SANITATION(2015)

项　目	Item	单位	Unit	2015
市容环卫专用车辆总数	Number of Special Vehicles for Environmental Sanitation	辆	unit	3 184
生活垃圾清运量	Volume of Garbage Disposal	万吨	10000 tons	185
生活垃圾无害化处理厂(场)数	Number of Bio-safety Disposal Plant of Garbage	座	unit	5
生活垃圾无害化处理能力	Bio-safety Disposal Capacity of Garbage	吨/日	ton/day	3 316
生活垃圾无害化处理量	Bio-safety Disposal Volume of Garbage	万吨	10000 tons	185
道路清扫保洁面积	Area under Cleaning Program	万平方米	10000 sq. m	5 795
#机械化	of which:Mechanization	万平方米	10000 sq. m	2 269
粪便清运量	Volume of Excrement and Urine Disposal	万吨	10000 tons	8.19
粪便无害化处理量	Bio-safety Disposal Volume of Excrement and Urine	万吨	10000 tons	5.87
公共厕所	Public Toilets	个	unit	529

6-8 城市道路、下水道及绿化(2015 年)
URBAN ROAD,SEWAGE AND GREEN(2015)

项　目	Item	单位	Unit	2015
道路	**Road**			
年末道路长度	Length of Roads at Year-end	公里	km	4 375
年末道路面积	Area of Roads at Year-end	万平方米	10000 sq. m	7 940
#人行道面积	of which:Area of Pavements	万平方米	10000 sq. m	1 819
排水管道长度	Length of Sewage Pipes	公里	km	6 993
园林绿化	**Greening**			
绿化覆盖面积	Area of Green Coverage Areas	公顷	hectare	30 201
绿地面积	Area of Green Areas	公顷	hectare	29 117
公园绿地面积	Area of Park Green Areas	公顷	hectare	4 802
公园数	Number of Parks and Zoos	个	unit	87
公园面积	Area of Parks and Zoos	公顷	hectare	3 163
游人量	Number of Tourists	万人次	10000 person-times	
城市每人平均公园绿地面积	Per Capita Park Green Area	平方米	sq. m	14.2
建成区绿化覆盖率	Green Coverage Rate of Developed Areas	%	%	39.44

6 -9 环境保护基本情况(2015 年)
BASIC CONDITIONS OF ENVIRONMENTAL PROTECTION(2015)

项　目	Item	单位	Unit	2015	2014	2015 年比 2014 年增(+)减(-)% 2015 Compared to 2014(+/-)
二氧化硫排放总量	Sulphur Dioxide Emission	吨	ton	91 119	91 119	0
氮氧化物排放总量	Discharge Amount of Nitrogenoxides	吨	ton	101 657.45	101 657.45	0
烟(粉)尘排放总量	Soot(Dust) Emission	吨	ton	41 491.43	45 772.19	-9.35
工业固体废物排放总量	Industrial Solid Wastes Discharged	吨	ton	0	0	
化学需氧量排放总量	Discharge Amount of Chemical Oxygen Demand	吨	ton	143 690.51	143 690.51	0
氨氮排放总量	Discharge Amount of Ammonia and Nitrogen	吨	ton	12 193.35	12 193.35	0
废水排放总量	Waste Water Discharged	万吨	10 000 tons	53 235.21	50 870.00	4.65

6 -10 环境质量状况(2015 年)
ENVIRONMENT CONDITION(2015)

项　目	Item	单位	Unit	2015	2014	2015 年比 2014 年增(+)减(-)% 2015 Compared to 2014(+/-)
市区空气质量优良率	The Percentages of Excellent Or Good Air Quality of Urban Area	%	%	80.3	71.8	11.84
近岸海域功能区达标率	The Reaching Rate of The Offshore Sea Water for Corresponding Functional Regions	%	%	84.4	84.4	0
市区区域环境噪声平均等效声级	The Average Equivalent Sound Level of the Urban Regional Environmental Noise	分贝(A)	db(A)	56.7	58.2	-2.58
市区道路交通噪声平均等效声级	The Average Equivalent Sound Level of the Urban Road Traffic Noise	分贝(A)	db(A)	68.4	67.8	0.88

6－11 工业"三废"排放情况(2015 年)
DISCHARGE CONDITIONS OF INDUSTRIAL WASTE WATER, WASTE GAS AND SOLID WASTE(2015)

项　目	Item	单位	Unit	2015	2014	2015 年比 2014 年增(＋)减(－)% 2015 Compared to 2014(＋/－)
工业废水排放总量	Industrial Waste Water Discharged	万吨	10000 tons	10 566	10 989.4	－3.85
废水治理设施数	Number of Facilities for Treatment of Waste Water	套	set	422	459	－8.06
废水治理设施处理能力	Capacity of Facilities for Treatment of Waste Water	万吨/日	10000 tons/day	145.78	156.59	－6.90
进入城市污水处理厂量	Volume Handled by Sewage Treatment Plant	万吨	10000 tons	7 207.02	7 388.84	－2.46
化学需氧量排放量	Discharge Amount of Chemical Oxygen Demand	吨	ton	8 128.42	8 128.42	0
氨氮排放量	Discharge Amount of Ammonia and Nitrogen	吨	ton	693.3	693.3	0
工业废气排放总量	Industrial Waste Air Discharged	万标立方米	10000 cu. m	22 136 892	20 848 629	6.18
废气治理设施数	Number of Facilities for Treatment of Waste Air	套	set	1 375	1 396	－1.50
其中:脱硫设施数	of which: Desulphurization Facilities	套	set	293	286	2.45
废气治理设施处理能力	Capacity of Facilities for Treatment of Waste Air	万标立方米/时	10000 cu. m/hr	6 749.1	6 978.07	－3.28
其中:脱硫能力	of which: Desulphurization Capacity	千克/时	kg/hr	54 946.7	50 692	8.39
二氧化硫去除量	Sulphur Dioxide Removed	吨	ton	232 754.71	217 848.33	6.84
二氧化硫排放量	Sulphur Dioxide Emission	吨	ton	64 029.23	64 029.23	0
烟(粉)尘排放量	Soot (Dust) Emission	吨	ton	28 767.13	32 196.05	－10.65
工业固体废物产生量	Industrial Solid Wastes Producted	万吨	10000 tons	707.97	865.57	－18.21
其中:危险废物	of which: Hazardous Wastes	吨	ton	65 634	41 808	56.99
工业固体废物综合利用量	Industrial Solid Wastes Comprehensive Utilized	万吨	10000 tons	664.48	842.39	－21.12
工业固体废物排放量	Industrial Solid Wastes Discharged	万吨	10000 tons	0	0	
其中:危险废物	of which: Hazardous Wastes	吨	ton	0	0	
污染治理项目完成投资	Investment in Treatment Projects of Pollution	万元	10000 yuan	20 466.3	76 250.4	－73.16
污染治理项目数	Number of Treatment Projects of Pollution	个	item	7	21	－66.67
当年竣工治理项目数	Number of Completed Treatment Projects in the Year	个	item	7	17	－58.82

主要统计指标解释

供水综合生产能力 指按供水设施取水、净化、送水、出厂输水干管等环节设计能力计算的综合生产能力。

年末供水管道长度 指从送水泵至用户水表之间所有管道的长度。不包括新安装尚未使用的管道。

用水普及率 指城市用水人口数与城市人口总数的比率。计算公式：

$$\text{用水普及率}=\frac{\text{城市用水人口数}}{\text{城市人口总数}}\times100\%$$

全年供水总量 指报告期供水企业(单位)供出的全部水量。包括有效供水量和漏损水量。

全年供气总量 指全年燃气企业(单位)向用户供应的燃气数量。包括销售量和损失量。

用气普及率 指报告期末使用燃气的城市人口数与城市人口总数的比率。计算公式为：

$$\text{用气普及率}=\frac{\text{城市用气人口数}}{\text{城市人口总数}}\times100\%$$

年末道路长度 指年末道路长度和与道路相通的广场、桥梁、隧道的长度，按车行道中心线计算。在统计时只统计路面宽度在3.5米(含3.5米)以上的各种铺装道路，包括开放型工业区和住宅区道路在内。

工业废气排放量 指报告期内企业厂区内燃料燃烧和生产工艺过程中产生的各种排入大气的含有污染物的气体的总量，以标准状态(273K，101325Pa)计算。

工业废水排放量 指经过企业厂区所有排放口排到企业外部的工业废水量。包括生产废水、外排的直接冷却水、超标排放的矿井地下水和与工业废水混排的厂区生活污水，不包括外排的间接冷却水(清污不分流的间接冷却水应计算在内)。

工业废水排放达标量 指各项指标都达到国家或地方排放标准的外排工业废水量，包括未经处理外排达标的和经过处理后外排达标的和两部分。国家排放标准见GB8978—88。

工业固体废物产生量 指企业在生产过程中产生的固体状、半固体状和高浓度液体状废弃物的总量，包括危险废物、冶炼废渣、粉煤灰、炉渣、煤矸渣、尾矿、放射性废物和其他废物等；不包括矿山开采的剥离废石和掘进废石(煤矸石和呈酸性或碱性的废石除外)酸性或碱性废石是指采掘的废石其流经水、雨淋水的pH值小于4或pH值大于10.5者。

工业粉尘排放量 指企业在生产工艺过程中排放的能在空气中悬浮一定时间的固体颗粒物排放量。如钢铁企业的耐火材料粉尘、焦化企业的筛焦系统粉尘、烧结机的粉尘、石灰窑的粉尘、建材企业的水泥粉尘等。不包括电厂排入大气的烟尘。

化学需氧量(COD) 测量有机和无机物质化学分解所消耗氧的质量浓度的水污染指数。

Explanatory Notes on Main Statistical Indicators

Production Capacity of Water Supply refers to the designed comprehensive production capacity of water facilities, covering the 4 links of water collection, purification, conveyance, and outflow through trunk pipelines.

Length of Water Supply Pipelines at the Year-end refers to the total length of all the pipelines between the water pumps and the user water meters, excluding pipelines newly installed but not used yet.

Coverage Rate of Urban Population with Access to Tap Water refers to the ratio of the urban population with access to tap water to the total urban population. The formula is:

Coverage rate of urban population with access to tap water = (Urban population with access to tap water)/(Urban population) × 100%

Annual Volume of Water Supply refers to the total volume of water supplied by water-works(units) during the reference period, including both the effective water supply and loss during the water supply.

Annual Volume of Gas Supply refers to the total volume of gas provided to users by gas-producing enterprises(units) in a year, including the volume sold and the volume lost.

Coverage Rate of Urban Population with Access to Gas refers to the ratio of the urban population with access to gas to the total urban population at the end of the reference period. The formula is:

Coverage rate of urban population with access to gas = (Urban population with access to gas/Urban population) ×100%

Length of Paved Roads at the Year-end refers to the length of roads with paved surface including squares bridges and tunnels connected with roads by the end of the year. Length of the roads is measured by the central lines for vehicles for paved roads with a width of 3.5 meters and over, including roads in open-ended factory compounds and residential quarters.

Industrial Waste Air Emission refers to discharge into atmosphere of waste air containing pollutants generated from fuel burning and production process in enterprises within a given period of time. It is calculated at standard status(273K, 101325Pa).

Waste Water Discharged by Industry refers to the volume of waste water discharged by industrial enterprises through all their outlets, including waste water from production process, directly cooled water, groundwater from mining wells which does not meet discharge standards and sewage from households mixed with waste water produced by industrial activities, but excluding indirectly cooled water discharged(It should be included if the discharge is not separated with waste water).

Industrial Waste Water Meeting Discharge Standards refers to volume of industrial waste water discharge which, with or without treatment, reaches national or local standards with regard to all pollutants. National Discharge standards see GB8978—88.

Industrial Solid Wastes Produced refers to total volume of solid, semi-solid and high concentration liquid residues produced by industrial enterprises from production process in a given period of time, including hazardous wastes, slag, coal ash, gangue, tailings, radioactive residues and other wastes, but excluding stones stripped or dug out in mining(gangue and acid or alkaline stones not included). A stone is acid or alkaline depending on the pH value of the water below 4 or above 10.5 when the stone is in, or soaked by, the water.

Industrial Dust Emission refers to volume of dust emitted by production process of enterprises and suspended in the air for a given period of time, including dust from refractory material of iron and steel works, dust from coke-screening systems and sintering machines of coke plants, dust from lime kilns and dust from cement production in building material enterprises, but excluding soot and dust emitted from power plants.

Chemical Oxygen Demand(COD) refers to index of water pollution measuring the mass concentration of oxygen consumed by the chemical breakdown of organic and inorganic matter.

7 能源消耗
CONSUMPTION OF ENERGY

简要说明

一、本篇资料的主要内容

本篇资料主要反映了全市规模以上工业主要能源消费与库存情况，主要包括规模以上工业主要能源消费与库存、规模以上工业主要能源分行业消费量、重点耗能工业企业能源加工转换、规模以上工业主要能源工业消费量等方面的资料。

二、本篇资料的来源

本篇资料来源于规模以上工业能源统计年报，由市统计局能源统计处整理提供。

Brief Introduction

I. Main Content

Data in this chapter show the consumption and stock of major energy of industry above designated size, including consumption and stock of major energy of industry above designated size, major energy consumption of industry above designated size grouped by sector, energy conversion of major energy-consuming industrial enterprises and major energy consumption of industry above designated size, etc.

II. Source of Data

Data in this chapter are based on the annual report of energy consumed by industrial enterprises above designated size. The data are provided by the Division of Energy Statistics of Qingdao Municipal Bureau of Statistics.

7-1 规模以上工业主要能源消费与库存(2015年)
CONSUMPTION AND STOCK OF MAJOR ENERGY OF INDUSTRY ABOVE DESIGNATED SIZE(2015)

名称	Name	计算单位	Unit	年初库存 Stock at Year-beginning	本年消费 Consumption in the Year			年末库存 Stock at Year-end
						#工业 Industry	#非工业 Non-industry	
原煤	Raw Coal	吨	ton	1 811 691.17	12 826 075.36	12 807 956.98	18 118.38	1 252 620.68
焦炭	Coke	吨	ton	36 839.16	1 217 422.46	1 217 416.46	6.00	2 375.00
焦炉煤气	Coking Gas	万立方米	10 000 cu. m					
高炉煤气	Blast Furnace Gas	万立方米	10 000 cu. m		18 088.87	18 088.87		
原油	Crude Oil	吨	ton	514 818.98	12 920 700.50	12 920 699.65	0.85	505 408.36
汽油	Petrol	吨	ton	444.72	143 367.94	123 677.77	19 690.18	239.25
煤油	Kerosene	吨	ton	92.16	377.53	254.99	122.54	
柴油	Diesel Oil	吨	ton	2 857.55	135 370.22	117 942.42	17 427.86	2 071.27
燃料油	Fuel Oil	吨	ton	4 687.93	205 624.89	205 243.94	380.95	8 159.89
液化石油气	Liquefied Petroleum Gas	吨	ton	495.16	134 653.01	134 626.39	26.62	240.70
炼厂干气	Refinery Dry Gas	吨	ton		471 941.00	471 941.00		
热力	Heat	百万千焦	million kJ		28 317 657.69	27 830 902.05	486 755.63	
电力	Electricity	万千瓦时	10 000 kW·h		2 115 121.13	2 093 715.49	21 405.53	

补充资料:2015年综合能源消费量1483.7万吨标准煤。

Note: In 2015, comprehensive energy consumption is 1483.7 million tons SCE.

7-2 规模以上工业主要能源分行业消费量(2015年)

MAJOR ENERGY CONSUMPTION OF INDUSTRY ABOVE DESIGNATED SIZE BY SECTOR (2015)

名称	Name	原煤（吨）Raw Coal (ton)	焦炭（吨）Coke (ton)	焦炉煤气（万立方米）Coking Gas (10 000 cu. m)	原油（吨）Crude Oil (ton)	汽油（吨）Petrol (ton)
总　计	**Total**	**12 826 075**	**1 217 422**		**12 920 701**	**143 368**
采掘业	Mining	763				481
制造业	Manufacturing	3 213 053	1 217 422		12 920 701	139 488
电力煤气及水生产供应业	Production and Supply of Electricity, Gas and Water	9 612 260				3 399

7-2 续表

continued

名称	Name	煤油（吨）Kerosene (ton)	柴油（吨）Diesel Oil (ton)	燃料油（吨）Fuel Oil (ton)	液化石油气（吨）Liquefied Petroleum Gas (ton)	热力（百万千焦）Heat (million kJ)	电力（万千瓦时）Electricity (10 000 kW·h)
总　计	**Total**	**378**	**135 370**	**205 625**	**134 653**	**28 317 658**	**2 115 121**
采掘业	Mining		857				9 546
制造业	Manufacturing	378	132 298	204 322	134 651	23 790 276	1 768 162
电力煤气及水生产供应业	Production and Supply of Electricity, Gas and Water		2 215	1 303	2	4 527 381	337 413

7-3 重点耗能工业企业能源加工转换(2015年)

ENERGY CONVERSION OF MAJOR ENERGY-CONSUMING INDUSTRIAL ENTERPRISES(2015)

名称	Name	单位	Unit	能源消费合计 Total Energy Consumption	#加工转换投入 Conversion Input	火电 Thermal Power	供热 Heating	炼油 Petrolume Refining	制气 Gas Production	能源加工转换产出 Conversion Output of Energy
原煤	Raw Coal	吨	ton	10 720 320.51	10 270 571.51	5 928 308.47	4 342 262.86			
洗精煤	Dressing Coal	吨	ton							
煤制品	Coal Products	吨	ton							
焦炭	Coke	吨	ton	1 185 555.01						
其他焦化产品	Other Coking Products	吨	ton	85 665.79						
焦炉煤气	Coking Gas	万立方米	10 000 cu. m							
高炉煤气	Blast Furnace Gas	万立方米	10 000 cu. m	18 088.87	18 088.87		18 088.87			
原油	Raw Oil	吨	ton	12 920 606.51	12 909 300.51			12 909 300.51		
汽油	Petrol	吨	ton	232.94						3 634 831.76
煤油	Kerosene	吨	ton							1 264 819.00
柴油	Diesel Oil	吨	ton	4 388.06						3 656 346.16
燃料油	Fuel Oil	吨	ton	152 987.77	148 885.85	684.85	114.00	148 087.00		308 266.41
液化石油气	Liquefied Petroleum Gas	吨	ton							917 676.15
炼厂干气	Refinery Dry Gas	吨	ton	471 941.00	1 193.00	119.00	1 074.00			471 941.00
其他石油制品	Other Petroleum Products	吨	ton	461 982.00	123 501.00			123 501.00		965 272.21
热力	Heat	百万千焦	million kJ	12 081 046.00						75 579 030.58
电力	Electricity	万千瓦时	10 000 kW · h	424 073.27						1 613 883.25
其他燃料	Other Fuel	吨标准煤	ton SCE							
能源合计	**Total**	**吨标准煤**	**ton SCE**	**30 674 925.04**	**26 871 065.90**	**4 585 527.99**	**3 458 852.58**	**18 826 685.20**		**23 081 782.51**

7－4 规模以上工业主要能源工业消费量(2015 年)

MAJOR ENERGY CONSUMPTION OF INDUSTRY ABOVE DESIGNATED SIZE(2015)

行业	Sector
总　　计	**Total**
煤炭开采和洗选业	Mining and Washing of Coal
石油和天然气开采业	Extraction of Petroleum and Natural Gas
黑色金属矿采选业	Mining of Ferrous Metal Ores
有色金属矿采选业	Mining of Non-ferrous Metal Ores
非金属矿采选业	Mining and Processing of Nonmetal Ores
开采辅助活动	Auxiliary Activities of Mining
其他采矿业	Mining of Other Ores
农副食品加工业	Processing of Food from Agricultural Products
食品制造业	Manufacture of Foods
酒、饮料和精制茶制造业	Manufacture of Liquor, Beverage and Refind Tea
烟草制品业	Manufacture of Tobacco
纺织业	Manufacture of Textile
纺织服装、服饰业	Manufacture of Textile Wearing Apparel
皮革、毛皮、羽毛及其制品和制鞋业	Manufacture of Leather, Fur, Feather & Its Products Footwear
木材加工和木、竹、藤、棕、草制品业	Processing of Timbers, Manufacture of Wood, Bamboo, Rattan, Palm and Straw Products
家具制造业	Manufacture of Furniture
造纸和纸制品业	Manufacture of Paper and Paper Products
印刷和记录媒介复制业	Printing, Reproduction of Recording Media
文教、工美、体育和娱乐用品制造业	Manufacture of Articles for Culture, Arts & Crafts, Sports and Entertainment
石油加工、炼焦和核燃料加工业	Processing of Petroleum, Coking, Processing of Nucleus Fuel
化学原料和化学制品制造业	Manufacture of Chemical Raw Material and Chemical Products
医药制造业	Manufacture of Medicines
化学纤维制造业	Manufacture of Chemical Fiber
橡胶和塑料制品业	Manufacture of Rubber and Plastic
非金属矿物制品业	Manufacture of Non-metallic Mineral Products
黑色金属冶炼和压延加工业	Smelting and Pressing of Ferrous Metals
有色金属冶炼和压延加工业	Smelting and Pressing of Non-ferrous Metals
金属制品业	Manufacture of Metal Products
通用设备制造业	Manufacture of General Purpose Machinery
专用设备制造业	Manufacture of Special Purpose Machinery
汽车制造业	Manufacture of Vehicle
铁路、船舶、航空航天和其他运输设备制造业	Manufacture of Transport Equipment for Railway, Shipping, Aerospace and other uses
电气机械和器材制造业	Manufacture of Electrical Machinery & Equipment
计算机、通信和其他电子设备制造业	Manufacture of Computer, Communication Equipment and Other Electronic Equipment
仪器仪表制造业	Manufacture of Measuring Instrument
其他制造业	Manufacture of Other Products
废弃资源综合利用业	Recycling and Disposal of Waste Resources
金属制品、机械和设备修理业	Maintenance of Metal Products, Machinery and Equipment
电力、热力的生产和供应业	Production and Supply of Electric Power and Heat Power
燃气生产和供应业	Production and Supply of Gas
水的生产和供应业	Production and Supply of Water

原煤 (吨) Raw Coal (ton)	洗精煤 (吨) Dressing Coal(ton)	其他洗煤 (吨) Other Dressing Coal(ton)	煤制品 (吨) Coal Products (ton)	焦炭 (吨) Coke (ton)
12 826 075	**74 904**	**3 652**	**7 867**	**1 217 422**
62				
701				
127 337	14 394		431	44
20 661	553	235		
49 598				
53 941				
122 778	38	3 407		
41 450				
9 921				
44 504				784
93 202			2 702	
91 388				
101 133	140			36
7 257				
703 269	59 587		58	74 208
5 907	130		1 904	
474 575	25			
246 005			106	
472 044				1 112 587
5 801				
223 402	12			18 387
92 098	12		800	4 063
53 913			1 842	7 204
22 322				40
24 520				70
89 993	13			
21 520		10	20	
5 971				
2 728				
5 816				
9 612 041				
219				

7-4 续表1
continued

行业	Sector
总　计	**Total**
煤炭开采和洗选业	Mining and Washing of Coal
石油和天然气开采业	Extraction of Petroleum and Natural Gas
黑色金属矿采选业	Mining of Ferrous Metal Ores
有色金属矿采选业	Mining of Non-ferrous Metal Ores
非金属矿采选业	Mining and Processing of Nonmetal Ores
开采辅助活动	Auxiliary Activities of Mining
其他采矿业	Mining of Other Ores
农副食品加工业	Processing of Food from Agricultural Products
食品制造业	Manufacture of Foods
酒、饮料和精制茶制造业	Manufacture of Liquor, Beverage and Refind Tea
烟草制品业	Manufacture of Tobacco
纺织业	Manufacture of Textile
纺织服装、服饰业	Manufacture of Textile Wearing Apparel
皮革、毛皮、羽毛及其制品和制鞋业	Manufacture of Leather, Fur, Feather & Its Products Footwear
木材加工和木、竹、藤、棕、草制品业	Processing of Timbers, Manufacture of Wood, Bamboo, Rattan, Palm and Straw Products
家具制造业	Manufacture of Furniture
造纸和纸制品业	Manufacture of Paper and Paper Products
印刷和记录媒介复制业	Printing, Reproduction of Recording Media
文教、工美、体育和娱乐用品制造业	Manufacture of Articles for Culture, Arts & Crafts, Sports and Entertainment
石油加工、炼焦和核燃料加工业	Processing of Petroleum, Coking, Processing of Nucleus Fuel
化学原料和化学制品制造业	Manufacture of Chemical Raw Material and Chemical Products
医药制造业	Manufacture of Medicines
化学纤维制造业	Manufacture of Chemical Fiber
橡胶和塑料制品业	Manufacture of Rubber and Plastic
非金属矿物制品业	Manufacture of Non-metallic Mineral Products
黑色金属冶炼和压延加工业	Smelting and Pressing of Ferrous Metals
有色金属冶炼和压延加工业	Smelting and Pressing of Non-ferrous Metals
金属制品业	Manufacture of Metal Products
通用设备制造业	Manufacture of General Purpose Machinery
专用设备制造业	Manufacture of Special Purpose Machinery
汽车制造业	Manufacture of Vehicle
铁路、船舶、航空航天和其他运输设备制造业	Manufacture of Transport Equipment for Railway, Shipping, Aerospace and other uses
电气机械和器材制造业	Manufacture of Electrical Machinery & Equipment
计算机、通信和其他电子设备制造业	Manufacture of Computer, Communication Equipment and Other Electronic Equipment
仪器仪表制造业	Manufacture of Measuring Instrument
其他制造业	Manufacture of Other Products
废弃资源综合利用业	Recycling and Disposal of Waste Resources
金属制品、机械和设备修理业	Maintenance of Metal Products, Machinery and Equipment
电力、热力的生产和供应业	Production and Supply of Electric Power and Heat Power
燃气生产和供应业	Production and Supply of Gas
水的生产和供应业	Production and Supply of Water

焦炉煤气 （万立方米） Coking Gas （10 000 cu. m）	高炉煤气 （万立方米） Blast Furnace Gas （10 000 cu. m）	原油 （吨） Crude Oil（ton）	汽油 （吨） Petrol （ton）	煤油 （吨） Kerosene （ton）
	18 089	**12 920 701**	**143 368**	**378**
			260	
			220	
			11 245	60
			1 510	
			1 827	
			43	
			3 149	
		89	12 931	63
			2 610	3
			306	
		1	1 851	
			973	4
			6 722	2
			14 241	11
		12 920 607	220	
			5 013	
			1 342	
			11	
			8 199	
			8 985	2
	18 089		1 277	
			1 277	
			20 490	11
			9 627	78
			8 046	22
			4 767	24
			2 589	95
		4	5 323	
			2 366	2
			1 314	2
			185	
			137	
			909	
			2 268	
			591	
			540	

7-4 续表2
continued

行业	Sector
总　计	**Total**
煤炭开采和洗选业	Mining and Washing of Coal
石油和天然气开采业	Extraction of Petroleum and Natural Gas
黑色金属矿采选业	Mining of Ferrous Metal Ores
有色金属矿采选业	Mining of Non-ferrous Metal Ores
非金属矿采选业	Mining and Processing of Nonmetal Ores
开采辅助活动	Auxiliary Activities of Mining
其他采矿业	Mining of Other Ores
农副食品加工业	Processing of Food from Agricultural Products
食品制造业	Manufacture of Foods
酒、饮料和精制茶制造业	Manufacture of Liquor, Beverage and Refind Tea
烟草制品业	Manufacture of Tobacco
纺织业	Manufacture of Textile
纺织服装、服饰业	Manufacture of Textile Wearing Apparel
皮革、毛皮、羽毛及其制品和制鞋业	Manufacture of Leather, Fur, Feather & Its Products Footwear
木材加工和木、竹、藤、棕、草制品业	Processing of Timbers, Manufacture of Wood, Bamboo, Rattan, Palm and Straw Products
家具制造业	Manufacture of Furniture
造纸和纸制品业	Manufacture of Paper and Paper Products
印刷和记录媒介复制业	Printing, Reproduction of Recording Media
文教、工美、体育和娱乐用品制造业	Manufacture of Articles for Culture, Arts & Crafts, Sports and Entertainment
石油加工、炼焦和核燃料加工业	Processing of Petroleum, Coking, Processing of Nucleus Fuel
化学原料和化学制品制造业	Manufacture of Chemical Raw Material and Chemical Products
医药制造业	Manufacture of Medicines
化学纤维制造业	Manufacture of Chemical Fiber
橡胶和塑料制品业	Manufacture of Rubber and Plastic
非金属矿物制品业	Manufacture of Non-metallic Mineral Products
黑色金属冶炼和压延加工业	Smelting and Pressing of Ferrous Metals
有色金属冶炼和压延加工业	Smelting and Pressing of Non-ferrous Metals
金属制品业	Manufacture of Metal Products
通用设备制造业	Manufacture of General Purpose Machinery
专用设备制造业	Manufacture of Special Purpose Machinery
汽车制造业	Manufacture of Vehicle
铁路、船舶、航空航天和其他运输设备制造业	Manufacture of Transport Equipment for Railway, Shipping, Aerospace and other uses
电气机械和器材制造业	Manufacture of Electrical Machinery & Equipment
计算机、通信和其他电子设备制造业	Manufacture of Computer, Communication Equipment and Other Electronic Equipment
仪器仪表制造业	Manufacture of Measuring Instrument
其他制造业	Manufacture of Other Products
废弃资源综合利用业	Recycling and Disposal of Waste Resources
金属制品、机械和设备修理业	Maintenance of Metal Products, Machinery and Equipment
电力、热力的生产和供应业	Production and Supply of Electric Power and Heat Power
燃气生产和供应业	Production and Supply of Gas
水的生产和供应业	Production and Supply of Water

柴油 (吨) Diesel Oil (ton)	燃料油 (吨) Fuel Oil (ton)	液化石油气 (吨) Liquefied Petroleum Gas(ton)	炼厂干气 (吨) Refinery Dry Gas(ton)
135 370	**205 625**	**134 653**	**471 941**
128			
729			
9 054		38	
1 350			
2 167		323	
5			
2 395	2 310	46	
8 170			
1 855	115		
184			
1 226			
1 333			
3 741			
5 901	970	1	
878	152 060	805	471 941
5 900	1 199	130 289	
1 837			
2			
5 402	4 553	7	
33 082	43 077	2	
3 599			
1 275			
11 647	33	79	
8 726			
5 469		5	
2 976		891	
4 814		0	
5 367		2 147	
1 932	6	19	
1 220			
169			
113			
509			
1 832	1 303	2	
83			
300			

7-4 续表3
continued

行业	Sector
总　计	**Total**
煤炭开采和洗选业	Mining and Washing of Coal
石油和天然气开采业	Extraction of Petroleum and Natural Gas
黑色金属矿采选业	Mining of Ferrous Metal Ores
有色金属矿采选业	Mining of Non-ferrous Metal Ores
非金属矿采选业	Mining and Processing of Nonmetal Ores
开采辅助活动	Auxiliary Activities of Mining
其他采矿业	Mining of Other Ores
农副食品加工业	Processing of Food from Agricultural Products
食品制造业	Manufacture of Foods
酒、饮料和精制茶制造业	Manufacture of Liquor, Beverage and Refind Tea
烟草制品业	Manufacture of Tobacco
纺织业	Manufacture of Textile
纺织服装、服饰业	Manufacture of Textile Wearing Apparel
皮革、毛皮、羽毛及其制品和制鞋业	Manufacture of Leather, Fur, Feather & Its Products Footwear
木材加工和木、竹、藤、棕、草制品业	Processing of Timbers, Manufacture of Wood, Bamboo, Rattan, Palm and Straw Products
家具制造业	Manufacture of Furniture
造纸和纸制品业	Manufacture of Paper and Paper Products
印刷和记录媒介复制业	Printing, Reproduction of Recording Media
文教、工美、体育和娱乐用品制造业	Manufacture of Articles for Culture, Arts & Crafts, Sports and Entertainment
石油加工、炼焦和核燃料加工业	Processing of Petroleum, Coking, Processing of Nucleus Fuel
化学原料和化学制品制造业	Manufacture of Chemical Raw Material and Chemical Products
医药制造业	Manufacture of Medicines
化学纤维制造业	Manufacture of Chemical Fiber
橡胶和塑料制品业	Manufacture of Rubber and Plastic
非金属矿物制品业	Manufacture of Non-metallic Mineral Products
黑色金属冶炼和压延加工业	Smelting and Pressing of Ferrous Metals
有色金属冶炼和压延加工业	Smelting and Pressing of Non-ferrous Metals
金属制品业	Manufacture of Metal Products
通用设备制造业	Manufacture of General Purpose Machinery
专用设备制造业	Manufacture of Special Purpose Machinery
汽车制造业	Manufacture of Vehicle
铁路、船舶、航空航天和其他运输设备制造业	Manufacture of Transport Equipment for Railway, Shipping, Aerospace and other uses
电气机械和器材制造业	Manufacture of Electrical Machinery & Equipment
计算机、通信和其他电子设备制造业	Manufacture of Computer, Communication Equipment and Other Electronic Equipment
仪器仪表制造业	Manufacture of Measuring Instrument
其他制造业	Manufacture of Other Products
废弃资源综合利用业	Recycling and Disposal of Waste Resources
金属制品、机械和设备修理业	Maintenance of Metal Products, Machinery and Equipment
电力、热力的生产和供应业	Production and Supply of Electric Power and Heat Power
燃气生产和供应业	Production and Supply of Gas
水的生产和供应业	Production and Supply of Water

其他油制品 （吨） Other Petroleum Products(ton)	热　力 （百万千焦） Heat (million kJ)	电　力 （万千瓦时） Electricity (10 000 kW·h)	其他燃料 （吨标准煤） Other Fuel (ton SCE)
464 766	**28 317 658**	**2 115 121**	**2 279**
		3 634	
		5 912	
	762 692	119 025	
	344 205	23 940	
	1 923 680	22 024	
	236 242	4 596	
	1 200 079	33 782	
	1 740 457	56 865	
	183 060	24 106	
		4 368	
	1 668	15 790	
	925 408	20 775	
	99 000	37 323	
1	239 040	54 128	38
461 982	3	110 813	
2 695	11 415 402	148 817	
	414 439	15 548	
	13 382	8 434	
	261 934	150 697	
	51 328	126 394	
	131 246	181 218	
	52 744	24 659	
8	460 346	125 210	224
70	69 547	97 175	
	11 046	61 797	
	1 351 799	79 348	12
10	824 670	60 280	2 001
	608 998	91 511	5
	375 804	55 697	
		9 014	
	92 060	2 345	
		369	
		2 114	
	4 513 477	311 693	
	13 904	5 294	
		20 427	

主要统计指标解释

工业企业能源消费量 工业企业能源消费包括工业企业在生产过程中作为燃料、动力、原料、辅助材料使用的能源以及工艺用能、非生产用能;作为能源加工转换企业,还要包括能源加工转换的投入量。工业企业能源消费量具体包括:

(1)用于本企业产品生产、工业性作业和其他生产性活动的能源。

(2)用于技术更新改造措施、新技术研究和新产品试制以及科学试验等方面的能源。

(3)用于经营维修、建筑及设备大修理、机电设备和交通运输工具等方面的能源。

(4)用于劳动保护的能源。

(5)其他非生产消费的能源。

不包括:

(1)由仓库发到车间,但在报告期最后一天没有消费的能源。这部分能源应在办理假退料手续后计入库存量。

(2)拨到外单位,委托外单位加工用的能源。

(3)调出本单位或借给外单位的能源。

工业生产能源消费 是指工业企业为进行工业生产活动所使用的能源。主要包括:

1. 用于本企业产品生产、工业性作业的能源,包括用作原料、材料、燃料、动力:作为能源加工转换企业,还包括用作加工转换的能源。

2. 产品生产过程中作为辅助材料使用的能源。

3. 生产工艺过程使用的能源。

4. 新技术研究、新产品试制、科学试验使用的能源。

5. 为了工业生产活动而在进行的各种修理过程中使用的能源。

6. 生产区内的劳动保护用能等。

Explanatory Notes on Main Statistical Indicators

Energy Consumption of Industrial Enterprises include energy in the production process as fuel, power, raw materials, supplementary materials, and for use of technology and non-production. As energy processing and conversion enterprises, also include energy processing and conversion of inputs. These specifically include: (1) Energy for the enterprise product, industrial production operations and other activities. (2) Energy for technical upgrading measures and new technology research and new product production and scientific experiments. (3) Energy for operation maintenance, construction and equipment overhaul, electrical and mechanical equipment and transport, and other aspects. (4) Energy for the protection of labor. (5) Energy for Other non-production and consumption. And these exclude: (1) Energy from the warehouse to the workshop, but out of consumption on the last day of the reporting period. This part of the energy should leave retreat materials handling procedures included stock. (2) Energy transferred to other units, entrusted with the processing. (3) Energy transferred out of the unit or loans to other units.

Energy Consumption for Industrial Production refers to energy for industrial enterprises in industrial production activities. These mainly include: 1. Energy for the enterprise products, industrial operations, including energy as raw materials, materials, fuels, and power. As energy processing and conversion enterprises, also include energy for processing and conversion. 2. Energy as supplementary material in product process. 3. Energy used in production process. 4. Energy for new technologies, new product production, and scientific experiment. 5. Energy in process of repairing for industrial production activities. 6. Energy for labor protection in production areas and so on.

8 财政、金融和保险业

GOVERNMENT FINANCE FINANCIAL INTERMEDIATION AND INSURANCE

简要说明

一、本篇资料的主要内容

本篇资料主要反映了全市财政收支、金融和保险方面的情况，主要包括财政收入、财政支出、金融机构存贷款、保险业务开展等方面的资料。

二、本篇资料的来源

1、财政部分的资料来源于市财政局。

2、金融方面的资料来源于中国人民银行青岛市中心支行。

3、保险方面的资料来源于中国保险监督管理委员会青岛监管局。

本篇资料由市统计局国民经济核算处整理提供。

Brief Introduction

I. Main Content

Data in this chapter show the conditions of local government budgetary finance, banking and insurance,and securities, including government revenue and expenditure, deposits and loans of financial institutions and statistics on insurance companies.

II. Source of Data

(1) Data on local government finance are provided by Qingdao Municipal Finance Bureau.

(2) Data on banking are provided by Qingdao Branch of the People's Bank of China.

(3) Data on insurance are provide by China Insurance Regulatory Commission of Qingdao Bureau.

Data in this chapter are prepared and compiled by the Division of National Accounts of Qingdao Municipal Bureau of Statistics.

8-1 主要年份地方财政收支

MAJOR YEAR'S REVENUE AND EXPENDITURE OF LOCAL GOVERNMENT FINANCE

单位:万元(10 000 yuan)

年份 Year	财政收入 Revenue of Government Finance	财政支出 Expenditure of Government Finance
1949	1 527	306
1952	19 809	2 226
1957	29 875	3 556
1962	32 869	4 327
1965	47 682	6 280
1970	95 778	7 825
1975	90 220	11 966
1978	130 749	19 427
1980	124 835	20 064
1985	165 155	41 996
1988	201 206	93 931
1989	221 183	113 585
1990	242 303	133 875
1991	259 377	137 716
1992	275 589	155 696
1993	182 348	211 938
1994	227 490	277 331
1995	294 771	376 982
1996	379 674	469 569
1997	476 804	564 787
1998	580 434	678 575
1999	680 089	740 937
2000	800 120	878 702
2001	987 080	1 097 848
2002	1 006 616	1 243 880
2003	1 201 398	1 471 747
2004	1 305 136	1 646 214
2005	1 763 412	2 030 622
2006	2 257 663	2 367 875
2007	2 925 798	3 211 777
2008	3 424 359	3 694 111
2009	3 769 896	4 335 754
2010	4 526 138	5 323 888
2011	5 661 400	6 580 605
2012	6 701 820	7 659 801
2013	7 889 313	10 142 273
2014	8 952 450	10 747 138
2015	10 063 220	12 228 664

注:1. 1993 年以后实行新制度,财政收入数与历年不可比。

2. 2002 年以后,财政收入、支出为一般预算数。

Note: 1. Since 1993, new regulations have been adopted in calculating revenue of government finance, the figures are not comparable with those over the years.

2. Since 2002, revenue of government finance and expenditure of government finance refer to general budgetary revenue and expenditure.

8-2 分市、区公共财政预算收入(2015年)
PUBLIC FINANCE BUDGET REVENUE BY CITY AND DISTRICT(2015)

单位:万元(10 000 yuan)

市、区名称	Region	公共财政预算收入 Public Finance Budget Revenue	#增值税 Value-added Tax	#营业税 Business Tax	#企业所得税 Enterprise Income Tax
全　市	**Whole Municipality**	**10 063 220**	**1 070 389**	**2 051 221**	**1 151 030**
市南区	Shinan District	1 113 719	134 015	349 549	166 691
市北区	Shibei District	1 000 667	103 797	249 803	159 763
李沧区	Licang District	576 013	45 401	206 905	27 504
崂山区	Laoshan District	1 190 145	141 553	211 354	267 654
黄岛区	Huangdao District	1 877 453	255 850	376 288	188 250
保税港区	Qingdao Free Trade Port Area of China	100 368	21 381	9 354	27 210
城阳区	Chengyang District	842 917	152 020	242 810	82 919
即墨市	Jimo	930 493	61 807	155 899	41 057
胶州市	Jiaozhou	800 616	61 777	107 692	45 523
平度市	Pingdu	450 856	42 263	65 136	49 219
莱西市	Laixi	475 080	26 435	45 655	16 904
红岛经济区	Qingdao National High-tech Industrial Development Zone	150 561	24 090	30 776	17 362
市本级	Municipal Level	554 332			60 974

8-2 续表
continued

单位：万元(10 000 yuan)

市、区名称	Region	#个人所得税 Personal Income Tax	#城市维护建设税 Urban Maintenance and Development Tax	#基金预算收入 Funds Budgetary Revenue
全　市	**Whole Municipality**	**471 907**	**470 700**	**4 685 055**
市南区	Shinan District	81 786	43 724	
市北区	Shibei District	32 766	49 788	
李沧区	Licang District	10 053	33 089	
崂山区	Laoshan District	87 976	83 692	368 809
黄岛区	Huangdao District	47 318	119 188	761 186
保税港区	Qingdao Free Trade Port Area of China	3 523	4 398	6 673
城阳区	Chengyang District	31 401	53 952	287 113
即墨市	Jimo	13 060	27 158	448 094
胶州市	Jiaozhou	144 787	22 661	117 972
平度市	Pingdu	7 818	15 365	122 938
莱西市	Laixi	5 316	9 885	5 000
红岛经济区	Qingdao National High-tech Industrial Development Zone	6 103	7 800	199 012
市本级	Municipal Level			2 368 258

8-3 分市、区公共财政预算支出(2015年)

PUBLIC FINANCE BUDGET EXPENDITURE BY CITY AND DISTRICT(2015)

单位:万元(10 000 yuan)

市、区名称	Region	公共财政预算支出 Public Finance Budget Expenditure	#一般公共服务支出 General Public Services	#公共安全 Public Security	#教育 Education	#科学技术 Science and Technology	#文化体育与传媒 Culture, Sport and Media
全　市	**Whole Municipality**	**12 228 664**	**1 269 558**	**622 868**	**2 340 929**	**285 793**	**163 757**
市南区	Shinan District	486 923	57 023	19 862	98 604	9 213	3 984
市北区	Shibei District	705 486	114 168	25 080	160 601	18 711	6 107
李沧区	Licang District	406 784	35 693	11 263	99 301	5 649	6 324
崂山区	Laoshan District	748 465	58 067	24 212	94 131	21 210	6 026
黄岛区	Huangdao District	1 704 415	228 855	49 320	371 183	16 014	14 587
保税港区	Qingdao Free Trade Port Area of China	73 803	16 376	1 972	0	314	14
城阳区	Chengyang District	672 272	64 770	19 149	165 672	12 671	6 537
即墨市	Jimo	1 148 887	98 015	28 626	300 384	5 786	9 389
胶州市	Jiaozhou	929 001	126 462	43 413	232 657	16 341	10 088
平度市	Pingdu	836 603	74 514	28 659	261 049	49 456	5 400
莱西市	Laixi	679 784	59 899	22 528	137 688	1 855	13 079
红岛经济区	Qingdao National High-tech Industrial Development Zone	166 396	16 161	1 993	24 279	33 937	499
市本级	Municipal Level	3 669 845	319 555	346 791	395 380	94 636	81 723

8－3 续表
continued

单位：万元(10 000 yuan)

市、区名称	Region	#社会保障和就业 Social Security and Employment	#医疗卫生 Health Care	#节能保护 Environment Protection	#城乡社区事务 Urban and Rural Community Affairs	#农林水事务 Affairs of Agiculture, Forest and Irrigation	#基金预算支出 Funds Budgetary Expenditure
全　市	**Whole Municipality**	**1 052 675**	**700 007**	**72 970**	**2 546 467**	**791 895**	**4 890 465**
市南区	Shinan District	48 732	26 445	981	109 619		2 688
市北区	Shibei District	61 241	46 299	4 278	237 127	4	230 348
李沧区	Licang District	45 366	22 199	3 550	140 516	3 173	122 378
崂山区	Laoshan District	31 900	28 551	4 947	260 754	55 789	383 419
黄岛区	Huangdao District	166 906	88 356	15 613	533 029	103 188	788 778
保税港区	Qingdao Free Trade Port Area of China	515	8		32 260	27	12 015
城阳区	Chengyang District	38 072	33 160	5 107	187 657	47 986	290 706
即墨市	Jimo	86 011	78 712	11 984	284 511	138 521	448 083
胶州市	Jiaozhou	62 324	65 117	21 647	117 452	93 342	126 665
平度市	Pingdu	112 465	92 078	7 601	75 779	110 071	105 932
莱西市	Laixi	80 236	64 206	3 491	24 755	92 672	42 788
红岛经济区	Qingdao National High-tech Industrial Development Zone	8 247	7 798	1 805	46 310	7 193	199 516
市本级	Municipal Level	310 660	147 078	－8 034	496 698	139 929	2 137 149

8-4 主要年份金融系统人民币存贷款(年末余额)

MAJOR YEAR'S DEPOSITS AND LOANS OF FINANCIAL INSTITUTIONS(YEAR-END BALANCE)

单位:万元(10 000 yuan)

年份 Year	存款合计 Total Deposits	#企业存款 Deposits by Enterprises	#储蓄存款 Savings Deposits	贷款合计 Total Loans
1949	693	239	28	278
1952	9 093	4 308	1 838	3 322
1957	10 372	3 359	4 037	30 690
1962	20 040	8 579	3 279	73 601
1965	27 331	11 830	6 347	64 555
1970	38 264	13 024	7 576	126 382
1975	60 622	22 568	15 637	207 006
1978	66 523	21 004	21 455	297 184
1980	120 644	38 105	38 609	379 666
1985	344 760	99 736	155 604	452 142
1988	754 442	206 541	366 483	955 351
1989	932 430	245 529	481 692	1 174 448
1990	1 235 562	321 542	655 895	1 535 751
1991	1 553 564	411 417	824 428	1 871 462
1992	2 076 667	612 868	1 044 165	2 352 449
1993	2 747 294	835 617	1 372 239	2 940 658
1994	3 769 019	1 399 110	1 918 734	3 610 564
1995	5 324 026	2 030 382	2 687 888	4 777 864
1996	6 991 289	2 630 958	3 499 219	5 941 281
1997	7 385 092	2 885 632	4 060 259	6 508 776
1998	8 183 471	3 018 063	4 591 012	7 239 231
1999	9 160 001	3 454 570	4 978 045	8 945 730
2000	10 560 624	4 386 316	5 353 215	9 564 293
2001	12 323 942	4 955 336	6 187 409	10 798 871
2002	15 225 733	5 819 655	7 449 408	13 044 792
2003	18 920 868	7 027 227	9 084 693	16 783 917
2004	22 462 592	7 924 690	10 894 941	18 472 613
2005	26 975 372	8 226 661	13 431 016	20 394 792
2006	32 453 583	10 144 296	15 676 197	25 779 442
2007	38 915 882	13 213 434	17 020 383	30 970 553
2008	47 353 803	14 641 948	21 233 637	37 483 209
2009	63 019 764	21 001 185	25 278 658	48 735 326
2010	76 592 065	27 271 963	29 123 256	58 862 263
2011	86 384 994	49 189 415	31 985 099	69 477 500
2012	94 348 924	50 978 985	37 576 007	79 465 532
2013	109 695 588	60 367 185	41 405 946	88 607 439
2014	113 703 085	60 791 933	44 358 964	97 200 532
2015	125 330 268	45 526 577	50 235 905	107 718 528

注:自2015年起,人民银行报表指标变化,企业存款指标暂用非金融企业存款,储蓄存款指标暂用住户存款,口径与以前年度不一致。

Note: Since 2015, the indexes in the People's Bank of China's statements have changed, enterprise deposit index provisionally uses non-financial corporate deposits, savings deposit index temporarily uses household deposits, the gauge is different with that for previous years.

8 -5 金融系统人民币存贷款(年末余额)

DEPOSITS AND LOANS OF FINANCIAL INSTITUTIONS(YEAR-END BALANCE)

单位:万元(10 000 yuan)

项目	Item	2015 年	比年初增减数 Incremental/Reductions Compared to the Beginning of the Year
一、存款总计	**Total Deposits**	**125 330 268**	**11 912 895**
住户存款	Household Deposits	50 235 905	3 815 572
非金融企业存款	Non-Financial Corporate Deposits	45 526 577	639 756
广义政府存款	General Government Deposits	17 779 703	269 086
非银行业金融机构存款	Non-Banking Financial Institutions' Deposits	11 340 704	7 179 568
二、贷款总计	**Total Loans**	**107 718 528**	**10 517 996**
住户贷款	Household Loans	26 534 147	3 097 120
#短期贷款	Short-Term Loans	4 448 463	-611 014
中长期贷款	Medium And Long-Term Loans	22 085 684	3 708 134
非金融企业及机关团体贷款	Non-Financial Enterprises And Institutions/Organizations' Loans	80 994 848	7 256 784
#短期贷款	Short-Term Loans	31 416 256	-307 023
中长期贷款	Medium&Long-term Loans	43 593 890	6 044 575
票据融资	Notes Financing	5 574 485	1 786 350
非银行业金融机构贷款	Non-Banking Financial Institutions' Loans	423	423

注:自 2015 年起,人民银行报表中指标发生变化,本表数据按照新指标提供。

Note:Since 2015, the indexes in the People's Bank of China's statements have changed, the data in the table are provided according to the new indexes.

8 -6 国内保险业务(2000 -2015 年)

DOMESTIC INSURANCE BUSINESS(2000 -2015)

项目	Item	2000	2005	2006	2007	2008
风险保障金额	**Total domestic insurance Value**	**38 357 485**	**91 691 581**	**119 396 881**	**228 774 417**	**276 989 344**
国内业务收入	**Domestic Business Income**	**220 780**	**495 701**	**605 143**	**776 031**	**1 027 258**
1. 保费收入	Premium Income	218 714	495 701	605 143	776 031	1 027 258
#财产险	Property Insurance	85 161	159 746	199 213	272 664	280 008
农业险	Agriculture Insurance	18	12	19	1 542	3 135
人身险	Personal Insurance	133 535	335 943	405 911	501 825	744 115
国内业务支出	**Domestic Business Expenditure**	**94 877**	**214 148**	**252 477**	**361 183**	**423 743**
1. 赔款支出	Claim Expenditure	62 275	111 385	131 321	171 613	196 318
#财产险	Property Insurance	58 361	92 700	115 214	138 739	164 415
农业险	Agriculture Insurance	5	11	3	53	907
人身险	Personal Insurance	3 909	18 674	16 104	32 821	30 996
2. 给付支出	Mature Payment	27 955	32 739	63 144	95 282	132 621
3. 退保	Surrender	4 647	70 024	58 012	94 288	94 804

注:本表由青岛市保监局提供,风险保障金额 2012 年之前为国内保险总值。

Note: This table was provided by the Qingdao Insurance Regulatory Bureau. The amount of risk protection before 2012 was the total value of domestic insurance.

单位:万元(10 000 yuan)

2009	2010	2011	2012	2013	2014	2015
293 519 697	**309 244 255**	**380 829 634**	**447 476 690**	**491 953 749**	**611 632 799**	**836 499 657**
1 153 101	1 538 526	1 457 269	1 602 881	1 789 854	2 031 421	2 441 172
1 153 101	1 538 526	1 457 269	1 602 881	1 789 854	2 031 421	2 441 172
339 314	492 190	556 257	644 269	744 470	872 805	920 229
4 066	3 261	3 587	5 046	6 824	8 395	12 100
809 721	1 043 075	897 425	953 566	1 038 560	1 150 220	1 508 843
476 377	497 832	463 751	592 167	757 404	1 031 415	1 236 281
219 546	279 019	307 564	360 085	432 494	492 693	539 320
188 723	250 966	286 214	328 877	392 860	442 168	492 573
3 452	2 808	1 087	1 833	3 820	5 519	9 724
27 371	25 245	20 263	29 375	35 814	45 006	37 023
123 056	109 318	156 188	154 922	194 592	274 790	340 786
133 775	109 496	69 275	77 159	130 318	263 932	356 175

主要统计指标解释

财政收入 指国家财政参与社会产品分配所取得的收入,是实现国家职能的财力保证。财政收入所包括的内容几经变化,目前主要包括:

(1)税收收入:包括增值税、营业税、企业所得税、个人所得税、资源税、固定资产投资方向调节税、城市维护建设税、房产税、印花税、城镇土地使用税、土地增值税、车船税、耕地占用税、契税、烟叶税、其他税收收入。

(2)非税收入:包括专项收入、行政事业性收费收入、罚没收入、国有资本经营收入、国有资源有偿使用收入、其他收入。

财政支出 国家财政将筹集起来的资金进行分配使用,以满足经济建设和各项事业的需要,主要包括:

(1)一般公共服务支出:反映政府提供一般公共服务的支出。

(2)公共安全:反映政府维护社会公共安全方面的支出,有关事务包括武装警察、公安、国家安全、检察、法院、司法行政、监狱、劳教、国家保密、缉私警察等。

(3)教育支出:反映政府教育事务支出。有关具体教育事务包括教育行政管理、学前教育、小学教育、初中教育、普通高中教育、普通高等教育、初等职业教育、中专教育、技校教育、职业高中教育、高等职业教育、广播电视教育、留学生教育、特殊教育、干部继续教育、教育机关服务等。

(4)科学技术:反映政府用于科学技术方面的支出。

(5)文化体育与传媒:反映政府在文化、文物、体育、广播电视、新闻出版等方面的支出。

(6)社会保障和就业:反映政府在社会保障与就业方面的支出。有关事项包括社会保障与就业管理事务、民政管理事务、财政对社会保险基金的补助、补充全国社会保障基金、行政事业单位离退休、企业改革补助、就业补助、抚恤、退役安置、社会福利、残疾人事业、城市居民最低生活保障、其他城镇社会救济、农村社会救济、自然灾害生活补助、红十字事务等。

(7)医疗卫生支出:反映政府医疗卫生方面的支出。具体包括医疗卫生管理事务支出、医疗服务支出、医疗保障支出、疾病预防控制支出、卫生监督支出、妇幼保健支出、农村卫生支出等。

(8)环境保护:反映政府环境保护支出。具体包括:环境保护管理事务支出、环境监测与监察支出、污染治理支出、自然生态保护支出、天然林保护工程支出、退耕还林支出、风沙荒漠治理支出、退牧还草支出、已垦草原退耕还草支出。

(9)城乡社区事务:反映政府城乡社区事务支出。具体包括:城乡社区管理事务支出、城乡社区规划与管理支出、城乡社区公共设施支出、城乡社区住宅支出、城乡社区环境卫生支出、建设市场管理与监督支出等。

(10)农林水事务:反映政府农林水事务方面的支出。具体包括农业、林业、水利、扶贫支出、农业综合开发支出等。

存款 指企业、机关、团体或居民根据资金必须收回的原则,把货币资金存入银行或其他信贷机构保管并取得一定利息的一种信用活动形式。根据存款对象或性质的不同可划分为企业存款、财政存款、机关团体存款、基本建设存款、储蓄存款、农村存款、委托存款、其他存款等科目。它是银行信贷资金的主要来源。

贷款 指银行或其他信贷机构根据资金必须归还的原则,按一定利率,为企业、个人等提供资金的一种信用活动形式。我国银行贷款分为短期贷款、中期流动资金贷款、中长期贷款、信托贷款、融资租赁、委托贷款、票据融资、各项垫款等。

保费 指投保人为取得保险人在约定范围内所承担赔偿责任而支付给保险人的费用。

Explanatory Notes on Main Statistical Indicators

Government Revenue refers to the revenue of the government finance by means of participating in the distribution of the social products, which is the financial resources for ensuring the government to function. The contents of government revenue have been changed several times. Now it includes the following main items:

(1) Various tax revenues, including value added tax, business tax, enterprise income tax, personal income tax, resources tax, fixed assets investment direction regulating tax, tax on city maintenance and construction, real estate tax, stamp tax, tax on use of urban land, land value added tax, vehicle and vessel tax, tax on occupancy of cultivated land, property tax, tobacco leaf tax, and other tax revenues.

(2) Non-tax Revenues including special revenues, revenues from Administrative and institutional fees, penalty and confiscatory revenues , revenues from state-owned capital operationg, revenues from paid use of state-owned resources, and other revenues.

Government Expenditure refers to the distribution and use of the funds the government finance has raised, so as to meet the needs of economic construction and various causes. It includes the following main items:

(1) Expenditure for general public services: It reflects the expenditure from the government for general public services.

(2) Expenditure on public security: It reflects the expenditure from the government towards safeguarding the public security, including the related affairs of armed police, public security, state security, procuratorial administration, law court, judicial administration, jail , reeducation through labor, state confidentiality, anti-smuggling Patrol, etc.

(3) Expenditure on education: It reflects the expenditure from the government on education, including the related affairs of educational administration management, preschool education, primary education, junior secondary educate, regular senior secondary educate, regular higher education, primary vocational education, specialized secondary educate, technical educate, vocational senior secondary educate, vocational higher education, radio and television education, foreign student educate, special education, cadre continuing education, education institution services, etc.

(4) Expenditure on science and technology: It reflects the expenditure from the government on science and technology.

(5) Expenditure on culture, sport and media: It reflects the expenditure from the government on culture, cultural relics, sport, radio and television, publication, etc.

(6) Expenditure on social security and employment: It reflects the expenditure from the government on social security and employment, including the related affairs of management of social security and employment, civil administration, subsidies to social insurance funds, supplement to national social security funds, retirees of government agencies and institutions, subsidies to enterprises reform, subsidies to employment, pension, settling down demobilized servicemen, social security, disabled person administration, minimum living allowance in urban area, other social relief in urban area, social relief in rural area, subsidies to natural disaster, Red Cross business, etc.

(7) Expenditure on health care: It reflects the expenditure from the government on health care, including expenditure on management of health care, medical services, medical security, disease control and prevention, public health supervision, rural health care, etc.

(8) Expenditure on environment protection: It reflects the expenditure from the government on environment protection, including expenditure on management of environment protection, environment monitoring and supervisory, pollution government, natural ecological protection, project of natural forest protection, returning farmland to forest, sandstorm and wilderness government, returning grazing land to grassland, returning cultivated grassland to grassland, etc.

(9) Expenditure on urban and rural community affairs: It reflects the expenditure from the government on urban and rural community affairs, including expenditure on management of urban and rural community affairs, plan and management of urban and rural community, public utility of urban and rural community, residential buildings of urban and rural community, environmental sanitation of urban and rural community, management and supervision of markets construction, etc.

(10) Expenditure on agriculture, forest and irrigation: It reflects the expenditure from the government on agriculture, forest and irrigation, including expenditure on agriculture, forest, irrigation, poverty alleviation, comprehensive development of agriculture, etc.

Deposit is a form of credit by which enterprises, institutions, organizations or households can put money into banks and other credit institutions for safekeeping and interest earning under the principle of free withdrawal. According to different depositors, deposits are divided into enterprise deposits, treasury deposits, deposits of government agencies and organizations, capital construction deposits, savings deposits, rural saving deposits, entrusted deposits and other deposits. Deposits are major sources of the credit funds of banks.

Loan is a form of credit by which banks and other credit institutions provide funds at certain interest rate to enterprises and individuals in the light of the principle of unconditional repayment. Loans from Chinese banks include circulating capital loans, fixed assets loans, loans to urban and rural individuals engaged in industrial and commercial business and agricultural loans.

Premium is the fee paid by the insurant to the insurer to obtain the obligation of compensation from the insurance within the agreed terms.

9 价格指数
PRICE INDEXES

简要说明

一、本篇资料的主要内容

本篇资料主要包括工业生产者出厂、工业生产者购进、固定资产投资、房地产、居民消费、商品零售等价格指数。

二、本篇资料的来源

1、工业生产者出厂、工业生产者购进、固定资产投资、房地产价格指数分别来源于生产、投资、房地产价格统计调查年报，由国家统计局青岛调查队生产投资价格调查处整理提供。

2、居民消费、商品零售价格指数来源于消费价格统计调查年报，由国家统计局青岛调查队消费价格调查处整理提供。

Brief Introduction

I. Main Content

Data in this chapter mainly include producer price indices for manufactured goods, purchasing price indices for industrial producers, price indices of investment in fixed assets, real estate price indices, consumer price indices and retail price indices.

II. Source of Data

(1) Data on producer price indices for manufactured goods, purchasing price indices for industrial producers, price indices of investment in fixed assets, real estate price indices are based on annual report of price survey on production,investment,real estate,and provided by the Division of Production Price Survey of Survey Office of the National Bureau of Statistics in Qingdao.

(2) Data on consumer price indices and retail price indices are based on annual report of consumer price survey, and provided by the Division of Consumer Price Survey of Survey Office of the National Bureau of Statistics in Qingdao.

9-1 主要年份居民消费和商品零售价格指数
MAJOR YEAR'S CONSUMER AND RETAIL PRICE INDEXES

(上年=100) (preceding year=100)

年份 Year	居民消费价格指数 Consumer Price Index	#食品类 Food	衣着类 Clothing	服务项目价格指数 Services Price Index	商品零售价格指数 Retail Price Index
1951	110.5	105.2	112.4		110.5
1952	99.8	99.6	98.7		99.8
1957	101.4	101.3	101.4	99.3	101.4
1962	102.6	102.0	100.2	99.9	102.6
1965	101.2	101.3	98.8	96.9	101.2
1970	98.9	99.7	100.0	99.5	98.9
1975	100.3	100.1	100.0	100.0	100.3
1978	100.5	100.2	99.8	100.0	100.5
1980	105.2	108.5	100.3	100.6	105.5
1985	110.4	115.2	102.3	102.7	110.9
1987	109.4	112.5	106.8	102.5	109.8
1988	120.7	125.2	117.3	118.3	120.9
1989	115.3	109.2	121.1	130.2	114.4
1990	104.5	103.4	103.4	118.8	103.6
1991	107.0	107.0	112.1	109.6	106.8
1992	111.4	115.1	108.6	119.9	110.8
1993	123.9	120.9	119.0	158.5	119.8
1994	126.9	135.2	130.1	117.9	122.8
1995	116.2	118.1	122.8	123.2	114.2
1996	112.6	110.1	104.3	130.4	106.0
1997	104.0	101.2	102.3	120.8	100.2
1998	100.0	93.7	94.5	136.2	94.9
1999	100.2	96.7	97.1	115.6	96.6
2000	103.3	100.0	108.3	112.0	99.7
2001	101.0	100.6	98.0	108.7	98.9
2002	98.9	97.8	100.2	101.0	99.5
2003	101.4	104.3	98.4	101.7	98.3
2004	102.1	104.0	103.6	104.7	99.0
2005	102.3	102.1	108.3	101.4	99.3
2006	100.9	101.7	99.4	100.8	99.7
2007	104.5	111.6	99.4	102.4	102.7
2008	104.7	111.7	103.9	99.8	103.9
2009	100.5	101.6	101.4	100.6	98.6
2010	102.2	106.4	101.0	100.4	101.4
2011	105.0	111.1	108.2	103.1	104.5
2012	102.7	104.3	106.3	102.1	101.7
2013	102.5	105.3	104.9	100.7	101.4
2014	102.6	104.4	103.2	101.9	102.3
2015	101.2	101.7	102.8	101.3	100.0

9－2 主要年份居民消费和商品零售价格指数(以1950年价格为100)

MAJOR YEAR'S CONSUMER AND RETAIL PRICE INDEXES (1950 = 100)

年份 Year	居民消费价格指数 Consumer Price Index	#食品类 Food	衣着类 Clothing	服务项目价格指数 Services Price Index	商品零售价格指数 Retail Price Index
1951	110.5	105.2	112.4		110.5
1952	110.3	104.8	110.9		110.3
1957	119.5	120.7	115.3	91.6	119.5
1962	127.4	128.8	115.1	94.2	127.4
1965	133.3	138.7	108.4	81.5	133.3
1970	129.0	137.6	110.3	76.8	129.0
1975	128.8	138.2	110.0	75.7	128.8
1978	129.1	138.7	109.8	75.7	129.1
1980	137.6	154.1	109.3	76.1	138.1
1985	160.8	196.1	103.8	80.5	162.5
1987	185.4	235.8	113.6	85.2	188.2
1988	223.8	295.2	133.2	100.8	227.6
1989	258.1	322.4	161.3	131.3	260.3
1990	269.7	333.3	166.8	155.9	269.7
1991	288.6	356.7	187.0	170.9	288.1
1992	321.5	410.5	203.1	204.9	319.2
1993	398.3	496.3	241.7	324.8	382.4
1994	505.4	671.1	314.4	382.9	469.5
1995	587.3	792.5	386.1	471.8	536.2
1996	661.3	872.6	402.7	615.2	568.4
1997	687.8	883.0	412.0	743.1	569.5
1998	687.8	827.4	389.3	1 012.1	540.5
1999	689.2	800.1	378.0	1 170.0	522.1
2000	711.9	800.1	409.4	1 310.4	520.5
2001	719.0	804.9	401.2	1 424.4	514.8
2002	711.1	787.2	402.0	1 438.7	512.2
2003	721.1	821.0	395.6	1 463.1	503.5
2004	736.2	853.9	409.8	1 531.9	498.5
2005	753.1	871.8	443.8	1 553.4	495.0
2006	759.9	886.6	441.2	1 565.8	493.5
2007	794.1	989.5	438.5	1 603.4	506.8
2008	831.4	1 105.3	455.6	1 600.2	526.6
2009	835.6	1 123.0	462.0	1 609.8	519.2
2010	854.0	1 194.9	466.6	1 616.2	526.5
2011	896.7	1 327.5	504.9	1 666.3	550.2
2012	920.9	1 384.6	536.7	1 701.3	559.6
2013	943.9	1 458.0	563.0	1 713.2	567.4
2014	968.4	1 522.2	581.0	1 745.8	580.5
2015	980.0	1 548.1	597.3	1 768.5	580.5

9 -3 主要年份生产投资价格指数

MAJOR YEAR'S PRICE INDEXES FOR PRODUCTION AND INVESTMENT

(上年 = 100) (preceding year = 100)

年份 Year	工业生产者出厂价格指数 Producer Price Indexes for Industrial Producers	工业生产者购进价格指数 Purchasing Price Indexes for Industrial Producers	房屋销售价格指数 Sales Price Indexes of Houses	房屋租赁价格指数 Renting Price Indexes of Houses	物业管理价格指数 Property Management Price Indexes	固定资产投资价格指数 Price Indexes for Investment in Fixed Assets
1990	104.33	108.64				
1991	101.68	108.10				
1992	105.46	107.13				
1993	115.49	126.91				
1994	121.62	120.30				
1995	112.70	114.25				
1996	103.81	103.25				
1997	100.22	101.93				
1998	94.96	92.77	100.1	94.0		
1999	96.93	95.88	103.7	104.3		
2000	101.89	106.81	102.3	95.8		
2001	98.00	97.81	104.1	107.0		
2002	97.37	96.78	107.6	94.4		
2003	100.97	106.51	114.6	99.4		
2004	102.92	113.62	115.2	98.6		105.8
2005	101.39	106.52	110.9	103.3	100.2	103.1
2006	101.08	105.80	106.9	110.1	99.8	102.6
2007	101.50	106.69	106.5	108.3	100.4	104.1
2008	105.33	115.91	105.1	106.5	102.1	111.0
2009	95.78	90.35	100.3	103.5	100.4	94.6
2010	103.75	112.21		103.0	100.5	104.9
2011	104.90	109.39				107.0
2012	98.61	97.00				100.0
2013	98.82	96.53				100.1
2014	99.20	97.40				99.9
2015	97.04	94.24				97.1

注:2010 年之前工业生产者出厂价格为工业品出厂价格;工业生产者购进价格为主要原材料、燃料、动力购进价格。

Note: Producer's prices at works were the prices of industrial products at works before 2010; producer's purchasing price refers to the purchasing price of main raw materials, fuels and power.

9－4 工业生产者出厂价格指数

PRODUCER PRICE INDEXES FOR INDUSTRIAL PRODUCERS

(上年＝100)

类　别	Item	2000	2005	2006	2007	2008
总 指 数	**General Index**	**101.89**	**101.39**	**101.08**	**101.50**	**105.33**
其中:轻工业	Light Industry	98.50	99.78	99.58	100.97	102.93
重工业	Heavy Industry	105.62	104.32	103.94	102.49	109.17
其中:生产资料	**Means of Production**	**105.03**	**103.24**	**102.49**	**102.41**	**108.76**
采掘	Excavation	95.67	114.74	104.73	99.85	115.24
原料	Raw Materials	113.82	106.91	104.05	104.01	108.81
加工	Processing	97.58	101.45	101.86	101.91	108.59
生活资料	**Means of Livelihood**	**98.25**	**99.13**	**99.74**	**100.64**	**101.72**
食品	Food	96.59	98.80	101.52	106.55	108.42
衣着	Clothing	99.37	101.48	102.16	102.46	103.36
一般日用品	Articles for Daily Use	104.52	101.97	101.82	103.21	103.03
耐用消费品	Durable Consumer Goods	97.70	97.43	97.23	96.10	97.13

(preceding year = 100)

2009	2010	2011	2012	2013	2014	2015
95.78	**103.75**	**104.90**	**98.61**	**98.82**	**99.20**	**97.04**
97.21	100.80	103.46	99.70	99.11	99.62	99.85
93.45	107.57	105.89	97.87	98.62	98.91	95.10
94.25	**106.43**	**105.54**	**97.55**	**98.58**	**98.87**	**95.23**
93.44	130.94	132.07	93.35	91.72	100.65	95.12
90.67	115.24	111.52	99.05	99.26	98.87	88.59
95.34	103.50	103.49	97.20	98.50	98.84	97.06
97.45	**99.61**	**103.82**	**100.42**	**99.21**	**99.76**	**100.07**
98.21	105.06	109.71	99.91	95.34	98.34	102.53
102.03	101.56	107.44	102.03	102.74	100.34	100.39
99.39	99.96	108.02	101.64	101.42	101.01	99.59
94.52	93.23	94.34	98.79	98.41	99.65	98.26

9－5 工业生产者购进价格指数

PURCHASING PRICE INDEXES FOR INDUSTRIAL PRODUCERS

（上年＝100）

名　称	Item	2000	2005	2006	2007	2008
总 指 数	**General Index**	**106.81**	**106.52**	**105.8**	**106.69**	**115.91**
燃料、动力类	Fuel and Power	113.82	117.34	117.17	103.14	126.19
黑色金属材料类	Ferrous Metals	102.66	107.84	95.83	109.61	122.19
#钢材	Rolled-steel	105.44	106.57	96.11	108.14	119.10
其他	Others	101.1	112.88	94.91	114.43	132.40
有色金属材料及电线类	Nonferrous Metals and Electric Wire	106.75	108.06	131.58	106.51	93.41
化工原料类	Raw Chemical Materials	106.9	112.47	99.71	111.09	123.00
木材及纸浆类	Timber and Paper Pulp	108.98	103.8	104.29	107.23	103.58
建筑材料及非金属矿类	Building Materials and Nonmetals	99.5	115.54	92.83	95.8	124.52
其他工业原材料及半成品	Other Industrial Raw Materials and Semi-finished Goods	105.32	97.87	103.33	104.43	109.65
农副产品	Agricultural Products	92.73	101.55	110.87	112.49	117.68
纺织原料类	Textile Materials	104.03	98.15	100.15	104.01	101.44

(preceding year = 100)

2009	2010	2011	2012	2013	2014	2015
90.35	**112.21**	**109.39**	**97.00**	**96.53**	**97.40**	**94.24**
90.53	115.43	111.29	100.64	95.18	97.65	88.51
82.38	111.97	113.08	93.20	93.76	95.81	87.26
85.25	108.67	107.95	92.33	92.87	96.87	89.99
72.73	122.64	129.01	94.64	96.57	92.49	78.70
86.24	122.65	108.45	93.64	96.23	96.24	92.34
87.66	111.04	113.79	96.72	96.47	99.51	96.44
89.16	117.06	103.78	93.12	98.79	102.42	98.33
100.98	107.61	116.71	102.48	100.13	97.36	95.52
92.70	106.41	103.31	98.05	96.65	96.25	96.95
88.60	121.30	115.04	98.21	98.54	97.62	99.75
98.69	112.90	111.11	95.61	99.60	97.38	95.86

9-6 按工业行业分工业生产者出厂价格指数

PRODUCER PRICE INDEXES FOR INDUSTRIAL PRODUCERS BY SECTOR

(上年=100)

行业	Sector
工业生产者出厂价格指数	**Producer Price Indexes for Manufactured Goods**
黑色金属矿采选业	Mining of Ferrous Metal Ores
有色金属矿采选业	Mining of Non-ferrous Metal Ores
非金属矿采选业	Mining and Processing of Nonmetal Ores
农副食品加工业	Processing of Food from Agricultural Products
食品制造业	Manufacture of Foods
酒、饮料和精制茶制造业	Manufacturing Industry of Alcohol, Beverage and Refined Tea
纺织业	Manufacture of Textile
纺织服装、服饰业	Industry of Textile and Garment, and Apparel
皮革、毛皮、羽毛及其制品和制鞋业	Industry of Leather, Furs, Down and Related Products, and Shoes Making
木材加工和木、竹、藤、棕、草制品业	Processing of Timbers, Manufacture of Wood, Bamboo, Rattan, Palm, and Straw Products
家具制造业	Manufacture of Furniture
造纸和纸制品业	Manufacture of Paper and Paper Products
印刷和记录媒介复制业	Printing, Reproduction of Recording Media
文教、工美、体育和娱乐用品制造业	Industry of Culture and Education, Arts and Crafts, and Entertainment Products Manufacturing
石油加工、炼焦和核燃料加工业	Processing of Petroleum, Coking, Processing of Nucleus Fuel
化学原料和化学制品制造业	Manufacture of Chemical Raw Material and Chemical Products
医药制造业	Manufacture of Medicines
化学纤维制造业	Manufacture of Chemical Fiber
橡胶和塑料制品业	Industry of Rubber and Plastic Products
非金属矿物制品业	Manufacture of Non-metallic Mineral Products
黑色金属冶炼和压延加工业	Smelting and Pressing of Ferrous Metals
有色金属冶炼和压延加工业	Smelting and Pressing of Non-ferrous Metals
金属制品业	Manufacture of Metal Products
通用设备制造业	Manufacture of General Purpose Machinery
专用设备制造业	Manufacture of Special Purpose Machinery
汽车制造业	Vehicle Manufacturing Industry
铁路、船舶、航空航天和其他运输设备制造业	Maufacturing Industry of Railroads, Vessels, Aerospace and Other Transporation Equipment
电气机械和器材制造业	Manufacture of Electrical Machinery & Equipment
计算机、通信和其他电子设备制造业	Computer, Communications and Other Electronic Equipment Manufacturing
仪器仪表制造业	Instruments Manufacturing Industry
其他制造业	Other Manufacturing Industry
金属制品、机械和设备修理业	Industry of Metal Products, and Repair of Machinery and Equipment
电力、热力生产和供应业	Production and Supply of Electric Power and Heat Power
燃气生产和供应业	Production and Supply of Gas
水的生产和供应业	Production and Supply of Water

注:2012年国民经济行业分类调整,本表中2011年-2015年数据采用新国民经济行业分类GB/T 4754-2011。

Note: Classification of national economic industries was adjusted in 2012. The new national economic industries classification by GB/T 4754-2011 applies to data from 2011 to 2015 in this table.

(preceding year = 100)

2011	2012	2013	2014	2015
104.90	**98.61**	**98.82**	**99.20**	**97.04**
104.33	99.93	100.00	99.86	100.00
111.39	102.48	98.72	95.57	89.94
145.13	89.33	87.06	102.14	94.85
111.34	98.69	93.46	97.58	102.47
112.52	103.11	103.08	101.78	100.66
104.14	105.89	100.48	98.76	99.01
105.09	96.15	100.18	100.27	99.41
105.43	101.66	104.17	101.74	100.84
104.79	102.59	101.83	98.56	99.72
108.13	103.21	99.67	100.96	100.35
101.11	102.00	100.02	100.00	99.91
105.71	95.59	96.13	101.96	99.78
110.06	107.10	108.65	96.97	95.96
100.61	101.47	100.47	100.00	99.96
114.95	104.26	99.49	97.38	76.03
114.60	89.61	98.04	99.70	96.53
107.33	95.05	105.08	127.56	100.73
123.72	92.56	95.65	96.69	90.31
114.68	99.67	95.40	95.50	94.93
108.19	98.39	99.82	100.91	101.62
111.00	86.47	93.52	94.45	83.44
108.26	89.14	93.87	94.43	87.95
99.79	99.82	104.14	96.62	96.59
101.39	100.07	103.87	101.02	100.37
101.69	101.26	99.99	99.81	99.72
99.27	98.97	98.59	102.49	101.04
99.17	99.66	97.65	100.96	100.03
103.10	98.40	98.82	99.24	98.61
84.65	95.43	94.31	98.88	96.31
102.01	98.72	98.01	98.43	97.05
95.16	98.52	99.94	100.12	99.89
102.17	98.43	88.75	91.69	90.21
101.49	104.36	99.81	99.15	98.10
107.34	103.32	102.54	109.38	98.88
100.15	100.25	100.05	100.34	103.46

9-7 固定资产投资价格指数

PRICE INDEXES FOR INVESTMENT IN FIXED ASSETS

(上年=100) (preceding year=100)

项目名称	Item	2005	2006	2007	2008	2009	2010	2011	2012	2013	2014	2015
总　计	**Total**	**103.1**	**102.6**	**104.1**	**111.0**	**94.6**	**104.9**	**107.0**	**100.0**	**100.1**	**99.9**	**97.1**
建筑安装、装饰工程	Construction and Installation Project	103.7	103.5	105.4	115.5	92.1	107.5	110.1	99.8	100.0	99.6	95.5
其中:人工费	of which:Labor Cost	112.7	110.0	111.0	112.7	104.9	112.0	115.9	110.4	107.8	104.8	103.1
材料费	Materials Expenses	101.0	100.7	103.9	120.5	87.5	107.0	109.6	96.7	97.6	97.7	92
机械使用费	Expenses on Machinery Use	104.2	109.1	107.2	106.9	100.0	104.3	105.0	102.3	101.0	100.8	100.9
设备、工器具购置	Purchase of Equipment,Tools and Instruments	99.7	100.6	100.8	102.5	98.0	100.2	101.8	99.2	99.3	99.9	99.2
其他费用	Others	105.5	100.9	103.9	105.9	98.5	102.2	103.0	102.0	101.4	101.4	101.2

9-8 住宅销售价格指数(2015 年)

SALES PRICE INDEXES FOR RESIDENCE(2015)

(上年=100) (preceding year=100)

项目	Item	2015
新建住宅销售价格指数	**Sales Price Indexes for Newly Constructed Residence**	
一月	January	92.7
二月	February	91.7
三月	March	91.1
四月	April	90.7
五月	May	90.6
六月	June	91.2
七月	July	92.5
八月	August	93.4
九月	September	94.7
十月	October	95.9
十一月	November	96.7
十二月	December	97.8
二手住宅销售价格指数	**Sales Price Indexes for Second-hand Residence**	
一月	January	94.2
二月	February	93.5
三月	March	93.2
四月	April	93.4
五月	May	93.7
六月	June	94.3
七月	July	95.5
八月	August	96.4
九月	September	97.5
十月	October	98.6
十一月	November	99.3
十二月	December	99.7

9－9 居民消费价格分类指数(2015 年)

CONSUMER PRICE INDEXES BY CATEGORY(2015)

(上年＝100) (preceding year＝100)

项　目	Item	指　数 Indexes
居民消费价格总指数	**Consumer Price Index**	**101.2**
非食品价格指数	Non-food Price Index	101.0
服务项目价格指数	Services Price Index	101.3
扣除鲜菜鲜果总指数	Price Index Without Fresh Vegetables and Fresh Fruits	101.3
消费品价格指数	Consumer Goods Price Index	101.2
一、食品	**Food**	**101.7**
1. 粮食	Grain	101.5
2. 淀粉及制品	Starch and Products	100.7
3. 干豆类及豆制品	Beans and Bean Products	104.6
4. 油脂	Oil or Fat	98.0
5. 肉禽及其制品	Meat Poultry and Its Products	104.3
6. 蛋类	Eggs	90.1
7. 水产品	Aquatic Products	101.0
8. 菜	Vegetables	109.1
9. 调味品	Flavoring	102.3
10. 糖	Carbohydrate	100.5
11. 茶及饮料	Tea and Beverages	102.3
12. 干鲜瓜果类	Dried and Fresh Melons and Fruits	95.0
13. 糕点饼干面包	Cake, Biscuit and Bread	102.7
14. 液体乳及乳制品	Milk and Its Products	101.1
15. 在外用膳食品	Outward Dinner Food	103.3
16. 其它食品及食品加工服务	Other Foods and Manufacturing Services	101.2
二、烟酒	**Tobacco Liquor**	**102.3**
1. 烟草	Tobacco	104.8
2. 酒	Liquor	100.4

9-9 续表
continued

项　目	Item	指数 Indexes
三、衣着	**Clothing**	**102.8**
1. 服装	Garments	101.7
2. 衣着材料	Clothing Materials	101.6
3. 鞋袜帽	Footgear and Hats	105.3
4. 衣着加工服务	Clothing Manufacturing Services	103.3
四、家庭设备用品及维修服务	**Household Facilities, Articles and services**	**100.6**
1. 耐用消费品	Durable Consumer Goods	100.0
2. 室内装饰品	Interior Decorations	94.0
3. 床上用品	Bed Articles	101.2
4. 家庭日用杂品	Daily Use Household Articles	100.4
5. 家庭服务及加工维修服务	Household Services and Maintenance and Renovation	107.3
五、医疗保健和个人用品	**Health Care and Personal Articles**	**103.8**
1. 医疗保健	Health Care	105.5
2. 个人用品及服务	Personal Articles and Services	100.1
六、交通和通讯	**Transportation and Communication**	**97.2**
1. 交通	Transportation	95.9
2. 通讯	Communication	99.8
七、娱乐教育文化用品及服务	**Recreation, Education and Culture Articles and Services**	**101.2**
1. 文娱用耐用消费品及服务	Durable Consumer Goods for Cultural and Recreational Use and Services	98.3
2. 教育	Education	105.8
3. 文化娱乐	Cultural	102.6
4. 旅游	Touring	87.5
八、居住	**Residence**	**100.3**
1. 建房及装修材料	Building and Building Decoration Materials	100.1
2. 租房	Renting	100.0
3. 自有住房	Private Housing	100.5
4. 水、电、燃料	Water, Electricity and Fuels	100.0

9－10 商品零售价格分类指数(2015 年)

RETAIL PRICE INDEXES BY CATEGORY(2015)

(上年＝100) (preceding year＝100)

项　目	Item	指　数 Indexes
商品零售价格总指数	**Retail Price Index**	**100.0**
一、食品	**Food**	**101.7**
1. 粮食	Grain	101.0
2. 淀粉及制品	Starch and Products	100.7
3. 干豆类及豆制品	Beans and Bean Products	104.5
4. 油脂	Oil or Fat	98.0
5. 肉禽及其制品	Meat Poultry and Its Products	104.1
6. 蛋	Eggs	90.4
7. 水产品	Aquatic Products	101.7
8. 菜	Vegetables	109.1
9. 调味品	Flavoring	102.0
10. 糖	Carbohydrate	100.4
11. 干鲜瓜果	Dried and Fresh Melons and Fruits	95.5
12. 糕点饼干面包	Cake, Biscuit and Bread	102.7
13. 液体乳及乳制品	Milk and Its Products	100.9
14. 在外用膳食品	Outward Dinner Food	103.0
15. 其他食品	Other Foods	101.2
二、饮料、烟酒	**Beverages, Tobacco and Liquor**	**102.3**
1. 茶及饮料	Tea and Beverages	102.3
2. 烟草	Tobacco	104.8
3. 酒	Liquor	100.4
三、服装、鞋帽	**Clothing**	**103.1**
1. 服装	Garments	101.7
2. 鞋袜帽	Footgear and Hats	105.3
3. 其他	Others	95.3
四、纺织品	**Textiles**	**101.0**
1. 衣着材料	Cotton Cloth	101.6
2. 床上用品	Blend Cloth	100.8
五、家用电器及音像器材	**Household Appliances, Music and Video Equipment**	**98.4**
1. 家庭设备	Household Facilities	98.4
2. 文娱用耐用消费品	Durable Consumer Goods for Cultural and Recreational Use and Services	98.4
3. 专业音像器材	Professional Audio and Video Equipment	99.1

9-10 续表
continued

项　　目	Item	指　数 Indexes
六、文化办公用品	**Culture and office Articles**	**99.6**
七、日用品	**Articles for Daily Use**	**100.4**
1. 日用百货	General Merchandise for Daily Use	101.4
2. 日用杂品	Miscellaneous for Daily Use	101.5
3. 洗涤用品	Cleaning Products	102.7
4. 其他日用品	Other Articles for Daily Use	96.9
八、体育娱乐用品	**Sports and Recreation Articles**	**100.5**
1. 体育用品	Sports Articles	100.5
2. 娱乐用品	Recreation Articles	100.4
九、交通、通信用品	**Transportation and Communication Appliances**	**99.3**
1. 交通运输机械	Transportation Machines	99.4
2. 通信器材	Communication Equipment	98.7
十、家具	**Furniture**	**102.7**
十一、化妆品	**Cosmetics**	**100.9**
十二、金银珠宝	**Gold, Silver and Jewelry**	**90.0**
十三、中西药品及医疗保健用品	**Traditional Chinese and Western Medicals and Health Care Articles**	**104.3**
1. 医疗器具及用品	Medical Apparatus and Articles	100.9
2. 中药材及中成药	Traditional Chinese Medicinal Materials and Medicines	103.0
3. 西药	Western Medicines	103.1
4. 保健器具及用品	Health Care Articles	108.4
十四、书报杂志及电子出版物	**Books, Newspapers, Magazines and Electronic Publications**	**107.2**
1. 教材及参考书	Teaching Material and Reference Books	105.5
2. 书报杂志	Books, Newspapers and Magazines	107.6
3. 电子音像制品	Electronic Music and Video Products	109.8
十五、燃料	**Fuels**	**89.4**
1. 煤炭及制品	Coal and Its Products	100.0
2. 石油及制品	Petroleum and Its Products	88.5
十六、建筑材料及五金电料	**Building Materials and Hardware**	**100.2**
1. 建筑装璜材料	Building Decoration Materials	99.9
2. 五金电料	Hardware	100.8

主要统计指标解释

居民消费价格指数 是反映一定时期内城乡居民所购买的生活消费品价格和服务项目价格变动趋势和程度的相对数，是对城市居民消费价格指数和农村居民消费价格指数进行综合汇总计算的结果。该指数可以观察和分析消费品的零售价格和服务价格变动对城乡居民实际生活费支出的影响程度。

商品零售价格指数 是反映一定时期内城乡商品零售价格变动趋势和程度的相对数。商品零售价格的变动直接影响到城乡居民的生活支出和国家的财政收入，影响居民购买力和市场供需的平衡，影响到消费与积累的比例关系。因此，该指数可以从一个侧面对上述经济活动进行观察和分析。

工业生产者出厂价格指数 是反映一定时期内全部工业产品出厂价格总水平的变动趋势和程度的相对数，包括工业企业售给本企业以外所有单位的各种产品和直接售给居民用于生活消费的产品。该指数可以观察出厂价格变动对工业总产值及增加值的影响。

工业生产者购进价格指数 是反映工业企业作为生产投入，而从物资交易市场和能源、原材料生产企业购买原材料、燃料和动力产品时，所支付的价格水平变动趋势和程度的统计指标，是扣除工业企业物质消耗成本中的价格变动影响的重要依据。

房地产价格指数 是反映一定时期内房地产价格变动趋势和程度的相对数，包括新建住宅销售价格指数、二手住宅销售价格指数。

Explanatory Notes on Main Statistical Indicators

Consumer Price Indices reflect the trend and degree of changes in prices of consumer goods and services purchased by urban and rural households during a given period. They are obtained by combining the Urban Consumer Price Indices and the Rural Consumer Price Indices. The Indices enable the observation and analysis of the degree of impact of the changes in the prices of retailed goods and services on the actual living expenses of urban and rural residents.

Retail Price Indices reflect the trend and degree of change in retail prices of commodities during a given period. The change in retail prices of commodities directly affect the living expenditure of urban and rural residents, government revenue, purchasing power of residents and the equilibrium of market supply and demand, and the ratio of consumption to accumulation. Therefore, the retail price indices are useful to analyze the changes of the above economic activities.

Producer Price Indices for Industrial Producers reflect the trend and degree of changes in general ex-factory prices of all industrial products during a given period, including sales of industrial products by an industrial enterprise to all units outside the enterprise, as well as sales of consumer goods to residents. It can be used to analyze the impact of ex-factory prices on gross output value and value-added of the industrial sector.

Purchasing Price Indices for Industrial Producers reflect changes in the level and degree of prices paid by industrial enterprises when they purchase production input such as raw materials, fuels and power from the market or from other energy or raw materials producing enterprises. These indices provide important basis for measuring the material consumption of industrial enterprises after removing influence of price changes.

Price Indices for Real Estate reflect the trend and degree of changes in prices of real estate during a given period, including sales price indices for newly constructed residential buildings and secondhand residential buildings.

主要统计指标解释

Explanatory Notes on Main Statistical Indicators

10 人民生活

PEOPLE'S LIVING CONDITIONS

简要说明

一、本篇资料的主要内容

本篇资料主要反映了全体居民的家庭收支、居住、家庭消费构成、耐用消费品拥有量等方面的情况。

二、本篇资料的来源

1、本篇资料中城乡居民家庭相关资料来源于青岛市住户一体化收支调查年报，由国家统计局青岛调查队住户专项调查处提供。

2、自2015年开始，全市城乡住户调查统一使用一体化改革后的数据，与原数据相比，城乡居民收支指标的调查范围和口径均存在较大变化。原“城市居民人均可支配收入”调整为“城镇居民人均可支配收入”；原“农民人均纯收入”调整为“农村居民人均可支配收入”。

Brief Introduction

I. Main Content

This section mainly reflects the residents' household income and expenditure, housing, household consumption structure, quantity of durable consumer goods possessed and other information.

II. Source of Data

(1)The information contained on this section on urban and rural households comes from the annual report on the integrated survey of income and expenditure of residents in Qingdao, provided by the Household Survey Department of National Bureau of Statistics Qingdao Survey Office.

(2)From 2015 on, the data used are statistics of the integrated survey of residents in urban and rural areas across Qingdao. Compared with previous data, there is a significant change in statistic coverage and gauge for indicators of urban and rural residents' income and expenditure. The 'per capita disposable income of residents in cities' was changed to 'per capita disposable income of urban residents'; the 'per capita net income of farmers' was changed to 'per capita disposable income of rural residents.

10－1 城市居民收支(1978—2014 年)
INCOME AND EXPENDITURE OF URBAN RESIDENTS (1978－2014)

年份 Year	城市居民人均可支配收入(元) Annual Per Capita Disposable Income of Urban Households(yuan)	城市居民人均消费性支出(元) Per Capita Consumption Expenditure of Urban Households(yuan)	城市恩格尔系数(%) Engel coefficient (%)
1978	336	321	
1979	380	360	
1980	537	495	
1981	500	490	57.8
1982	528	484	61.6
1983	549	510	63.7
1984	665	580	62.8
1985	733	681	58.6
1986	882	806	59.2
1987	1 089	996	58.1
1988	1 225	1 278	55.9
1989	1 455	1 439	57.8
1990	1 624	1 507	58.4
1991	1 856	1 767	57.4
1992	2 138	1 956	57.0
1993	2 668	2 445	51.8
1994	3 880	3 479	53.2
1995	5 357	4 606	52.5
1996	5 602	5 079	51.8
1997	6 222	5 525	48.2
1998	6 554	5 565	46.4
1999	7 282	5 981	44.5
2000	8 016	6 677	42.5
2001	8 731	6 849	41.9
2002	8 721	7 344	40.5
2003	10 075	8 056	39.3
2004	11 089	9 002	38.0
2005	12 920	9 883	37.6
2006	15 328	11 945	36.4
2007	17 856	13 376	37.0
2008	20 464	14 999	37.4
2009	22 368	16 080	38.5
2010	24 998	17 531	37.4
2011	28 567	19 297	37.5
2012	32 145	20 391	36.5
2013	35 227	22 060	36.5
2014	38 294	24 016	35.7

注:2002 年开始城市居民可支配收入为新计算口径。

Note: From 2002 on, disposable income of urban residents are counted by new gauges.

10 -2 农村居民收支(1978—2014 年)
INCOME AND EXPENDITURE OF RURAL RESIDENTS(1978 -2014)

年份 Year	农民人均纯收入(元) Annual Per Capita Net Income of Rural Households(yuan)	农村居民人均生活消费支出(元) Per Capita Consumption Expenditure of Rural Households(yuan)	农村恩格尔系数(%) Engel coefficient (%)
1978	146	109	59.3
1979	153	129	58.4
1980	209	142	54.9
1981	218	163	44.3
1982	273	199	52.9
1983	399	277	52.8
1984	452	304	50.0
1985	567	376	47.8
1986	647	474	46.4
1987	730	462	42.9
1988	820	439	38.8
1989	876	510	38.9
1990	952	494	41.5
1991	1 021	546	41.3
1992	1 029	572	41.7
1993	1 255	743	42.7
1994	1 694	1 384	54.5
1995	2 225	1 641	55.7
1996	2 625	2 173	50.5
1997	2 599	2 150	52.9
1998	3 177	2 119	49.5
1999	3 415	2 150	47.3
2000	3 637	2 380	43.2
2001	3 901	2 618	41.2
2002	4 195	2 820	38.9
2003	4 530	2 988	38.0
2004	5 080	3 353	38.7
2005	5 806	3 737	37.5
2006	6 546	4 203	36.6
2007	7 477	4 736	37.2
2008	8 509	5 303	37.7
2009	9 249	5 832	36.4
2010	10 550	6 662	35.5
2011	12 370	7 661	36.6
2012	13 990	8 653	36.2
2013	15 731	9 786	34.9
2014	17 461	10 808	33.8

10 -3 城乡居民住房面积(1990—2014 年)
HOUSING AREA OF URBAN AND RURAL RESIDENTS(1990 - 2014)

年份 Year	城市居民人均现住房建筑面积(平方米) Per Capita Home Floor Area of Urban Residents (square meter)	农村居民人均居住面积(平方米) Per Capita Housing Area of Rural Residents (square meter)
1990	14.16	19.60
1995	17.12	23.03
2000	20.76	25.88
2001	21.86	26.59
2002	22.76	27.00
2003	23.73	27.00
2004	24.22	27.99
2005	22.96	29.54
2006	23.73	30.82
2007	23.72	30.95
2008	26.83	30.73
2009	26.71	31.39
2010	27.42	30.97
2011	27.67	31.73
2012	27.86	32.32
2013	29.12	33.50
2014	29.80	34.20

10－4 全体居民家庭基本情况(2015 年)
BASIC INFORMATION ON ALL HOUSEHOLDS (2015)

指标名称	Name	单位	Unit	2015	2014	2015 年比 2014 年增长(±%) 2015/2014(±%)
人均可支配收入	**Per Capita Disposable Income**	元	**yuan**	**32 885**	**30 273**	**8.6**
(一)工资性收入	Income from Wages and Salaries	元	yuan	20 068	18 348	9.4
(二)经营性净收入	Net Income from Household Operations	元	yuan	6 480	6 035	7.4
(三)财产性收入	Income from Properties	元	yuan	2 522	2 396	5.2
(四)转移性收入	Income from Transfers	元	yuan	3 815	3 494	9.2
人均消费支出	**Per Capita Consumption Expenditure**	元	**yuan**	**21 326**	**19 653**	**8.5**
(一)食品烟酒	Food, Tobacco and Liquor	元	yuan	6 459	5 970	8.2
(二)衣着	Clothing	元	yuan	2 096	1 944	7.8
(三)居住	Residence	元	yuan	4 584	4 316	6.2
(四)生活用品及服务	Household Facilities, Articles and Services	元	yuan	1 485	1 374	8.1
(五)交通通信	Transportation and Communication	元	yuan	3 226	2 905	11.0
(六)教育文化娱乐	Education, Cultural and Recreation Services	元	yuan	1 830	1 654	10.6
(七)医疗保健	Health Care and Medical Services	元	yuan	1 115	1 002	11.2
(八)其他用品和服务	Other Goods and Services	元	yuan	531	488	8.8
城镇居民人均现住房建筑面积	**Per Capita Building Space in Urban Areas**	平方米	**sq. m**	**31.5**		
农村居民人均现住房建筑面积	**Per Capita Living Space in Rural Areas**	平方米	**sq. m**	**32.4**		

注:自 2015 年开始,全市城乡住户调查统一使用一体化改革后的数据,与原数据相比,城乡居民收支指标的调查范围和口径均存较大变化。原"城市居民人均可支配收入"调整为"城镇居民人均可支配收入";原"农民人均纯收入"调整为"农村居民人均可支配收入"。2014 年数据也为新口径,与去年年鉴数据不一致。2014 年农村居民住房为拥有面积,2015 年为现住房建筑面积。

Note: From 2015 on, the data used are statistics of the integrated survey of residents in urban and rural areas. Compared with previous data, there is a significant change in statistic coverage and gauge for indicators of urban and rural residents' income and expenditure. The 'per capita disposable income of residents in cities was changed to 'per capita disposable income of urban residents'; the 'per capita net income of farmers' was changed to 'per capita disposable income of rural residents. Data in 2014 are counted by new gauge and they are different from the data in last year's yearbook. As for the statistics of rural resident homes, the owned house area was taken in 2014, but in 2015, the construction area was counted.

10－5 城镇居民家庭基本情况（2015 年）

BASIC CONDITIONS OF URBAN HOUSEHOLDS(2015)

单位：元(yuan)

指标名称	Name	2015	2014	2015 年比 2014 年增长(±%) 2015/2014(±%)
人均可支配收入	**Per Capita Disposable Income**	**40 370**	**37 346**	**8.1**
（一）工资性收入	Income from Wages and Salaries	25 040	23 034	8.7
（二）经营性净收入	Net Income from Household Operations	6 277	5 818	7.9
（三）财产性收入	Income from Properties	3 580	3 436	4.2
（四）转移性收入	Income from Transfers	5 473	5 058	8.2
人均消费支出	**Per Capita Consumption Expenditure**	**26 052**	**24 122**	**8.0**
（一）食品烟酒	Food, Tobacco and Liquor	7 856	7 295	7.7
（二）衣着	Clothing	2 685	2 497	7.5
（三）居住	Residence	5 607	5 302	5.8
（四）生活用品及服务	Household Facilities, Articles and Services	1 819	1 686	7.9
（五）交通通信	Transportation and Communication	3 810	3 455	10.3
（六）教育文化娱乐	Education, Cultural and Recreation Services	2 264	2 057	10.0
（七）医疗保健	Health Care and Medical Services	1 352	1 227	10.2
（八）其他用品和服务	Other Goods and Services	659	603	9.3

注：本表数据为新口径，2014 年与去年年鉴数据不一致。

Note: Data in this table are measured by new gauge and they are different from the figures in last year's yearbook.

10-6 农村居民家庭基本情况(2015年)
BASIC CONDITIONS OF RURAL HOUSEHOLDS(2015)

单位:元(yuan)

指标名称	Name	2015	2014	2015年比2014年增长(±%) 2015/2014(±%)
人均可支配收入	**Per Capita Disposable Income**	**16 730**	**15 434**	**8.4**
(一)工资性收入	Income from Wages and Salaries	9 337	8 517	9.6
(二)经营性净收入	Net Income from Household Operations	6 919	6 489	6.6
(三)财产性收入	Income from Properties	236	216	9.3
(四)转移性收入	Income from Transfers	238	212	12.4
人均消费支出	**Per Capita Consumption Expenditure**	**11 127**	**10 277**	**8.3**
(一)食品烟酒	Food, Tobacco and Liquor	3 442	3 188	8.0
(二)衣着	Clothing	826	784	5.3
(三)居住	Residence	2 377	2 248	5.8
(四)生活用品及服务	Household Facilities, Articles and Services	765	720	6.2
(五)交通通信	Transportation and Communication	1 965	1 751	12.2
(六)教育文化娱乐	Education, Cultural and Recreation Services	895	809	10.6
(七)医疗保健	Health Care and Medical Services	604	532	13.5
(八)其他用品和服务	Other Goods and Services	253	245	3.3

注:本表数据为新口径,2014年与去年年鉴数据不一致。

Note: Data in this table are measured by new gauge and they are different from the figures in last year's yearbook.

10－7 全体居民家庭消费构成
HOUSEHOLD CONSUMPTION STRUCTURE

项　目	Item	2015		2014	
		年人均支出金额(元) Per Capita Annual Expenditure(yuan)	占消费支出的比重(%) Percentage to Consumption Expenditure(%)	年人均支出金额(元) Per Capita Annual Expenditure(yuan)	占消费支出的比重(%) Percentage to Consumption Expenditure(%)
消费支出	**Consumption Expenditure**	**21 326**	**100**	**19 653**	**100**
(一)食品烟酒	Food, Tobacco and Liquor	6 459	30.3	5 970	30.4
(二)衣着	Clothing	2 096	9.8	1 944	9.9
(三)居住	Residence	4 584	21.5	4 316	21.9
(四)生活用品及服务	Household Facilities, Articles and Services	1 485	7.0	1 374	7.0
(五)交通通信	Transportation and Communication	3 226	15.1	2 905	14.8
(六)教育文化娱乐	Education, Cultural and Recreation Services	1 830	8.6	1 654	8.4
(七)医疗保健	Health Care and Medical Services	1 115	5.2	1 002	5.1
(八)其他用品和服务	Other Goods and Services	531	2.5	488	2.5

10 -8 城镇居民家庭消费构成
COMPOSITION OF URBAN HOUSEHOLDS CONSUMPTION

项 目	Item	2015		2014	
		年人均支出金额(元) Per Capita Annual Expenditure(yuan)	占消费支出的比重(%) Percentage to Consumption Expenditure(%)	年人均支出金额(元) Per Capita Annual Expenditure(yuan)	占消费支出的比重(%) Percentage to Consumption Expenditure(%)
消费支出	**Consumption Expenditure**	**26 052**	**100**	**24 122**	**100**
(一)食品烟酒	Food,Tobacco and Liquor	7 856	30.2	7 295	30.2
(二)衣着	Clothing	2 685	10.3	2 497	10.4
(三)居住	Residence	5 607	21.5	5 302	22.0
(四)生活用品及服务	Household Facilities, Articles and Services	1 819	7.0	1 686	7.0
(五)交通通信	Transportation and Communication	3 810	14.6	3 455	14.3
(六)教育文化娱乐	Education,Cultural and Recreation Services	2 264	8.7	2 057	8.5
(七)医疗保健	Health Care and Medical Services	1 352	5.2	1 227	5.1
(八)其他用品和服务	Other Goods and Services	659	2.5	603	2.5

10 -9 农村居民家庭消费构成
COMPOSITION OF RURAL HOUSEHOLDS CONSUMPTION

项　目	Item	2015		2014	
		年人均支出金额(元) Per Capita Annual Expenditure(yuan)	占消费支出的比重(%) Percentage to Consumption Expenditure(%)	年人均支出金额(元) Per Capita Annual Expenditure(yuan)	占消费支出的比重(%) Percentage to Consumption Expenditure(%)
消费支出	**Consumption Expenditure**	**11 127**	**100**	**10 277**	**100**
(一)食品烟酒	Food,Tobacco and Liquor	3 442	30.9	3 188	31.0
(二)衣着	Clothing	826	7.4	784	7.6
(三)居住	Residence	2 377	21.4	2 248	21.9
(四)生活用品及服务	Household Facilities, Articles and Services	765	6.9	720	7.0
(五)交通通信	Transportation and Communication	1 965	17.7	1 751	17.0
(六)教育文化娱乐	Education,Cultural and Recreation Services	895	8.0	809	7.9
(七)医疗保健	Health Care and Medical Services	604	5.4	532	5.2
(八)其他用品和服务	Other Goods and Services	253	2.3	245	2.4

10-10 城市住户每百户家庭主要耐用品拥有量(1980-2015年)
OWNERSHIP OF MAJOR DURABLE CONSUMER GOODS PER 100 URBAN HOUSEHOLDS(1980-2015)

年份 Year	家用电脑(台) Computer (set)	钢琴(架) Piano (set)	空调器(台) Air Conditioner (set)	淋浴热水器(台) Water Heater (set)	洗衣机(台) Washing Machine (set)	电冰箱(台) Refrigerator (set)	家用汽车(辆) Automobile (unit)	彩色电视机(台) Color TV (set)	移动电话(部) Cell Phone (unit)	照相机(架) Camera (set)
1980										2.0
1981					12.0			1.0		2.0
1982					22.0			2.0		4.0
1983					27.0	1.0		6.0		6.0
1984					30.0	2.0		8.0		8.0
1985					35.5	3.5		17.5		13.5
1986					40.0	4.5		24.5		15.0
1987					51.5	18.0		33.5		17.5
1988					60.5	33.0		47.0		20.5
1989					67.0	50.0		59.0		22.0
1990					66.0	62.0		68.0		26.0
1991					70.0	76.0		82.0		33.0
1992		1.0		12.5	72.5	83.0		81.0		38.5
1993		2.0	0.5	18.0	82.5	85.5		87.5		49.5
1994		4.0	1.0	17.0	81.0	88.5		92.0		51.0
1995		4.0	3.0	33.5	81.5	89.0		100.0		60.5
1996		4.5	6.5	39.5	83.0	91.5		105.0		63.0
1997	1.0	4.5	9.0	46.5	83.0	93.0		110.5	2.5	63.0
1998	8.3	5.3	16.5	53.0	83.0	91.8		110.8	6.8	69.4
1999	10.5	3.8	21.8	61.3	83.0	93.5		117.3	15.0	68.5
2000	19.3	2.0	24.5	65.8	83.3	94.3		120.0	30.3	69.5
2001	20.0	2.3	24.3	65.8	84.0	92.8		127.5	36.0	68.5
2002	31.5	2.3	38.3	75.3	89.3	93.0	0.5	123.3	80.0	72.8
2003	40.8	3.3	47.5	76.3	90.5	92.8	0.3	124.8	105.5	70.0
2004	46.0	3.0	55.0	79.0	92.5	92.5	2.0	123.5	128.0	68.3
2005	55.0	4.3	69.3	83.8	91.8	94.8	3.8	118.3	152.8	72.3
2006	71.3	7.8	89.3	88.0	97.3	98.5	6.3	124.5	187.0	81.8
2007	75.4	7.4	98.3	93.3	99.8	106.7	7.9	121.8	193.8	82.9
2008	75.0	5.0	93.8	90.3	94.5	102.8	12.8	116.0	190.8	67.0
2009	81.8	6.5	98.3	90.5	96.3	105.0	18.0	117.5	199.0	70.8
2010	86.0	7.5	99.3	90.8	97.3	106.8	20.3	118.5	207.5	71.0
2011	95.0	8.0	103.0	91.5	98.0	108.3	22.0	117.3	218.8	76.5
2012	100.8	9.0	103.5	92.8	97.5	108.0	28.5	115.0	230.5	78.8
2013	105.0	10.0	104.0	93.0	98.0	107.0	32.0	118.0	232.0	79.0
2014	105.0	10.0	104.0	98.0	99.0	105.0	34.0	109.0	235.0	79.0
2015	80.0	9.0	91.0	91.0	91.0	94.0	50.0	101.0	215.0	57.0

10-11 农村住户每百户家庭主要耐用品拥有量(1985-2015年)

OWNERSHIP OF MAJOR DURABLE CONSUMER GOODS PER 100 RURAL HOUSEHOLDS(1985-2015)

年份 Year	家用电脑(台) Computer (unit)	空调器(台) Air Conditioner (unit)	热水器(台) Water Heater (unit)	自行车(辆) Bicycle (unit)	洗衣机(台) Washing Machine (unit)	电冰箱(台) Household Refrigerator (unit)	彩色电视机(台) Color TV Set (unit)	移动电话(部) Cell Phone (unit)	照相机(架) Camera (unit)	家用汽车(辆) Automobile (unit)
1985				147	0.3		3		1	
1986				165	1.1	0.3	4.5		1	
1987				148	2.4	0.5	7		2	
1988				154	2.4	1	9		2	
1989				170	3	1	12		2	
1990				164	4	2	13		2	
1991				173	5	4	16		2	
1992				178	5	7	20		2	
1993				203	7	14	26		2	
1994				204	9	21	35		7	
1995				203	16	28	43		6	
1996				198	13	33	46		8	
1997				191	15	36	56		13	
1998				184	17	39	63		15	
1999				185	20	42	74		10	
2000				165	28	47	86		13	
2001				153	28	53	92		13	
2002				152	36	58	98		16	
2003	6	5	33	137	39	60	100	45	16	2
2004	8	8	39	142	48	68	105	68	21	2
2005	14	14	53	138	57	77	109	91	21	5
2006	17	15	54	116	63	87	112	114	14	7
2007	19	19	63	118	70	94	113	132	17	8
2008	25	23	68	124	76	97	114	148	19	9
2009	28	25	71	127	79	99	115	160	21	11
2010	34	30	75	128	82	102	117	170	21	12
2011	44	32	76	114	85	100	112	202	18	15
2012	55	37	85	119	91	102	114	216	21	16
2013	61	45	88	111	93	105	116	221	26	23
2014	61	49	85		93	102	106	225	24	26
2015	46	54	86		92	105	110	219	21	41

主要统计指标解释

常住人员 指住户成员中,经常在家居住、或者调查期内居住时间超过一半的人员,以及本住户供养的学生。

可支配收入 指调查户在调查期内获得的、可用于最终消费支出和储蓄的总和,即调查户可以用来自由支配的收入。可支配收入既包括现金,也包括实物收入。按照收入的来源,可支配收入包含四项,分别为:工资性收入、经营净收入、财产净收入和转移净收入。计算公式为:

可支配收入 = 工资性收入 + 经营净收入 + 财产净收入 + 转移净收入

居民人均可支配收入是按居民家庭常住人口计算的平均每人可支配收入。

消费支出 指住户用于满足家庭日常生活消费需要的全部支出。根据用途不同,消费支出可划分为食品烟酒、衣着、居住、生活用品及服务、交通通信、教育文化娱乐、医疗保健、其他用品及服务八大类。根据来源不同,消费支出可划分为现金消费支出、实物消费支出(含自产自用、来自单位、来自政府和其他社会组织)。

Explanatory Notes on Main Statistical Indicators

Permanent resident(s) refer to the member(s) of household(s) who often live at home or reside at the household(s) for more than half the time of the survey period during the survey period or the student(s) who are supported by the household(s).

Disposable income is the sum of spending and savings which were obtained by a household surveyed during the survey period which can be used for final consumption, that is the income which can be freely disposed of by the household. Disposable income, including cash and income in kind. By source of income, disposable income includes four items, namely, salary income, net operating income, net income from property and net transfer income, its calculating formula is:

Disposable income = Salary income + Net operating income + Net income from property + Net transfer income

The per capita disposable income of residents means the average disposable income per capita based on the permanent resident population of households.

Consumer spending refers to all expenditures a household spends to meet its daily consumption needs. By purposes, consumer spending is classified in eight categories, namely, food, tobacco and liquor, clothing, housing, daily necessities and services, transportation and communication, education, culture and entertainment, medical and health care, other product and services. By sources, consumer spending can be classified into consumer spending in cash and consumer spending in kind (including those produced for self-use, from organizations, from governments and other social organizations).

11 农 业

AGRICULTURE

简要说明

一、本篇资料的主要内容

本篇资料主要反映了全市农业生产和农村经济的基本情况，主要包括农林牧渔业总产值、中间消耗、增加值、农村劳动力、耕地、主要农产品产量、农业机械年末拥有量、农业机械化和电气化以及农田水利建设等方面的资料。

二、本篇资料的来源

1、本篇资料中耕地面积资料来源于市国土资源房屋管理局。

2、水产品产量等相关资料来源于市海洋与渔业局。

3、农业机械化等相关资料来源于市农机局。

4、农田水利灌溉等相关资料来源于市水利局。

5、植树造林等相关资料来源于市林业局。

本篇资料由市统计局农村统计处、国家统计局青岛调查队农村调查处整理提供。

Brief Introduction

I. Main Content

Data in this chapter show the basic conditions of agricultural production and rural economy, mainly including agricultural output, intermediate consumption, value added, rural labor force, cultivated land, output of main agricultural produces, agricultural machinery and electrification in rural areas and basic construction on irrigation and drainage.

II. Source of Data

(1)Data on area of cultivated land are provided by Qingdao Municipal Bureau of Land Resources and Housing Management.

(2)Data on output of aquatic products are provided by Qingdao Municipal Bureau of Ocean and Fishery.

(3)Data on Agricultural machinery are provided by Qingdao Municipal Bureau of Agricultural Machinery.

(4)Data on farmland water conservancy are provided by Qingdao Municipal Bureau of Water Conservancy.

(5)Data on forest planting are provided by Qingdao Municipal Forestry Bureau.

Data in this chapter are compiled by the Division of Countryside Statistics of Qingdao Municipal Bureau of Statistics and Division of Rural Household Survey of Survey Office of the National Bureau of Statistics in Qingdao.

11 -1 农村基本情况(2000 -2015 年)
BASIC STATISTICS ON RURAL AREA(2000 - 2015)

项目	Item	单位	Unit	2000	2005	2006	2007	2008	2009
一、乡村户数、人口、劳动力	**Rural Households, Population and Labor Force**								
乡村户数	Rural Households	万户	10000 households	148.20	151.06	151.1	151.19	151.75	152
乡村人口	Rural Population	万人	10000 persons	483.39	478.78	478.32	478.06	480.22	485
乡村劳动力	Rural Labor Force	万人	10000 persons	254.62	257.87	264.7	268.31	270.71	275
男劳动力	Male	万人	10000 persons	137.09	137.66	141.27	144.04	144.36	146
女劳动力	Female	万人	10000 persons	117.53	120.21	123.43	124.27	126.35	129
二、年末实有耕地面积	**Year-end Area of Cultivated Land**	**万公顷**	**10000 hectares**	**47.75**	**42.1**	**41.29**	**41.31**	**41.79**	**41.87**
三、农用机械总动力	**Total Agricultural Machinery Power**	**万千瓦**	**10000 kW**	**459.21**	**619.69**	**650.65**	**680.16**	**697.38**	**719**
拖拉机	Tractors	台	unit	126 981	163 032	171 155	173 326	176 156	180 171
四、农村用电量	**Electricity Consumed in Rural Areas**	**万千瓦时**	**10000 kW·h**	**189 651**	**372 645**	**413 762**	**425 715**	**424 292**	**426 306**
五、农用化肥施用量(折纯)	**Consumption of Chemical Fertilizer (convert to pure amount)**	**万吨**	**10000 tons**	**32.53**	**33.01**	**32.64**	**33.89**	**31.05**	**30**
六、有效灌溉面积	**Irrigated Area**	**万公顷**	**10000 hectares**	**29.52**	**29.65**	**30.31**	**30.58**	**31.39**	**32**

11－1 续表
continued

项目	Item	单位	Unit	2010	2011	2012	2013	2014	2015
一、乡村户数、人口、劳动力	**Rural Households, Population and Labor Force**								
乡村户数	Rural Households	万户	10000 households	155	155	156	155	157	155
乡村人口	Rural Population	万人	10000 persons	487	489	491	491	494	495
乡村劳动力	Rural Labor Force	万人	10000 persons	276	277	277	277	277	275
男劳动力	Male	万人	10000 persons	147	147	146	147	147	145
女劳动力	Female	万人	10000 persons	129	131	130	131	130	130
二、年末实有耕地面积	**Year-end Area of Cultivated Land**	**万公顷**	**10000 hectares**			**52.81**	**52.55**	**52.42**	**52.22**
三、农用机械总动力	**Total Agricultural Machinery Power**	**万千瓦**	**10000 kW**	**764**	**784**	**798**	**809**	**827**	**854**
拖拉机	Tractors	台	unit	200 208	202 022	206 290	206 300	205 065	207 809
四、农村用电量	**Electricity Consumed in Rural Areas**	**万千瓦时**	**10000 kW·h**	**426 819**	**431 646**	**426 815**	**359 139**	**404 380**	**401 122**
五、农用化肥施用量(折纯)	**Consumption of Chemical Fertilizer (convert to pure amount)**	**万吨**	**10000 tons**	**30**	**29**	**29**	**29**	**29**	**28**
六、有效灌溉面积	**Irrigated Area**	**万公顷**	**10000 hectares**	**33**	**33**	**33**	**30**	**32**	**32**

11 -2 农村劳动力(1985 -2015 年)
RURAL LABOR FORCE(1985 -2015)

单位:万人(10 000 persons)

年份 Year	合计 Total	农林牧渔业 Farming, Forestry, Animal Husbandry and Fishery	工业 Industry	建筑业 Construction
1985	225.09	147.89	32.92	15.62
1988	238.93	146.00	44.46	17.51
1989	242.70	151.16	44.65	16.46
1990	247.29	155.20	44.48	16.17
1991	253.01	160.31	45.49	15.87
1992	258.23	160.04	47.00	17.25
1993	259.18	159.22	44.04	20.20
1994	258.34	155.74	43.70	21.52
1995	258.66	154.08	44.06	22.33
1996	256.34	151.10	43.08	21.80
1997	258.60	153.07	41.66	22.02
1998	258.50	152.79	40.79	21.68
1999	256.82	149.11	42.18	22.32
2000	254.62	143.59	42.76	22.99
2001	253.98	132.46	47.76	24.66
2002	254.08	119.98	53.66	26.52
2003	257.67	118.27	55.65	26.65
2004	258.91	112.05	60.32	28.36
2005	257.87	103.03	65.59	29.03
2006	264.70	102.28	71.46	28.16
2007	268.31	100.63	74.70	30.97
2008	270.71	100.90	74.82	30.87
2009	274.74	102.64	75.42	31.23
2010	276.04	102.45	76.32	32.10
2011	277.24	102.73	76.87	32.57
2012	276.97	102.24	76.82	32.36
2013	277.32	104.48	76.42	31.15
2014	276.90			
2015	274.77			

11-2 续表
continued

单位:万人(10 000 persons)

年 份 Year	交通运输仓储和邮政业 Transport, Postal and Telecommunication Services	批发零售贸易、餐饮业 Wholesale and Retail Trades and Catering Services	金融保险业 Finance and Insurance	其他劳动力 Other Labor Force
1985	5.23	0.06	19.76	3.61
1988	5.89	0.09	20.40	4.58
1989	6.00	0.12	19.95	4.36
1990	6.11	0.12	20.71	4.50
1991	6.09	0.13	20.52	4.60
1992	7.02	0.16	21.74	5.02
1993	8.93	0.16	20.65	5.98
1994	6.48	10.10		20.80
1995	7.11	10.71		20.37
1996	7.33	11.78		21.25
1997	7.62	12.40		21.83
1998	8.02	13.32		21.90
1999	8.19	14.03		20.99
2000	8.39	16.10		20.79
2001	9.02	17.80		22.28
2002	10.00	20.07		23.85
2003	9.96	20.60		26.54
2004	10.20	24.08		22.96
2005	10.70	25.88		22.34
2006	11.66	25.31		24.37
2007	11.61	27.61		21.16
2008	11.06	28.76		22.09
2009	11.40	29.03		22.75
2010	11.78	28.85		22.01
2011	11.89	29.34		21.02
2012	11.96	29.56		21.11
2013	11.92	29.48		20.33
2014				
2015				

11－3 分市、区乡村户数、人口、劳动力(2015 年)
RURAL HOUSEHOLDS, POPULATION AND LABOR FORCE BY REGION(2015)

市、区名称	Region	乡村户数(万户) Rural Households (10000 households)	乡村人口(万人) Rural Population (10000 persons)	乡村劳动力(万人) Labor Force of Village (10000 persons)	男劳动力 Male Laborer	女劳动力 Female Laborer	#种植业 Planting
全　市	**Whole Municipality**	**155.4**	**495.1**	**274.8**	**145.0**	**129.8**	**81.3**
崂山区	Laoshan District	4.5	13.1	7.8	4.1	3.7	1.2
黄岛区	Original Huangdao District	27.4	89.7	45.7	24.3	21.3	10.0
城阳区	Chengyang District	15.6	42.1	22.6	11.7	10.9	1.5
即墨市	Jimo	29.7	99.1	53.7	28.4	25.3	14.1
胶州市	Jiaozhou	19.8	63.7	36.9	19.3	17.6	9.6
平度市	Pingdu	37.8	123.8	71.0	37.6	33.3	28.1
莱西市	Laixi	20.6	63.7	37.2	19.5	17.6	16.8

11－4 主要年份农、林、牧、渔业总产值(按现价计算)

MAJOR YEAR'S GROSS OUTPUT VALUE OF FARMING, FORESTRY, ANIMAL HUSBANDRY AND FISHERY(CURRENT PRICE)

单位:万元(10 000 yuan)

年 份 Year	农、林、牧、渔业总产值 Gross Output Value of Farming, Forestry, Animal Husbandry and Fishery	农业产值 Farming	林业产值 Forestry	牧业产值 Animal Husbandry	渔业产值 Fishery
1949	16 511	14 755	325	1 200	231
1952	24 428	21 353	479	1 888	708
1957	26 189	22 717	644	2 218	610
1962	15 356	13 257	230	1 243	626
1965	25 123	21 488	854	2 110	671
1970	44 078	36 889	1 851	3 817	1 521
1975	93 213	79 208	2 144	7 923	3 938
1978	121 497	94 397	3 112	17 293	6 695
1980	149 436	117 547	2 953	22 215	6 721
1985	299 139	215 729	8 986	53 894	20 530
1987	378 981	263 066	5 949	73 271	36 695
1989	463 952	303 679	19 134	91 885	49 254
1990	579 877	381 287	13 801	119 208	65 581
1991	664 779	417 111	12 875	144 909	89 884
1992	703 433	400 471	15 252	150 942	136 768
1993	989 763	509 601	20 845	232 143	227 174
1994	1 424 074	763 366	23 101	356 734	280 873
1995	1 923 771	1 021 413	26 765	503 999	371 594
1996	2 317 434	1 145 399	29 100	692 362	450 573
1997	2 047 712	939 922	24 052	578 443	505 295
1998	2 386 303	1 198 043	16 760	633 735	537 765
1999	2 382 320	1 169 596	17 122	618 020	577 582
2000	2 483 256	1 116 397	19 102	692 782	654 975
2001	2 615 228	1 135 816	20 433	758 313	700 666
2002	2 688 532	1 110 671	23 157	796 007	758 697
2003	2 759 692	1 062 576	36 183	859 915	801 018
2004	2 967 389	1 181 009	32 831	937 494	816 055
2005	3 205 057	1 265 695	25 246	1 070 831	843 285
2006	3 396 096	1 360 755	23 546	1 076 254	855 131
2007	3 429 877	1 483 733	20 842	975 032	830 479
2008	4 008 540	1 778 404	24 452	1 214 648	856 227
2009	4 086 146	1 856 753	22 264	1 160 558	898 608
2010	4 831 806	2 339 238	19 241	1 264 028	1 051 452
2011	5 359 343	2 365 300	19 237	1 560 108	1 232 720
2012	5 665 217	2 492 493	20 461	1 582 549	1 370 622
2013	6 118 581	2 841 323	22 178	1 640 755	1 394 753
2014	6 300 421	2 998 853	22 620	1 657 075	1 372 771
2015	6 601 353	3 375 921	27 106	1 624 718	1 300 632

11－5 分市、区农、林、牧、渔业总产值(2015 年,现价)
GROSS OUTPUT VALUE OF FARMING,FORESTRY,ANIMAL HUSBANDRY AND FISHERY BY REGION(2015,CURRENT PRICE)

单位:万元(10 000 yuan)

市、区名称	Region	农、林、牧、渔业总产值 Gross Output Value of Farming,Forestry,Animal Husbandry and Fishery	农　业 Farming	林　业 Forestry	牧　业 Animal Husbandry	渔　业 Fishery	服务业 Services
全　市	**Whole Municipality**	**6 601 353**	**3 375 921**	**27 106**	**1 624 718**	**1 300 632**	**272 977**
崂山区	Laoshan District	109 194	9 077	435	6 596	81 051	12 035
黄岛区	Original Huangdao District	1 107 303	483 199	4 240	134 022	436 339	49 503
城阳区	Chengyang District	61 280	21 026	870	20 532	18 759	93
即墨市	Jimo	1 108 338	435 019	4 583	233 061	366 036	69 639
胶州市	Jiaozhou	941 998	495 046	5 008	215 830	180 424	45 690
平度市	Pingdu	1 873 252	1 276 161	5 117	522 240	17 734	52 000
莱西市	Laixi	1 197 222	654 671	6 767	484 431	9 243	42 110
高新区	Hi-tech Area	202 765	1 721	86	8 006	191 045	1 907

注:本表按当年价格计算。
Note:Data in this form are calculated at current price.

11 -6 农、林、牧、渔业总产值、增加值(2015 年)
VALUE-ADDED OF FARMING,FORESTRY,ANIMAL HUSBANDRY AND FISHERY(2015)

单位:万元(10 000 yuan)

		总 计 Total	农 业 Farming	林 业 Forestry	牧 业 Animal Husbandry	渔 业 Fishery	服务业 Services
总产值	**Gross Output Value**	**6 601 353**	**3 375 920**	**27 105**	**1 624 720**	**1 300 631**	**272 977**
中间消耗	**Intermediate Expenditure**	**2 810 756**	**1 316 362**	**12 320**	**866 984**	**492 893**	**122 198**
中间物质消耗	Intermediate Expenditure of Matter	2 031 512	1 004 118	7 040	660 004	300 821	59 529
对非农生产部门的劳动支出	Expenditure of Labor Services to Nonagricultural Production Development	779 244	312 244	5 280	206 980	192 072	62 668

11 -7 分市、区农、林、牧、渔业增加值(2015 年)
VALUE-ADDED OF FARMING,FORESTRY,
ANIMAL HUSBANDRY FISHERY BY REGION(2015)

单位:亿元(100 million yuan)

市、区名称	Region	增加值 Added Value	农 业 Farming	林 业 Forestry	牧 业 Animal Husbandry	渔 业 Fishery	服务业 Services
全 市	**Whole Municipality**	**3 790 597**	**2 059 558**	**14 785**	**757 736**	**807 738**	**150 779**
崂山区	Laoshan District	64 063	5 590	223	2 972	48 873	6 404
黄岛区	Original Huangdao District	644 570	289 385	2 373	62 120	263 110	27 582
城阳区	Chengyang District	34 170	13 036	454	8 942	11 687	51
即墨市	Jimo	639 330	261 053	2 611	108 025	230 233	37 408
胶州市	Jiaozhou	558 232	309 898	2 701	100 145	118 667	26 820
平度市	Pingdu	1 068 524	779 600	2 659	247 284	11 048	27 933
莱西市	Laixi	657 135	399 936	3 719	224 537	5 481	23 462
高新区	Hi-tech Area	124 573	1 060	45	3 711	118 637	1 120

11 -8 主要年份耕地面积与播种面积
MAJOR YEAR'S CULTIVATED AND SOWN AREA

单位:万公顷(10 000 hectares)

年份 Year	年末实有耕地面积 Year - end Area of Cultivated Land	农作物播种面积 Sown Area of Farm Crops	#粮食作物 Grain Crops	经济作物 Economic Crops
1949		93.47	84.00	7.20
1952		97.53	85.07	10.80
1957		97.87	87.07	10.53
1962		81.47	72.53	5.80
1965		82.80	71.80	8.33
1970		80.73	68.27	10.07
1975		79.82	65.84	11.01
1978		77.60	63.60	10.40
1980		75.87	60.33	12.00
1985		78.27	57.33	15.73
1987		76.67	55.87	15.93
1989		74.78	54.28	16.06
1990		76.85	56.99	15.53
1991		76.98	56.89	15.69
1992		76.96	56.37	15.64
1993	56.90	77.75	56.22	15.71
1994		76.61	54.08	16.20
1995		76.54	53.71	15.65
1996	55.01	77.26	54.81	14.90
1997		75.04	52.32	14.40
1998		77.18	53.05	14.54
1999		77.56	50.61	13.24
2000		76.47	45.07	13.98
2001		73.69	41.91	14.54
2002		72.32	40.83	13.95
2003		67.82	36.05	14.50
2004		71.33	41.40	14.11
2005	42.10	75.02	49.93	11.89
2006	41.29	74.86	49.79	11.75
2007	41.31	72.79	47.56	12.11
2008	41.79	74.09	51.06	11.29
2009	41.87	75.00	52.92	11.34
2010		75.39	53.56	11.00
2011		75.70	54.56	10.69
2012	52.81	74.96	54.08	10.69
2013	52.55	70.99	50.04	10.83
2014	52.42	69.96	49.55	9.92
2015	52.22	68.95	49.31	9.19

注:2009 年前由统计局提供。

Note: Those of before 2009 were provided by the National Bureau of Statistics.

11－9 分市、区耕地面积(2015 年)

AREA OF CULTIVATED LAND BY REGION(2015)

单位:万公顷(10 000 hectares)

市、区名称	Region	年末耕地面积 Year-end Area of Cultivated Land	#旱田 Dry Farmland	当年增加的耕地 Area of Cultivated Land Increased in the Year	#新开荒地 Wasteland Newly Opened up
全 市	**Whole Municipality**	**52.22**	**27.58**	**0.0025**	**0.0015**
崂山区	Laoshan District	0.1	0.1		
黄岛区	Original Huangdao District	7.5	7.3		
城阳区	Chengyang District	0.7	0.5		
即墨市	Jimo	10.0	8.7		
胶州市	Jiaozhou	6.5	2.4		
平度市	Pingdu	18.5	1.2	0.0004	
莱西市	Laixi	9.0	7.3	0.0021	0.0015

11－9 续表

continued

单位:公顷(hectare)

市、区名称	Region	当年减少的耕地 Area of Cultivated Land Decreased in the Year	国家基建占地 Government Capital Construction	乡镇集体基建占地 Rural Capital Construction	农民个人建房占地 Private Building
全 市	**Whole Municipality**	**742.2**	**59.2**	**69.1**	**133.9**
崂山区	Laoshan District	1.1	0.6		0.2
黄岛区	Original Huangdao District	279.9	23.8	26.4	20.4
城阳区	Chengyang District	20.9	4.0	3.7	3.4
即墨市	Jimo	147.8	8.6	20.9	70.7
胶州市	Jiaozhou	38.3	6.0	8.2	9.2
平度市	Pingdu	163.2	3.3	5.8	14.1
莱西市	Laixi	78.2	0.1	4.2	15.9

11－10 分市、区农作物播种面积(2015 年)

SOWN AREA OF FARM CROPS BY REGION(2015)

单位:万公顷(10 000 hectares)

市、区名称	Region	总播种面积 Total Sown Area	#粮食 Grain	#棉花 Cotton	#花生 Peanut	#烟叶 Tobacco	#蔬菜 Vegetable
全　市	**Whole Municipality**	**68.95**	**49.31**	**0.14**	**8.20**	**0.03**	**10.45**
崂山区	Laoshan District	0.1	0.02		0.02		0.03
黄岛区	Original Huangdao District	7.8	5.0		1.9	0.03	0.9
城阳区	Chengyang District	0.6	0.4		0.01		0.2
即墨市	Jimo	10.7	8.1		1.5		1.0
胶州市	Jiaozhou	9.6	6.7		0.7		2.1
平度市	Pingdu	27.2	20.1	0.14	2.3		4.3
莱西市	Laixi	13.0	9.0		1.8		2.0

11 -11 分市、区部分农作物产量(2015 年)
OUTPUT OF FARM CROPS BY REGION(2015)

单位:吨(ton)

市、区名称	Region	粮 食 Grain	棉 花 Cotton	花 生 Peanut	烟 叶 Tobacco	蔬 菜 Vegetable
全 市	**Whole Municipality**	**3 214 000**	**2 220**	**345 515**	**817**	**5 790 950**
崂山区	Laoshan District	1 100		542		9 425
黄岛区	Original Huangdao District	252 500		71 316	651	410 013
城阳区	Chengyang District	19 695		114		75 074
即墨市	Jimo	478 000	59	63 268		564 095
胶州市	Jiaozhou	405 205	72	29 893	51	1 120 624
平度市	Pingdu	1 456 500	2 089	102 956	116	2 449 274
莱西市	Laixi	601 000		77 426		1 162 445

11－12 分市、区部分农作物播公顷单产量(2015年)
OUTPUT OF FARM CROPS PER HECTARE BY REGION(2015)

单位:千克(kg)

市、区名称	Region	粮食 Grain	棉花 Cotton	花生 Peanut	烟叶 Tobacco	蔬菜 Vegetable
全　市	**Whole Municipality**	**6 519**	**1 554**	**4 214**	**2 484**	**55 415**
崂山区	Laoshan District	6 111		2 825		34 694
黄岛区	Original Huangdao District	5 036		3 755	2 340	47 327
城阳区	Chengyang District	4 712		2 111		41 708
即墨市	Jimo	5 898	2 475	4 137		58 682
胶州市	Jiaozhou	6 021	2 025	4 334	3 300	53 274
平度市	Pingdu	7 260	1 526	4 478	3 255	56 439
莱西市	Laixi	6 710		4 407		58 941

11－13 主要年份农作物总产量
MAJOR YEAR'S OUTPUT OF FARM CROPS

单位：吨（ton）

年份 Year	粮食 Grain	#小麦 Wheat	#玉米 Corn	棉花 Cotton	花生 Peanut	水果 Fruit	蔬菜 Vegetable
1949	723 190	158 815	25 810	1 280	71 080	9 955	356 015
1952	967 640	200 380	58 130	6 025	115 585	13 468	284 050
1957	921 920	210 690	141 540	3 520	90 445	18 869	625 220
1962	628 930	104 340	53 010	1 280	35 470	8 366	524 455
1965	917 635	180 610	135 595	6 090	88 390	16 034	465 850
1970	1 175 985	243 945	244 530	16 490	96 280	33 907	541 145
1975	1 899 540	430 135	420 095	15 390	98 495	59 206	693 970
1978	1 900 850	514 570	510 635	8 720	114 370	82 819	921 140
1980	2 164 415	520 045	819 930	19 630	160 670	80 840	996 565
1985	2 331 060	961 055	739 455	19 335	475 270	200 515	1 253 075
1987	2 626 029	996 165	1 030 926	13 819	394 296	249 655	1 489 250
1989	2 654 334	993 406	1 084 441	14 638	391 782	288 757	1 664 238
1990	2 998 246	1 265 157	1 210 687	17 490	413 636	292 366	1 786 041
1991	3 180 893	1 421 143	1 285 043	25 965	446 880	294 349	1 837 265
1992	2 675 641	1 235 755	981 490	8 160	321 145	341 415	2 030 327
1993	3 164 812	1 463 759	1 248 780	15 344	419 109	383 368	2 705 349
1994	3 106 562	1 392 977	1 252 952	8 326	494 827	423 024	3 002 318
1995	3 291 587	1 480 385	1 365 167	8 177	510 662	478 685	3 221 507
1996	3 390 033	1 513 479	1 466 668	4 001	486 574	505 711	3 405 056
1997	2 523 064	1 584 478	743 199	2 000	308 233	438 398	3 333 181
1998	3 469 821	1 627 261	1 484 182	4 159	546 786	529 592	4 036 992
1999	3 331 124	1 501 182	1 499 775	3 668	572 941	606 800	5 459 140
2000	2 780 481	1 353 445	1 169 649	2 077	534 174	651 591	6 649 322
2001	2 539 257	1 143 679	1 178 851	3 409	579 441	675 244	6 250 361
2002	2 383 802	1 085 936	1 094 731	3 755	557 714	579 703	6 847 570
2003	2 221 697	931 787	1 117 704	5 324	568 798	677 361	7 305 618
2004	2 650 952	1 301 791	1 202 063	7 216	580 290	748 516	6 720 886
2005	3 150 203	1 535 471	1 478 616	4 042	503 941	737 300	5 792 110
2006	3 039 266	1 548 928	1 372 166	3 954	471 853	827 755	6 051 239
2007	3 007 443	1 395 643	1 497 343	4 330	495 972	793 859	6 157 471
2008	3 336 643	1 620 734	1 620 910	4 173	471 447	806 815	6 118 876
2009	3 539 075	1 727 966	1 723 279	4 529	468 022	820 887	5 679 434
2010	3 514 081	1 646 745	1 795 187	3 952	441 443	803 092	5 807 761
2011	3 630 046	1 653 376	1 906 374	3 917	443 713	805 192	5 838 183
2012	3 699 600			4 301	459 464	798 685	5 697 564
2013	3 223 879	1 518 351	1 658 129	3 429	443 909	749 501	5 754 180
2014	3 230 238	1 520 990	1 667 630	2 467	398 028	751 757	5 953 466
2015	3 214 000	1 535 245	1 636 611	2 220	345 515	1 187 297	5 790 950

11－14 分市、区部分蔬菜产量(2015 年)
PRODUCTION OF SOME VEGETABLES BY CITY AND DISTRICT (2015)

单位:万吨(10 000 tons)

市、区名称	Region	蔬　菜 Vegetable	#大白菜 Cabbage	#芹菜 Celery	#胡萝卜 Carrot	#马铃薯 Potato
全　市	**Whole Municipality**	**5 790 950**	**1 274 303**	**183 604**	**276 404**	**963 669**
崂山区	Laoshan District	9 425	4 342	129	159	2 330
黄岛区	Original Huangdao District	410 013	187 811	21 724	1 033	73 192
城阳区	Chengyang District	75 074	29 807	7 696		2 135
即墨市	Jimo	564 095	186 415	16 803	21 162	70 141
胶州市	Jiaozhou	1 120 624	254 074	11 275	4 169	352 253
平度市	Pingdu	2 449 274	457 910	57 257	88 848	425 306
莱西市	Laixi	1 162 445	153 944	68 720	161 032	38 311

11－14 续表
continued

单位:万吨(10 000 tons)

市、区名称	Region	#黄瓜 Cucumber	#西红柿 Tomato	#大葱 Green onion	#蒜头 Garlic	#食用菌 Edible fungi
全　市	**Whole Municipality**	**384 900**	**390 640**	**613 891**	**165 731**	**8 810**
崂山区	Laoshan District	313	32	71	50	
黄岛区	Original Huangdao District	7 488	36 950	2 622	1 073	2 089
城阳区	Chengyang District	11 648	4 031	624		442
即墨市	Jimo	59 518	18 554	60 745	10 971	2 383
胶州市	Jiaozhou	14 341	12 622	53 883	2 611	
平度市	Pingdu	36 079	109 573	474 833	130 902	3 007
莱西市	Laixi	255 512	208 879	21 113	20 125	888

11－15 分市、区牛头数(2015年)
THE NUMBER OF CATTLE BY CITY AND DISTRICT(2015)

单位:万头(10 000 head)

市、区名称	Region	年末大牲畜头数 Number of Large Livestock (year-end)	牛 Cattle and Buffaloes	#奶 牛 Cows
全 市	**Whole Municipality**	**19.26**	**19.26**	**10.71**
崂山区	Laoshan District	0.01	0.01	0.01
黄岛区	Original Huangdao District	0.91	0.91	0.07
城阳区	Chengyang District	0.51	0.51	0.48
即墨市	Jimo	1.58	1.58	1.20
胶州市	Jiaozhou	1.20	1.20	0.38
平度市	Pingdu	5.41	5.41	0.76
莱西市	Laixi	9.63	9.63	7.80

11－16 分市、区猪、羊及家禽存养量(2015年)
HOGS,SHEEP,GOATS AND POULTRY IN STOCK BY REGION(2015)

单位:万只(10 000 head)

市、区名称	Region	年末生猪存养量 Hogs in Stock (year-end)	年末羊存养量 Sheep and Goats in Stock (year-end)	#山 羊 Goats	家 禽 Poultry
全 市	**Whole Municipality**	**187.3**	**20.3**	**12.6**	**5 268.5**
崂山区	Laoshan District	0.2	0.1	0.1	40.3
黄岛区	Original Huangdao District	32.6	4.6	3.7	304.5
城阳区	Chengyang District	4.4	0.2	0.2	161.8
即墨市	Jimo	22.2	1.1	0.7	840.3
胶州市	Jiaozhou	29.3	3.4	2.2	335.8
平度市	Pingdu	57.5	7.4	2.7	1 525.1
莱西市	Laixi	41.2	3.6	3.2	2 060.7

11－17 分市、区肉、蛋、奶产量(2015 年)
OUTPUT OF MEAT, EGGS AND MILK BY REGION (2015)

单位:万吨(10 000 tons)

市、区名称	Region	肉类产量 Output of Meat	#猪肉 Pork	#牛肉 Beef	#禽肉 Poultry Meat	禽　蛋 Poultry Eggs	牛羊奶 Milk
全　市	**Whole Municipality**	**54.7**	**22.2**	**0.8**	**30.8**	**18.3**	**35.4**
崂山区	Laoshan District	0.1	0.02		0.1	0.4	0.1
黄岛区	Original Huangdao District	6.0	3.9	0.1	1.4	1.3	1.2
城阳区	Chengyang District	0.9	0.6		0.3	1.6	1.4
即墨市	Jimo	6.1	2.5	0.1	3.5	4.3	3.6
胶州市	Jiaozhou	4.6	3.4	0.1	1.1	2.7	1.7
平度市	Pingdu	16.8	6.7	0.3	9.7	3.8	2.9
莱西市	Laixi	20.2	5.1	0.3	14.8	4.3	24.4

11－18 分市、区渔业养殖面积
AQUACULTURE AREA BY REGION

单位:公顷(hectare)

市、区名称	Region	2015			2014		
		养殖面积 Aquaculture Area	#海 水 Seawater	#淡 水 Fresh Water	养殖面积 Aquaculture Area	#海 水 Seawater	#淡 水 Fresh Water
全　市	**Whole Municipality**	**49 028**	**33 255**	**15 773**	**50 088**	**33 829**	**16 259**
崂山区	Laoshan District	1 600	1 600		1 600	1 600	
黄岛区	Original Huangdao District	13 458	11 398	2 060	13 927	11 518	2 409
城阳区	Chengyang District	9 393	7 637	1 756	9 690	7 934	1 756
即墨市	Jimo	12 063	10 889	1 174	12 063	10 889	1 174
胶州市	Jiaozhou	4 332	1 731	2 601	4 332	1 888	2 444
平度市	Pingdu	3 800		3 800	3 800		3 800
莱西市	Laixi	4 382		4 382	4 676		4 676

11－19 分市、区水产品总产量(2015 年)
OUTPUT OF AQUATIC PRODUCTS BY REGION(2015)

单位:吨(ton)

市、区名称	Region	水产品总产量 Output of Aquatic Products	#养殖产量 Aquaculture Output	#捕捞产量 Catch	鱼类 Fish	甲壳类 Crust	贝类 Shellfish	藻类 Algae
全市	**Whole Municipality**	**1 091 278**	**830 614**	**260 664**	**208 200**	**66 574**	**722 550**	**13 693**
崂山区	Laoshan District	73 007	22 014	50 993	21 518	8 570	19 263	3 461
黄岛区	Original Huangdao District	349 495	266 880	82 615	94 666	21 060	201 053	3 800
城阳区	Chengyang District	242 597	210 828	31 769	16 658	2 999	202 704	6 300
即墨市	Jimo	298 318	233 270	65 048	19 396	28 427	234 881	132
胶州市	Jiaozhou	107 673	77 434	30 239	35 821	5 490	64 649	
平度市	Pingdu	10 600	10 600		10 568	28		
莱西市	Laixi	9 588	9 588		9 573			

11－20 分市、区植树及造林面积(2015 年)
AREA OF FORESTATION AND AFFORESTATION BY REGION(2015)

市、区名称	Region	当年造林面积(公顷) Area of Afforestation in the Year(hectare)	育苗面积(公顷) Seedling Area (hectare)	森林抚育作业面积(公顷) Forest Tending Area (hectare)	零星(四旁)植树(万株) Surrounding Tree Planting(10 000 trees)
全市	**Whole Municipality**	**10 070**	**16 090**	**18 720**	**484**
崂山区	Laoshan District	54	120	7 333	1.5
黄岛区	Original Huangdao District	2 133	2 268	667	11
城阳区	Chengyang District	152	632	600	15
即墨市	Jimo	1 667	2 500	1 333	80
胶州市	Jiaozhou	1 735	1 283	467	14.6
平度市	Pingdu	2 316	2 145	8 320	128
莱西市	Laixi	2 013	7 142		234

11 －21 分市、区果园面积、水果总产量(2015 年)
AREA OF ORCHARDS AND OUTPUT OF FRUITS BY REGION(2015)

单位:吨(ton),公顷(hectare)

市、区名称	Region	果园总面积(公顷) Area of Orchards (hectare)	水果总产量(吨) Output of Fruits(ton)	#园林水果 Garden Fruits	#瓜果类水果 Melon Fruits
全　市	**Whole Municipality**	**27 203**	**1 187 297**	**758 675**	**428 622**
崂山区	Laoshan District	598	5 844	5 810	34
黄岛区	Original Huangdao District	5 255	105 962	82 971	22 991
城阳区	Chengyang District	744	14 462	10 802	3 660
即墨市	Jimo	557	60 158	15 397	44 761
胶州市	Jiaozhou	1 403	70 896	44 267	26 629
平度市	Pingdu	10 522	560 908	357 718	203 189
莱西市	Laixi	8 125	369 068	241 711	127 357

11 －21 续表
continued

单位:吨(ton),公顷(hectare)

市、区名称	Region	#苹果 Apple	#梨 Pear	#桃 Peach	#葡萄 Grape	#杏 Apricot	#山楂 Hawthorn	#西瓜 Watermelon	#甜瓜 Muskmelon
全　市	**Whole Municipality**	**444 633**	**72 998**	**68 659**	**123 086**	**8 742**	**3 663**	**281 551**	**114 808**
崂山区	Laoshan District	330	108	2 449	13	1 403	19	17 964	1 001
黄岛区	Original Huangdao District	47 938	4 699	14 343	2 369	299	165		
城阳区	Chengyang District	202	53	4 873	2 864	997	1		
即墨市	Jimo	4 528	477	1 936	1 084	27	215	24 487	1 148
胶州市	Jiaozhou	18 332	4 376	10 617	4 414	5 644	62	32 747	11 557
平度市	Pingdu	220 764	15 205	27 206	80 880	370	1 110	178 115	9 533
莱西市	Laixi	152 539	48 079	7 235	31 461	2	2 090	28 238	91 569

11－22 分市、区果园、茶园面积和茶叶产量(2015 年)

AREA OF ORCHARD AND TEA GARDEN AND PRODUCTION OF TEA BY CITY AND DISTRICT(2015)

单位:公顷(hectare),吨(ton)

市、区名称	Region	果园面积(公顷) Area of Orchards (hectare)	#苹果园 Apple Orchard	#梨园 Pear Orchard	#葡萄园 Vineyard	#桃园 Peach Orchard
全 市	**Whole Municipality**	**27 203**	**12 544**	**2 020**	**4 286**	**4 144**
崂山区	Laoshan District	598	15	7	1	104
黄岛区	Original Huangdao District	5 255	1 359	170	195	1 853
城阳区	Chengyang District	744	10	6	142	280
即墨市	Jimo	557	159	16	84	91
胶州市	Jiaozhou	1 403	408	105	118	396
平度市	Pingdu	10 522	5 731	488	2 635	790
莱西市	Laixi	8 125	4 863	1 228	1 111	628

11－22 续表

continued

单位:公顷(hectare),吨(ton)

市、区名称	Region	茶园面积(公顷) Area of Tea Plantations(hectare)	茶叶产量(吨) Output of Tea(ton)
全 市	**Whole Municipality**	**4 284**	**2 064**
崂山区	Laoshan District	1 198	1 172
黄岛区	Original Huangdao District	2 760	475
城阳区	Chengyang District	83	28
即墨市	Jimo	233	386
胶州市	Jiaozhou		
平度市	Pingdu	9	4
莱西市	Laixi		

11－23 主要年份主要农业机械拥有量

MAJOR YEAR'S OWNERSHIP OF AGRICULTURAL MACHINERY

年　份 Year	农业机械总动力(万千瓦) Total Agricultural Machinery Power (10 000 kW)	农用拖拉机 Agricultural Tractors		大、中型机引农具(万台) Large and Medium Towing Farm Machinery(10 000 sets)	排灌机械 Drainage and Irrigation Machinery	
		混合台 set	千　瓦 kW		台 set	万千瓦 10 000 kW
1949						
1952						
1957	0.22	59	2.2	0.01		
1962	2.47	254	11.47	0.06		
1965	3.49	296	13.2	0.08		
1970	10.40	602	7 963	0.07		
1975	43.94	6 447	103 476	0.48		
1978	75.45	15 576	309 287	1.02		
1980	110.44	24 278	502 731	1.72		
1985	174.76	33 097	506 217	1.71	67 794	54.92
1990	253.52	55 363	680 903	2.03	105 574	74.63
1991	250.58	57 404	691 332	2.20	134 900	73.77
1992	253.94	57 182	684 182	2.28	124 800	82.68
1993	261.24	56 335	678 161	2.34	144 460	78.96
1994	278.41	58 698	688 886	2.39	147 259	80.81
1995	289.23	56 391	657 025	2.28	138 625	73.98
1996	303.57	59 698	680 447	2.32	148 313	81.53
1997	326.72	66 841	744 424	2.42	155 629	88.09
1998	364.21	87 226	894 985	2.48	156 565	86.68
1999	411.44	105 743	1 075 907	3.06	170 875	96.20
2000	459.21	126 981	1 253 210	3.30	182 646	108.26
2001	496.27	141 409	1 394 114	4.33	178 437	104.18
2002	534.92	152 920	1 537 544	4.79	182 799	107.35
2003	560.94	160 676	1 666 185	5.07	192 930	109.44
2004	599	168 061	1 818 276	5	192 144	110
2005	620	163 032	1 757 177	6	188 689	112
2006	651	171 155	1 890 402	6	192 010	116
2007	680	173 326	1 958 047	7	195 050	118
2008	697	176 156	2 034 453	8	208 711	134
2009	719	180 171	2 266 697	9	207 648	134
2010	764	200 208	2 331 867	10	190 770	123
2011	784	202 022	2 649 283	10	189 834	127
2012	798	206 290	2 759 004	10	190 134	127
2013	809	206 309	2 968 332	10	190 433	127
2014	827	205 065	2 960 438	10	190 584	128
2015	854	207 809	3 176 870	10	191 152	128

11 -24 主要年份农业机械化、用电量、化肥施用量

MAJOR YEAR'S MECHANIZATION, ELECTRICITY AND CHEMICAL FERTILIZER CONSUMPTION

年份 Year	有效灌溉面积(公顷) Irrigated Area (hectare)	配套机电井(眼) Number of Electromechanical Well(well)	机耕面积(公顷) Area of Motorized Cultivation (hectare)	机播面积(公顷) Area of Motorized Planting (hectare)	机收面积(公顷) Area of Motorized Harvesting (hectare)	农村用电量(万千瓦时) Electricity Consumption in Rural Area (10 000 kW · h)	化肥施用量(折纯万吨) Chemical Fertilizer Consumption (convert to 10 000 tons)
1949	8 340						
1952	14 980						
1957	59 353		12 800	13			0.19
1962	55 213	191	65 680	927	927	55	0.10
1965	80 000	125	11 433	573	247	128	0.55
1970	147 613	3 947	143 700	2 527	133	1 208	1.76
1975	233 980	12 820	248 867	54 507	953	2 522	2.77
1978	276 660	21 017	329 213	178 533	15 060	13 975	3.64
1980	296 606	22 472	444 800	187 980	55 333	20 492	12.06
1985	302 647	42 925	366 786	148 433	56 447	41 524	11.66
1987	260 800	48 497	410 820	187 680	104 240	58 280	13.87
1989	267 440	61 570	540 413	208 527	107 320	62 859	17.91
1990	274 680	56 821	426 680	220 593	143 133	67 616	20.47
1991	281 500	58 987	431 293	254 266	192 946	81 200	22.53
1992	281 610	62 100	438 533	270 453	207 780	88 024	22.60
1993	284 080	63 954	439 300	260 287	225 807	102 501	28.04
1994	286 750	64 877	436 820	262 846	238 693	121 307	28.73
1995	287 020	64 651	435 213	271 707	250 267	134 284	31.45
1996	289 320	65 237	438 947	280 480	235 933	143 740	31.36
1997	292 130	66 783	442 213	308 267	266 147	150 971	28.99
1998	294 120	64 109	442 920	359 447	285 513	153 113	31.95
1999	294 790	64 734	440 967	396 180	286 367	169 337	32.58
2000	295 190	65 179	439 980	346 480	292 787	189 651	32.53
2001	296 980	65 547	436 576	382 870	265 730	228 069	31.73
2002	294 310	65 588	433 660	364 680	267 690	256 453	31.07
2003	292 410	65 406	415 790	404 980	256 600	299 425	31.89
2004	292 520	65 501	415 220	454 800	314 680	330 609	32.45
2005	296 450	65 303	409 610	493 240	367 740	372 644	33.01
2006	303 070	65 981	403 980	493 750	398 700	413 762	32.64
2007	305 760	66 400	400 480	499 590	429 630	425 715	33.89
2008	313 920	66 828	404 080	517 540	455 120	424 292	31.05
2009	322 710	67 027	404 080	538 220	481 176	426 306	30.17
2010	328 960	67 242		558 611	499 248	426 819	29.89
2011	331 690	62 104		567 947	547 108	431 646	29.37
2012	333 850	62 112	410 440	627 701	566 653	426 815	29.09
2013	302 790	170 008	410 601	627 701	566 653	359 138	29.12
2014	321 670	169 491	411 355	590 798	545 360	404 380	28.94
2015	323 400	155 074	417 991	640 022	600 696	401 122	28.49

11－25 分市、区农业机械化和电气化(2015 年)
MECHANIZATION AND ELECTRIFICATION IN AGRICULTURE BY REGION(2015)

市、区名称	Region	农村用电量（万千瓦小时）Electricity Consumed in Rural Areas (10 000 kW·h)	机耕作业面积（公顷）Area of Motorized Cultivation(hectare)	机播地面积（公顷）Area of Motorized Planting(hectare)	机收面积（公顷）Area of Motorized Harvesting(hectare)
全 市	**Whole Municipality**	**401 122**	**417 991**	**640 022**	**600 696**
崂山区	Laoshan District	12 273			
黄岛区	Original Huangdao District	56 703	51 924	62 011	56 103
城阳区	Chengyang District	48 021	4 639	6 389	4 305
即墨市	Jimo	69 214	71 427	110 816	101 400
胶州市	Jiaozhou	96 578	63 275	98 277	8 953
平度市	Pingdu	80 815	164 330	245 251	240 716
莱西市	Laixi	37 519	62 396	117 278	108 219

11 -26 分市、区农用化肥施用量(2015 年)
CONSUMPTION OF CHEMICAL FERTILIZERS BY REGION(2015)

单位:折纯吨(ton converted to pure amount)

市、区名称	Region	农用化肥施用量 Consumption of Chemical Fertilizers	氮 肥 Nitrogenous Fertilizer	磷 肥 Phosphate Fertilizer	钾 肥 Potash Fertilizer	复合肥 Compound Fertilizer	附:平均每公顷耕地施用化肥量(*) Annotation:Consumption of Chemical Fertilizer Per Hectare
全 市	**Whole Municipality**	**284 923**	**49 657**	**12 643**	**15 594**	**207 028**	**546**
崂山区	Laoshan District	969	196	55	56	662	1 071
黄岛区	Original Huangdao District	35 215	8 386	3 070	4 233	19 526	469
城阳区	Chengyang District	1 446	344	103	103	896	211
即墨市	Jimo	37 495	15 048	2 463	1 158	18 826	374
胶州市	Jiaozhou	37 887	6 438	996	4 385	26 068	587
平度市	Pingdu	121 141	8 383	1 953	5 401	105 404	656
莱西市	Laixi	50 770	10 860	4 005	258	35 646	565

注:(*)单位为[折纯千克]

Note:The(*)mark refers to kilogram converted to pure amount.

11 -27 分市、区农田水利(2015 年)
FARMLAND WATER CONSERVANCY BY REGION(2015)

市、区名称	Region	有效灌溉面积(公顷) Irrigated Area (hectare)	有效灌溉面积占耕地面积比重(%) Percentage of Irrigated Area to Area of Cultivated Land(%)	农业排灌机械拥有量(万台/万千瓦) Ownership of Drainage and Irrigation Machinery (10 000 sets/10 000 kW)	农用水泵(万台) Agricultural Pump (10 000 sets)	喷灌机械(万套) Spraying Irrigation Machinery (10 000 sets)	机电井数(眼) Number of Electromechanical Well (well)
全 市	**Whole Municipality**	**323 400**	**61.9**	**19.1/128**	**14.3**	**8.9**	**155 074**
崂山区	Laoshan District	500	55.2				1 307
黄岛区	Original Huangdao District	41 500	55.2	0.7/6	1.2	0.9	22 247
城阳区	Chengyang District	3 700	54.0	0.6/4	0.4	0.3	1 027
即墨市	Jimo	59 000	58.8	2.1/15	2.1	1.9	17 726
胶州市	Jiaozhou	38 200	59.1	1.4/11	0.8	1.4	35 436
平度市	Pingdu	127 400	69.0	12.5/80	7.4	1.8	50 785
莱西市	Laixi	53 100	59.1	1.8/12	2.4	2.6	26 546

11－28 分市、区主要农业机械拥有量(2015 年)

OWNERSHIP OF MAJOR AGRICULTURAL MACHINERY BY REGION(2015)

市、区名称	Region	农业机械总动力(万千瓦) Agricultural Machinery Power (10 000 kW)	平均每公顷耕地拥有量(千瓦) Power Per Hectare of Cultivated Land(kW)	大中型拖拉机 Large and Medium Tractors		小型拖拉机 Small Tractors	
				台 set	千瓦 kW	台 set	千瓦 kW
全　市	**Whole Municipality**	**854**	**16.4**	**44 402**	**1 805 251**	**163 407**	**1 371 619**
崂山区	Laoshan District						
黄岛区	Original Huangdao District	93	12.4	3 692	105 359	43 414	287 610
城阳区	Chengyang District	34	49.6	443	14 881	1 547	10 639
即墨市	Jimo	133	13.3	7 402	248 486	31 450	259 632
胶州市	Jiaozhou	121	18.7	5 590	278 402	18 377	257 278
平度市	Pingdu	336	18.2	20 875	927 161	33 723	320 365
莱西市	Laixi	137	15.3	6 400	230 962	34 896	236 095

11-28 续表 1
continued

市、区名称	Region	大、中、小播种机（部）Large, Medium and Small Seeders (set)	机引犁（部）Towing Ploughs (unit)	机引耙（部）Towing Rakes (unit)	脱粒机（部）Threshers (unit)
全 市	**Whole Municipality**	**59 504**	**125 639**	**28 868**	**34 564**
崂山区	Laoshan District				
黄岛区	Original Huangdao District	2 060	32 913	1 000	7 300
城阳区	Chengyang District	772	1 200	207	
即墨市	Jimo	12 645	19 952	1 680	6 574
胶州市	Jiaozhou	8 876	15 113	5 242	3 390
平度市	Pingdu	26 850	21 850	16 500	12 000
莱西市	Laixi	8 301	34 611	4 239	5 300

11－28 续表 2
continued

市、区名称	Region	粮食加工机械（台）Grain Processing Machinery(unit)	棉花加工机械（部）Cotton Processing Machinery(unit)	油料加工机械（部）Oil Processing Machinery(unit)	饲料粉碎机（部）Pulverizers (unit)
全　市	**Whole Municipality**	**25 677**	**132**	**9 142**	**23 011**
崂山区	Laoshan District				
黄岛区	Original Huangdao District	1 112		255	3 544
城阳区	Chengyang District	1 605	17	520	338
即墨市	Jimo	3 259		1 472	1 449
胶州市	Jiaozhou	3 050		2 125	3 570
平度市	Pingdu	4 371	6	1 420	7 520
莱西市	Laixi	12 280	109	3 350	6 590

主要统计指标解释

农业总产值　是以货币表现的农、林、牧、渔业全部产品的总量,它反映一定时期内农业生产的总规模和总成果。

农、林、牧、渔业的统计范围是:

(1)农业包括农作物种植业和其他农业。

农作物种植业包括谷物、豆类、薯类、棉、油料、糖料、麻类、烟叶、蔬菜、药材、瓜类和其他农作物的种植,以及茶园、桑园、果园的生产经营。其他农业包括采集野生植物的果实、纤维、树胶、树脂、油料以及柴草、野生药材、菌类等及农民家庭兼营的商品性工业。

(2)林业包括林木的栽培(不包括茶园、桑园和果园的栽培、管理和收获等活动)、林产品的采集和村及村以下合作经济组织和农户的竹木采伐。

(3)牧业包括除渔业养殖以外的一切动物饲养和放牧,以及野生动物的捕猎和饲养。

(4)渔业包括水生动物和海藻类植物的养殖和捕捞。

粮食产量　指稻谷、小麦、玉米、高粱等谷物及薯类和豆类的全社会产量。包括国有经济经营的、集体统一经营的和农民家庭经营的粮食产量,还包括工矿企业办的农场和其他生产单位的产量。其产量计算方法,豆类按去豆荚后的干豆计算;薯类(包括甘薯,不包括芋头和木薯)按 5 公斤鲜薯折 1 公斤粮食计算。城市郊区作为蔬菜的薯类(如马铃薯等)按鲜品计算,并且不作粮食统计。其他粮食一律按脱粒后的原粮计算。

水产品产量　指人工养殖的水产品和天然生长的水产品的捕捞量.包括海水的鱼类、虾蟹类、贝类和藻类以及内陆水域的鱼类、虾蟹类和贝类,不包括淡水生植物。

猪、牛、羊肉产量　指当年出栏并已屠宰、除去头蹄下水后带骨头肉(即胴体重)的重量。其统计范围为全社会。

农用化肥施用量　指本年内实际用于农业生产的化肥数量,包括氮肥、磷肥、钾肥和复合肥。化肥施用量要求按折纯量计算数量。折纯量是指把氮肥、磷肥、钾肥分别按含氮、含五氧化二磷、含氧化钾的百分之百成分进行折算后的数量。复合肥按其所含主要成分折算。

公式:折纯量 = 实物量 × 某种化肥有效成分含量的百分比

农业机械总动力　指用于农、林、牧、渔业生产的各种动力机械的动力总和。动力机械包括耕作、排灌、种植、植物保护、收获、农产品加工、运输、畜牧、渔业、农田水利等各种机械。不包括专门用于乡办工业、基本建设、非农业运输、科学试验和教学等非农业生产方面用的动力机械与作业机械的数量。

Explanatory Notes on Main Statistical Indicators

Gross Output Value of Agriculture　refers to the total volume of products of farming, forestry, animal husbandry, and fishery expressed in the monetary terms. It reflects the overall scale and achievements of agricultural production during a given period of time.

The scope of statistics on farming, forestry, animal husbandry, and fishery are as follows:

(1) Farming includes cultivation of farm crops and other agricultural activities.

Cultivation of farm crops include cultivation of grain crops, legume crops, tuber-crops, cotton, oil-bearing crops, sugar crops, and cultivation and management of tea plantations, mulberry fields and orchards.

Other agricultural activities include harvesting wild fruits, fiber, tree gum, resin, oil-bearing plants, firewood, wild medicinal herbs, fungus, and rural-household commodity industries.

(2) Forestry refers to planting trees of various kinds (excluding tea plantations, mulberry fields and orchards), collection of forestry products and cutting and felling of bamboo and trees by villages and other cooperative organizations under village level.

(3) Animal husbandry refers to raising and grazing of all kinds of farm animals except fishing and aquatic cultivating, and hunting and rising of wild animals.

(4) Fishery refers to cultivation and catching of fish and other aquatic products and cultivation and collection of seaweed and other aquatic plants.

Grain Output refers to the total output of rice, wheat, corn, sorghum, millet and other miscellaneous grains as well as tubers and bean in the whole country including grains produced by states farms, collective unit, industrial enterprises and mines, output of beans refers to dry beans without pods, the output of tubers (sweet potatoes, excluding taros and cassava) was converted into that of grain at the ratio 5∶ 1, i. e. 5 kilograms of fresh tubers was equivalent to 1 kilogram of grain, tubers supplies as vegetable (such as potatoes) in cities and suburbs are calculated as fresh vegetables and their output is not included in the output of grain output of all other grains refers to husked grain.

Output of Aquatic Products refers to catches of both artificially cultured and naturally grown aquatic products, including fish, shrimps, crabs and shellfish in sea and inland water as well as seaweed. Freshwater plants are not included.

Output of Pork, Beef, and Mutton refers to the meat of slaughtered hogs, cattle, sheep and goats with head, feet, and offal taken away. Data refers to the production of the whole country.

Consumption of Chemical Fertilizers in Agriculture refers to the quantity of chemical fertilizers applied in agriculture in the year, including nitrogenous fertilizer, phosphate fertilizer, potash fertilizer, and compound fertilizer. The consumption of chemical fertilizers is required in calculation to convert the gross weight into weight containing 100% effective component (e. g. 100% nitrogen content in nitrogenous fertilizer, 100% phosphorous pent oxide contents in phosphate fertilizer, 100% potassium oxide contents in potash fertilizer). Compound fertilizer is converted with its major component. The formula is:

Volume of effective component = physical quantity × effective component of certain chemical fertilizer (%)

Total Power of Agriculture Machinery Refers to the total mechanical power of machinery used in farming forestry animal husbandry and fishery, including machines used for ploughing, irrigation and drainage, crop growing, plant protection, harvesting, farm product processing, transport, stock breeding, fishery and water conservancy, Machinery employed for non agricultural purposes such as township industry, capital construction, non-agricultural transport, scientific experiments and for teaching is excluded.

12 工业 INDUSTRY

简要说明

一、本篇资料的主要内容

本篇资料主要反映了全市工业生产和基本效益情况，主要包括工业企业单位数、历年工业总产值、规模以上工业、国有控股工业、国有工业、集体工业、外商投资和港澳台投资工业、大中型工业企业的主要经济指标、相关的财务分析指标和主要工业产品产量等方面的内容。

二、本篇资料的来源

1、本篇中规模以上工业资料来源于工业统计年报，由市统计局工业统计处整理提供。

2、规模以下工业资料产值与单位数均来源于抽样调查推算，工业单位数除普查年度外无分市（区）数据，由国家统计局青岛调查队工业与投资建筑业调查处整理提供。

Brief Introduction

I. Main Content

Data in this chapter show the basic condition of industrial production and benefit in Qingdao, mainly including the number of industrial enterprises, gross industrial output value and indices, the output of major industrial products and major economic and relevant financial indicators of industrial enterprises. Industrial enterprises include enterprises above designated size, state share-holding enterprises, state owned enterprises, collective owned enterprises, foreign funded enterprises, enterprises with funds from Hong Kong, Macao and Taiwan, large and medium sized enterprises.

II. Source of Data

(1)Data on industry above designated size are based on the annual report of industrial statistics, and prepared by the Division of Industry Statistics of Qingdao Municipal Bureau of Statistics.

(2)Data on output value and unit number of industry below designated size are based on the sample survey, and there is no data on number of enterprises by region except census year. The Data are complied by the Division of Industry, Investment and Construction Survey of Survey Office of the National Bureau of Statistics in Qingdao.

12 -1 规模以上工业企业单位数
NUMBER OF INDUSTRIAL ENTERPRISES ABOVE DESIGNATEO SIZE

单位:个(unit)

项 目	Item	1985	1990	1995	2000	2005	2006
总 计	**Total**	**2 411**	**2 997**	**4 987**	**1 504**	**3 697**	**4 567**
一、按隶属关系分	**Grouped by Subordination**						
中央工业	Central Industry	24	16	102	18	26	17
省属工业	Provincial Industry	26	22	64	7	37	33
地方工业	Local Industry	2 361	2 959	4 821	1 479	3 634	4 517
二、按经济类型分	Grouped by Economic Types						
国有企业	State-owned	502	568	1 084	179	76	74
集体企业	Collective-owned	1 907	2 386	2 731	226	87	72
其他经济类型企业	Other Economic Types	2	43	1 172	1 099	3 534	4 421
#外商及港澳台商投资企业	Foreign Funded Enterprises and Enterprises with Funds from Hong Kong, Macao and Taiwan		35	1 027	593	1 658	1 952
三、按轻重工业分	Grouped by Light and Heavy Industries						
轻工业	Light Industry	1 398	1 730	2 858	891	1 942	2 313
重工业	Heavy Industry	1 013	1 267	2 129	613	1 755	2 254
四、按企业规模分	Grouped by Size of Enterprises						
大型企业	Large	26	42	89	202	51	51
中型企业	Medium	80	168	216	229	441	469
小型企业	Small	2 305	2 787	4 480	1 073	3 205	4 047
五、按行业分	Grouped by Sectors						
黑色金属矿采选业	Mining of Ferrous Metal Ores		4	6	1	2	5
有色金属矿采选业	Mining of Non-ferrous Metal Ores	2	7	9	7	5	5
非金属矿采选业	Mining and Processing of Nonmetal Ores	43	70	87	29	34	31
食品制造业	Manufacture of Foods	244	324	437	170	121	137
#粮食及饲料加工	Processing of Grain and Feed	62	57	60	27		
饮料制造业	Manufacture of Beverage	31	44	74	23	29	28
#饮料酒	Beverage Liquor	20	28	27	19	20	25

注：1.规模以上工业企业为年主营业务收入2000万元及以上的工业法人企业。
2.2010年以前为国有及年主营业务收入500万元以上的非国有工业企业。
3.本表1998年以前为乡及乡以上工业企业单位数 。
4.2012年行业分类按2011年发布的《国民经济行业分类》(GB/T4754－2011)重新划分。

Note:1. Industrial enterprises above designated size refers to industrial enterprises with revenue from principal business over 20 million yuan.
2. Before 2010, industrial enterprises above designated size refered to all the state-owned enterprises and non-state enterprises with revenue from principal business over 5 million yuan.
3. Before 1998, the number of industial enterprises refer to those at and above county level.
4. The sectors are grouped by "Classification and Code of the Sectors of the National Economy" (GB/T4754 - 2011) in 2012.

12－1 续表1

项　目	Item	2007	2008	2009	2010	2011
总　计	**Total**	**5 032**	**5 628**	**5 895**	**5 674**	**4 727**
一、按隶属关系分	**Grouped by Subordination**					
中央工业	Central Industry	9	40	44	31	31
省属工业	Provincial Industry	34	28	25	25	17
地方工业	Local Industry	4 989	5 560	5 826	5 618	4 679
二、按经济类型分	Grouped by Economic Types					
国有企业	State-owned	63	65	163	61	147
集体企业	Collective-owned	72	61	59	53	31
其他经济类型企业	Other Economic Types	4 897	5 502	5 673	5 560	4 549
#外商及港澳台商投资企业	Foreign Funded Enterprises and Enterprises with Funds from Hong Kong, Macao and Taiwan	2 091	2 217	2 244	2 037	1 618
三、按轻重工业分	Grouped by Light and Heavy Industries					
轻工业	Light Industry	2 489	2 704	2 805	2 635	2 131
重工业	Heavy Industry	2 543	2 924	3 090	3 039	2 596
四、按企业规模分	Grouped by Size of Enterprises					
大型企业	Large	53	48	50	52	50
中型企业	Medium	489	519	502	525	516
小型企业	Small	4 490	5 061	5 343	5 097	4 161
五、按行业分	Grouped by Sectors					
黑色金属矿采选业	Mining of Ferrous Metal Ores	7	23	22	12	12
有色金属矿采选业	Mining of Non-ferrous Metal Ores	5	6	6	4	
非金属矿采选业	Mining and Processing of Nonmetal Ores	33	30	26	26	23
食品制造业	Manufacture of Foods	156	158	174	167	127
#粮食及饲料加工	Processing of Grain and Feed					
饮料制造业	Manufacture of Beverage	33	40	42	42	36
#饮料酒	Beverage Liquor					

12 -1 续表 2
continued

单位:个(unit)

项　目	Item	1985	1990	1995	2000	2005	2006
烟草制品业	Manufacture of Tobacco	2	2	5	3	2	2
纺织业	Manufacture of Textile	169	225	330	132	300	327
纺织服装、鞋、帽制造业	Manufacture of Textile Wearing Apparel, Footware and Caps	171	194	322	95	272	339
皮革、毛皮、羽毛(绒)及其制品业	Manufacture of Leather, Fur, Feather and Related Products	56	64	161	64	167	194
木材加工制品业	Processing of Wood and Wood Products	71	89	116	19	40	53
家具制造业	Manufacture of Furniture	61	72	88	10	72	103
造纸及纸制品业	Manufacture of Paper and Paper Products	66	74	110	56	102	128
印刷业和记录媒介的复制	Printing, Reproduction of Recording Media	61	81	215	23	44	59
文教体育用品制造业	Manufacture of Articles For Culture, Education and Sport Activities	31	27	93	48	89	91
石油加工、炼焦及核燃料加工业	Processing of Petroleum, Coking, Processing of Nuclear Fuel	2	3	13	5	10	6
化学原料及制品	Manufacture of Raw Chemical Materials and Chemical Products	106	156	278	81	178	233
医药制造业	Manufacture of Medicines	16	14	39	20	30	46
化学纤维制造业	Manufacture of Chemical Fibers	2	4	26	15	14	13
橡胶制品业	Manufacture of Rubber	53	57	143	48	116	170
塑料制品业	Manufacture of Plastics	103	131	237	64	153	179
非金属矿物制品业	Manufacture of Non-metallic Mineral Products	230	245	275	62	161	218
黑色金属压延加工业	Smelting and Pressing of Ferrous Metals	11	13	31	15	41	45
有色金属压延加工业	Smelting and Pressing of Non-ferrous Metals	6	8	19	9	28	40
金属制品业	Manufacture of Metal Products	161	186	372	88	186	250
通用设备制造业	Manufacture of General Purpose Machinery	320	398	320	94	299	397
交通运输制造业	Manufacture of Transport Equipment	104	114	358	52	151	194
电气机械及器材制造业	Manufacture of Electrical Machinery and Equipment	86	96	211	79	214	249
通信设备、计算机及其他电子设备制造业	Manufacture of Communication Equipment, Computers and Other Electronic Equipment	32	31	79	34	123	140
仪器仪表及文化、办公用机械制造业	Manufacture of Measuring Instruments and Machinery for Cultural Activity and Office Work	28	33	70	20	40	44
水的生产和供应业	Production and Supply of Water	8	12	12	8	10	10
电力、热力的生产和供应业	Production and Supply of Electric Power and Heat Power	10	16	20	17	27	32
燃气生产和供应业	Production and Supply of Gas	1	4	3	2	5	6
其他工业	Other Industrial Sectors	46	48	209	63	166	534

12－1 续表3
continued

单位:个(unit)

项　目	Item	2007	2008	2009	2010	2011
烟草制品业	Manufacture of Tobacco	2	2	2	1	1
纺织业	Manufacture of Textile	340	330	322	287	229
纺织服装、鞋、帽制造业	Manufacture of Textile Wearing Apparel, Footware and Caps	362	418	434	392	295
皮革、毛皮、羽毛(绒)及其制品业	Manufacture of Leather, Fur, Feather and Related Products	197	209	210	211	160
木材加工制品业	Processing of Wood and Wood Products	64	66	68	68	49
家具制造业	Manufacture of Furniture	119	130	133	117	97
造纸及纸制品业	Manufacture of Paper and Paper Products	126	133	133	138	101
印刷业和记录媒介的复制	Printing, Reproduction of Recording Media	63	74	79	92	58
文教体育用品制造业	Manufacture of Articles For Culture, Education and Sport Activities	97	96	99	90	75
石油加工、炼焦及核燃料加工业	Processing of Petroleum, Coking, Processing of Nuclear Fuel	7	7	9	8	7
化学原料及制品	Manufacture of Raw Chemical Materials and Chemical Products	261	276	275	262	231
医药制造业	Manufacture of Medicines	48	49	56	52	44
化学纤维制造业	Manufacture of Chemical Fibers	12	13	14	12	10
橡胶制品业	Manufacture of Rubber	183	211	214	196	187
塑料制品业	Manufacture of Plastics	199	227	234	233	169
非金属矿物制品业	Manufacture of Non-metallic Mineral Products	259	311	320	327	303
黑色金属压延加工业	Smelting and Pressing of Ferrous Metals	39	24	27	31	29
有色金属压延加工业	Smelting and Pressing of Non-ferrous Metals	40	41	40	35	34
金属制品业	Manufacture of Metal Products	271	347	376	361	294
通用设备制造业	Manufacture of General Purpose Machinery	473	535	592	597	521
交通运输制造业	Manufacture of Transport Equipment	217	264	290	296	263
电气机械及器材制造业	Manufacture of Electrical Machinery and Equipment	274	303	300	281	230
通信设备、计算机及其他电子设备制造业	Manufacture of Communication Equipment, Computers and Other Electronic Equipment	152	163	168	167	124
仪器仪表及文化、办公用机械制造业	Manufacture of Measuring Instruments and Machinery for Cultural Activity and Office Work	47	47	55	54	39
水的生产和供应业	Production and Supply of Water	10	13	14	14	11
电力、热力的生产和供应业	Production and Supply of Electric Power and Heat Power	34	36	39	38	36
燃气生产和供应业	Production and Supply of Gas	7	13	13	14	11
其他工业	Other Industrial Sectors	895	1 033	1 109	1 049	921

12 -1 续表4
continued

单位:个(unit)

项　目	Item	2012	2013	2014	2015
总　计	**Total**	**4 817**	**4917**	**4 790**	**4 876**
一、按隶属关系分	**Grouped by Subordination Relation**				
中央工业	Central Industry	15	30	28	33
省属工业	Provincial Industry	18	16	15	12
地方工业	Local Industry	4 784	4 871	4 747	4 831
二、按经济类型分	**Grouped by Economic Types**				
国有企业	State-owned	144	140	132	141
集体企业	Collective-owned	28	24	19	15
其他经济类型企业	Other Economic Types	4 645	4 753	4 639	4 720
#外商及港澳台商投资企业	Foreign Funded Enterprises and Enterprises with Funds from Hong Kong, Macao and Taiwan	1 599	1 551	1 445	1 361
三、按轻重工业分	**Grouped by Light and Heavy Industries**				
轻工业	Light Industry	2 153	2 190	2 080	2 095
重工业	Heavy Industry	2 664	2 727	2 710	2 781
四、按企业规模分	**Grouped by Size of Enterprises**				
大型企业	Large	98	97	91	89
中型企业	Medium	596	599	568	566
小型企业	Small	4 123	4 221	4 131	4 221
五、按行业分	**Grouped by Sectors**				
黑色金属矿采选业	Mining of Ferrous Metal Ores	10	11	8	7
非金属矿采选业	Mining and Processing of Nonmetal Ores	14	13	7	6
农副食品加工业	Processing of Food from Agricultural Products	454	468	444	458
食品制造业	Manufacture of Foods	129	123	109	116
酒、饮料和精制茶制造业	Manufacture of Liquor, Beverage and Refind Tea	34	35	34	38
烟草制品业	Manufacture of Tobacco	1	1	1	1
纺织业	Manufacture of Textile	181	175	146	133
纺织服装、服饰业	Manufacture of Textile Wearing Apparel	312	283	249	244
皮革、毛皮、羽毛及其制品和制鞋业	Manufacture of Leather, Fur, Feather & Its Products Footwear	177	148	124	116

12－1 续表5
continued

单位:个(unit)

项 目	Item	2012	2013	2014	2015
木材加工和木、竹、藤、棕、草制品业	Processing of Timbers, Manufacture of Wood, Bamboo, Rattan, Palm and Straw Products	34	40	32	34
家具制造业	Manufacture of Furniture	103	107	96	98
造纸和纸制品业	Manufacture of Paper and Paper Products	100	71	54	52
印刷和记录媒介复制业	Printing, Reproduction of Recording Media	80	121	150	156
文教、工美、体育和娱乐用品制造业	Manufacture of Articles for Culture, Arts & Crafts, Sports and Entertainment	263	335	348	345
石油加工、炼焦和核燃料加工业	Processing of Petroleum, Coking, Processing of Nucleus Fuel	8	8	9	9
化学原料和化学制品制造业	Manufacture of Chemical Raw Material and Chemical Products	224	240	246	249
医药制造业	Manufacture of Medicines	45	49	50	54
化学纤维制造业	Manufacture of Chemical Fiber	9	8	8	8
橡胶和塑料制品业	Manufacture of Rubber and Plastic	350	345	331	310
非金属矿物制品业	Manufacture of Non-metallic Mineral Products	325	333	330	338
黑色金属冶炼和压延加工业	Smelting and Pressing of Ferrous Metals	105	93	87	83
有色金属冶炼和压延加工业	Smelting and Pressing of Non-ferrous Metals	37	36	38	39
金属制品业	Manufacture of Metal Products	399	389	380	388
通用设备制造业	Manufacture of General Purpose Machinery	362	382	395	402
专用设备制造业	Manufacture of Special Purpose Machinery	312	322	314	336
汽车制造业	Manufacture of Vehicle	136	141	145	158
铁路、船舶、航空航天和其他运输设备制造业	Manufacture of Transport Equipment for Railway, Shipping, Aerospace and other uses	145	146	152	168
电气机械和器材制造业	Manufacture of Electrical Machinery & Equipment	202	212	217	226
计算机、通信和其他电子设备制造业	Manufacture of Computer, Communication Equipment and Other Electronic Equipment	137	136	141	147
仪器仪表制造业	Manufacture of Measuring Instrument	41	49	52	58
其他制造业	Manufacture of Other Products	18	17	13	15
废弃资源综合利用业	Recycling and Disposal of Waste Resources	4	6	6	5
金属制品、机械和设备修理业	Maintenance of Metal Products, Machinery and Equipment	7	7	7	6
电力、热力的生产和供应业	Production and Supply of Electric Power and Heat Power	36	39	40	43
燃气生产和供应业	Production and Supply of Gas	12	13	12	14
水的生产和供应业	Production and Supply of Water	11	15	15	16

12－2 分市、区全部工业企业单位数(2015 年)
NUMBER OF ALL INDUSTRIAL ENTERPRISES BY REGION(2015)

单位:个(unit)

市、区名称	Region	规模以上 Above Designated Size	按轻重工业分 Grouped by Light and Heavy Industries		按企业规模分 Grouped by Size of Enterprises		
			轻工业 Light Industry	重工业 Heavy Industry	大型企业 Large	中型企业 Medium	小型企业 Small
全　市	**Total**	**4 876**	**2 095**	**2 781**	**89**	**566**	**4 221**
市内三区	Three Districts in Urban Area	166	57	109	15	30	121
崂山区	Laoshan District	97	35	62	5	17	75
黄岛区	Huangdao District	862	260	602	21	116	725
保税港区	Qingdao Free Trade Port Area of China	23	7	16	1	5	17
城阳区	Chengyang District	456	202	254	10	78	368
即墨市	Jimo	869	450	419	13	91	765
胶州市	Jiaozhou	986	414	572	8	111	867
平度市	Pingdu	642	276	366	7	58	577
莱西市	Laixi	673	362	311	5	42	626
红岛经济区	Qingdao National High-tech Industrial Development Zone	102	32	70	4	18	80

12－2 续表
continued

单位:个(unit)

市、区名称	Region	按经济类型分 Grouped by Economic Types			
		国有企业 State-owned	集体企业 Collective-owned	其他经济 Others	#外资及港澳台商企业 Foreign Funded Enterprises and Enterprises with Funds from Hong Kong, Macao and Taiwan
全　市	**Total**	**141**	**15**	**4 720**	**1 361**
市内三区	Three Districts in Urban Area	42	2	122	46
崂山区	Laoshan District	5	1	91	30
黄岛区	Huangdao District	35	2	825	237
保税港区	Qingdao Free Trade Port Area of China			23	11
城阳区	Chengyang District	11	1	444	205
即墨市	Jimo	9	2	858	225
胶州市	Jiaozhou	8	1	977	219
平度市	Pingdu	15	4	623	167
莱西市	Laixi	5	2	666	176
红岛经济区	Qingdao National High-tech Industrial Development Zone	11	0	91	45

12 -3 历年全部工业总产值

GROSS INDUSTRIAL OUTPUT VALUE OVER THE YEARS

单位:万元(10 000 yuan)

年 份 Year	工业总产值 Gross Industrial Output Value	轻工业产值 Light Industry	重工业产值 Heavy Industry
1949	21 605	18 494	3 111
1950	34 010	28 720	5 290
1951	53 538	44 600	8 938
1952	84 295	69 258	15 037
1953	115 222	74 716	40 506
1954	126 064	80 604	45 460
1955	118 935	86 956	31 979
1956	144 833	93 809	51 024
1957	142 920	101 202	41 718
1958	217 648	92 407	125 241
1959	282 610	84 376	198 234
1960	291 451	77 043	214 408
1962	120 738	64 233	56 505
1963	139 542	83 630	55 912
1964	177 273	108 884	68 389
1965	215 536	141 765	73 771
1966	252 896	152 304	100 592
1967	287 739	163 627	124 112
1968	299 814	175 791	123 489
1969	296 814	188 860	107 954
1970	345 212	202 903	142 309

注:本表按当年价格计算,1995 年开始工业总产值按新规定计算。

Note: The data in this form are calculated at current price. Since 1995, new regulations have been adopted in calculating gross industrial output value.

12 -3 续表 1
continued

单位:万元(10 000 yuan)

年 份 Year	工业总产值 Gross Industrial Output Value	轻工业产值 Light Industry	重工业产值 Heavy Industry
1971	365 770	216 172	149 598
1972	378 266	230 309	147 957
1973	377 943	245 371	132 572
1974	237 219	154 054	83 165
1975	402 541	261 418	141 123
1976	439 793	278 514	161 279
1977	490 669	296 728	193 941
1978	565 503	336 817	228 686
1979	625 227	379 276	245 951
1980	677 690	442 078	235 612
1981	707 434	479 954	227 480
1982	732 705	474 767	257 938
1983	816 793	513 759	303 034
1984	918 364	569 080	349 284
1985	1 113 891	699 524	414 367
1986	1 316 230	833 864	482 366
1987	1 703 830	1 065 873	637 957
1988	2 481 594	1 451 215	1 030 379
1989	3 191 643	1 857 019	1 334 624
1990	3 571 845	2 057 968	1 513 878
1991	3 986 427	2 318 257	1 668 170
1992	4 826 834	2 835 728	1 991 106
1993	5 929 236	3 422 107	2 507 129

12 -3 续表 2
continued

单位:万元(10 000 yuan)

年 份	Year	工业总产值 Gross Industrial Output Value	轻工业产值 Light Industry	重工业产值 Heavy Industry
1994	1994	8 456 974	4 931 262	3 525 712
1995	1995	9 412 635	5 579 637	3 832 998
1996	1996	11 173 672	6 793 007	4 380 665
1997	1997	13 704 735	8 620 710	5 084 025
1998	1998	15 794 106	10 153 634	5 640 472
1999	1999	16 822 436	10 918 827	5 903 609
2000	2000	19 408 338	12 433 214	6 975 124
2001	2001	22 398 464	14 368 582	8 029 882
2002	2002	25 794 324	14 811 106	10 983 218
2003	2003	31 195 595	17 306 539	13 889 056
2004	2004	39 590 783	21 473 202	18 117 581
2005	2005	50 017 829	24 697 792	25 320 037
2006	2006	59 188 120	28 686 826	30 501 294
2007	2007	74 306 364	33 463 071	40 843 293
2008	2008	89 467 300	37 871 227	51 596 073
2009	2009	102 556 155	42 715 781	59 840 374
2010	2010	116 148 345	44 954 630	71 193 715
2011	2011	132 779 629	50 854 938	81 924 691
2012	2012	153 102 565	60 521 444	92 581 121
2013	2013	168 971 805	66 799 317	102 172 488
2014	2014	174 442 125	67 683 545	106 758 580
2015	2015	180 194 299	71 176 748	109 017 551
“一五”时期合计	“First Five-Year Plan”Period	647 974	437 287	210 687
“二五”时期合计	“Second Five-Year Plan”Period	1 077 075	388 406	688 669
1963-1965 年合计	1963-1965	532 351	334 279	198 072
“三五”时期合计	“Third Five-Year Plan”Period	1 481 941	883 485	598 456
“四五”时期合计	“Fourth Five-Year Plan”Period	1 761 739	1 107 324	654 415
“五五”时期合计	“Fifth Five-Year Plan”Period	2 798 882	1 733 413	1 065 469
“六五”时期合计	“Sixth Five-Year Plan”Period	4 289 187	2 737 084	1 552 103
“七五”时期合计	“Seventh Five-Year Plan”Period	12 265 142	7 265 939	4 999 204
“八五”时期合计	“Eighth Five-Year Plan”Period	32 612 106	19 087 323	13 524 783
“九五”时期合计	“Ninth Five-Year Plan”Period	76 903 287	48 919 392	27 983 895
“十五”时期合计	“Tenth Five-Year Plan”Period	168 996 995	92 657 221	76 339 774
“十一五”时期合计	“Eleventh Five-Year Plan”Period	175 336 465	73 641 456	101 695 009
“十二五”时期合计	“Twelveth Five-Year Plan”Period	809 490 422	317 030 889	492 420 143

12 -4 分市、区全部工业总产值(2015 年)
GROSS INDUSTRIAL OUTPUT VALUE BY REGION(2015)

单位:万元(10 000 yuan)

市、区名称	Region	工业总产值 Gross Industrial Output Value	规模以上 Above Designated Size	#外商及港澳台商投资企业 Foreign Funded Enterprises and Enterprises with Funds from Hong Kong, Macao and Taiwan	规模以下 Below Designated Size
全　市	**Whole Municipality**	**180 194 299**	**168 118 299**	**43 853 395**	**12 076 000**
市内三区	The Three Districts of Qingdao City	6 903 523	6 270 223	1 704 014	633 300
崂山区	Laoshan District	5 455 959	5 004 559	812 353	451 400
黄岛区	Huangdao District	55 082 476	52 984 676	12 850 717	2 097 800
保税港区	Qingdao Free Trade Port Area of China	409 764	409 764	320 627	
城阳区	Chengyang District	17 539 534	15 628 734	4 679 823	1 910 800
即墨市	Jimo	33 247 042	31 084 742	9 272 725	2 162 300
胶州市	Jiaozhou	27 966 140	26 226 640	5 126 643	1 739 500
平度市	Pingdu	18 242 624	16 664 724	4 543 439	1 577 900
莱西市	Laixi	12 723 950	11 335 450	3 186 469	1 388 500
红岛经济区	Qingdao National High-tech Industrial Development Zone	2 623 287	2 508 787	1 356 585	114 500

注:规模以下工业资料产值与单位数均来源于抽样调查推算,工业单位数除普查年度外无分市(区)数据。

Note:The output and unit numbers of industrial enterprises under designed size all come from the counting based upon sampling survey. There is no city (district) data on the number of industrial enterprisers other than census year.

12－5 分市、区规模以上工业总产值(2015 年)
GROSS INDUSTRIAL OUTPUT VALUE ABOVE DESIGNATED SIZE BY REGION(2015)

指　标	Indicator	总计 Total	市内三区 The Three Districts of Qingdao City	崂山区 Laoshan District	黄岛区 Huangdao District
总　计	**Total**	**168 118 299**	**6 270 223**	**5 004 559**	**52 984 676**
按隶属关系分	**Grouped by Subordination**				
中央	Centrality	15 411 059	1 650 999	250 357	7 042 592
省(自治区、直辖市)	Province(Autonomous Region, Municipality)	516 018	20 137		191 763
市(地级)	Municipality(local level)	18 815 257	2 294 972	3 124 664	10 153 440
县级市(区)	Municipality at County Level(District)	4 572 262	219 489	273 180	1 071 683
镇、街道	Town and Subdistrict Office	5 537 705	57 732	29 334	1 476 490
乡	Country	71 912			
其它	Others	123 194 085	2 026 894	1 327 024	33 048 709
按登记注册类型分	**Grouped by Status of Registration**				
国有经济	State-owned	28 932 010	2 968 532	293 524	16 236 274
集体经济	Collective-owned	8 550 363	4 808	2 508 451	5 502 694
其他经济	Others	130 635 926	3 296 883	2 202 585	31 245 708
#外资与港澳台企业	Foreign Funded Enterprises and Enterprises with Funds from Hong Kong, Macao and Taiwan	43 853 395	1 704 014	812 353	12 850 717
按轻重工业分	**Grouped by Light and Heavy Industries**				
轻工业	Light Industry	66 481 319	1 641 731	3 344 447	18 036 973
重工业	Heavy Industry	101 636 980	4 628 491	1 660 112	34 947 703
按企业规模分	**Grouped by Size of Enterprises**				
大型企业	Large	44 892 541	3 319 113	3 565 188	20 676 958
中型企业	Medium	36 294 333	1 241 370	759 152	13 515 940
小型企业	Small	86 931 425	1 709 739	680 219	18 791 778

注:部分数据因四舍五入的原因,存在着分项合计不等的情况。
Note: Some of the data are unequal to subtotal due to rounding.

单位:万元(10 000 yuan)

保税港区 Qingdao Free Trade Port Area of China	城阳区 Chengyang District	即墨市 Jimo	胶州市 Jiaozhou	平度市 Pingdu	莱西市 Laixi	红岛经济区 Qingdao National High-tech Industrial Development Zone
409 764	**15 628 734**	**31 084 742**	**26 226 640**	**16 664 724**	**11 335 450**	**2 508 787**
	5 161 094	781 317	200 696	185 331		138 673
	17 878	276 516		9 724		
13 852	892 492	492 302	123 492	1 294 611	18 302	407 131
	830 403	1 292 508	216 861	433 548	224 400	10 190
	638 142	766 118	2 078 717	411 407	21 687	58 080
					71 912	
395 912	8 088 726	27 475 981	23 606 874	14 330 103	10 999 149	1 894 714
	5 708 079	1 283 256	387 258	1 357 817	141 883	555 388
	45 622	257 014	44 900	138 072	48 802	
409 764	9 875 033	29 544 472	25 794 482	15 168 835	11 144 765	1 953 399
320 627	4 679 823	9 272 725	5 126 643	4 543 439	3 186 469	1 356 585
149 357	3 807 999	15 538 383	9 172 792	7 362 414	6 465 276	961 946
260 407	11 820 736	15 546 359	17 053 848	9 302 310	4 870 173	1 546 842
118 114	7 816 263	4 371 905	1 025 229	1 637 502	1 696 784	665 485
103 538	3 944 955	7 199 202	4 936 947	2 591 713	1 295 458	706 057
188 112	3 867 516	19 513 635	20 264 464	12 435 510	8 343 208	1 137 245

12－5 续表
continued

指　标	Indicator	总计 Total	市内三区 The Three Districts of Qingdao City
按行业分	**Grouped by Industrial Sector**	**168 118 299**	**6 270 223**
煤炭开采和洗选业	Mining and Washing of Coal		
石油和天然气开采业	Extraction of Petroleum and Natural Gas		
黑色金属矿采选业	Mining of Ferrous Metal Ores	173 262	
有色金属矿采选业	Mining of Non-ferrous Metal Ores		
非金属矿采选业	Mining and Processing of Nonmetal Ores	141 304	
开采辅助活动	Auxiliary Activities of Mining		
其他采矿业	Mining of Other Ores		
农副食品加工业	Processing of Food from Agricultural Products	13 711 575	334 345
食品制造业	Manufacture of Foods	3 223 596	52 579
酒、饮料和精制茶制造业	Manufacture of Liquor, Beverage and Refind Tea	1 795 106	572 898
烟草制品业	Manufacture of Tobacco		
纺织业	Manufacture of Textile	2 377 867	32 736
纺织服装、服饰业	Manufacture of Textile Wearing Apparel	5 695 037	32 877
皮革、毛皮、羽毛及其制品和制鞋业	Manufacture of Leather, Fur, Feather & Its Products Footwear	2 491 889	14 339
木材加工和木、竹、藤、棕、草制品业	Processing of Timbers, Manufacture of Wood, Bamboo, Rattan, Palm, and Straw Products	691 286	
家具制造业	Manufacture of Furniture	1 736 847	16 913
造纸和纸制品业	Manufacture of Paper and Paper Products	946 353	7 498
印刷和记录媒介复制业	Printing, Reproduction of Recording Media	3 720 502	116 741
文教、工美、体育和娱乐用品制造业	Manufacture of Articles for Culture, Arts & Crafts, Sports and Entertainment	7 266 444	90 061
石油加工、炼焦和核燃料加工业	Processing of Petroleum, Coking, Processing of Nucleus Fuel	6 415 753	899 105
化学原料和化学制品制造业	Manufacture of Chemical Raw Material and Chemical Products	8 434 967	890 312
医药制造业	Manufacture of Medicines	1 860 712	33 673
化学纤维制造业	Manufacture of Chemical Fiber	160 742	20 298
橡胶和塑料制品业	Manufacture of Rubber and Plastic	9 395 680	43 993
非金属矿物制品业	Manufacture of Non-metallic Mineral Products	6 494 354	105 015
黑色金属冶炼和压延加工业	Smelting and Pressing of Ferrous Metals	3 174 974	708 477
有色金属冶炼和压延加工业	Smelting and Pressing of Non-ferrous Metals	1 376 959	
金属制品业	Manufacture of Metal Products	13 539 036	20 387
通用设备制造业	Manufacture of General Purpose Machinery	11 897 585	373 611
专用设备制造业	Manufacture of Special Purpose Machinery	9 009 610	49 409
汽车制造业	Manufacture of Vehicle	7 540 888	128 810
铁路、船舶、航空航天和其他运输设备制造业	Manufacture of Transport Equipment for Railway, Shipping, Aerospace and other uses	11 800 121	588 979
电气机械和器材制造业	Manufacture of Electrical Machinery & Equipment	17 675 087	274 646
计算机、通信和其他电子设备制造业	Manufacture of Computer, Communication Equipment and Other Electronic Equipment	10 528 236	135 532
仪器仪表制造业	Manufacture of Measuring Instrument	1 457 932	27 117
其他制造业	Manufacture of Other Products	220 360	12 492
废弃资源综合利用业	Recycling and Disposal of Waste Resources	90 088	
金属制品、机械和设备修理业	Maintenance of Metal Products, Machinery and Equipment	168 306	
电力、热力生产和供应业	Production and Supply of Electric Power and Heat Power	2 184 376	534 882
燃气生产和供应业	Production and Supply of Gas	529 391	56 564
水的生产和供应业	Production and Supply of Water	192 077	95 932

单位:万元(10 000 yuan)

崂山区 Laoshan District	黄岛区 Huangdao District	保税区 Qingdao Free Trade Port Area of China	城阳区 Chengyang District	即墨市 Jimo	胶州市 Jiaozhou	平度市 Pingdu	莱西市 Laixi	红岛经济区 Qingdao National High-tech Industrial Development Zone
5 004 559	**52 984 676**	**409 764**	**15 628 734**	**31 084 742**	**26 226 640**	**16 664 724**	**11 335 450**	**2 508 787**
						123 795	49 467	
				4 449		92 161	44 693	
44 235	2 437 861	11 648	1 190 776	1 688 497	2 033 790	2 462 663	3 333 742	174 018
109 581	1 199 780	73 319	195 169	127 014	642 649	313 741	485 442	24 322
263 463	362 979		3 055	183 326	21 418	334 181	53 786	
5 999	112 198	27 040	163 664	891 513	611 508	277 378	252 896	2 936
8 415	574 904		262 791	3 798 836	391 339	282 019	316 782	27 073
8 718	382 416		58 344	907 355	523 609	58 461	538 647	
	164 467			24 941	282 017	67 647	152 215	
5 751	77 801		229 552	96 844	988 206	219 839	95 880	6 062
22 588	387 133		107 562	2 281	186 926	188 216	44 150	
3 331	708 735		203 625	2 226 320	253 113	10 186	150 998	47 454
9 499	734 856	15 070	325 447	1 570 072	2 070 179	1 712 043	730 397	8 820
72 085	4 919 431		503 536	2 691	16 598	2 307		
25 465	2 634 970	2 701	449 468	1 346 052	1 424 220	785 537	548 576	327 666
159 301	326 303		103 122	405 124	442 204	136 467	157 901	96 617
	11 659		13 690		115 095			
54 661	4 984 705	20 021	348 154	1 063 337	1 048 948	1 065 912	663 813	102 138
71 075	1 157 824	17 879	490 745	207 866	1 140 158	1 782 953	1 502 796	18 045
	1 047 438		11 756	211 232	307 921	867 454	20 696	
	88 815		16 459	234 823	448 739	474 409		113 713
8 503	2 020 832	23 459	564 536	7 098 655	2 904 801	481 434	328 785	87 645
26 260	3 871 310		449 854	1 035 845	4 051 617	1 478 767	396 171	214 149
60 254	3 835 884	16 189	870 289	943 519	1 974 817	856 989	342 311	59 950
23 446	4 403 937	17 412	645 054	1 135 360	409 986	347 996	148 556	280 331
149 622	3 591 005	8 000	5 570 987	434 483	642 028	340 098	171 050	303 870
3 145 140	7 964 151	5 692	456 487	3 106 947	2 292 777	70 806	302 209	56 234
291 433	3 865 200	163 127	2 201 175	1 698 707	252 960	1 252 497	181 752	485 853
405 240	199 559	8 208	85 463	33 706	371 969	247 703	26 354	52 613
4 630			20 677	44 842	52 644	51 933	26 355	6 786
							90 088	
	89 254			79 051				
25 863	645 772		32 799	321 020	219 800	269 079	122 665	12 495
	151 909		43 348	142 636	100 406	3 488	31 040	
	31 588		11 151	17 400	4 201	6 568	25 238	

12-6 规模以上工业企业主要指标(2015年)
MAIN INDICATORS OF INDUSTRIAL ENTERPRISES ABOVE DESIGNATED SIZE(2015)

项　目	Indicator	企业单位数(个) Number of Enterprises (unit)
总　计	**Total**	**4 876**
按注册登记类型分	**Grouped by Status of Registration**	
国有及国有控股企业	State-owned and State-holding Enterprises	141
集体企业	Collective-owned Enterprises	15
股份有限公司	Share-holding Corporations Ltd	107
外商投资企业	Foreign Funded Enterprises	1 112
港澳台商投资企业	Invested by HongKong, Macao and Taiwan	249
按轻重工业分	**Grouped by Light and Heavy Industries**	
轻工业	Light Industry	2 095
重工业	Heavy Industry	2 781
按企业规模分	**Grouped by Size of Enterprises**	
大型企业	Large	89
中型企业	Medium	566
小型企业	Small	4 221
按所在地分	**Grouped by Location**	
市　区	Urban Area	1 604
#崂山区	Laoshan District	97
黄岛区	Huangdao District	862
保税港区	Qingdao Free Trade Port Area of China	23
城阳区	Chengyang District	456
即墨市	Jimo	869
胶州市	Jiaozhou	986
平度市	Pingdu	642
莱西市	Laixi	673
红岛经济区	Qingdao National High-tech Industrial Development Zone	102
按行业分	**Grouped by Sector**	
煤炭开采和洗选业	Mining and Washing of Coal	
石油和天然气开采业	Extraction of Petroleum and Natural Gas	
黑色金属矿采选业	Mining of Ferrous Metal Ores	7
有色金属矿采选业	Mining of Non-ferrous Metal Ores	
非金属矿采选业	Mining and Processing of Nonmetal Ores	6
开采辅助活动	Auxiliary Activities of Mining	
其他采矿业	Mining of Other Ores	

单位:万元(10 000 yuan)

工业总产值 Gross Industrial Output Value	资产合计 Total Assets	流动资产合计 Total Current Assets	固定资产净值 Net Value of Fixed Assets
168 118 299	**116 228 626**	**62 885 521**	**33 714 645**
28 932 010	31 674 779	18 150 147	8 096 391
8 550 363	17 794 562	13 889 042	1 117 536
11 189 631	10 421 667	7 002 063	1 736 935
34 756 124	23 367 825	12 946 464	7 212 836
9 097 271	4 462 153	2 803 060	1 259 908
66 481 319	47 034 713	28 495 545	11 045 336
101 636 980	69 193 913	34 389 976	22 669 309
44 673 593	51 241 882	35 037 497	7 950 599
36 441 373	26 072 913	12 571 581	8 543 257
87 003 333	38 913 832	15 276 443	17 220 790
80 297 957	74 505 022	46 276 579	14 856 434
5 004 559	9 345 116	6 734 117	1 004 262
52 984 676	40 566 009	24 689 325	8 786 390
409 764	1 212 696	788 072	116 166
15 628 734	13 508 713	9 151 933	2 025 058
31 084 742	9 726 654	4 764 820	3 514 583
26 226 640	16 792 634	4 662 037	9 396 059
16 664 724	7 434 966	3 326 637	2 894 590
11 335 450	4 708 142	2 102 580	2 145 770
2 508 787	3 061 209	1 752 869	907 209
173 262	38 405	7 951	21 658
141 304	37 429	15 054	19 504

12 -6 续表 1
continued

项 目	Indicator	主营业务收入 Revenue from Principal Business
总 计	**Total**	**166 979 333**
按注册登记类型分	**Grouped by Status of Registration**	
国有及国有控股企业	State-owned and State-holding Enterprises	30 082 809
集体企业	Collective-owned Enterprises	9 851 669
股份有限公司	Share-holding Corporations Ltd	10 746 993
外商投资企业	Foreign Funded Enterprises	34 022 866
港澳台商投资企业	Invested by HongKong Macao and Taiwan	9 097 213
按轻重工业分	**Grouped by Light and Heavy Industries**	
轻工业	Light Industry	68 034 098
重工业	Heavy Industry	98 945 235
按企业规模分	**Grouped by size of Enterprises**	
大型企业	Large	46 952 688
中型企业	Medium	35 716 051
小型企业	Small	84 310 594
按所在地分	**Grouped by Location**	
市 区	Urban Area	80 214 190
#崂山区	Laoshan District	5 777 334
黄岛区	Huangdao District	51 624 493
保税港区	Qingdao Free Trade Port Area of China	412 386
城阳区	Chengyang District	14 490 338
即墨市	Jimo	30 233 794
胶州市	Pingdu	25 889 416
平度市	Pingdu	17 061 600
莱西市	Pingdu	11 078 355
红岛经济区	Qingdao National High – tech Industrial Development Zone	2 501 978
按行业分	**Grouped by Sector**	
煤炭开采和洗选业	Mining and Washing of Coal	
石油和天然气开采业	Extraction of Petroleum and Natural Gas	
黑色金属矿采选业	Mining of Ferrous Metal Ores	171 096
有色金属矿采选业	Mining of Non-ferrous Metal Ores	
非金属矿采选业	Mining and Processing of Nonmetal Ores	140 253
开采辅助活动	Auxiliary Activities of Mining	
其他采矿业	Mining of Other Ores	

单位：万元(10 000 yuan)

主营业务成本 Cost of Principal Business	主营业务税金及附加 Taxes and Extra Charges on Principal Business	利润总额 Total Profits	全部从业人员年平均人数(人) Annual Average Employed Persons(person)
141 083 895	**2 971 243**	**9 365 604**	**1 022 811**
25 040 401	1 319 134	1 423 279	122 646
6 965 997	73 166	865 169	21 499
9 114 861	66 796	576 740	65 752
28 945 316	434 751	1 946 330	292 908
7 904 287	74 532	471 203	55 485
56 580 331	722 636	4 266 634	494 836
84 503 564	2 248 607	5 098 970	527 975
38 712 630	592 875	2 805 991	266 553
30 209 542	1 146 153	1 670 057	302 374
72 161 723	1 232 215	4 889 556	453 884
67 493 520	1 920 522	4 033 888	427 079
4 220 781	45 764	495 404	37 118
43 863 469	1 441 273	2 485 878	205 672
303 871	2 325	58 468	8 318
12 417 488	97 702	710 238	115 415
26 135 465	454 337	1 738 472	184 390
21 170 131	442 202	1 757 298	171 015
14 503 846	119 166	1 106 808	104 479
9 744 167	26 196	612 387	109 602
2 036 767	8 821	116 752	26 246
140 297	1 781	15 585	855
110 688	1 963	9 116	1 062

12-6 续表2
continued

项　目	Indicator	企业单位数(个) Number of Enterprises (unit)
农副食品加工业	Processing of Food from Agricultural Products	458
食品制造业	Manufacture of Foods	116
酒、饮料和精制茶制造业	Manufacture of Liquor, Beverage and Refind Tea	38
烟草制品业	Manufacture of Tobacco	1
纺织业	Manufacture of Textile	133
纺织服装、服饰业	Manufacture of Textile Wearing Apparel	244
皮革、毛皮、羽毛及其制品和制鞋业	Manufacture of Leather, Fur, Feather & Its Products Footwear	116
木材加工和木、竹、藤、棕、草制品业	Processing of Timbers, Manufacture of Wood, Bamboo, Rattan, Palm, and Straw Products	34
家具制造业	Manufacture of Furniture	98
造纸和纸制品业	Manufacture of Paper and Paper Products	52
印刷和记录媒介复制业	Printing, Reproduction of Recording Media	156
文教、工美、体育和娱乐用品制造业	Manufacture of Articles for Culture, Arts & Crafts, Sports and Entertainment	345
石油加工、炼焦和核燃料加工业	Processing of Petroleum, Coking, Processing of Nucleus Fuel	9
化学原料和化学制品制造业	Manufacture of Chemical Raw Material and Chemical Products	249
医药制造业	Manufacture of Medicines	54
化学纤维制造业	Manufacture of Chemical Fiber	8
橡胶和塑料制品业	Manufacture of Rubber and Plastic	310
非金属矿物制品业	Manufacture of Non-metallic Mineral Products	338
黑色金属冶炼和压延加工业	Smelting and Pressing of Ferrous Metals	83
有色金属冶炼和压延加工业	Smelting and Pressing of Non-ferrous Metals	39
金属制品业	Manufacture of Metal Products	388
通用设备制造业	Manufacture of General Purpose Machinery	402
专用设备制造业	Manufacture of Special Purpose Machinery	336
汽车制造业	Manufacture of Vehicle	158
铁路、船舶、航空航天和其他运输设备制造业	Manufacture of Transport Equipment for Railway, Shipping, Aerospace and other uses	168
电气机械和器材制造业	Manufacture of Electrical Machinery & Equipment	226
计算机、通信和其他电子设备制造业	Manufacture of Computer, Communication Equipment and Other Electronic Equipment	147
仪器仪表制造业	Manufacture of Measuring Instrument	58
其他制造业	Manufacture of Other Products	15
废弃资源综合利用业	Recycling and Disposal of Waste Resources	5
金属制品、机械和设备修理业	Maintenance of Metal Products, Machinery and Equipment	6
电力、热力生产和供应业	Production and Supply of Electric Power and Heat Power	43
燃气生产和供应业	Production and Supply of Gas	14
水的生产和供应业	Production and Supply of Water	16

单位:万元(10 000 yuan)

工业总产值 Gross Industrial Output Value	资产合计 Total Assets	流动资产合计 Total Current Assets	固定资产净值 Net Value of Fixed Assets
13 711 575	5 534 426	2 675 437	2 211 110
3 223 596	2 152 165	1 140 333	834 393
1 795 106	2 339 119	758 048	429 883
2 377 867	818 528	394 012	345 382
5 695 037	2 890 874	1 461 602	1 023 011
2 491 889	890 110	423 727	337 145
691 286	342 858	69 212	187 011
1 736 847	768 733	285 992	391 225
946 353	503 792	278 410	156 571
3 720 502	1 177 671	541 925	477 809
7 266 444	2 230 765	838 199	1 125 709
6 415 753	2 523 673	815 141	1 369 914
8 434 967	5 440 992	2 309 300	1 807 933
1 860 712	1 314 708	633 278	431 972
160 742	144 684	89 562	38 495
9 395 680	4 953 309	2 015 383	2 052 606
6 494 354	3 759 881	1 871 322	1 418 942
3 174 974	4 787 286	1 867 022	1 135 701
1 376 959	719 661	308 076	363 362
13 539 036	4 965 760	2 059 212	2 080 321
11 897 585	6 689 081	2 979 693	2 795 031
9 009 610	4 993 175	2 211 168	1 851 381
7 540 888	8 133 971	5 974 777	1 383 415
11 800 121	11 011 054	7 298 353	2 114 504
17 675 087	23 112 576	16 547 125	2 334 680
10 528 236	6 564 268	4 477 629	1 102 920
1 457 932	1 486 082	1 006 668	244 216
220 360	142 488	83 680	51 649
90 088	95 821	56 152	31 491
168 306	48 734	31 855	12 687
2 184 376	3 696 909	963 384	2 315 619
529 391	1 049 285	153 212	731 284
192 077	870 353	243 627	486 112

12-6 续表3
continued

项 目	Indicator	主营业务收入 Revenue from Principal Business
农副食品加工业	Processing of Food from Agricultural Products	13 722 080
食品制造业	Manufacture of Foods	3 069 601
酒、饮料和精制茶制造业	Manufacture of Liquor, Beverage and Refind Tea	2 418 050
烟草制品业	Manufacture of Tobacco	
纺织业	Manufacture of Textile	2 319 998
纺织服装、服饰业	Manufacture of Textile Wearing Apparel	5 578 089
皮革、毛皮、羽毛及其制品和制鞋业	Manufacture of Leather, Fur, Feather & Its Products Footwear	2 413 955
木材加工和木、竹、藤、棕、草制品业	Processing of Timbers, Manufacture of Wood, Bamboo, Rattan, Palm, and Straw Products	673 856
家具制造业	Manufacture of Furniture	1 711 919
造纸和纸制品业	Manufacture of Paper and Paper Products	917 040
印刷和记录媒介复制业	Printing, Reproduction of Recording Media	3 502 747
文教、工美、体育和娱乐用品制造业	Manufacture of Articles for Culture, Arts & Crafts, Sports and Entertainment	6 995 718
石油加工、炼焦和核燃料加工业	Processing of Petroleum, Coking, Processing of Nucleus Fuel	6 485 374
化学原料和化学制品制造业	Manufacture of Chemical Raw Material and Chemical Products	8 083 157
医药制造业	Manufacture of Medicines	1 789 004
化学纤维制造业	Manufacture of Chemical Fiber	166 260
橡胶和塑料制品业	Manufacture of Rubber and Plastic	9 139 767
非金属矿物制品业	Manufacture of Non-metallic Mineral Products	6 394 643
黑色金属冶炼和压延加工业	Smelting and Pressing of Ferrous Metals	3 828 640
有色金属冶炼和压延加工业	Smelting and Pressing of Non-ferrous Metals	1 446 656
金属制品业	Manufacture of Metal Products	13 162 736
通用设备制造业	Manufacture of General Purpose Machinery	11 760 847
专用设备制造业	Manufacture of Special Purpose Machinery	8 242 565
汽车制造业	Manufacture of Vehicle	6 662 409
铁路、船舶、航空航天和其他运输设备制造业	Manufacture of Transport Equipment for Railway, Shipping, Aerospace and other uses	11 924 970
电气机械和器材制造业	Manufacture of Electrical Machinery & Equipment	18 742 432
计算机、通信和其他电子设备制造业	Manufacture of Computer, Communication Equipment and Other Electronic Equipment	10 786 945
仪器仪表制造业	Manufacture of Measuring Instrument	1 449 788
其他制造业	Manufacture of Other Products	233 628
废弃资源综合利用业	Recycling and Disposal of Waste Resources	87 558
金属制品、机械和设备修理业	Maintenance of Metal Products, Machinery and Equipment	135 629
电力、热力生产和供应业	Production and Supply of Electric Power and Heat Power	2 102 855
燃气生产和供应业	Production and Supply of Gas	525 156
水的生产和供应业	Production and Supply of Water	193 911

单位：万元(10 000 yuan)

主营业务成本 Cost of Principal Business	主营业务税金及附加 Taxes and Extra Charges on Principal Business	利润总额 Total Profits	全部从业人员年平均人数(人) Annual Average Employed Persons(person)
12 168 992	112 366	622 635	96 091
2 446 755	42 983	248 617	19 275
1 818 158	63 897	277 374	17 557
			1 433
1 987 329	28 068	123 390	21 543
4 764 275	59 927	340 356	88 859
2 044 488	24 282	154 026	46 971
571 502	9 172	47 607	4 430
1 460 510	21 968	94 653	16 445
811 868	9 277	37 080	7 331
3 011 253	55 332	199 380	18 206
6 015 492	93 251	465 237	56 164
4 986 600	1 201 960	95 547	3 381
7 006 304	85 503	314 765	38 217
1 326 471	19 242	171 500	11 579
141 473	2 137	3 532	1 159
8 096 074	91 249	387 615	57 707
5 457 248	56 822	372 611	37 628
3 359 829	25 505	127 044	20 428
1 291 424	9 750	63 740	5 933
11 467 002	199 644	700 888	61 195
10 037 196	127 046	647 207	66 416
6 948 743	158 441	452 838	49 829
5 711 225	70 424	405 290	47 033
10 125 161	91 059	725 084	55 873
14 487 935	202 437	1 369 082	69 305
9 301 694	68 414	542 876	58 767
1 143 410	16 979	126 534	13 873
194 316	2 917	15 301	3 793
70 518	570	6 973	912
107 091	1 417	13 350	487
1 810 628	11 545	168 565	17 085
463 856	2 993	25 895	2 107
198 092	923	-5 689	3 880

12－7 按行业分国有及国有控股工业企业主要指标(2015年)

MAIN INDICATORS OF STATE-OWNED AND STATE-HOLDING INDUSTRIAL ENTERPRISES BY INDUSTRIAL SECTOR(2015)

项 目	Indicator	企业单位数(个) Number of Enterprises(unit)
总 计	**Total**	**141**
煤炭开采和洗选业	Mining and Washing of Coal	
石油和天然气开采业	Extraction of Petroleum and Natural Gas	
黑色金属矿采选业	Mining of Ferrous Metal Ores	
有色金属矿采选业	Mining of Non-ferrous Metal Ores	
非金属矿采选业	Mining and Processing of Nonmetal Ores	1
开采辅助活动	Auxiliary Activities of Mining	
其他采矿业	Mining of Other Ores	
农副食品加工业	Processing of Food from Agricultural Products	1
食品制造业	Manufacture of Foods	1
酒、饮料和精制茶制造业	Manufacture of Liquor, Beverage and Refind Tea	2
烟草制品业	Manufacture of Tobacco	1
纺织业	Manufacture of Textile	
纺织服装、服饰业	Manufacture of Textile Wearing Apparel	1
皮革、毛皮、羽毛及其制品和制鞋业	Manufacture of Leather, Fur, Feather & Its Products Footwear	1
木材加工和木、竹、藤、棕、草制品业	Processing of Timbers, Manufacture of Wood, Bamboo, Rattan, Palm, and Straw Products	
家具制造业	Manufacture of Furniture	
造纸和纸制品业	Manufacture of Paper and Paper Products	1
印刷和记录媒介复制业	Printing, Reproduction of Recording Media	1
文教、工美、体育和娱乐用品制造业	Manufacture of Articles for Culture, Arts & Crafts, Sports and Entertainment	
石油加工、炼焦和核燃料加工业	Processing of Petroleum, Coking, Processing of Nucleus Fuel	4
化学原料和化学制品制造业	Manufacture of Chemical Raw Material and Chemical Products	17
医药制造业	Manufacture of Medicines	2
化学纤维制造业	Manufacture of Chemical Fiber	
橡胶和塑料制品业	Manufacture of Rubber and Plastic	5
非金属矿物制品业	Manufacture of Non-metallic Mineral Products	11
黑色金属冶炼和压延加工业	Smelting and Pressing of Ferrous Metals	4
有色金属冶炼和压延加工业	Smelting and Pressing of Non-ferrous Metals	3
金属制品业	Manufacture of Metal Products	2
通用设备制造业	Manufacture of General Purpose Machinery	10
专用设备制造业	Manufacture of Special Purpose Machinery	2
汽车制造业	Manufacture of Vehicle	6
铁路、船舶、航空航天和其他运输设备制造业	Manufacture of Transport Equipment for Railway, Shipping, Aerospace and other uses	18
电气机械和器材制造业	Manufacture of Electrical Machinery & Equipment	3
计算机、通信和其他电子设备制造业	Manufacture of Computer, Communication Equipment and Other Electronic Equipment	1
仪器仪表制造业	Manufacture of Measuring Instrument	1
其他制造业	Manufacture of Other Products	1
废弃资源综合利用业	Recycling and Disposal of Waste Resources	
金属制品、机械和设备修理业	Maintenance of Metal Products, Machinery and Equipment	
电力、热力生产和供应业	Production and Supply of Electric Power and Heat Power	28
燃气生产和供应业	Production and Supply of Gas	2
水的生产和供应业	Production and Supply of Water	11

单位:万元(10 000 yuan)

工业总产值 Gross Industrial Output Value	资产合计 Total Assets	流动资产合计 Total Current Assets	固定资产净值 Net Value of Fixed Assets
28 932 010	**31 674 778**	**18 150 147**	**8 096 391**
6 145	9 382	5 775	1 654
12 634	24 058	15 021	2 761
7 759	7 433	5 953	1 259
286 203	153 639	87 744	55 558
15 284	23 889	12 019	10 624
11 116	12 027	8 375	1 957
149 806	73 043	36 878	33 200
4 712	10 094	2 840	6 567
6 322 072	2 448 200	776 682	1 344 008
763 172	1 640 526	483 529	343 860
191 003	175 946	93 896	50 567
472 985	714 045	408 568	95 666
184 400	319 713	235 495	38 974
979 894	3 504 695	1 371 077	531 415
35 202	193 503	8 591	165 305
27 302	88 992	35 227	49 817
506 403	525 942	333 966	137 188
44 419	100 606	54 900	37 180
4 020 037	4 918 939	4 186 891	545 050
7 857 152	7 975 508	5 803 851	1 267 193
624 853	548 753	318 424	74 663
4 153 685	3 703 709	2 859 652	327 180
5 958	3 633	3 564	69
12 492	26 008	22 729	1 489
2 017 018	2 998 159	742 781	1 997 804
69 116	662 510	27 252	511 378
151 189	811 828	208 467	464 005

12 -7 续表
continued

项　目	Indicator	主营业务收入 Revenue from Principal Business
总　计	**Total**	**30 082 809**
煤炭开采和洗选业	Mining and Washing of Coal	
石油和天然气开采业	Extraction of Petroleum and Natural Gas	
黑色金属矿采选业	Mining of Ferrous Metal Ores	
有色金属矿采选业	Mining of Non-ferrous Metal Ores	
非金属矿采选业	Mining and Processing of Nonmetal Ores	6 691
开采辅助活动	Auxiliary Activities of Mining	
其他采矿业	Mining of Other Ores	
农副食品加工业	Processing of Food from Agricultural Products	12 040
食品制造业	Manufacture of Foods	7 759
酒、饮料和精制茶制造业	Manufacture of Liquor, Beverage and Refind Tea	195 846
烟草制品业	Manufacture of Tobacco	
纺织业	Manufacture of Textile	
纺织服装、服饰业	Manufacture of Textile Wearing Apparel	30 020
皮革、毛皮、羽毛及其制品和制鞋业	Manufacture of Leather, Fur, Feather & Its Products Footwear	12 442
木材加工和木、竹、藤、棕、草制品业	Processing of Timbers, Manufacture of Wood, Bamboo, Rattan, Palm, and Straw Products	
家具制造业	Manufacture of Furniture	
造纸和纸制品业	Manufacture of Paper and Paper Products	129 636
印刷和记录媒介复制业	Printing, Reproduction of Recording Media	4 591
文教、工美、体育和娱乐用品制造业	Manufacture of Articles for Culture, Arts & Crafts, Sports and Entertainment	
石油加工、炼焦和核燃料加工业	Processing of Petroleum, Coking, Processing of Nucleus Fuel	6 393 852
化学原料和化学制品制造业	Manufacture of Chemical Raw Material and Chemical Products	646 872
医药制造业	Manufacture of Medicines	166 431
化学纤维制造业	Manufacture of Chemical Fiber	
橡胶和塑料制品业	Manufacture of Rubber and Plastic	458 937
非金属矿物制品业	Manufacture of Non-metallic Mineral Products	189 352
黑色金属冶炼和压延加工业	Smelting and Pressing of Ferrous Metals	1 743 590
有色金属冶炼和压延加工业	Smelting and Pressing of Non-ferrous Metals	34 711
金属制品业	Manufacture of Metal Products	35 175
通用设备制造业	Manufacture of General Purpose Machinery	489 998
专用设备制造业	Manufacture of Special Purpose Machinery	49 017
汽车制造业	Manufacture of Vehicle	3 468 732
铁路、船舶、航空航天和其他运输设备制造业	Manufacture of Transport Equipment for Railway, Shipping, Aerospace and other uses	8 043 624
电气机械和器材制造业	Manufacture of Electrical Machinery & Equipment	878 468
计算机、通信和其他电子设备制造业	Manufacture of Computer, Communication Equipment and Other Electronic E-quipment	4 878 398
仪器仪表制造业	Manufacture of Measuring Instrument	5 958
其他制造业	Manufacture of Other Products	22 921
废弃资源综合利用业	Recycling and Disposal of Waste Resources	
金属制品、机械和设备修理业	Maintenance of Metal Products, Machinery and Equipment	
电力、热力生产和供应业	Production and Supply of Electric Power and Heat Power	1 959 689
燃气生产和供应业	Production and Supply of Gas	66 008
水的生产和供应业	Production and Supply of Water	152 053

单位:万元(10 000 yuan)

主营业务成本 Cost of Principal Business	主营业务 税金及附加 Taxes and Extra Charges on Principal Business	利润总额 Total Profits	全部从业人员 年平均人数(人) Annual Average Employed Persons(person)
25 040 401	**1 319 134**	**1 423 279**	**122 645**
4 900	370	153	185
10 374	23	2 260	70
5 746	73	1 519	358
165 916	3 781	3 621	2 004
			1 433
30 004	121	-1 669	988
8 999	53	603	176
123 088	233	1 365	1 162
3 357	142	107	141
4 923 432	1 200 580	83 735	2 795
509 272	8 421	28 624	6 537
77 884	1 153	36 024	1 333
404 960	1 199	2 941	6 404
150 260	716	9 782	1 765
1 626 451	871	7 464	10 818
20 561	63	2 821	1 186
29 697	171	873	336
449 221	3 053	6 263	4 202
45 944	100	-5 059	727
2 977 660	27 430	256 746	9 581
6 801 930	35 744	468 902	27 554
769 604	3 519	13 878	6 430
3 964 051	19 757	348 016	18 249
3 888	39	19	81
21 459	224	467	126
1 689 965	10 585	167 773	14 320
55 449	94	-2 044	266
166 328	621	-11 902	3 418

12-8 按行业分规模以上外商投资和港澳台商投资工业企业主要指标（2015年）

MAIN INDICATORS OF FOREIGN FUNDED ENTERPRISES AND ENTERPRISES WITH FUNDS FROM HONG KONG, MACAO AND TAIWAN ABOVE DESIGNATED SIZE BY INDUSTRIAL SECTOR(2015)

项 目	Indicator	企业单位数(个) Number of Enterprises(unit)
总 计	**Total**	**1 361**
煤炭开采和洗选业	Mining and Washing of Coal	
石油和天然气开采业	Extraction of Petroleum and Natural Gas	
黑色金属矿采选业	Mining of Ferrous Metal Ores	1
有色金属矿采选业	Mining of Non-ferrous Metal Ores	
非金属矿采选业	Mining and Processing of Nonmetal Ores	
开采辅助活动	Auxiliary Activities of Mining	
其他采矿业	Mining of Other Ores	
农副食品加工业	Processing of Food from Agricultural Products	143
食品制造业	Manufacture of Foods	49
酒、饮料和精制茶制造业	Manufacture of Liquor, Beverage and Refind Tea	11
烟草制品业	Manufacture of Tobacco	
纺织业	Manufacture of Textile	52
纺织服装、服饰业	Manufacture of Textile Wearing Apparel	113
皮革、毛皮、羽毛及其制品和制鞋业	Manufacture of Leather, Fur, Feather & Its Products Footwear	60
木材加工和木、竹、藤、棕、草制品业	Processing of Timbers, Manufacture of Wood, Bamboo, Rattan, Palm, and Straw Products	4
家具制造业	Manufacture of Furniture	29
造纸和纸制品业	Manufacture of Paper and Paper Products	14
印刷和记录媒介复制业	Printing, Reproduction of Recording Media	36
文教、工美、体育和娱乐用品制造业	Manufacture of Articles for Culture, Arts & Crafts, Sports and Entertainment	144
石油加工、炼焦和核燃料加工业	Processing of Petroleum, Coking, Processing of Nucleus Fuel	1
化学原料和化学制品制造业	Manufacture of Chemical Raw Material and Chemical Products	77
医药制造业	Manufacture of Medicines	9
化学纤维制造业	Manufacture of Chemical Fiber	5
橡胶和塑料制品业	Manufacture of Rubber and Plastic	70
非金属矿物制品业	Manufacture of Non-metallic Mineral Products	54
黑色金属冶炼和压延加工业	Smelting and Pressing of Ferrous Metals	17
有色金属冶炼和压延加工业	Smelting and Pressing of Non-ferrous Metals	6
金属制品业	Manufacture of Metal Products	92
通用设备制造业	Manufacture of General Purpose Machinery	73
专用设备制造业	Manufacture of Special Purpose Machinery	50
汽车制造业	Manufacture of Vehicle	48
铁路、船舶、航空航天和其他运输设备制造业	Manufacture of Transport Equipment for Railway, Shipping, Aerospace and other uses	37
电气机械和器材制造业	Manufacture of Electrical Machinery & Equipment	54
计算机、通信和其他电子设备制造业	Manufacture of Transport Equipment for Railway, Shipping, Aerospace and other uses	80
仪器仪表制造业	Manufacture of Measuring Instrument	15
其他制造业	Manufacture of Other Products	4
废弃资源综合利用业	Recycling and Disposal of Waste Resources	1
金属制品、机械和设备修理业	Maintenance of Metal Products, Machinery and Equipment	2
电力、热力生产和供应业	Production and Supply of Electric Power and Heat Power	1
燃气生产和供应业	Production and Supply of Gas	7
水的生产和供应业	Production and Supply of Water	2

单位:万元(10 000 yuan)

工业总产值 Gross Industrial Output Value	资产合计 Total Assets	流动资产合计 Total Current Assets	固定资产净值 Net Value of Fixed Assets
43 853 395	**27 829 979**	**15 749 523**	**8 472 744**
89 624	10 755	732	10 023
4 377 414	2 278 287	1 247 296	875 786
2 015 909	1 574 493	896 421	554 294
1 125 820	2 046 311	619 020	318 639
901 872	377 239	182 454	169 612
1 743 390	821 025	405 519	327 192
1 277 864	450 778	227 810	174 054
95 122	157 942	3 136	85 858
534 065	235 191	97 401	125 419
275 166	241 739	168 753	63 356
1 019 446	501 835	264 680	172 625
2 848 235	866 847	388 918	408 926
72 085	48 904	28 530	9 622
3 072 831	2 236 023	1 115 752	887 271
535 559	141 053	69 685	24 124
45 647	116 897	79 710	20 922
1 404 261	1 063 841	487 006	530 955
1 032 236	705 796	368 674	294 178
585 014	629 574	337 982	268 651
215 773	116 704	74 131	40 167
5 247 938	1 756 629	856 078	704 380
2 336 947	1 535 615	889 997	519 577
1 124 949	760 446	432 133	223 300
4 075 577	4 759 634	4 099 552	559 281
1 005 827	842 913	540 721	198 905
1 795 566	1 018 952	448 452	206 379
4 052 714	1 912 840	1 035 780	504 659
436 108	290 214	226 033	49 829
64 946	55 212	38 580	13 966
23 440	11 871	6 813	5 058
28 086	10 246	9 249	975
5 529	32 651	1 331	31 171
367 199	196 933	94 674	78 068
21 236	24 591	6 521	15 522

12 -8 续表
continued

项 目	Indicator	主营业务收入 Revenue from Principal Business
总 计	**Total**	**43 120 078**
煤炭开采和洗选业	Mining and Washing of Coal	
石油和天然气开采业	Extraction of Petroleum and Natural Gas	
黑色金属矿采选业	Mining of Ferrous Metal Ores	87 624
有色金属矿采选业	Mining of Non-ferrous Metal Ores	
非金属矿采选业	Mining and Processing of Nonmetal Ores	
开采辅助活动	Auxiliary Activities of Mining	
其他采矿业	Mining of Other Ores	
农副食品加工业	Processing of Food from Agricultural Products	4 790 333
食品制造业	Manufacture of Foods	1 890 111
酒、饮料和精制茶制造业	Manufacture of Liquor, Beverage and Refind Tea	1 850 264
烟草制品业	Manufacture of Tobacco	
纺织业	Manufacture of Textile	898 538
纺织服装、服饰业	Manufacture of Textile Wearing Apparel	1 701 926
皮革、毛皮、羽毛及其制品和制鞋业	Manufacture of Leather, Fur, Feather & Its Products Footwear	1 236 251
木材加工和木、竹、藤、棕、草制品业	Processing of Timbers, Manufacture of Wood, Bamboo, Rattan, Palm, and Straw Products	96 065
家具制造业	Manufacture of Furniture	507 039
造纸和纸制品业	Manufacture of Paper and Paper Products	275 269
印刷和记录媒介复制业	Printing, Reproduction of Recording Media	997 188
文教、工美、体育和娱乐用品制造业	]Manufacture of Articles for Culture, Arts & Crafts, Sports and Entertainment	2 680 323
石油加工、炼焦和核燃料加工业	Processing of Petroleum, Coking, Processing of Nucleus Fuel	70 622
化学原料和化学制品制造业	Manufacture of Chemical Raw Material and Chemical Products	2 983 998
医药制造业	Manufacture of Medicines	510 709
化学纤维制造业	Manufacture of Chemical Fiber	52 995
橡胶和塑料制品业	Manufacture of Rubber and Plastic	1 397 033
非金属矿物制品业	Manufacture of Non-metallic Mineral Products	1 021 375
黑色金属冶炼和压延加工业	Smelting and Pressing of Ferrous Metals	519 706
有色金属冶炼和压延加工业	Smelting and Pressing of Non-ferrous Metals	315 793
金属制品业	Manufacture of Metal Products	5 080 698
通用设备制造业	Manufacture of General Purpose Machinery	2 388 837
专用设备制造业	Manufacture of Special Purpose Machinery	919 548
汽车制造业	Manufacture of Vehicle	3 492 645
铁路、船舶、航空航天和其他运输设备制造业	Manufacture of Transport Equipment for Railway, Shipping, Aerospace and other uses	995 368
电气机械和器材制造业	Manufacture of Electrical Machinery & Equipment	1 740 061
计算机、通信和其他电子设备制造业	Manufacture of Computer, Communication Equipment and Other Electronic E-quipment	3 672 185
仪器仪表制造业	Manufacture of Measuring Instrument	436 266
其他制造业	Manufacture of Other Products	67 799
废弃资源综合利用业	Recycling and Disposal of Waste Resources	23 317
金属制品、机械和设备修理业	Maintenance of Metal Products, Machinery and Equipment	26 320
电力、热力生产和供应业	Production and Supply of Electric Power and Heat Power	5 529
燃气生产和供应业	Production and Supply of Gas	367 058
水的生产和供应业	Production and Supply of Water	21 284

单位:万元(10 000 yuan)

主营业务成本 Cost of Principal Business	主营业务税金及附加 Taxes and Extra Charges on Principal Business	利润总额 Total Profits	全部从业人员年平均人数(人) Annual Average Employed Persons(person)
36 849 603	**509 282**	**2 417 533**	**348 392**
74 426	1 043	7 436	287
4 296 995	42 734	165 820	33 590
1 448 010	30 343	174 117	9 405
1 361 528	53 922	241 919	13 030
773 731	10 771	38 204	10 632
1 482 212	21 973	88 951	36 481
1 074 958	14 723	50 438	31 409
82 047	1 158	7 679	383
431 450	5 458	28 889	5 054
244 479	2 197	6 334	2 154
842 061	18 238	47 242	6 555
2 325 712	28 773	160 229	28 041
46 411	1 097	10 219	403
2 592 537	22 234	68 107	12 339
425 622	3 874	37 743	1 670
45 529	254	-4 460	810
1 167 462	16 891	78 413	15 233
864 780	6 084	52 922	8 276
448 954	2 496	18 624	2 989
275 284	1 176	14 870	1 050
4 448 758	78 735	227 957	21 934
2 019 148	17 517	124 371	18 653
783 867	10 293	47 484	6 961
2 853 649	29 632	343 714	20 208
786 968	19 184	83 481	7 688
1 536 805	30 532	66 327	15 125
3 343 854	30 957	133 204	28 581
324 291	4 197	63 163	5 258
61 851	239	859	2 535
20 117	1	2 660	256
22 650	86	2 978	173
3 257		1 891	29
325 606	2 382	22 627	944
14 596	90	3 122	256

12－9 按行业分大中型工业企业主要指标（2015年）

MAIN INDICATORS OF LARGE AND MEDIUM-SIZED INDUSTRIAL ENTERPRISES BY INDUSTRIAL SECTOR(2015)

项　目	Indicator	企业单位数(个) Number of Enterprises(unit)
总　计	**Total**	**655**
煤炭开采和洗选业	Mining and Washing of Coal	
石油和天然气开采业	Extraction of Petroleum and Natural Gas	
黑色金属矿采选业	Mining of Ferrous Metal Ores	
有色金属矿采选业	Mining of Non-ferrous Metal Ores	
非金属矿采选业	Mining and Processing of Nonmetal Ores	1
开采辅助活动	Auxiliary Activities of Mining	
其他采矿业	Mining of Other Ores	
农副食品加工业	Processing of Food from Agricultural Products	60
食品制造业	Manufacture of Foods	19
酒、饮料和精制茶制造业	Manufacture of Liquor, Beverage and Refind Tea	6
烟草制品业	Manufacture of Tobacco	
纺织业	Manufacture of Textile	12
纺织服装、服饰业	Manufacture of Textile Wearing Apparel	51
皮革、毛皮、羽毛及其制品和制鞋业	Manufacture of Leather, Fur, Feather & Its Products Footwear	29
木材加工和木、竹、藤、棕、草制品业	Processing of Timbers, Manufacture of Wood, Bamboo, Rattan, Palm, and Straw Products	2
家具制造业	Manufacture of Furniture	9
造纸和纸制品业	Manufacture of Paper and Paper Products	2
印刷和记录媒介复制业	Printing, Reproduction of Recording Media	8
文教、工美、体育和娱乐用品制造业	Manufacture of Articles for Culture, Arts & Crafts, Sports and Entertainment	46
石油加工、炼焦和核燃料加工业	Processing of Petroleum, Coking, Processing of Nucleus Fuel	4
化学原料和化学制品制造业	Manufacture of Chemical Raw Material and Chemical Products	26
医药制造业	Manufacture of Medicines	9
化学纤维制造业	Manufacture of Chemical Fiber	2
橡胶和塑料制品业	Manufacture of Rubber and Plastic	38
非金属矿物制品业	Manufacture of Non-metallic Mineral Products	15
黑色金属冶炼和压延加工业	Smelting and Pressing of Ferrous Metals	7
有色金属冶炼和压延加工业	Smelting and Pressing of Non-ferrous Metals	5
金属制品业	Manufacture of Metal Products	44
通用设备制造业	Manufacture of General Purpose Machinery	51
专用设备制造业	Manufacture of Special Purpose Machinery	31
汽车制造业	Manufacture of Vehicle	34
铁路、船舶、航空航天和其他运输设备制造业	Manufacture of Transport Equipment for Railway, Shipping, Aerospace and other uses	32
电气机械和器材制造业	Manufacture of Electrical Machinery & Equipment	41
计算机、通信和其他电子设备制造业	Manufacture of Computer, Communication Equipment and Other Electronic E-quipment	38
仪器仪表制造业	Manufacture of Measuring Instrument	9
其他制造业	Manufacture of Other Products	2
废弃资源综合利用业	Recycling and Disposal of Waste Resources	
金属制品、机械和设备修理业	Maintenance of Metal Products, Machinery and Equipment	
电力、热力生产和供应业	Production and Supply of Electric Power and Heat Power	18
燃气生产和供应业	Production and Supply of Gas	1
水的生产和供应业	Production and Supply of Water	3

单位:万元(10 000 yuan)

工业总产值 Gross Industrial Output Value	资产合计 Total Assets	流动资产合计 Total Current Assets	固定资产净值 Net Value of Fixed Assets
81 186 874	**77 379 837**	**47 657 680**	**16 499 575**
41 446	8 727	1 862	6 865
6 135 121	2 566 546	1 348 273	970 784
1 280 986	962 833	602 888	248 616
1 312 086	2 054 137	627 910	335 590
568 219	193 652	99 991	80 735
3 113 952	1 853 126	1 061 998	541 554
1 273 876	566 978	263 633	214 803
96 359	41 902	12 872	29 031
372 189	168 354	84 231	72 564
196 893	83 643	38 778	41 900
411 595	217 546	137 704	76 138
1 477 333	633 861	237 002	315 362
6 213 331	2 415 758	780 874	1 317 077
2 666 629	2 990 962	1 256 124	807 496
622 427	832 019	460 691	233 501
31 957	68 691	49 322	11 914
4 433 161	2 988 503	1 287 408	1 011 177
718 057	790 784	476 117	205 480
1 108 666	3 589 292	1 405 137	562 398
229 124	337 224	91 483	215 002
3 994 814	2 041 320	1 033 311	747 155
4 638 312	2 809 881	1 777 184	765 608
2 187 937	1 933 060	1 243 924	309 827
5 901 657	7 090 707	5 460 108	1 068 036
9 238 237	9 274 343	6 528 272	1 514 835
11 984 541	20 902 577	15 864 234	1 541 028
8 213 378	5 545 086	3 862 947	819 279
716 278	1 017 587	712 310	122 985
57 745	52 132	35 897	13 658
1 825 765	2 789 061	732 733	1 878 059
56 564	167 470	23 572	127 179
68 241	392 077	58 892	293 942

12－9 续表
continued

项 目	Indicator	主营业务收入 Revenue from Principal Business
总 计	**Total**	**82 756 350**
煤炭开采和洗选业	Mining and Washing of Coal	
石油和天然气开采业	Extraction of Petroleum and Natural Gas	
黑色金属矿采选业	Mining of Ferrous Metal Ores	
有色金属矿采选业	Mining of Non-ferrous Metal Ores	
非金属矿采选业	Mining and Processing of Nonmetal Ores	41 352
开采辅助活动	Auxiliary Activities of Mining	
其他采矿业	Mining of Other Ores	
农副食品加工业	Processing of Food from Agricultural Products	6 231 571
食品制造业	Manufacture of Foods	1 133 466
酒、饮料和精制茶制造业	Manufacture of Liquor, Beverage and Refind Tea	1 916 345
烟草制品业	Manufacture of Tobacco	
纺织业	Manufacture of Textile	575 376
纺织服装、服饰业	Manufacture of Textile Wearing Apparel	3 087 811
皮革、毛皮、羽毛及其制品和制鞋业	Manufacture of Leather, Fur, Feather & Its Products Footwear	1 218 822
木材加工和木、竹、藤、棕、草制品业	Processing of Timbers, Manufacture of Wood, Bamboo, Rattan, Palm, and Straw Products	93 683
家具制造业	Manufacture of Furniture	362 423
造纸和纸制品业	Manufacture of Paper and Paper Products	175 148
印刷和记录媒介复制业	Printing, Reproduction of Recording Media	378 131
文教、工美、体育和娱乐用品制造业	Manufacture of Articles for Culture, Arts & Crafts, Sports and Entertainment	1 449 084
石油加工、炼焦和核燃料加工业	Processing of Petroleum, Coking, Processing of Nucleus Fuel	6 292 756
化学原料和化学制品制造业	Manufacture of Chemical Raw Material and Chemical Products	2 608 153
医药制造业	Manufacture of Medicines	598 774
化学纤维制造业	Manufacture of Chemical Fiber	31 678
橡胶和塑料制品业	Manufacture of Rubber and Plastic	4 261 529
非金属矿物制品业	Manufacture of Non-metallic Mineral Products	700 733
黑色金属冶炼和压延加工业	Smelting and Pressing of Ferrous Metals	1 812 981
有色金属冶炼和压延加工业	Smelting and Pressing of Non-ferrous Metals	215 930
金属制品业	Manufacture of Metal Products	3 866 154
通用设备制造业	Manufacture of General Purpose Machinery	4 718 512
专用设备制造业	Manufacture of Special Purpose Machinery	1 994 249
汽车制造业	Manufacture of Vehicle	5 040 684
铁路、船舶、航空航天和其他运输设备制造业	Manufacture of Transport Equipment for Railway, Shipping, Aerospace and other uses	9 400 578
电气机械和器材制造业	Manufacture of Electrical Machinery & Equipment	13 333 853
计算机、通信和其他电子设备制造业	Manufacture of Computer, Communication Equipment and Other Electronic Equipment	8 559 430
仪器仪表制造业	Manufacture of Measuring Instrument	716 031
其他制造业	Manufacture of Other Products	60 598
废弃资源综合利用业	Recycling and Disposal of Waste Resources	
金属制品、机械和设备修理业	Maintenance of Metal Products, Machinery and Equipment	
电力、热力生产和供应业	Production and Supply of Electric Power and Heat Power	1 756 208
燃气生产和供应业	Production and Supply of Gas	56 564
水的生产和供应业	Production and Supply of Water	67 742

单位:万元(10 000 yuan)

主营业务成本 Cost of Principal Business	主营业务 税金及附加 Taxes and Extra Charges on Principal Business	利润总额 Total Profits	全部从业人员 年平均人数(人) Annual Average Employed Persons(person)
68 994 454	**1 739 355**	**4 481 341**	**569 305**
26 205	383	3 430	423
5 683 893	41 230	168 163	54 821
796 616	12 804	125 786	8 007
1 433 875	54 484	239 352	14 705
496 267	3 609	32 266	7 127
2 627 017	20 040	186 121	65 335
1 012 656	6 633	85 620	34 506
79 718	1 233	8 101	912
318 458	2 689	10 646	5 874
163 858	489	5 421	1 530
325 723	1 636	20 534	3 487
1 257 100	18 602	94 913	22 281
4 815 948	1 182 390	100 918	3 012
2 263 638	19 273	42 943	16 582
332 236	5 704	92 135	6 115
28 673	119	-4 944	776
3 803 831	15 548	132 175	28 330
602 367	5 679	35 274	8 653
1 674 636	1 584	10 165	12 270
179 679	183	2 914	2 310
3 393 644	46 243	185 181	26 013
4 166 947	28 359	225 879	28 980
1 681 248	24 790	73 896	18 376
4 333 372	44 368	330 317	33 216
7 980 683	46 939	541 550	43 308
9 919 308	96 169	1 066 763	50 176
7 331 233	42 187	461 030	45 527
542 140	5 816	71 658	8 163
55 403	224	668	2 401
1 515 830	9 678	144 161	13 264
54 478	9	2 781	621
97 778	263	-14 476	2 204

12-10 按行业分规模以上工业企业主要经济效益指标(2015年)

MAIN INDICATORS ON ECONOMIC BENEFIT OF INDUSTRIAL ENTERPRISES ABOVE DESIGNATED SIZE BY INDUSTRIAL SECTOR(2015)

行 业	Sector	总资产贡献率(%) Ratio of Total Assets to Industrial Output Value(%)
总 计	**Total**	**15.7**
按轻重工业分	**Grouped by Light and Heavy Industries**	
轻工业	Light Industry	15.78
重工业	Heavy Industry	15.65
按行业分	**Grouped by Sector**	
煤炭开采和洗选业	Mining and Washing of Coal	
石油和天然气开采业	Extraction of Petroleum and Natural Gas	
黑色金属矿采选业	Mining of Ferrous Metal Ores	53.82
有色金属矿采选业	Mining of Non-ferrous Metal Ores	
非金属矿采选业	Mining and Processing of Nonmetal Ores	45.1
开采辅助活动	Auxiliary Activities of Mining	
其他采矿业	Mining of Other Ores	
农副食品加工业	Processing of Food from Agricultural Products	20.79
食品制造业	Manufacture of Foods	20.17
酒、饮料和精制茶制造业	Manufacture of Liquor, Beverage and Refind Tea	18.9
烟草制品业	Manufacture of Tobacco	
纺织业	Manufacture of Textile	31.59
纺织服装、服饰业	Manufacture of Textile Wearing Apparel	21.13
皮革、毛皮、羽毛及其制品和制鞋业	Manufacture of Leather, Fur, Feather & Its Products Footwear	31.68
木材加工和木、竹、藤、棕、草制品业	Processing of Timbers, Manufacture of Wood, Bamboo, Rattan, Palm, and Straw Products	24.74
家具制造业	Manufacture of Furniture	24.39
造纸和纸制品业	Manufacture of Paper and Paper Products	17.69
印刷和记录媒介复制业	Printing, Reproduction of Recording Media	34.34
文教、工美、体育和娱乐用品制造业	Manufacture of Articles for Culture, Arts & Crafts, Sports and Entertainment	36.9
石油加工、炼焦和核燃料加工业	Processing of Petroleum, Coking, Processing of Nucleus Fuel	63.8
化学原料和化学制品制造业	Manufacture of Chemical Raw Material and Chemical Products	10.69
医药制造业	Manufacture of Medicines	22.54
化学纤维制造业	Manufacture of Chemical Fiber	9.28
橡胶和塑料制品业	Manufacture of Rubber and Plastic	15.45
非金属矿物制品业	Manufacture of Non-metallic Mineral Products	17.75
黑色金属冶炼和压延加工业	Smelting and Pressing of Ferrous Metals	5.9
有色金属冶炼和压延加工业	Smelting and Pressing of Non ferrous Metals	17.15
金属制品业	Manufacture of Metal Products	28.31
通用设备制造业	Manufacture of General Purpose Machinery	18.37
专用设备制造业	Manufacture of Special Purpose Machinery	19.41
汽车制造业	Manufacture of Vehicle	8.01
铁路、船舶、航空航天和其他运输设备制造业	Manufacture of Transport Equipment for Railway, Shipping, Aerospace and other uses	10.34
电气机械和器材制造业	Manufacture of Electrical Machinery & Equipment	9.25
计算机、通信和其他电子设备制造业	Manufacture of Computer, Communication Equipment and Other Electronic Equipment	14.08
仪器仪表制造业	Manufacture of Measuring Instrument	14.68
其他制造业	Manufacture of Other Products	18.8
废弃资源综合利用业	Recycling and Disposal of Waste Resources	10.68
金属制品、机械和设备修理业	Maintenance of Metal Products, Machinery and Equipment	50.39
电力、热力生产和供应业	Production and Supply of Electric Power and Heat Power	8.3
燃气生产和供应业	Production and Supply of Gas	5.2
水的生产和供应业	Production and Supply of Water	0.7

资产负债率 (%) Assets-Liability Ratio(%)	流动资产周转次数(次/年) Number of Times of Annualof Turnover Current Assets(time/year)	工业成本费用利润率(%) Ratio of Profits to Industrial Costs(%)	产品销售率 (%) Ratio of Sales to Output(%)
57.23	**2.69**	**5.94**	**98.58**
59.29	2.44	6.57	99.31
55.83	2.9	5.5	98.1
36.45	21.52	10.14	99.26
42.38	9.32	7.11	97.92
52.7	5.14	4.78	97.72
41.16	2.83	8.81	99.35
34.84	3.36	11.51	133.58
58.33	5.9	5.69	97.54
41.88	3.85	6.5	98.11
48.59	5.7	6.88	97.1
36.87	9.74	7.73	98.27
48.22	5.99	5.94	98.93
43.52	3.33	4.21	97.85
45.37	6.48	6.11	96.76
41.32	8.37	7.22	98.47
78.84	8.13	1.8	99.54
55	3.52	4.05	97.8
40.77	2.83	10.66	97.34
60.72	2.02	2.01	99.55
51.97	4.58	4.42	98.92
53.23	3.44	6.21	98.22
62.16	2.06	3.44	99.12
54.33	4.73	4.62	97.61
44.72	6.4	5.7	96.82
46.76	3.98	5.86	98.09
45.52	3.75	5.89	97.82
59.04	1.15	6.31	98.78
64.98	1.64	6.52	98.47
71.26	1.15	7.73	98.67
53.92	2.56	4.97	98.38
55.07	1.46	9.59	98.24
55.16	2.82	7.04	99.47
69.49	1.56	8.72	96.53
49.27	4.34	10.77	89.31
61.82	2.29	7.93	99.47
58.58	3.57	4.8	99.97
63.53	0.91	-2.2	99.41

12－11 按行业分国有控股工业企业主要经济效益指标(2015 年)

MAIN INDICATORS ON ECONOMIC BENEFIT OF STATE-OWNED AND STATE-HOLDING INDUSTRIAL ENTERPRISES BY INDUSTRIAL SECTOR(2015)

行 业	Sector	总资产贡献率(%) Ratio of Total Assets to Industrial Output Value(%)
总 计	**Total**	**11.84**
煤炭开采和洗选业	Mining and Washing of Coal	
石油和天然气开采业	Extraction of Petroleum and Natural Gas	
黑色金属矿采选业	Mining of Ferrous Metal Ores	
有色金属矿采选业	Mining of Non-ferrous Metal Ores	
非金属矿采选业	Mining and Processing of Nonmetal Ores	10.66
开采辅助活动	Auxiliary Activities of Mining	
其他采矿业	Mining of Other Ores	
农副食品加工业	Processing of Food from Agricultural Products	9.49
食品制造业	Manufacture of Foods	31.58
酒、饮料和精制茶制造业	Manufacture of Liquor, Beverage and Refind Tea	6.62
烟草制品业	Manufacture of Tobacco	
纺织业	Manufacture of Textile	
纺织服装、服饰业	Manufacture of Textile Wearing Apparel	-0.56
皮革、毛皮、羽毛及其制品和制鞋业	Manufacture of Leather, Fur, Feather & Its Products Footwear	10.37
木材加工和木、竹、藤、棕、草制品业	Processing of Timbers, Manufacture of Wood, Bamboo, Rattan, Palm, and Straw Products	
家具制造业	Manufacture of Furniture	
造纸和纸制品业	Manufacture of Paper and Paper Products	7.21
印刷和记录媒介复制业	Printing, Reproduction of Recording Media	11.77
文教、工美、体育和娱乐用品制造业	Manufacture of Articles for Culture, Arts & Crafts, Sports and Entertainment	
石油加工、炼焦和核燃料加工业	Processing of Petroleum, Coking, Processing of Nucleus Fuel	65.02
化学原料和化学制品制造业	Manufacture of Chemical Raw Material and Chemical Products	2.61
医药制造业	Manufacture of Medicines	27.05
化学纤维制造业	Manufacture of Chemical Fiber	
橡胶和塑料制品业	Manufacture of Rubber and Plastic	2.53
非金属矿物制品业	Manufacture of Non-metallic Mineral Products	6.48
黑色金属冶炼和压延加工业	Smelting and Pressing of Ferrous Metals	1.78
有色金属冶炼和压延加工业	Smelting and Pressing of Non-ferrous Metals	2.62
金属制品业	Manufacture of Metal Products	1.46
通用设备制造业	Manufacture of General Purpose Machinery	3.43
专用设备制造业	Manufacture of Special Purpose Machinery	-4.08
汽车制造业	Manufacture of Vehicle	7.19
铁路、船舶、航空航天和其他运输设备制造业	Manufacture of Transport Equipment for Railway, Shipping, Aerospace and other uses	8.50
电气机械和器材制造业	Manufacture of Electrical Machinery & Equipment	7.63
计算机、通信和其他电子设备制造业	Manufacture of Computer, Communication Equipment and Other Electronic Equipment	14.88
仪器仪表制造业	Manufacture of Measuring Instrument	12.43
其他制造业	Manufacture of Other Products	4.74
废弃资源综合利用业	Recycling and Disposal of Waste Resources	
金属制品、机械和设备修理业	Maintenance of Metal Products, Machinery and Equipment	
电力、热力生产和供应业	Production and Supply of Electric Power and Heat Power	9.66
燃气生产和供应业	Production and Supply of Gas	1.31
水的生产和供应业	Production and Supply of Water	-0.27

资产负债率 (%) Assets-Liability Ratio(%)	流动资产周转次数(次/年) Number of Times of Annual of Turnover Current Assets(time/year)	工业成本费用利润率(%) Ratio of Profits to Industrial Costs(%)	产品销售率 (%) Ratio of Sales to Output(%)
64.54	**1.72**	**4.95**	**99.12**
83.02	1.16	2.49	75.6
37.41	0.84	20.29	99.95
29.77	1.93	15.41	100
61.63	2.23	1.92	98.08
116.68	3.97	-3.39	98.15
50.07	1.51	5.04	96.64
63.59	3.52	1.07	96
6.57	1.62	2.47	97.44
80.25	8.42	1.60	99.56
58.24	1.37	4.53	97.42
39.02	1.79	26.33	96.76
58.67	1.20	0.60	98.95
76.14	0.81	5.47	102.53
74.43	1.27	0.43	100.32
59.76	4.22	8.50	100
60.73	1.04	2.50	112.98
62.42	1.49	1.26	98.66
79.23	0.92	-9.14	92.45
58.65	0.87	7.62	98.76
69.06	1.39	6.22	98.49
65.01	2.80	1.59	101.75
51.28	1.93	6.65	99.87
19.57	1.68	0.31	100
71.47	1.01	2.09	100
62.00	2.77	8.51	98.98
54.61	2.55	-2.86	100
64.28	0.86	-5.33	99.72

12－12 按行业分规模以上外商及港澳台商投资工业企业主要经济效益指标(2015 年)

MAIN INDICATORS ON ECONOMIC BENEFIT OF FOREIGN FUNDED ENTERPRISES AND ENTERPRISES WITH FUNDS FROM HONG KONG, MACAO AND TAIWAN ABOVE DESIGNATED SIZE BY INDUSTRIAL SECTOR(2015)

行　业	Sector	总资产贡献率(%) Ratio of Total Assets to Industrial Output Value(%)
总　计	**Total**	**15.53**
煤炭开采和洗选业	Mining and Washing of Coal	
石油和天然气开采业	Extraction of Petroleum and Natural Gas	
黑色金属矿采选业	Mining of Ferrous Metal Ores	89.60
有色金属矿采选业	Mining of Non-ferrous Metal Ores	
非金属矿采选业	Mining and Processing of Nonmetal Ores	
开采辅助活动	Auxiliary Activities of Mining	
其他采矿业	Mining of Other Ores	
农副食品加工业	Processing of Food from Agricultural Products	14.02
食品制造业	Manufacture of Foods	18.93
酒、饮料和精制茶制造业	Manufacture of Liquor, Beverage and Refind Tea	18.40
烟草制品业	Manufacture of Tobacco	
纺织业	Manufacture of Textile	21.69
纺织服装、服饰业	Manufacture of Textile Wearing Apparel	21.55
皮革、毛皮、羽毛及其制品和制鞋业	Manufacture of Leather, Fur, Feather & Its Products Footwear	23.44
木材加工和木、竹、藤、棕、草制品业	Processing of Timbers, Manufacture of Wood, Bamboo, Rattan, Palm, and Straw Products	8.56
家具制造业	Manufacture of Furniture	25.34
造纸和纸制品业	Manufacture of Paper and Paper Products	8.98
印刷和记录媒介复制业	Printing, Reproduction of Recording Media	23.46
文教、工美、体育和娱乐用品制造业	Manufacture of Articles for Culture, Arts & Crafts, Sports and Entertainment	33.42
石油加工、炼焦和核燃料加工业	Processing of Petroleum, Coking, Processing of Nucleus Fuel	31.67
化学原料和化学制品制造业	Manufacture of Chemical Raw Material and Chemical Products	5.57
医药制造业	Manufacture of Medicines	46.52
化学纤维制造业	Manufacture of Chemical Fiber	1.05
橡胶和塑料制品业	Manufacture of Rubber and Plastic	14.28
非金属矿物制品业	Manufacture of Non-metallic Mineral Products	14.49
黑色金属冶炼和压延加工业	Smelting and Pressing of Ferrous Metals	5.41
有色金属冶炼和压延加工业	Smelting and Pressing of Non-ferrous Metals	19.09
金属制品业	Manufacture of Metal Products	26.92
通用设备制造业	Manufacture of General Purpose Machinery	13.68
专用设备制造业	Manufacture of Special Purpose Machinery	10.61
汽车制造业	Manufacture of Vehicle	10.01
铁路、船舶、航空航天和其他运输设备制造业	Manufacture of Transport Equipment for Railway, Shipping, Aerospace and other uses	19.05
电气机械和器材制造业	Manufacture of Electrical Machinery & Equipment	15.85
计算机、通信和其他电子设备制造业	Manufacture of Computer, Communication Equipment and Other Electronic E-quipment	12.05
仪器仪表制造业	Manufacture of Measuring Instrument	31.33
其他制造业	Manufacture of Other Products	3.40
废弃资源综合利用业	Recycling and Disposal of Waste Resources	25.22
金属制品、机械和设备修理业	Maintenance of Metal Products, Machinery and Equipment	40.49
电力、热力生产和供应业	Production and Supply of Electric Power and Heat Power	6.76
燃气生产和供应业	Production and Supply of Gas	17.30
水的生产和供应业	Production and Supply of Water	17.32

资产负债率 (%) Assets-Liability Ratio(%)	流动资产周转次数(次/年) Number of Times of Annual of Turnover Current Assets(time/year)	工业成本费用利润率(%) Ratio of Profits to Industrial Costs(%)	产品销售率 (%) Ratio of Sales to Output(%)
47.50	**2.78**	**5.91**	**99.63**
7.69	119.69	9.40	100
55.21	3.85	3.61	98.13
42.16	2.28	10.08	99.67
31.69	3.19	12.83	155.46
53.92	4.93	4.49	97.47
40.42	4.21	5.57	98.24
50.86	5.43	4.31	96.69
31.99	30.64	8.80	99.78
55.36	5.21	6.13	99.51
39.95	1.68	2.30	99.79
48.08	3.78	5.05	97.53
38.91	6.91	6.42	98.71
29.14	2.48	17.23	98.01
59.73	2.71	2.31	99.18
36.17	7.34	8.03	95.88
69.29	0.85	-6.19	98.41
45.08	2.90	5.96	99.86
37.81	2.80	5.45	98.94
27.45	1.57	3.65	99.48
49.17	4.26	4.96	99.01
45.34	5.95	4.76	96.42
43.77	2.72	5.51	97.64
48.08	2.15	5.41	97.59
55.17	0.88	10.69	99.55
55.90	1.85	9.34	99.42
28.37	3.88	4.04	98.85
56.73	3.57	3.77	96.17
28.44	1.95	16.92	100.7
79.96	1.79	1.27	104.4
20.27	3.42	12.88	99.48
18.47	2.85	12.48	86.15
15.30	4.15	51.98	100
60.48	3.88	6.53	99.99
39.13	3.26	17.26	100

12－13 按行业分大中型工业企业主要经济效益指标（2015年）

MAIN INDICATORS ON ECONOMIC BENEFIT OF LARGE AND MEDIUM-SIZED INDUSTRIAL ENTERPRISES BY INDUSTRIAL SECTOR(2015)

行　业	Sector	总资产贡献率(%) Ratio of Total Assets to Industrial Output Value(%)
总　计	**Total**	**11.25**
煤炭开采和洗选业	Mining and Washing of Coal	
石油和天然气开采业	Extraction of Petroleum and Natural Gas	
黑色金属矿采选业	Mining of Ferrous Metal Ores	
有色金属矿采选业	Mining of Non-ferrous Metal Ores	
非金属矿采选业	Mining and Processing of Nonmetal Ores	49.85
开采辅助活动	Auxiliary Activities of Mining	
其他采矿业	Mining of Other Ores	
农副食品加工业	Processing of Food from Agricultural Products	13.83
食品制造业	Manufacture of Foods	22.08
酒、饮料和精制茶制造业	Manufacture of Liquor, Beverage and Refind Tea	17.99
烟草制品业	Manufacture of Tobacco	
纺织业	Manufacture of Textile	29.92
纺织服装、服饰业	Manufacture of Textile Wearing Apparel	16.89
皮革、毛皮、羽毛及其制品和制鞋业	Manufacture of Leather, Fur, Feather & Its Products Footwear	25.76
木材加工和木、竹、藤、棕、草制品业	Processing of Timbers, Manufacture of Wood, Bamboo, Rattan, Palm, and Straw Products	26.78
家具制造业	Manufacture of Furniture	15.00
造纸和纸制品业	Manufacture of Paper and Paper Products	13.79
印刷和记录媒介复制业	Printing, Reproduction of Recording Media	17.49
文教、工美、体育和娱乐用品制造业	Manufacture of Articles for Culture, Arts & Crafts, Sports and Entertainment	25.76
石油加工、炼焦和核燃料加工业	Processing of Petroleum, Coking, Processing of Nucleus Fuel	65.53
化学原料和化学制品制造业	Manufacture of Chemical Raw Material and Chemical Products	2.50
医药制造业	Manufacture of Medicines	17.87
化学纤维制造业	Manufacture of Chemical Fiber	-0.98
橡胶和塑料制品业	Manufacture of Rubber and Plastic	8.13
非金属矿物制品业	Manufacture of Non-metallic Mineral Products	7.79
黑色金属冶炼和压延加工业	Smelting and Pressing of Ferrous Metals	1.89
有色金属冶炼和压延加工业	Smelting and Pressing of Non-ferrous Metals	3.92
金属制品业	Manufacture of Metal Products	17.15
通用设备制造业	Manufacture of General Purpose Machinery	13.49
专用设备制造业	Manufacture of Special Purpose Machinery	9.42
汽车制造业	Manufacture of Vehicle	6.95
铁路、船舶、航空航天和其他运输设备制造业	Manufacture of Transport Equipment for Railway, Shipping, Aerospace and other uses	8.80
电气机械和器材制造业	Manufacture of Electrical Machinery & Equipment	7.02
计算机、通信和其他电子设备制造业	Manufacture of Computer, Communication Equipment and Other Electronic Equipment	13.51
仪器仪表制造业	Manufacture of Measuring Instrument	11.55
其他制造业	Manufacture of Other Products	3.21
废弃资源综合利用业	Recycling and Disposal of Waste Resources	
金属制品、机械和设备修理业	Maintenance of Metal Products, Machinery and Equipment	
电力、热力生产和供应业	Production and Supply of Electric Power and Heat Power	9.10
燃气生产和供应业	Production and Supply of Gas	4.31
水的生产和供应业	Production and Supply of Water	-2.78

资产负债率 (%) Assets-Liability Ratio(%)	流动资产周转次数(次/年) Number of Times of Annual of Turnover Current Assets(time/year)	工业成本费用利润率(%) Ratio of Profits to Industrial Costs(%)	产品销售率 (%) Ratio of Sales to Output(%)
63.50	**1.78**	**5.66**	**99.1**
3.44	22.21	9.38	99.77
58.89	4.64	2.77	96.71
54.41	2.12	12.23	99
32.72	3.25	12.26	148.49
63.57	5.75	5.99	98.6
44.60	2.94	6.35	98.75
51.57	4.63	7.62	95.28
18.45	7.28	9.60	98.35
71.87	4.31	3.04	99.48
61.64	4.52	3.20	96.06
42.70	2.76	5.74	93.3
39.63	6.15	7.06	98.92
81.09	8.24	1.96	100.8
65.01	2.09	1.66	97.49
37.12	1.31	18.08	97.62
68.28	0.65	-13.46	97.72
54.52	3.37	3.14	98.83
62.33	1.53	5.21	97.95
73.51	1.30	0.56	100.72
55.57	2.43	1.31	99.29
44.55	3.76	5.07	96.62
56.44	2.69	4.97	95.87
51.88	1.62	3.83	97.41
59.97	0.96	6.76	98.83
68.43	1.44	6.14	98.45
75.05	0.86	8.40	99.3
53.39	2.39	5.23	98.19
66.26	1.02	11.06	96.31
81.27	1.72	1.10	104.95
59.36	2.52	8.10	97.72
73.76	3.16	3.11	100
54.53	1.39	-11.78	99.39

12-14 主要年份主要工业产品产量
MAJOR YEAR'S PRODUCTS OUTPUT OF INDUSTRY ABOVE DESIGNATED SIZE

年 份 Year	原 盐 (万吨) Salt (10000 tons)	发电量 (亿千瓦小时) Electricity (100 million kW·h)	饮料酒 (万吨) Beverage Liquor (10000 tons)	#啤 酒 Beer	卷 烟 (万箱) Cigarettes (10000 cases)	罐 头 (吨) Canned Food (ton)	化学纤维 (吨) Chemical Fiber (ton)	纱 (吨) Yarn (ton)
1949	15.16	1.21	0.18	0.12	2.36			27 447
1952	35.08	2.11	0.37	0.18	12.27			59 674
1957	44.34	2.92	0.96	0.58	23.41			50 699
1962	38.60	3.86	1.58	0.79	16.59		28	17 939
1965	41.34	6.80	2.04	1.34	31.34		205	68 082
1970	29.96	10.57	3.39	2.55	42.16		621	85 591
1975	34.52	10.98	5.30	2.98	36.00		357	79 516
1978	60.68	13.63	6.25	3.75	44.00	4 743	1 413	85 233
1980	41.19	12.50	8.49	4.84	48.79	3 521	2 116	83 389
1985	47.34	26.97	13.76	10.05	51.81	6 400	1 747	91 839
1987	50.64	28.97	23.40	13.85	55.84	16 000	3 442	108 003
1988	53.28	29.35	26.61	15.58	57.01	27 200	3 393	107 720
1989	55.37	29.87	24.57	15.40	58.64	13 200	3 700	118 379
1990	35.70	40.22	29.18	19.61	61.94		2 900	100 381
1991	31.39	54.60	36.75	27.38	56.19	130 510	5 200	96 271
1992	46.24	58.63	44.59	37.01	59.37	3 200	6 000	99 043
1993	48.88	59.39	54.74	45.92	63.46	1 900	27 100	91 351
1994	53.02	59.62	60.00	50.92	69.20	2 300	21 400	86 744
1995	50.84	64.69	60.85	54.16	70.96	4 609	20 973	79 492
1996	41.39	83.02	61.79	54.40	73.04	1 719	22 945	66 832
1997	34.11	95.12	66.64	56.06	88.32	554	26 300	70 402
1998	19.08	79.65	47.33	42.79	77.10		23 858	66 504
1999	30.30	82.00	126.21	120.10	149.00	379	29 967	56 431
2000	41.83	90.84	211.47	206.50	148.10	225	65 362	69 561
2001	31.40	85.73	279.37	274.28	142.95	99	89 989	72 933
2002	42.50	89.70	323.20	320.60	138.10	11 690	91 394	70 888
2003	36.85	87.69	353.90	351.80	148.00		101 752	65 919
2004	34.36	89.01	393.30	390.60	147.10	10 889	115 187	71 931
2005	10.00	98.63	439.70	435.20	150.70	10 097	95 887	72 140
2006	15.30	124.54	101.60(本地)	95.60(本地)	95.16(本地)	1 668	72 381	56 128
2007	19.23	155.30	118.10(本地)	112.50(本地)	100.08(本地)	1 850	68 746	47 850
2008	15.90	164.58	132.07(本地)	124.75(本地)	100.02(本地)	1 510	51 751	43 102
2009	5.90	172.66	137.21(本地)	127.12(本地)	100.08(本地)	4 706	59 852	38 566
2010	11.25	181.93	144.66(本地)	141.65(本地)	102.55(本地)	1 092	68 654	35 278
2011		173.69	164.04(本地)	156.50(本地)	104.51(本地)	41 204	38 640	18 556
2012		174.72	174.03(本地)	163.95(本地)	106.03(本地)	35 026	32 371	19 404
2013	1.28	180.11	194.22(本地)	185.17(本地)	108.36(本地)	30 204	23 647	33 687
2014		178.29	169.85(本地)	164.59(本地)	112.06(本地)	23 970	22 053	32 336
2015			162.66(本地)	157.83(本地)	111.48(本地)	36 179	17 419	27 721

注:1998 年以前为乡及乡以上工业。

Note: Before 1998, the data refer to those at and above county level.

12 -14 续表 1
continued

年　份 Year	布(万米) Cloth (10000 m)	印染布 (万米) Printed Fabric (10000 m)	机制纸及纸板(万吨) Machine-made Paper and Paperboards (10000 tons)	硫　酸 (万吨) Sulfuric Acid (10000 tons)	烧　碱 (万吨) Caustic Soda (10000 tons)	纯　碱 (万吨) Soda Ash (10000 tons)
1949	10 608	2 947	0.98		0.01	
1952	30 069	13 658	0.44		0.17	
1957	27 806	16 053	1.54		0.74	
1962	7 444	7 375	1.45	0.06	0.89	
1965	29 538	13 670	2.22		1.66	5.32
1970	33 660	21 994	3.14	0.04	2.14	12.01
1975	31 242	22 828	3.10	0.53	2.36	9.15
1978	36 877	25 797	4.55	1.32	3.61	14.04
1980	34 937	22 900	5.25	4.11	4.33	18.18
1985	34 998	17 679	6.20	3.34	5.52	26.03
1987	38 155	21 833	6.52	4.40	6.15	29.53
1988	35 890	21 213	7.42	4.88	6.62	31.12
1989	36 188	19 842	6.20	4.30	6.95	32.25
1990	34 066	21 446	6.02	4.86	6.73	30.48
1991	34 076	19 999	5.99	5.62	5.99	29.50
1992	33 682	21 534	5.95	6.70	5.62	34.60
1993	35 912	16 606	8.84	6.96	6.07	40.43
1994	43 241	16 387	12.36	8.33	6.48	43.36
1995	41 170	17 864	11.06	9.69	7.90	43.20
1996	39 023	16 881	11.31	10.12	7.30	46.91
1997	43 615	15 722	7.78	10.16	8.45	50.55
1998	40 440	9 864	6.91	10.33	9.25	52.80
1999	39 576	4 340	7.77	12.56	8.96	53.70
2000	41 783	3 526	10.96	12.96	10.24	56.20
2001	40 640	3 402	23.05	13.03	11.44	58.47
2002	47 609	5 592	29.92	5.00	13.80	60.70
2003	35 922	10 131	31.76	4.50	13.53	62.50
2004	50 111	7 718	36.38	14.70	14.86	60.80
2005	51 307	16 027	31.95	14.80	16.10	62.50
2006	55 093	20 867	15.50	7.00	15.90	63.95
2007	44 251	18 708	24.04	9.22	14.91	71.02
2008	48 399	58 907	22.41	13.02	12.78	72.03
2009	31 048	27 998	34.59	1.40	12.24	68.21
2010	17 457	29 631	35.43	4.07	13.87	69.35
2011	49 617	28 449	32.28	5.06	13.20	70.07
2012	48 987	32 478	22.27	7.22	13.71	63.35
2013	51 646	34 381	17.95	4.32	11.06	61.66
2014	44 593	33 653	18.26			67.85
2015	28 040	25 458	18.29			68.95

12 -14 续表 2
continued

年 份 Year	合成氨 （万吨） Synthetic Ammonia （10000 tons）	化学肥料 （万吨） Chemical Fertilizer （10000 tons）	化学农药 （吨） Chemical Pesticides （ton）	油 漆 （吨） Paint （ton）	染 料 （吨） Dye （ton）
1949				30	599
1952				480	2 855
1957			1 226	1 247	4 307
1962		0.45	213	910	3 560
1965		1.42	2	4 727	8 667
1970	0.98	5.89	2 313	6 380	9 347
1975	3.46	12.46	4 439	7 016	5 967
1978	7.17	23.66	9 714	8 786	5 877
1980	7.24	7.82	8 333	14 556	2 159
1985	6.31	5.16	2 000	26 055	4 448
1987	8.20	8.32	2 200	28 323	5 316
1988	8.72	9.41	2 400	28 943	5 527
1989	8.47	8.84	2 500	27 713	5 784
1990	7.56	7.55	2 500	29 075	5 119
1991	8.52	8.04	2 800	33 548	5 263
1992	10.45	7.85	3 400	35 058	4 821
1993	10.70	8.02	3 600	33 054	4 550
1994	13.04	12.39	3 600	29 437	5 097
1995	14.98	12.62	4 934	37 772	7 185
1996	18.67	12.62	4 976	26 762	7 668
1997	16.94	12.52	4 600	19 743	11 189
1998	22.36	15.30	6 755	17 594	8 274
1999	26.09	20.19	4 480	3 730	7 866
2000	24.64	20.04	3 758	693	9 306
2001	35.53	28.07	3 915	1 349	9 757
2002	20.30	9.80	4 020	1 701	9 826
2003	21.55	9.70	2 039	2 106	10 734
2004	30.30	19.60	5 061	1 955	3 961
2005	33.80	22.10	6 524	1 687	13 979
2006	33.30	21.30	12 544		26 544
2007	28.22	25.70	16 433	2 957	28 269
2008	17.93	21.51	12 848	12 105	18 263
2009	17.71	21.23	49 684		24 893
2010	16.84	14.10	16 450		41 383
2011	10.78	9.26	23 286		
2012	7.71	6.98	28 801		
2013	6.48	5.10	27 715		
2014			27 160		
2015			36 853		

12－14 续表3
continued

年 份 Year	化学原料药 （吨） Chemical Medicines(ton)	水 泥 （万吨） Cement （10000 tons）	平板玻璃 （万重量箱） Plate Glass （10000 weight cases）	耐火材料 （万吨） Refractory Material （10000 tons）	粗钢 （万吨） Crude Steel （10000 tons）	钢 材 （万吨） Rolled-steel （10000 tons）
1949						0.06
1952				0.78	0.36	0.41
1957				3.39	1.77	4.30
1962		2.09		2.41	4.59	2.94
1965		6.59		2.91	11.72	8.43
1970		7.35	16.31	3.23	19.38	14.56
1975	55	20.93	19.44	4.88	21.25	20.01
1978	185	35.40	8.86	5.93	31.06	27.61
1980	123	44.66	70.13	5.38	37.14	32.82
1984	7 228	70.27	91.25	7.98	37.81	32.43
1985	4 222	82.70	77.00	4.35	37.51	32.68
1987	7 457	117.20	87.00	4.90	46.51	38.09
1988	7 655	141.00	108.81	4.56	50.17	38.26
1989	8 348	135.00	96.49	3.68	54.64	39.38
1990	6 913	139.48	83.13	3.91	54.55	38.04
1991	4 754	165.66	96.90	3.71	56.96	39.02
1992	5 743	191.50	120.00	3.86	63.75	50.09
1993	6 566	221.30	148.71	3.55	61.75	44.88
1994	4 238	246.50	145.12	3.06	60.82	46.95
1995	1 993	213.82	426.40	3.88	67.27	49.60
1996	5 505	181.45	423.60	3.54	72.02	50.60
1997	1 693	208.04	570.85	2.45	75.71	51.06
1998	910	131.51	509.38	0.99	84.02	64.93
1999	1 691	149.41	576.50	0.59	108.10	86.58
2000	2 131	137.52	556.58	0.62	101.17	93.35
2001	2 534	148.67	421.51	0.51	124.45	119.77
2002	2 712	140.30	405.40	0.45	145.90	142.20
2003	3 288	154.90	361.40	0.47	204.80	204.30
2004	4 394	181.19	163.30	0.69	225.70	230.97
2005	4 430	210.80	297.50	1.04	309.70	330.30
2006	32 232	232.72	418.74	1.21	325.82	375.52
2007	14 139	425.53	397.79	2.38	327.00	365.55
2008	17 910	363.57	599.87	3.65	300.19	350.14
2009	19 086	397.66	681.02	18.46	307.89	349.63
2010	26 170	442.66	662.04	8.17	300.04	333.46
2011	29 337	588.08	510.05	20.02	318.27	325.89
2012	49 290	556.57	494.54	33.44	252.78	274.67
2013	49 081	575.66	610.21	42.34	235.53	230.39
2014	50 713	597.35	612.40	39.37	214.43	212.79
2015	45 923	532.36	534.99	41.13	154.56	140.63

12－14 续表 4
continued

年 份 Year	金属切削机床 (台) Metal-cutting Machine Tools(unit)	锻压机械 (台) Metal Forming Machinery(unit)	汽 车 (辆) Motor Vehicles (set)	交流电动机 (万千瓦) AC Motors (10000 kW)
1949				0.02
1952	105			0.50
1957	76			3.61
1962	167	77		3.85
1965	526	111	13	6.48
1970	2 353	531	120	14.53
1975	3 213	788	490	15.56
1978	2 558	379	22	21.72
1980	595	444	1 644	20.11
1985	900	607	4 575	26.08
1987	1 175	887	2 304	27.02
1988	1 336	737	3 722	39.60
1989	1 107	1 010	3 404	38.60
1990	1 049	440	2 317	34.28
1991	869	764	1 514	44.17
1992	1 018	982	3 287	61.08
1993	1 532	919	4 828	64.13
1994	1 505	860	2 793	37.71
1995	972	2 563	5 210	39.18
1996	1 084	584	12 247	22.65
1997	449	416	13 020	20.74
1998	280		15 475	6.43
1999	251		20 038	11.10
2000	384		30 053	38.70
2001	472	2 477	40 658	42.72
2002	588		70 079	68.25
2003	990		65 612	95.63
2004	1 287		62 572	96.13
2005	1 347		31 055	63.50
2006	3 636		50 278	702.02
2007	3 392	1 869	61 016	119.23
2008	8 381	1 230	70 161	96.89
2009	668		458 900	728.03
2010	1 120		566 211	101.10
2011	1 194		488 330	74.08
2012	1 014		574 729	104.48
2013	2 689		708 966	126.82
2014	2 563		770 245	114.46
2015	618		861 250	104.30

12 -14 续表 5
continued

年 份 Year	钢芯铝绞线(吨) Steel-cored Aluminum Stranded Wire(ton)	家用电冰箱(万台) Home Refrigerators (10000 sets)	家用洗衣机(万台) Home Washing Machines (10000 sets)	彩色电视机 (万部) Color TV Sets (10000 sets)
1949				
1952				
1957				
1962				
1965	250			
1970	34			
1975	188			
1978	684			
1980	1 232			
1985	2 327	1.66	0.48	6.60
1987	2 849	9.08	22.08	14.20
1988	1 571	15.22	42.38	17.00
1989	2 805	21.65	35.02	18.11
1990	1 880	27.41	45.86	18.50
1991	2 463	31.51	45.70	22.27
1992	2 248	54.84	46.31	28.07
1993	1 144	50.48	56.59	36.08
1994	287	62.50	71.34	60.15
1995	1 659	107.91	64.34	60.53
1996	2 265	193.80	100.94	56.68
1997	2 616	257.10	171.95	124.86
1998	1 725	219.23	183.67	96.83
1999	2 805	259.60	256.30	285.20
2000	4 202	311.10	318.50	379.40
2001	4 498	396.30	367.89	455.40
2002	5 825	518.20	408.60	593.20
2003	4 940	598.30	471.50	671.70
2004	6 608	815.03	575.06	957.90
2005	116 592	908.80	614.90	1 324.30
2006	46 974	1 290.00	649.40	1 205.60
2007	22 564	1 421.40	769.40	1 243.10
2008	29 507	723.19	407.54	836.66
2009		827.21	488.72	1 064.70
2010		801.22	580.87	1 111.19
2011		718.54	604.55	1 154.20
2012		575.01	583.60	1 439.98
2013		524.35	606.65	1 512.05
2014		610.07	590.95	1 714.93
2015		872.09	595.11	1 736.20

12 –15 规模以上工业主要产品产量

OUTPUT OF MAJOR INDUSTRIAL PRODUCTS OF INDUSTRY ABOVE DESIGNATED SIZE

产品名称	Name	计量单位	Unit	2015	2014	2015 年比 2014 年 (±%) 2015/2014 (±%)
冶金工业产品	**Products of Metallurgical Industry**					
粗钢	Crude Steel	万吨	10000 tons	154.56	214.43	-27.92
钢材	Rolled-steel	万吨	10000 tons	140.63	212.79	-33.91
耐火材料制品	Refractory Material	万吨	10000 tons	41.13	39.37	4.48
电力工业产品	**Products of Electricity Industry**					
发电量	Electricity	亿千瓦小时	100 million kW · h	173.53	178.29	-2.04
化学工业产品	**Products of Chemical Industry**					
原油加工量	Processing Amount of Crude Oil	万吨	10000 tons	1288.11	1544.57	-16.60
汽油	Petrol	万吨	10000 tons	363.48	447.51	-18.78
柴油	Diesel Oil	万吨	10000 tons	365.63	465.68	-21.48
燃料油	Fuel Oil	万吨	10000 tons	30.83	30.84	-0.03
纯碱	Soda Ash	万吨	10000 tons	68.95	67.85	1.63
化学农药	Chemical Pesticides	万吨	10000 tons	3.69	3.11	18.33
塑料制品	Plastic	万吨	10000 tons	30.93	34.64	-10.71
化学药品(原料)	Chemical Medicines(Raw Materials)	万吨	10000 tons	4.59	5.07	-9.44

12 －15 续表 1
continued

产品名称	Name	计量单位	Unit	2015	2014	2015 年比 2014 年（±%） 2015/2014（±%）
橡胶轮胎外胎	Tires	万条	10000 tires	5 179.46	4 875.76	6.23
机械工业产品	**Products of Machinery Industry**					
工业锅炉	Industrial Boiler	蒸发量吨	ton(evaporation amount)	11 830.95	22 139.82	－46.56
交流电动机	AC Motors	万千瓦	10000 kW	104.30	114.46	－8.88
金属切削机床	Metal-cutting Machine	台	set	618	2 563	－75.89
汽车	Motor Vehicles	辆	set	861 250	770 245	11.82
改装汽车	Refitted Motor Vehicles	辆	set	12 770	14 222	－10.21
民用钢质船舶	Civil Steel Ships	载重吨	syn-ton	820 795	729 108	12.58
电子产品	**Electronic Products**					
彩电电视机	Color TV Sets	万台	10000 sets	1 376.20	1 714.93	1.24
电子元件	Electronics	万只	10000 units	436 217.24	478 597.64	－8.86
建材工业产品	**Products of Construction Industry**					
水泥	Cement	万吨	10000 tons	532.36	592.56	－10.16
平板玻璃	Plate Glass	万重量箱	10000 weight cases	534.99	612.40	－12.64
砖（折标准砖）	Bricks	万块	10000 pieces	102 323.00	130 538.00	－21.61

12－15 续表2
continued

产品名称	Name	计量单位	Unit	2015	2014	2015年比2014年(±%) 2015/2014(±%)
纺织工业产品	**Products of Textile Industry**					
纱	Yarn	吨	ton	27 720.98	29 609.26	-6.38
布	Cloth	万米	10000 m	28 040.05	33 798.01	-17.04
印染布	Printed Fabric	万米	10000 m	25 458.30	33 279.80	-23.50
化学纤维	Chemical Fibers	万吨	10000 tons	1.74	2.21	-21.02
轻工产品	**Products of Light Industry**					
机制纸及纸板	Machine-made Paper and Paperboards	万吨	10000 tons	18.29	18.29	-0.01
家用洗衣机	Home Washing Machines	万台	10000 sets	595.11	590.95	0.70
糖果	Sugar	吨	ton	10 656.00	12 100.00	-11.93
卷烟	Cigarette	万箱	10000 cases	111.48	112.06	-0.52
食用植物油	Vegetable Oil	万吨	10000 tons	44.24	40.49	9.26
饮料酒	Beverage Liquor	万吨	10000 tons	162.66	169.85	-4.23
#白酒	Wine	万吨	10000 tons	1.83	1.79	2.12
#啤酒	Beer	万吨	10000 tons	157.83	164.59	-4.10
塑料制品	Plastic Products	万吨	10000 tons	30.93	34.64	-10.71
家具	Furniture	万件	10000 units	674.98	819.12	-17.60
家用电冰箱	Home Refrigerators	万台	10000 sets	872.09	773.21	12.79
皮革鞋靴	Leather Shoes	万双	10000 pairs	6 310.61	6 041.28	4.46
服装	Clothing	万件	10000 articles	68 955.80	68 358.39	0.87

12－16 规模以上工业主要产品生产能力

PRODUCTION CAPACITY OF MAJOR PRODUCTS OF INDUSTRY ABOVE DESIGNATED SIZE

产品名称	Name	计算单位	Unit	2015 生产能力 Production Capacity of 2015	2014 生产能力 Production Capacity of 2014
发电设备容量总计/发电量	Total Capacity of Generation Equipment	万千瓦/万千瓦小时	10000 kW/10000 kW·h	363	388
卷烟	Cigarettes	万支	10000 pieces	7 141 500	6 885 000
化学纤维	Chemical Fiber	吨	ton	19 800	26 800
棉纺锭/纺纱量	Knitting Spindle	锭/吨	spindle/ton	155 160	156 707
棉布织机/布	Cotton Cloth Loom	台/万米	set/10000 m	22 488	22 077
焦炭	Coke	吨	ton	600 000	600 000
农用氮、磷、钾化学肥料总计(折纯)	Chemical Fertilizer	吨	ton		
水泥	Cement	吨	ton	10 700 000	8 885 516
平板玻璃	Plate Glass	重量箱	weight cases	6 000 000	7 150 000
生铁	Pig Iron	吨	ton	4 000 000	4 000 000
粗钢	Crude Steel	吨	ton	4 000 000	4 000 000
钢材	Rolled-steel	吨	ton	3 700 000	3 738 000
金属切削机床	Metal-cutting Machine	台	set	1 880	1 718
汽车	Motor Vehicles	辆	set	1 200 000	680 000
家用电冰箱	Home Refrigerators	台	set	7 550 000	7 500 000
房间空气调节器	Air Conditioner	台	set	9 960 000	9 660 000
移动通信手持机(手机)	Cell Phone	台	set	41 000 000	33 500 000
彩色电视机	Color TV Sets	台	set	19 070 000	17 570 000

说明:2014 年报汽车生产能力为载货汽车的生产能力。

Note:In 2014,the statistical scope of production capcity of motor vehicles is the production capcity of trucks.

主要统计指标解释

工业总产值　是以货币表现的工业企业在一定时期内生产的已出售或可供出售工业产品总量,它是反映一定时间内工业生产的总规模和总水平。

工业销售产值　是以货币表现的工业企业在一定时期内销售的本企业生产的工业产品产量。包括已销售的成品、半成品价值,以及对外提供的工业性作业价值和对本单位基本建设部门、生活福利部门等提供的产品和工业性作业及自制设备的价值。

工业增加值　指工业企业在报告期内以货币表现的工业生产活动的最终成果。是企业全部生产活动的总成果扣除了在生产过程中消耗或转移的物质产品和劳务价值后的余额,是企业生产过程中新增加的价值。

资产总计　指企业拥有或控制的能以货币计量的经济资源,包括各种财产、债权和其他权利。资产按其流动性(即资产的变现能力和支付能力)划分为:流动资产、长期投资、固定资产、无形资产、递延资产和其他资产。

负债合计　指企业所承担的能以货币计量,将以资产或劳务偿付的债务,偿还形式包括货币、资产或提供劳务。负债一般按偿还期长短分为流动负债和长期负债。

利润总额　指企业生产经营活动的最终成果,是企业在一定时期内实现的盈亏相抵后的利润总额(亏损以"-"号表示),它等于营业利润加上补贴收入加上投资收益加上营业外净收入再加上以前年度损益调整。

Explanatory Notes on Main Statistical Indicators

Gross Industrial Output Value　is the total volume of final industrial products produced and industrial services provided during a given period. It reflects the total achievements and overall scale of industrial production during a given period.

Sales Output Value of Industry　refers to total sales of products produced by industrial enterprises during a given period, including sales of fished goods, value of semi-products, value of industrial services provided to other units, value of products, industrial services provided for capital construction sector, welfare and self produced equipments within enterprise.

Value-added of Industry　refers to the final results of industrial production of industrial enterprises in money terms during the reference period.

Total Assets　refer to all economic resources, in monetary terms, that is owned or controlled by enterprises, including properties, creditors equity and other economic rights of all forms. Classified by the degree of equitability, total assets include circulating assets, long-term investment, fixed assets, intangible assets and deferred assets, and other assets.

Total Liabilities　refer to payable liabilities of enterprises that have to repay in terms of money, assets or labour services. In terms of payment, it can be divided into liquid liabilities and long-term liabilities.

Total Profits　refer to the final achievements of production and operation of the enterprises, represented by the total profits after deducting losses (loss is expressed by the negative figure). It is the sum of profits from operation, income from subsidies, investment earnings, net income from activities other than operation, and adjustment of profits and losses of previous years.

13 建筑业 CONSTRUCTION

简要说明

一、本篇资料的主要内容

本篇资料主要反映了全市建筑业基本情况，主要包括建筑业总产值、增加值、建筑企业生产指标、财务指标、重点建筑企业名单等方面的内容。

二、本篇资料的来源

本篇资料来源于建筑业统计年报，由市统计局固定资产投资统计处整理提供。

Brief Introduction

I. Main Content

Data in this chapter show the basic conditions of construction of the whole city, mainly including the gross output value of construction, value added, major production and financial indicators and list of key enterprises of construction, etc.

II. Source of Data

Data in this chapter are based on the annual report of construction industry, and complied by the Division of Investment and Construction Statistics of Qingdao Municipal Bureau of Statistics.

13 -1 建筑业企业生产情况(2015 年)

PRODUCTION SITUATION OF CONSTRUCTION ENTERPRISES(2015)

项　目	Item	单位	Unit	合计 Total	#中央 of which: Central Enterprises	国有企业 State-owned Enterprises	集体企业 Collective-owned Enterprises	其他所有制企业 Other Ownership Enterprises
施工企业单位数	Number of Construction Enterprises	个	unit	562	10	23	14	525
建筑业总产值	Gross Output Value of Construction	万元	10000 yuan	13 386 271	2 674 310	847 251	72 294	12 466 726
#建筑工程	of which: Construction	万元	10000 yuan	11 346 349	1 771 857	499 521	60 480	10 786 348
安装工程	Installation	万元	10000 yuan	1 528 916	626 745	333 926	11 290	1 183 700
建筑业增加值	Value Added of Construction	万元	10000 yuan	4 868 300				
全年竣工产值	Output Value of Buildings Completed in the Year	万元	10000 yuan	5 506 894	850 787	432 085	27 279	5 047 531
施工房屋面积	Floor Space of Buildings under Construction	万平方米	10000 sq. m	11 210	1 358	93	38	11 079
#新开工	of which: Newly Operating	万平方米	10000 sq. m	3 011	349	27	18	2 966
投标承包	Bidding and Contracting	万平方米	10000 sq. m	7 455	1 358	93	37	7 326
竣工房屋面积	Floor Space of Buildings Completed	万平方米	10000 sq. m	2 108	235	17	8	2 083
#住宅	of which: Residential Buildings	万平方米	10000 sq. m	1 375	179	0	6	1 369
计算建筑业劳动生产率平均人数	Average Number of Persons for Calculating the Labor Productivity	人	person	392 603	48 667	14 959	5 122	372 522

13－2 建筑业企业财务状况(2015年)

FINANCIAL SITUATION OF CONSTRUCTION ENTERPRISES(2015)

项　目	Item	单位	Unit	合计 Total
流动资产	Circulating Funds	万元	10000 yuan	13 301 527
#存货	of which:Inventory	万元	10000 yuan	2 335 786
年末固定资产原价	Original Value of Fixed Assets(year-end)	万元	10000 yuan	1 608 253
本年固定资产折旧	Depreciation of Fixed Assets in the Year	万元	10000 yuan	106 246
年末固定资产净值	Net Value of Fixed Assets(year-end)	万元	10000 yuan	840 948
年末资产合计	Total Assets(year-end)	万元	10000 yuan	15 575 332
年末负债合计	Total Liabilities(year-end)	万元	10000 yuan	11 639 658
所有者权益合计	Total Owners' Equity	万元	10000 yuan	3 935 673
#实收资本	Paid-in Capitals	万元	10000 yuan	2 287 441
主营业务收入	Revenue from Principal Business	万元	10000 yuan	14 670 089
主营业务成本	Cost of Principal Business	万元	10000 yuan	13 107 016
主营业务税金及附加	Taxes and Extra Charges on Principal Business	万元	10000 yuan	360 890
管理费用	Management Expenses	万元	10000 yuan	430 290
利润总额	Total Profits	万元	10000 yuan	469 835
利税总额	Total Pre-tax Profits	万元	10000 yuan	868 239
年末应收工程款	Account Receivable(year-end)	万元	10000 yuan	4 271 855

#中央 of which: Central Enterprises	国有企业 State-owned Enterprises	集体企业 Collective-owned Enterprises	其他所有制企业 Other Ownership Enterprises
3 482 395	1 659 335	23 237	11 618 956
715 130	371 066	5 161	1 959 559
604 169	222 783	8 094	1 377 376
50 629	12 521	426	93 299
255 658	121 574	3 350	716 024
4 122 320	1 956 295	31 110	13 587 927
3 577 189	1 635 410	19 171	9 985 077
545 131	320 884	11 939	3 602 850
308 753	145 250	9 882	2 132 309
3 966 546	1 751 919	62 415	12 855 755
3 648 555	1 624 248	56 037	11 426 730
81 704	17 422	2 217	341 251
117 952	51 645	1 659	376 985
90 892	48 115	1 772	419 948
176 802	67 477	4 140	796 622
1 218 491	387 120	10 053	3 874 683

13 –3 建筑业企业主要经济效益指标(2015 年)
MAIN INDICATORS ON ECONOMIC BENEFIT OF CONSTRUCTION ENTERPRISES(2015)

项 目	Item	单位	Unit	合计 Total	#中央 of which: Central Enterprises	国有企业 State-owned Enterprises	集体企业 Collective-owned Enterprises	其他所有制企业 Other Ownership Enterprises
建筑业劳动生产率	Labor Productivity of Construction							
按总产值计算	In Terms of Gross Output Value	元/人	yuan/person	340 962	549 512	566 382	14 1144	334 657
竣工率	Rate of Buildings Completed							
按产值计算	In Terms of Gross Output Value	%	%	41.1	31.8	51.0	37.7	40.5
产值工资率	Ratio of Wages to Gross Output Value	%	%	12.6	12.4	19.0	32.7	12.1
资金利润率	Ratio of Profit to Funds	%	%	3.6	2.9	2.7	3.6	3.8
产值利润率	Ratio of Profit to Gross Output Value	%	%	3.8	3.4	5.7	2.5	3.7
流动比率	Current Ratio	%	%	128.7	115.5	141.1	149.6	127.2
资产负债率	Assets-Liability Ratio	%	%	74.7	86.7	83.6	61.6	73.5

13 -4 建筑业增加值(2015 年)
VALUE ADDED OF CONSTRUCTION(2015)

单位:亿元(100 million yuan)

市、区名称	Region	增加值 Value Added
全　市	Whole Municipal	486.83
市南区	Shinan District	42.91
市北区	Shibei District	55.68
李沧区	Licang District	11.10
崂山区	Laoshan District	59.00
黄岛区	Huangdao District	129.24
城阳区	Chengyang District	12.40
即墨市	Jimo	53.81
胶州市	Jiaozhou	57.99
平度市	Pingdu	28.58
莱西市	Laixi	35.12
红岛经济区	Qingdao National High-tech Industrial Development Zone	1.00

13 -5 重点建筑企业一览表(2015 年)
LIST OF KEY CONSTRUCTION ENTERPRISES(2015)

序号 Precedence	企业单位名称	Name	所在地区 Location	资质等级 Qualification Criteria
1	青建集团股份公司	Qingjian Group Co. ,Ltd.	市北区 Shibei District	A001
2	中铁二十局集团第四工程有限公司	China Railway 20th Bureau Group 4th Engineering Co. ,Ltd.	崂山区 Laoshan	A103
3	青岛建安建设集团有限公司	Qingdao Jianan Construction Group Co. Ltd.	市南区 Shinan	A101
4	中启胶建集团有限公司	Zhongqi Jiaozhou Construction Group Co. , Ltd.	胶州市 Jiaozhou	A001
5	青岛博海建设集团有限公司	Qingdao Bohai Construction Group Co. , Ltd.	市南区 Shinan	A101
6	青岛海尔家居集成股份有限公司	Qingdao Haier Home Corp.	崂山区 Laoshan	B103
7	中建八局第四建设有限公司	China Construction 8th Devision Corp. Ltd. (Qingdao Branch)	市南区 Shinan	A101
8	青岛海川建设集团有限公司	Qingdao Haichuan Construction Group Co. , Ltd.	市北区 Shibei District	A101
9	中建筑港集团有限公司	China State Construction Port Engineering Group Co. ,Ltd.	市北区 Shibei District	A104
10	山东莱钢建设有限公司	Shandong Laigang Gonstruction Co. ,Ltd.	市南区 Shinan	A108
11	莱西市建筑总公司	Laixi Construction Corp.	莱西市 Laixi	A001
12	青岛东亚装饰股份有限公司	Qingdao Dongya Decoration Co. , Ltd.	市南区 Shinan	B103
13	青岛一建集团有限公司	Qingdao Yijian Group Co. ,Ltd.	市北区 Shibei District	A101
14	山东电力建设第三工程公司	Shandong Power Construction No. 3 Engineering Co. ,Ltd.	崂山区 Laoshan	A106
15	中交一航局第二工程有限公司	China Communications 1nd Navigational Bureau 2nd Engineering Co. , Ltd.	市南区 Shinan	A104
16	中石化第十建设有限公司	Sinopec Tenth Construction Co. , Ltd.	黄岛区 Huangdao District	A109
17	中铁建工集团青岛工程有限公司	China Railway Construction Engineering Group Qingdao Engineering Co. , Ltd.	崂山区 Laoshan	A301
18	青岛温泉建设集团有限公司	Qingdao Hot Spring Construction Group Co. ,Ltd.	即墨市 Jimo	A101
19	中铁二十五局集团第五工程有限公司	No. 5 Engineering Co. , Ltd. of China Railway 25th Bureau Group	崂山区 Laoshan	A110
20	中国石油天然气第七建设公司	China Petroluem 7th Construction Company	崂山区 Laoshan	A109
21	通广建工集团有限公司	Qingdao Tongguang Construction Engineering Co. ,Ltd.	即墨市 Jimo	A101
22	青岛公路建设集团有限公司	Qingdao Highway Construction Group Co. , Ltd.	崂山区 Laoshan	A102
23	青岛第一市政工程有限公司	Qingdao No. 1 Municipal Construction Engineering Co. ,Ltd.	市北区 Shibei District	A110
24	青岛平建建筑安装股份有限公司	Qingdao Pingjian Construction and Installation Co. ,Ltd.	平度市 Pingdu	A101
25	青岛胶城建设集团有限公司	Qingdao Jiaocheng Construction Co. ,Ltd.	胶州市 Jiaozhou	A101
26	青岛亿联集团股份有限公司	Qingdao Yilian Group Co. ,Ltd.	黄岛区 Huangdao District	A101
27	德才装饰股份有限公司	Decai Decoration Co. ,Ltd.	崂山区 Laoshan	B103
28	青岛安装建设股份有限公司	Qingdao Installation and Construction Co. , Ltd.	市北区 Shibei District	A112
29	青岛星火建筑工程有限公司	Qingdao Xinghuo Construction Engineering Co. ,Ltd.	黄岛区 Huangdao District	A101
30	青建国际集团有限公司	China Qingdao Construction International Group Co. , Ltd.	市北区 Shibei District	A101
31	青岛建工集团有限公司	Qingdao Jiangong Group Co. ,Ltd.	崂山区 Laoshan	A102
32	青岛即建建设集团有限公司	Qingdao Jijian Construction Group Co. , Ltd.	即墨市 Jimo	A101
33	青岛福瀛建设集团有限公司	Qingdao Fuying Construction Group Co. , Ltd.	黄岛区 Huangdao District	A101

13 –5 续表 1
continued

序号 Precedence	企业单位名称	Name	所在地区 Location	资质等级 Qualification Criteria
34	青岛城建集团有限公司	Qingdao City Construction Co. ,Ltd.	市北区 Shibei District	A110
35	青岛利民建筑安装有限公司	Qingdao Limin Construction and Installation Co. Ltd.	市北区 Shibei District	A301
36	青岛市市政工程集团有限公司	Qingdao Municipal Engineering Co. ,Ltd.	市南区 Shinan	A110
37	青岛瑞源工程集团有限公司	Qingdao Ruiyuan Engineering Group Co. , Ltd.	黄岛区 Huangdao District	A105
38	山东兴华建设集团有限公司	Shandong Xinghua Construction Co. ,Ltd.	黄岛区 Huangdao District	A101
39	青岛滨海建设集团有限公司	Qingdao Binhai Construction Group Co. , Ltd.	黄岛区 Huangdao District	A101
40	青岛土木建工集团有限公司	Qingdao Civil Engineering Group Co. ,Ltd.	黄岛区 Huangdao District	A101
41	青岛海德路桥工程股份有限公司	Qingdao Haide Highway & Bridge Engineering Co. ,Ltd.	市南区 Shinan	A210
42	青岛营上建设集团有限公司	Qingdao Yingshang Construction Co. ,Ltd.	即墨市 Jimo	A101
43	青岛恒生源集团建设有限公司	Qingdao Hengshengyuan Construction Engineering Co. ,Ltd.	即墨市 Jimo	A101
44	青岛新华友建工集团股份有限公司	Qingdao Xinhuayou Construction Engineering Group Co. ,Ltd.	崂山区 Laoshan	A101
45	山东电建铁军电力工程有限公司	Shandong Tiejun Electric Power Engineering Co. ,Ltd.	崂山区 Laoshan	B148
46	青岛胶州湾建设集团有限公司	Qingdao Jiaozhouwan Construction Group Co. ,Ltd.	胶州市 Jiaozhou	A101
47	青岛环海工程贸易发展有限公司	Qingdao Huanhai Engineering Trade Development Co. ,Ltd.	市北区 Shibei District	A201
48	青岛通力建设集团有限公司	Qingdao Tongli Construction Group Co. , Ltd.	市南区 Shinan	A101
49	青岛颐金建筑装饰工程有限公司	Qingdao Yijin Construction and Installation Co. , Ltd.	市南区 Shinan	B103
50	青岛青房建安集团有限公司	Qingdao Qingfang Construction and Installation Co. ,Ltd.	市南区 Shinan	A101
51	青岛福海洋建设集团有限公司	Qingdao Fuhaiyuang Construction Co. ,ltd.	胶州市 Jiaozhou	A201
52	胶南市建筑工程公司	Jiaonan Construction Engineering Co. ,Ltd.	黄岛区 Huangdao District	A101
53	青岛阳光东辉建设集团有限公司	Qingdao Yangguang Donghui Construction Group Co. ,Ltd.	胶州市 Jiaozhou	A201
54	山东巴龙建设集团有限公司	Shandong Ballon Construction Group Co. , Ltd.	市南区 Shinan	A201
55	青岛地矿岩土工程有限公司	Qingdao Mine Engineering Co. ,Ltd.	市南区 Shinan	B101
56	青岛建国工程集团有限公司	Qingdao Jianguo Engineering Co. ,Ltd.	黄岛区 Huangdao District	A201
57	青岛建祥建设集团有限公司	Qingdao Jianxiang Construction Group Co. , Ltd.	胶州市 Jiaozhou	A201
58	青岛高新建筑安装工程有限公司	Qingdao Gaoxin Construction and Installation Co. ,Ltd.	崂山区 Laoshan	A101
59	青岛营海建设集团有限公司	Qingdao Yinghai Construction Co. ,Ltd.	胶州市 Jiaozhou	A101
60	青岛德泰建设工程有限公司	Qingdao Detai Construction Engineering Co. ,Ltd.	黄岛区 Huangdao District	A101
61	青岛建设集团有限公司	Qingdao Construction Group Co. , Ltd.	市南区 Shinan	A201
62	青岛新城发展建筑工程有限公司	Qingdao New City Development Construction Engineering Co. ,Ltd.	市北区 Shibei District	A201
63	青岛恒源送变电工程有限公司	Qingdao Hengyuan Transmission and Distribution Project Co. ,Ltd.	城阳区 Chengyang District	A201
64	青岛百果山建筑安装有限公司	Qingdao Baiguoshan Construction and Installation Co. , Ltd.	李沧区 Licang District	A301
65	青岛九龙建设集团有限公司	Qingdao Jiulong Construction Co. ,Ltd.	胶州市 Jiaozhou	A201
66	青岛施运机械施工有限责任公司	Qingdao Shiyun Mechanized Construction Co. ,Ltd.	市北区 Shibei District	B101

13 -5 续表 2
continued

序号 Precedence	企业单位名称	Name	所在地区 Location		资质等级 Qualification Criteria
67	青岛东捷建设工程有限公司	Qingdao Dongjie Construction Engineering Co. ,Ltd.	市北区	Shibei District	A101
68	青岛港务局港务工程公司	Qingdao Port Engineering Co. ,Ltd.	黄岛区	Huangdao District	A204
69	青岛爱华工程有限公司	Qingdao Aihua Engineering Co. ,Ltd.	市北区	Shibei District	A201
70	青岛天一建设集团有限公司	Qingdao Tianyi Construction Group Co. ,Ltd.	黄岛区	Huangdao District	A201
71	青岛裕和建设有限公司	Qingdao Yuhe Construction Co. , Ltd.	黄岛区	Huangdao District	A204
72	青岛金沙滩建设集团有限公司	Qingdao Jinsha Beach Construction Co. ,Ltd.	黄岛区	Huangdao District	A101
73	青岛环城建工集团有限公司	Qingdao Huancheng Construction Engineering Group Co. ,Ltd.	黄岛区	Huangdao District	A201
74	青岛市热电工程公司	Qingdao Thermal Power Engineering Company	市北区	Shibei District	A210
75	山东国建工程集团有限公司	Shandong Guojian Construction Project Co. ,Ltd.	崂山区	Laoshan	B201
76	青岛建设集团建兴工程有限公司	Qingdao Construction Group Jianxing Engineering Co. ,Ltd.	市南区	Shinan	A201
77	山东省即墨市第二建筑工程公司	Shandong Jimo Second Construction Engineering Company	即墨市	Jimo	A201
78	青岛林海建设工程有限公司	Qingdao Linhai Construction and Engineering Co. , Ltd.	黄岛区	Huangdao District	A210
79	青岛田横建筑工程有限公司	Qingdao Tianheng Construction Project Co. ,Ltd.	即墨市	Jimo	A201
80	平度市金泰建筑有限公司	Pingdu Jintai Construction Engineering Co. ,Ltd.	平度市	Pingdu	A201
81	青岛万怡东方建设集团有限公司	Qingdao Wanyi Dongfang Construction Group Co. ,Ltd.	黄岛区	Huangdao District	A101
82	青岛金星科技工程有限公司	Qingdao Jinxing Science and Technology Enginnering Co. ,Ltd.	市南区	Shinan	B111
83	青岛多元建设集团有限公司	Qingdao Duoyuan Construction Group Co. , Ltd.	黄岛区	Huangdao District	A210
84	青岛市崂山区古建建筑工程有限公司	Qingdao Laoshan Gujian Construction Engineering Co. ,Ltd.	崂山区	Laoshan	A201
85	青岛腾达建筑工程有限公司	Qingdao Tengda Construction Engineering Co. ,Ltd.	即墨市	Jimo	A201
86	青岛市房屋建筑集团股份有限公司	Qingdao Housing Construction Group Co. , Ltd.	市北区	Shibei District	A101
87	青岛市黄岛区园林绿化工程有限公司	Qingdao Huangdao Green Enginnering Co. , Ltd.	黄岛区	Huangdao District	B101
88	青岛新世纪路桥工程有限公司	Qingdao New Century Highway & Bridge Engineering Co. ,Ltd.	即墨市	Jimo	A202
89	青岛铁路工程建筑有限公司	Qingdao Railway Engineering Co. ,Ltd.	市南区	Shinan	A203
90	青岛望城三宝建设有限公司	Qingdao Wangcheng Sanbao Construction Co. ,Ltd.	莱西市	Laixi	A101
91	青岛亿佰建工集团有限公司	Qingdao Yibai Construction Engineering Co. ,Ltd.	黄岛区	Huangdao District	A201
92	青岛经济技术开发区市政工程总公司	Municipal Engineering Company of Qingdao Economic and Technological Development Zone	黄岛区	Huangdao District	A210
93	山东红建建安集团公司	Shandong Hongjian Construction and Installation Co. ,Ltd.	黄岛区	Huangdao District	A201
94	青岛泰能工程股份有限公司	Qingdao Taineng Engineering Co. ,Ltd.	市北区	Shibei District	A210
95	青岛铁路红宇建设集团有限公司	Qingdao Railway Hongyu Construction Group Co. ,Ltd.	市南区	Shinan	A301
96	青岛建设装饰集团有限公司	Qingdao Construction and Decoration Group Co. , Ltd.	市南区	Shinan	B103
97	青岛润佳建设集团有限公司	Qingdao Runjia Construction Group Co. , Ltd.	即墨市	Jimo	A201
98	青岛昶德建设集团有限公司	Qingdao Changde Construction Co. ,Ltd.	胶州市	Jiaozhou	A101
99	青岛经济技术开发区建筑安装工程总公司	Qingdao Development Zone Construction and Installation Co. ,Ltd.	黄岛区	Huangdao District	A201
100	青岛万福建筑工程有限公司	Qingdao Wanfu Construction Engineering Co. Ltd.	莱西市	Laixi	A301

主要统计指标解释

建筑业统计单位　指从事房屋、构筑物建造和设备安装活动的法人企业。建筑业法人企业应具有建筑业资质并能够独立核算，同时其应具备以下条件：①依法成立，有自己的名称、组织机构和场所，能够承担民事责任；②独立拥有和使用资产，承担负债，有权与其他单位签订合同；③独立核算盈亏，能够编制资产负债表。

建筑业总产值　是以货币形式表现的建筑业企业在一定时期内生产的建筑业产品和提供的服务的总和。建筑业总产值包括：

（1）建筑工程产值：指列入建筑工程预算内的各种工程价值。

（2）安装工程产值：指设备安装工程价值，不包括被安装设备本身的价值。

（3）其他产值：建筑业总产值中除建筑工程、安装工程以外的产值。包括房屋构筑物修理产值、非标准设备制造产值、总包企业向分包企业收取的管理费以及不能明确划分的施工活动所完成的产值。

建筑业增加值　指建筑业企业在报告期内以货币形式表现的建筑业生产经营活动的最终成果。

建筑业现价增加值　按生产法和分配法（收入法）两种方法计算，以收入法的计算结果为准，即从收入的角度出发，根据生产要素在生产过程中应得的收入份额计算。具体计算方法：经济普查年度建筑业增加值按照《经济普查年度 GDP 核算方案》计算，非经济普查年度建筑业增加值按照《非经济普查年度 GDP 核算方案》计算。

Explanatory Notes on Main Statistical Indicators

Statistical Unit in Construction　refers to corporate enterprise engaged in the construction of buildings and structures and in the installation of equipment. A corporate construction enterprise should have qualification certificates with independent accounting system, and should meet the following 3 requirements: a) being set up in line with relevant legal basis, having its full name, organization and location, and capable of taking civil liabilities; b) independently possessing and using its assets and assuming its liabilities, and entitled to sign contracts with other institutions; and c) making independent accounts of its profits and losses, and capable of compiling its own balance sheet.

Gross Output Value of Construction　refers to total of construction products and services, expressed in money terms, produced or rendered by construction and installation enterprises during a given period of time. It includes:

(1) Output value of construction projects, that is the value of projects covered by the project budgets;

(2) Output value of installation projects, that is the value of the installation of equipment, (excluding the value of the equipment to be installed);

(3) Output value of others, that is the output value of construction industry excluding that of construction projects and installation projects. It includes: output value of repair of buildings and structures; output value of non-standard equipment manufacturing; overhead expenses received by contracted enterprises to the sub-contracted enterprises and the completed output value of construction activities that have no clear definition.

The added value of the building industry　refers to the final results of production and operation activities of enterprises in the building industry, expressed in monetary form, during the reporting period.

The construction industry's added value at current price is calculated　by the production method and distribution method (income method), based on the result of income method, that is from the point of view of income, the calculation is based on the share of income to be received by the production factors during the production process. The specific calculation method: For the economic census year, construction industry's added value is based on the Economic Census Year's GDP Accounting Scheme; for the non-economic census year, construction industry's added value is based on the Non-economic Census Year's GDP Accounting Scheme.

Explanatory Notes on Main Statistical Indicators

14 运 输、邮 电
TRANSPORT, POSTAL AND TELECOMMUNICATION SERVICES

简要说明

一、本篇资料的主要内容

本篇资料主要反映了全市交通运输业和邮电业通讯业发展的基本情况，主要包括客货运输及港口吞吐量、民用汽车拥有量、独立核算运输邮电单位主要财务指标、邮电通讯基本情况等方面的内容。

二、本篇资料的来源

1、本篇资料中交通运输资料来源于全市交通运输业统计年报。

2、邮电通讯业资料来源于邮电通讯基本情况统计年报。

3、民用汽车拥有量资料来源于青岛市公安局交警支队车辆管理所。

本篇资料由市统计局服务业处整理提供。

Brief Introduction

I. Main Content

Data in this chapter show the basic conditions of the development of transport, post and telecommunications in Shandong Province, mainly including the freight traffic and passenger traffic, cargo handled at port, possession of civil motor vehicles, major financial indices and basic conditions of transport, postal and telecommunication services.

II. Source of Data

(1)Data on transport are based on the annual report of transport.

(2)Data on postal and telecommunication are based on the annual report of postal and telecommunication.

(3)Data on possession of civil motor vehicles are provided by Traffic Police Office of Vehicle Management of Qingdao Municipal Bureau of Public Security.

Data in this chapter are prepared and provide by the Division of Service Statistics of Qingdao Municipal Bureau of Statistics.

14－1 主要年份客货运输及港口吞吐量

MAJOR YEAR'S PASSENGER & FREIGHT TRAFFIC AND HANDLING CAPACITY OF THE PORTS

年份 Year	客运量(万人) Passenger Traffic(10000 persons)				货运量(万吨) Freight Traffic(10000 tons)				港口吞吐量(万吨) Cargo Handled at Ports (10000 tons)	集装箱吞吐量(万标箱) Containers (10000 TEU)
	铁路 Railways	公路 Highways	海运 Waterways	航空 Civil Aviation	铁路 Railways	公路 Highways	海运 Waterways	航空 Civil Aviation		
1949	327	14	9		386	162	22		73	
1952	571	49	13		447	399	44		181	
1957	1 054	149	13		747	548	118		269	
1962	3 100	141	39		909	524	97		391	
1965	1 424	230	19		1 257	690	158		524	
1970	1 329	373	20		1 856	736	232		695	
1975	1 803	159	30		2 325	817	282		1 542	
1978	1 986	274	49		2 917	1 561	528		2 081	
1980	1 896	713	73		2 596	1 642	941		1 779	
1985	2 063	1 894	86	1.0	3 009	2 303	919	0.03	2 610	
1987	2 019	2 133	159	7.0	3 288	4 948	1 085	0.04	3 070	
1988	2 083	3 300	234	8.8	3 418	6 486	1 160	0.04	3 153	
1989	1 802	3 441	308	11.3	3 717	8 926	1 450	0.10	3 145	
1990	1 488	3 639	316	14.1	3 741	6 433	1 556	0.20	3 068	
1991	1 453	4 144	366	19.0	3 774	6 896	1 789	0.31	3 194	
1992	1 488	4 965	437	27.0	3 899	6 822	1 981	0.45	3 240	
1993	1 499	6 436	499	35.3	4 044	7 685	1 910	0.64	3 650	
1994	1 564	6 787		47.0	4 112	8 336	1 804		4 331	
1995	1 480	9 785		66.6	4 205	11 788	2 185		5 165	
1996	1 230	10 738		79.9	4 415	10 749	474		6 056	81.1
1997	1 308	11 855			4 466	11 232	544		6 944	103.3
1998	1 549	11 754			4 028	14 311	1 792	1.44	7 044	121.3
1999	1 674	12 103			3 919	14 550	1 926	1.96	7 282	154.3
2000	1 780	12 145		124.1	4 256	17 234	2 998	2.30	8 661	212.0
2001	1 678	13 686		143.0	4 778	20 906	3 432	2.40	10 423	264.0
2002	1 530	14 516	777	163.7	5 079	24 480	2 530	3.00	12 252	341.0
2003	1 366	13 132	786	174.7	4 929	27 241	2 773	3.60	14 135	424.0
2004	1 496	16 420	862	241.9	5 119	29 937	3 503	5.30	16 303	514.0
2005	552	17 212	972	280.9	2 299	31 009	4 471	4.60	18 727	630.7
2006	810	17 752	999	320.2	2 790	32 047	4 768	5.10	22 438	770.0
2007	1 101	18 800	1 080	733.8	2 781	33 336	4 019	5.90	26 507	946.6
2008	1 278	19 909	1 055	755.8	3 225	34 172	5 080	7.20	30 029	1 037.7
2009	1 425	19 612	1 145	881.8	3 772	16 297	4 332	7.19	31 668	1 027.6
2010	1 537	20 460	1 302	1 010.9	5 031	17 525	4 407	8.44	35 012	1 201.0
2011	1 693	21 560	791	1 074.8	5 697	19 208	4 220	8.93	37 971	1 302.0
2012	1 881	22 724	414	1 173.1	6 126	21 312	1 791	9.06	41 465	1 450.0
2013	2 056	23 588	333	1 572.4	6 266	23 270	1 313	9.31	45 782	1 552.0
2014	2 301	5 588	324	1 641.2	5 564	19 043	1 434	10.22	47 701	1 658.0
2015	2 421	5 370	288	1 820.2	5 486	20 073	1 406	20.80	49 749	1 743.0

注:2014 年交通部调整公路客、货运统计口径,数据不可直接比。

Note: In 2014, the Ministry of Transportation made an adjustment to the statistical gauge for highway passenger and freight transportation and the data are not comparable directly.

14-2 民用车辆拥有量(2015 年底)
POSSESSION OF CIVIL MOTOR VEHICLES(END OF 2015)

单位:辆(unit)

项 目	Item	合计 Total 辆数 Number	#个人 of which: Private Vehicles 辆数 Number
一、汽车	**Automobile**	**1 947 370**	**1 667 538**
1.载客汽车	Passenger Vehicles	1 760 383	1 568 982
其中:轿车	of which:Sedan	1 137 017	1 035 706
2.载货汽车	Trucks	172 376	89 353
3.其他汽车	Other Automobile	14 620	9 203
二、电车	**Tram**	**63**	
三、摩托车	**Motorcycle**	**223 878**	**222 162**
四、农用运输车	**Agricultural Camion**		
五、挂车	**Trailer Trucks**	**20 343**	**370**
六、其他类型车	**Other Vehicles**	**215**	**14**

补充资料:机动车驾驶员(2831050 人)Motor drivers(2831050 person)
其中:汽车驾驶员(2768849 人)of which:Automobile drivers(2768849 person)

14－3 客货运输及港口吞吐量(2015年)
PASSENGER & FREIGHT TRAFFIC AND HANDLING CAPACITY OF THE PORTS(2015)

项目	Item	货运量（万吨）Freight Traffic (10000 tons)	货物周转量（亿吨公里）Freight Ton-kilometers(100 million tons·km)	客运量（万人）Passenger Traffic (10000 persons)	旅客周转量（亿人公里）Passenger-Kilometers(100 million person-km)	旅客吞吐量（万人）Volume of Passenger Handled (10000 persons)	货物吞吐量（万吨）Volume of Freight Handled (10000 tons)	集装箱（万标箱）Containers (10000 TEU)
总计	**Total**	**26 965**	**1 166.3**	**8 079.6**	**151.7**	**1 931.1**	**49 770.1**	**1 743**
铁路	Railways	5 486	166.8	2 421.0	73.8			
公路	Highways	20 073	443.8	5 370.0	77.6			
水运	Waterways	1 406	555.7	288.3	0.3			
机场	Civil Aviation					1 820.2	20.8	
港口	Ports					10.9	49 749.3	1 743

14－4 独立核算运输邮电单位主要财务指标(2015年)
MAIN FINANCIAL INDICATORS OF INDEPENDENT ACCOUNTING UNITS OF TRANSPORT, POSTAL AND TELECOMMUNICATION SERVICES(2015)

单位:万元(10 000 yuan)

项目	Item	主营业务收入 Revenue from principal Business	主营业务成本 Cost of principal Business	营业利润 Operating Profits	营业税金及附加 Operating Taxes and Extra Charges	利润总额 Total Profits
总计	**Total**	**5 258 034.8**	**3 845 308.2**	**790 050.2**	**52 071.7**	**1 011 129.9**
铁路	Railways					
公路	Highways	805 374	849 518.6	-199 283.6	6 852.1	-46 982.1
水运	Waterways	290 781.0	182 171.5	41 433.5	7 935.4	81 625.9
航空	Civil Aviation	187 209.7	158 539.9	6 311.3	953.7	8 417.1
港口	Ports	2 698 414.4	1 933 505.1	621 954.5	29 100.2	625 973.1
邮政	Postal Services	208 529.9	162 149.8	9 905.5	961.3	10 028.3
电信	Telecommunication Services	1 067 725.8	559 423.3	309 729	6 269	332 067.6

14－5 邮电通讯基本情况(2015 年)

BASIC CONDITIONS OF POSTAL AND TELECOMMUNICATION SERVICES(2015)

市、区名称	Region	邮电局(处) Post Office (unit)	#提供邮政全功能服务的 of which:Providing Omni-directional Services	邮路总长度(公里) Length of Postal Routes(km)	邮运汽车(辆) Vehicles for Postal Services(unit)	信筒、信箱(个) Post Boxes (unit)
总　计	**Total**	**651**	**217**	**5 381**	**279**	**755**
#市内三区	The Three Districts of Qingdao City	132	33	2 615	119	286
崂山区	Laoshan District	35	8	220	21	56
黄岛区	Huangdao District	109	31	683	40	92
即墨市	Jimo	97	34	522	29	75
胶州市	Jiaozhou	71	29	295	25	63
平度市	Pingdu	125	50	636	24	127
莱西市	Laixi	71	25	298	21	56

14-5 续表 1
continued

市、区名称	Region	固定电话市话交换机容量(门) Capacity of Urban Fixed Telephone Exchanges(line)	固定电话市话用户数(户) Urban Fixed Telephone Subscribers (subscriber)	固定电话农村交换机容量(门) Capacity of Rural Fixed Telephone Exchanges (line)	固定电话农村用户数(户) Rural Fixed Telephone Subscribers (subscriber)	移动电话交换机容量(户) Capacity of Mobile Telephone Exchanges (subscriber)	年末移动电话用户(户) Mobile Telephone Subscribersat Year-end (subscriber)
总　计	**Total**	**3 351 475**	**1 270 491**	**877 410**	**620 366**	**25 550 000**	**13 355 927**
#市内三区	The Three Districts of Qingdao City	190 863	876 719		283 511	9 640 000	5 816 249
崂山区	Laoshan District	5 917	70 303	1 249	27 810	1 320 000	896 800
黄岛区	Huangdao District	66 350	138 251	15 962	69 626	3 730 000	1 909 869
即墨市	Jimo	26 852	59 314	5 763	98 105	2 330 000	1 521 035
胶州市	Jiaozhou	29 690	64 534	2 611	46 608	1 630 000	1 063 775
平度市	Pingdu	21 225	34 511	1 251	65 745	1 560 000	1 178 664
莱西市	Laixi	23 665	26 859	1 029	28 961	1 030 000	701 357

14-5 续表2
continued

市、区名称	Region	函件（万件）Number of Letters (10000 pcs)	邮政储蓄期末余额(万元) Balance of Postal Savings at Term-end (10000 yuan)	特快专递（万件）Express Mail Services (10000 pcs)	邮电业务总量（万元2010年价）Business Volume of Postal and Telecommunication Services(10000 yuan at 2010 price)	报纸期发份数(万份) Issue of Newspapers (10000 copies)	杂志期发份数(万份) Issue of Magazines (10000 copies)
总　计	**Total**	**4 334.5**	**2 912 920.87**	**57.12**	**2 180 171.92**	**55.64**	**36.76**
#市内三区	The Three Districts of Qingdao City	839.3	250 203.92	18.17		17.72	18.53
崂山区	Laoshan District	123.87	110 934.55	5.7		4.63	2.86
黄岛区	Huangdao District	1 745.20	456 902.47	12.96		9.33	3.39
即墨市	Jimo	913.8	620 100.12	4.96		5.95	2.04
胶州市	Jiaozhou	256.7	508 407.2	4.94		6.7	2.49
平度市	Pingdu	140.5	694 450.51	6.32		6.96	6.34
莱西市	Laixi	315.1	271 992.1	4.07		4.35	1.11

主要统计指标解释

货(客)运量 指在一定时期内,各运输部门实际运送的货物(旅客)数量。是反映运输业为国民经济和人民生活服务的数量指标,也是制定和检查运输生产计划,研究运输发展规模和速度的重要指标。货运按吨计算,客运按人计算。货物不论运输距离长短,货物类别,均按实际重量统计;旅客不论行程远近或票价多少,均按一人一次作为客运量统计。半价票、小孩票也按一人统计。

货物(旅客)周转量 指在一定时期内,由各种运输工具运送的货物(旅客)数量与其相应运输距离的乘积之总和,是反映运输业生产总成果的重要指标,也是编制和检查运输生产计划,计算运输效益、劳动生产率以及核算运输单位成本的主要基础资料。通常以吨公里和人公里为计算单位。计算货物周转量通常按发出站与到达站之间的最短距离,也就是计费距离计算。

港口货物吞吐量 指经水运进出沿海主要港区范围,并经过装卸的货物数量,包括邮件及办理托运手续的行李、包裹以及补给运输船舶的燃、物料和淡水。货物吞吐量按货物流向分为进口、出口吞吐量,按货物交流性质分为外贸货物吞吐量和国内贸易货物吞吐量。货物吞吐量的货类构成及其流向,是衡量港口生产能力大小的重要指标。

邮电业务总量 指以货币表现的邮电部门用于传递信息和提供其他邮电服务的总数量。它综合反映了一定时期邮电工作的总成果,是研究邮电业务量构成和发展趋势的重要指标。它用各种邮电分类业务量,如函件件数、快递业务量、市内电话和农村电话的年均户数、订销报刊累计份数等,分别乘以相应的平均单位(不变价),加总后再加上出租电路和设备的收入、代用户维护电话交换机和线路等设备的收入、其他业务收入求得。

Explanatory Notes on Main Statistical Indicators

Freight (Passenger) Traffic refers to the volume of freight (passenger) transported with various means. Freight transport is calculated in tons and passenger traffic is calculated in the number of persons. Despite the type of freight and traveling distance, the freight transport is calculated in the actual weight of the goods; and despite the traveling distance and ticket price, the passenger traffic is calculated by the principle that one person can be counted only once in one travel. The passengers who travel with a half price ticket or a child ticket is also calculated as one person. The freight (passenger) traffic provides a quantitative measure to show how the transport industry serves the national economy and people, and is also an important indicator for planning the transport industry and for studying the development scale and speed of the transport industry.

Freight Ton-kilometers (Passenger-kilometers) refer to the sum of the products of the volume of transported cargo (passengers) multiplying by the transport distance. It is an important indicator to reflect the achievement of transportation industry. Normally, the shortest distance between the departure station and the destination station (i. e., the payable distance) is the basis to calculate the freight ton-kilometers. This is an important indicator to show the total results of the transport industry, to prepare and examine the transport plan and to measure the efficiency, the labour productivity and the unit cost of transport.

Volume of Freight Handled in Ports refers to the volume of cargo passing in and out the harbor area of the major coastal ports and having been loaded and unloaded. The volume includes that of the postal matters, registered luggage and fuels, materials and fresh water as supplies of the ships. The volume of freight handled may be classified by direction of flow as freight for import and freight for export, or by nature of cargo as freight for domestic trade and freight for foreign trade. As an important indicator, the volume of freight handled by type of cargo and by main flow direction reflects the production capacity of ports.

Business Volume of Postal and Telecommunication Services refers to the total amount of the information transmitted and other post and telecommunication services provided by the post and telecommunication departments. Expressed in monetary form, it is obtained by multiplying the business volume of different types, such as number of letters, couriers delivery volume, the annual average number of telephone subscribers in city and rural areas, the total number of newspapers and magazines subscribed, etc. by the corresponding average unit (fixed price), respectively, and then adding these products together, plus the income from the leased circuits and equipment and the income from maintenance of telephone switchboards, lines and other equipment, and the income from other business operations. It reflects the total achievements by the post and telecommunication departments during a given period of time in a comprehensive way, and is an important indicator to study the composition and development of the post and telecommunication business.

15 批发和零售业

WHOLESALE AND RETAIL TRADES

简要说明

一、本篇资料的主要内容

本篇资料主要反映了全市批发和零售业经营情况和效益情况，主要包括批发和零售业商品流转及财务情况、批发和零售业网点及从业人员、亿元以上商品交易市场、社会消费品零售总额等内容。

二、本篇资料的来源

本篇资料来源于批发和零售业统计年报和定期报表统计资料；网点资料依据第三次经济普查资料和市工商局提供的个体私营经济注册登记资料测算。由市统计局外经贸易统计处整理提供。

Brief Introduction

I. Main Content

Data in this chapter show the development of wholesale and retail trade of the whole city, mainly including the circulation and financial indices of commodities in the wholesale and retail trade, outlets and employment of wholesale and retail trade, commodity exchange markets over 100 million yuan, Total retail sales of consumer goods, etc.

II. Source of Data

Data in this chapter are based on annual report and regular reports of wholesale and retail trade. Outlet data are based on the information of the third economic census and the individual and private businesses' registration information provided by Qingdao Administration for Industry and Commerce. Data in this chapter are prepared and compiled by the Division of Trade and External Economic Relations Statistics of Qingdao Municipal Bureau of Statistics.

15 -1 社会消费品零售总额(1985 -2015 年)
TOTAL RETAIL SALES OF CONSUMER GOODS(1985 -2015)

单位:万元(10 000 yuan)

年份 Year	消费品零售总额 Total Retail Sales of Consumer Goods	批发零售业 Wholesale and Retail Trades	住宿餐饮业 Hotels and Catering Services	其他行业 Others
1985	307 222	231 477	16 996	18 753
1986	364 091	269 418	21 384	27 118
1987	432 569	310 658	23 319	32 617
1988	590 538	434 572	32 304	45 449
1989	619 941	450 812	34 083	56 303
1990	658 264	484 770	35 568	67 863
1991	760 562	566 767	43 320	56 812
1992	888 411	666 911	53 045	67 392
1993	1 384 533	1 031 794	80 077	96 759
1994	1 880 654	1 352 073	127 313	202 937
1995	2 376 776	1 637 349	186 028	305 947
1996	2 708 527	1 873 008	220 322	321 325
1997	3 008 981	2 105 728	241 928	361 248
1998	3 368 736	2 322 209	277 696	411 210
1999	3 762 754	2 715 635	315 307	391 388
2000	4 282 871	3 116 990	387 944	403 854
2001	4 911 735	3 561 731	507 012	433 851
2002	5 574 364	4 162 676	638 358	402 654
2003	6 455 113	5 283 584	849 032	322 497
2004	7 475 022	6 266 750	1 017 193	191 079
2005	8 701 057	7 304 660	1 176 539	219 858
2006	10 163 457	8 458 226	1 443 120	262 111
2007	12 162 246	9 995 772	1 837 754	328 720
2008	14 922 153	12 995 842	1 554 086	372 225
2009	17 302 231	14 232 954	2 549 203	520 074
2010	19 611 331	17 151 504	2 459 827	
2011	23 023 703	20 153 079	2 870 624	
2012	26 356 180	23 043 005	3 313 175	
2013	29 868 133	26 142 405	3 725 728	
2014	33 617 217	29 435 856	4 181 361	
2015	37 136 940	32 459 539	4 677 401	

注:1. 自 2003 年开始消费品零售总额不再包括制造业零售额和农民对非农居民的销售额分组。2. 自 2005 年起,住宿业从其它行业调整到住宿餐饮业中。
3. 根据第二次经济普查结果,对 2005 年以来的历史数据进行了调整。

Note:1. Since 2003, retail sales of manufacturing and retail sales of rural residents to urban residents are excluded in total retail sales of consumer goods.
2. Since 2005, hotels is adjusted to hotels and catering services from the others.
3. Historical data since 2005 have been adjusted according to results of the Second China Economic Census.

15 -2 分市、区社会消费品零售总额(2015 年)
TOTAL RETAIL SALES OF CONSUMER GOODS BY REGION(2015)

单位:万元(10 000 yuan)

市、区名称	Region	消费品零售总额 Total Retail Sales of Consumer Goods	按行业分 Grouped By Sector	
			批发零售业 Wholesale and Retail Trades	住宿餐饮业 Hotels and Catering Services
全　市	**Whole Municipality**	**37 136 940**	**32 459 539**	**4 677 401**
市南区	Shinan District	4 916 896	4 080 495	836 401
市北区	Shibei District	6 600 403	5 879 074	721 329
李沧区	Licang District	3 329 905	2 990 969	338 936
崂山区	Laoshan District	1 959 831	1 822 211	137 620
青岛(西海岸)黄岛新区	Qingdao (West Coast) Huangdao New District	4 765 807	4 076 430	689 377
黄岛区	Huangdao District	4 590 242	3 904 469	685 773
青岛前湾港保税港区	Qingdao Free Trade Port Area of China	175 565	171 961	3 604
城阳区	Chengyang District	2 122 932	1 851 414	271 518
即墨市	Jimo	3 870 665	3 522 332	348 333
胶州市	Jiaozhou	3 289 637	2 767 356	522 281
平度市	Pingdu	3 501 652	3 092 182	409 470
莱西市	Laixi	2 662 102	2 279 591	382 511
红岛经济区	Qingdao National High-tech Industrial Development Zone	117 110	97 485	19 625

15－3 限额以上批发和零售业商品购销存总额(2015 年)

TOTAL PURCHASES,SALES AND STOCK OF ENTERPRISES ABOVE DESIGNATED SIZE OF WHOLESALE AND RETAIL TRADES(2015)

单位:万元(10 000 yuan)

项目	Item	商品销售总额 Total Sales Value	#批发总额 Wholesale Value	零售总额 Retail Value	库存总额 Stock
总计	**Total**	**46 262 140**	**34 448 292**	**11 813 848**	**2 701 252**
国有企业	State-owned Enterprises	110 127	68 119	42 008	22 746
集体企业	Collective-owned Enterprises	439 008	409 638	29 370	7 924
其它企业	Other Enterprises	45 713 005	33 970 535	11 742 470	2 670 582
农、林、牧产品批发	Wholesale of Farm Produce and Livestock Products	1 167 015	1 160 956	6 060	71 709
食品、饮料及烟草制品批发	Wholesale of Food, Beverages and Tobaccos	3 143 097	3 002 479	140 618	307 423
纺织、服装及家庭用品批发	Retail of Textiles, Garments and Daily Consumer Articles	7 709 220	7 452 048	257 172	301 224
文化、体育用品及器材批发	Wholesale of Culture, Sports Appliances and Equipments	200 167	190 539	9 628	6 885
医药及医疗器材批发	Wholesale of Medicines and Medical Appliances	1 433 393	1 410 366	23 027	103 610
矿产品、建材及化工产品批发	Wholesale of Mineral Products, Building Materials and Chemical Products	17 166 227	16 930 428	235 799	670 758
机械设备、五金产品及电子产品批发	Wholesale of Machinery, Hardware and Electronic Equipment	2 567 117	2 522 507	44 610	151 069
贸易经纪与代理	Trade Broker and Agency	28 342	28 042	300	924
其它批发业	Other Wholesale not Classified Elsewhere	931 774	908 052	23 722	18 339
综合零售	Integrated Retail Trade	3 802 458	267 121	3 535 337	193 811
食品、饮料及烟草制品专门零售	Retail of Food, Beverages and Tobaccos	157 778	33 386	124 392	17 611
纺织、服装及日用品专门零售	Retail of Textiles, Garments and Daily Consumer Articles	756 590	127 613	628 977	195 768
文化、体育用品及器材专门零售	Retail of Culture, Sports Appliances and Equipments	196 457	51 634	144 824	57 402
医药及医疗器材专门零售	Retail of Medicines and Medical Appliances	418 754	64 621	354 133	63 197
汽车、摩托车、燃料及零配件专门零售	Retail of Motor Vehicles, Motorcycles, Fuel and Parts	4 826 485	120 044	4 706 441	436 792
家用电器及电子产品专门零售	Retail of Household Electric Appliances and Electronic Products	1 464 063	161 652	1 302 412	92 202
五金、家具及室内装饰材料专门零售	Retail of Hardware, Furniture and Decoration Materials	101 784	13 642	88 142	8 172
货摊、无店铺及其他零售业	Non-shop and Other Retails	191 418	3 164	188 254	4 357

15－4 限额以上批发和零售业商品分类销售额(2015 年)

SALES VALUE OF ENTERPRISES ABOVE DESIGNATED SIZE OF WHOLESALE AND RETAIL TRADES BY CATEGORY OF COMMODITIES(2015)

单位:万元(10 000 yuan)

项目	Item	销售总额 Total Sales Value	#批发总额 Wholesale Value	零售总额 Retail Value
销售总额	**Total Sales Value**	**46 372 222**	**34 929 324**	**11 442 898**
1. 粮油、食品类	Grain & Oil and Food	2 664 205	1 529 542	1 134 664
其中:粮油类	Grain and Oil	685 005	508 232	176 773
肉禽蛋类	Meat, Poultry and Eggs	376 015	189 146	186 869
水产品类	Aquatic Products	153 074	103 098	49 976
蔬菜类	Vegetable and Fruit	127 398	81 729	45 669
干鲜果品类	Dried and Fresh Fruit	181 122	100 177	80 945
2. 饮料类	Beverages	275 938	125 927	150 011
3. 烟酒类	Tobacco and Liquor	1 855 733	1 556 128	299 605
4. 服装、鞋帽、针纺织品类	Clothing, Shoes, Hats and Textiles	3 049 811	1 564 518	1 485 293
(1)服装类	Clothing	1 650 941	696 844	954 097
(2)鞋帽类	Shoes and Hats	627 935	157 345	470 590
(3)针纺织品类	Knitwear and Textiles	770 935	710 329	60 606
5. 化妆品类	Cosmetics	295 805	77 910	217 895
6. 金银珠宝类	Gold, Silver and Jewellery	410 334	82 031	328 303
7. 日用品类	Articles for Daily Use	595 877	271 919	323 959
其中:儿童玩具类	Children Toys	19 936	295	19 641
8. 五金、电料类	Hardware and Electrical Materials	387 429	292 676	94 753
9. 体育、娱乐用品类	Sports and Recreation Articles	102 978	10 938	92 041
其中:照相器材类	Photographic Apparatus	2 513	41	2 472
10. 书报杂志类	Newspapers and Magazines	111 266	34 388	76 878
11. 电子出版物及音像制品类	E-journals and Video Products	8 234	3 271	4 963
12. 家用电器和音像器材类	Household Appliances and Video Appliances	6 942 953	5 530 124	1 412 829
13. 中西药品类	Traditional Chinese and Western Medicines	1 548 157	1 178 365	369 791
其中:西药类	Western Medicines	1 336 158	1 046 359	289 799
中草药及中成药类	Traditional Chinese Medicines	169 987	123 654	46 333
14. 文化办公用品类	Cultural and Offices Appliances	448 502	213 398	235 104
其中:计算机及其配套产品	Computer and Related Products	153 501	88 910	64 590
15. 家具类	Furniture	42 701	14 292	28 409
16. 通讯器材类	Communication Appliances	431 948	222 195	209 754
17. 煤炭及制品类	Coal and Related Products	1 578 332	1 549 375	28 957
18. 木材及制品类	Wood and Wooden Products	247 325	247 325	
19. 石油及制品类	Petroleum and Related Products	5 651 397	4 120 606	1 530 791
20. 化工材料及制品类	Chemical Materials and Related Products	2 764 521	2 764 521	
其中:化肥类	Fertilizers	569 747	569 747	
21. 金属材料类	Metal Materials	7 607 266	7 607 266	
22. 建筑及装潢材料类	Building and Decoration Materials	1 171 141	1 038 085	133 056
23. 机电产品及设备类	Mechanical and Electrical Products	1 298 102	1 289 406	8 696
其中:农机类	Agricultural Machineries	80 631	80 631	
24. 汽车类	Automobiles	3 946 945	860 180	3 086 765
25. 种子饲料类	Seeds and Feedstuff	632 422	632 422	
26. 棉麻类	Cotton, Hemp	73 597	73 597	
27. 其他类	Others	2 229 303	2 038 920	190 383

注:此表为定期报表数据。

Note: The data are from regular reports.

15－5 限额以上批发业财务状况(2015 年)
FINANCIAL POSITION OF ENTERPRISES ABOVE DESIGNATED SIZE OF WHOLESALE TRADE(2015)

单位:万元(10 000 yuan)

指标	Indicator	合计 Total	国有经济 State-owned Enterprises	集体经济 Collective-owned Enterprises	外商及港澳台经济 Foreign Funded Enterprises and Enterprises with Funds from Hong Kong, Macao and Taiwan	其它 Other Enterprises
单位数	**Number of Enterprises**	**1 069**	**6**	**4**	**59**	**1 000**
年末资产负债	**Year-end Assets-Liability**					
资产总计	Total Assets	15 669 735	68 456	313 850	856 573	14 430 856
流动资产总计	Sub-total of Current Assets	13 589 500	43 838	300 790	749 877	12 494 995
负债合计	Total Liabilities	12 900 182	35 026	301 515	624 331	11 939 310
所有者权益合计	Total Owners' Equities	2 769 553	33 430	12 335	232 242	2 491 546
损益及分配	**Loss, Profits and Distribution**					
主营业务收入	Revenue from Principal Business	30 715 891	68 463	350 430	1 624 807	28 672 191
主营业务成本	Cost of Principal Business	28 819 369	64 139	324 322	1 556 733	26 874 175
主营业务税金及附加	Taxes and Extra Charges on Principal Business	181 897	212	381	1 345	179 959
营业利润	Profits from Principal Business	596 654	-133	3 714	2 653	590 420
其他业务利润	Profits from other Business	70 967	1 761	3 329	13 162	52 715
销售费用	Operating Costs	695 816	2 182	349	36 771	656 514
管理费用	Management Expenses	388 128	3 224	18 368	26 028	340 508
财务费用	Financial Expenses	134 637	1 019	3 944	7 113	122 561
利润总额	Total Profits	516 512	5 705	3 997	8 369	498 441
经济效益	**Economic Benefit**					
商品经营费用率%	Ratio of Operating Costs to Revenue from Principal Business	2.27	3.19	0.10	2.26	2.29
商品销售利润率%	Ratio of Profit to Sales Revenue	1.68	8.33	1.14	0.52	1.74

15－6 限额以上零售业财务状况(2015 年)

FINANCIAL POSITION OF ENTERPRISES ABOVE DESIGNATED SIZE OF RETAIL TRADE(2015)

单位:万元(10 000 yuan)

指标	Indicator	合计 Total	国有经济 State-owned Enterprises	集体经济 Collective-owned Enterprises	外商及港澳台经济 Foreign Funded Enterprises and Enterprises with Funds from Hong Kong, Macao and Taiwan	其它 Other Enterprises
单位数	**Number of Enterprises**	**648**	**5**	**2**	**34**	**607**
年末资产负债	**Year-end Assets-Liability**					
资产合计	Total Assets	5 883 434	26 378	18 318	738 770	5 099 968
流动资产合计	Sub-total of Current Assets	3 464 106	24 235	16 630	544 172	2 879 069
负债合计	Total Liabilities	4 602 716	25 448	18 158	496 040	4 063 070
所有者权益合计	Total Owners' Equities	1 280 718	930	159	242 730	1 036 899
损益及分配	**Loss, Profits and Distribution**					
主营业务收入	Revenue from Principal Business	10 010 399	36 272	25 086	1 404 040	8 545 001
主营业务成本	Cost of Principal Business	8 928 865	32 674	23 527	1 136 438	7 736 226
主营业务税金及附加	Taxes and Extra Charges on Principal Business	40 474	78	20	7 509	32 867
营业利润	Profits from Principal Business	201 429	974	-325	46 642	154 138
其他业务利润	Profits from other Business	136 117	247	153	31 611	104 106
销售费用	Operating Costs	564 248	178	402	150 849	412 819
管理费用	Management Expenses	370 625	2 523	1 372	94 767	271 963
财务费用	Financial Expenses	80 800	70	245	2 256	78 229
利润总额	Total Profits	228 918	996	-290	51 709	176 503
经济效益	**Economic Benefit**					
商品经营费用率%	Ratio of Operating Costs to Revenue from Principal Business	5.64	0.49	1.60	10.74	4.83
商品销售利润率%	Ratio of Profit to Sales Revenue	2.29	2.75	-1.16	3.68	2.07

15－7 分市、区城乡亿元商品交易市场分布情况(2015 年)

BASIC STATISTICS ON COMMODITY EXCHANGE MARKETS OF TRANSACTION VALUE OVER 100 MILLION YUAN BY REGION(2015)

市、区名称	Region	亿元商品交易市场数量(个) Number of Commodity Exchange Markets of Transaction Value over 100 Million Yuan(unit)			亿元商品交易市场成交额(亿元) Turnover of Commodity Exchange Markets of Transaction Value over 100 Million Yuan (100 million yuan)		
		合计 Total	#综合市场 Integrated Markets	#专业市场 Special Markets	合计 Total	#综合市场 Integrated Markets	#专业市场 Special Markets
全市	**Whole Municipality**	**70**	**12**	**58**	**1 109.7**	**254.6**	**855.1**
市南区	Shinan Area						
市北区	Shibei District	14	1	13	116.7	39.6	77.1
李沧区	Licang District	6	1	5	46.5	15.2	31.3
崂山区	Laoshan District	2		2	2.7		2.7
青岛(西海岸)黄岛新区	Qingdao (West Coast) Huangdao New District	8	2	6	71.9	17.8	54.1
黄岛区	Huangdao District	7	2	5	56.9	17.8	39.1
青岛前湾港保税港区	Qingdao Free Trade Port Area of China	1		1	15.0		15.0
城阳区	Chenyang District	4		4	139.2		139.2
即墨市	Jimo	11	1	10	498.4	117.0	381.4
胶州市	Jiaozhou	12	4	8	140.4	49.7	90.7
平度市	Pingdu	12	3	9	88.3	15.3	73.0
莱西市	Laixi	1		1	5.6		5.6
红岛经济区	Qingdao National High-tech Industrial Development Zone						

15-8 批发和零售业企业网点数(2015年底)

ENTERPRISES OUTLETS OF WHOLESALE AND RETAIL TRADES(END OF 2015)

单位:个(unit)

市、区名称	Region	合计 Total	批发业 Wholesale Trade	零售业 Retail Trade
全市	**Whole Municipality**	**77 590**	**61 119**	**16 471**
市南区	Shinan Area	12 674	10 815	1 859
市北区	Shibei District	18 888	15 503	3 385
李沧区	Licang District	5 548	4 351	1 197
崂山区	Laoshan District	3 925	2 815	1 110
青岛(西海岸)黄岛新区	Qingdao (West Coast) Huangdao New District	12 104	8 915	3 189
黄岛区	Huangdao District	11 723	8 538	3 185
青岛前湾港保税港区	Qingdao Free Trade Port Area of China	381	377	4
城阳区	Chenyang District	7 169	5 977	1 192
即墨市	Jimo	5 700	4 459	1 241
胶州市	Jiaozhou	5 603	4 226	1 377
平度市	Pingdu	3 028	2 115	913
莱西市	Laixi	2 838	1 880	958
红岛经济区	Qingdao National High-tech Industrial Development Zone	113	63	50

15－9 批发和零售业企业从业人员(2015 年底)

ENTERPRISES EMPLOYMENT OF WHOLESALE AND RETAIL TRADES(END OF 2015)

单位:人(person)

市、区名称	Region	合 计 Total	批发业 Wholesale Trade	零售业 Retail Trade
全市	**Whole Municipality**	**639 559**	**528 909**	**110 650**
市南区	Shinan Area	70 115	61 216	8 899
市北区	Shibei District	105 129	90 684	14 445
李沧区	Licang District	38 802	30 385	8 417
崂山区	Laoshan District	23 831	19 133	4 698
青岛(西海岸)黄岛新区	Qingdao (West Coast) Huangdao New District	135 452	106 917	28 535
黄岛区	Huangdao District	127 080	103 035	24 045
青岛前湾港保税港区	Qingdao Free Trade Port Area of China	8 372	3 882	4 490
城阳区	Chenyang District	50 401	44 910	5 491
即墨市	Jimo	69 651	57 499	12 152
胶州市	Jiaozhou	85 907	70 285	15 622
平度市	Pingdu	27 271	21 433	5 838
莱西市	Laixi	32 707	26 235	6 472
红岛经济区	Qingdao National High-tech Industrial Development Zone	293	212	81

15－10 批发和零售业个体网点数(2015 年底)

INDIVIDUAL OUTLETS OF WHOLESALE AND RETAIL TRADES(END OF 2015)

单位:个(unit)

市、区名称	Region	合 计 Total	批发业 Wholesale Trade	零售业 Retail Trade
全市	**Whole Municipality**	**420 935**	**77 170**	**343 765**
市南区	Shinan Area	17 063	628	16 435
市北区	Shibei District	50 679	8 348	42 331
李沧区	Licang District	17 467	1 604	15 863
崂山区	Laoshan District	10 286	835	9 451
青岛(西海岸)黄岛新区	Qingdao (West Coast) Huangdao New District	89 942	6 504	83 438
黄岛区	Huangdao District	89 720	6 492	83 228
青岛前湾港保税港区	Qingdao Free Trade Port Area of China	222	12	210
城阳区	Chenyang District	35 366	4 627	30 739
即墨市	Jimo	61 418	24 772	36 646
胶州市	Jiaozhou	58 891	9 693	49 198
平度市	Pingdu	45 216	12 045	33 171
莱西市	Laixi	33 188	8 059	25 129
红岛经济区	Qingdao National High-tech Industrial Development Zone	1 419	55	1 364

15－11 批发和零售业个体从业人员(2015 年底)

INDIVIDUAL EMPLOYMENT OF WHOLESALE AND RETAIL TRADES(END OF 2015)

单位:人(person)

市、区名称	Region	合计 Total	批发业 Wholesale Trade	零售业 Retail Trade
全市	**Whole Municipality**	**1 317 016**	**270 561**	**1 046 455**
市南区	Shinan Area	43 060	1 448	41 612
市北区	Shibei District	138 233	25 405	112 828
李沧区	Licang District	56 853	5 693	51 160
崂山区	Laoshan District	22 397	2 081	20 316
青岛(西海岸)黄岛新区	Qingdao (West Coast) Huangdao New District	247 869	20 337	227 532
黄岛区	Huangdao District	247 400	20 303	227 097
青岛前湾港保税港区	Qingdao Free Trade Port Area of China	469	34	435
城阳区	Chenyang District	152 938	21 031	131 907
即墨市	Jimo	228 774	98 055	130 719
胶州市	Jiaozhou	212 630	37 890	174 740
平度市	Pingdu	120 313	33 754	86 559
莱西市	Laixi	90 767	24 669	66 098
红岛经济区	Qingdao National High-tech Industrial Development Zone	3 182	198	2 984

主要统计指标解释

社会消费品零售总额 指各种经济类型的批发和零售业、住宿和餐饮业以及其他行业对城乡居民和社会集团的消费品零售额总和。该指标从2003年开始不再包括制造业零售额和农民对非农居民的零售额。

商品购进总额 指从本企业(单位)以外的单位和个人购进(包括从国外直接进口)作为转卖或加工后转卖的商品。这个指标反映批发零售贸易业从国内、国外市场上购进商品的总量。商品购进总额包括:(1)从工农业生产者购进的商品;(2)从出版社、报社的出版发行部门购进的图书、杂志和报纸;(3)从各种类型的批发零售贸易企业(单位)购进的商品;(4)从其他单位购进的商品,如从机关、团体、企业、单位购进的剩余物资,从餐饮业、服务业购进的商品,从海关、市场管理部门购进的缉私和没收的商品,向居民收购的废旧商品等;(5)从国(境)外直接进口的商品,但不包括企业(单位)为自身经营用和未通过买卖行为而收入的商品以及销售退回、商品损益等。

商品销售总额 指对本企业(单位)以外的单位和个人出售(包括对国(境)外直接出口)的商品。这个指标反映批发零售贸易业在国内市场上销售商品以及出口商品的总量。商品销售总额包括:(1)售给城乡居民和社会集团消费用的商品;(2)售给工业、农业、建筑业、运输邮电业、批发零售贸易业、餐饮业、服务业等作为生产、经营使用的商品;(3)售给批发零售贸易业作为转卖或加工后转卖的商品;(4)对国(境)外直接出口的商品。不包括:出售本企业(单位)自用的废旧包装用品,未通过买卖行为付出的商品,经本单位介绍,由买卖双方直接结算,本单位只收取手续费的业务,购货退出的商品以及商品损耗和损失等。

Explanatory Notes on Main Statistical Indicators

Total Retail Sales of Consumer Goods refers to the sum of retail sales of consumer goods sold by all sectors of the national economy to urban and rural residents and social groups. Sectors of the national economy include wholesale and retail trade, accommodation and catering trade and others. Since 2003, retail sales of manufacture and retail sales of rural residents to urban residents are excluded in total retail sales.

Total Purchases of Commodities refer to the total value of purchases of commodities by the enterprises (establishments) from other establishments or individuals (including direct import from abroad) for the purpose of re-selling, either with or without further processing of the commodities purchased. This indicator is used to show the total value of purchases of commodities by wholesale and retail establishments from domestic and overseas markets. The total purchases include: (1) agricultural and industrial products purchased from producers; (2) books, magazines and newspapers purchased from distribution departments of the publishers; (3) commodities purchased from wholesale and retail establishments of different status of registration; (4) commodities purchased from other units, such as surplus materials purchased from government agencies, enterprises or institutions, commodities purchased from catering and service establishments, confiscated goods purchased from customs authorities or market management agencies, second-hand goods and wastes purchased from residents; and (5) commodities directly imported from abroad. Excluded are commodities purchased by enterprises (establishments) for use in their own business operation, commodities obtained without buying or selling procedures, rejected commodities, etc.

Total Sales of Commodities refer to value of commodities sold by the establishments to other establishments and individuals (including direct export). This indicator is used to show the total value of sales of commodities at domestic markets and export. The total sales include: (1) commodities sold to urban and rural residents and social groups for their consumption; (2) commodities sold to establishments in industry, agriculture, construction, transportation, post and telecommunications, wholesale and retail trades, hotels and catering services, and public utility for their production and operation; (3) commodities sold to wholesale and retail establishments for re-selling, with or without further processing; and (4) commodities for direct export to other countries. Excluded are selling of waste packaging materials used by the establishments (units) themselves, commodities transferred without buying or selling procedures, commission income from brokerage in transactions for which settlement is directly handled by buyers and sellers, rejected commodities in the purchase, loss in commodities, etc.

16

住宿、餐饮业和旅游

HOTELS, CATERING SERVICES AND TOURISM

简要说明

一、本篇资料的主要内容

本篇资料主要反映了全市住宿和餐饮业的经营情况和效益情况以及旅游的基本情况，主要包括住宿和餐饮业经营情况和财务情况、网点及从业人员、涉外以及国内旅游基本情况等方面的内容。

二、本篇资料的来源

本篇资料中住宿和餐饮业经营情况和财务情况资料来源于住宿和餐饮业统计年报和定期报表统计资料；网点资料依据第三次经济普查资料和市工商局提供的个体私营经济注册登记资料测算。旅游资料来源于市旅游局。由市统计局外经贸易统计处整理提供。

Brief Introduction

I. Main Content

Data in this chapter show the development of wholesale and retail trade and tourism of the whole city, mainly including the circulation and financial indices of hotels and catering services, outlets and employment, international and domestic tourism, etc.

II. Source of Data

Data on hotels and catering services are based on annual report and regular reports of hotels and catering services. Outlet data are based on the information of the third economic census and the individual and private businesses' registration information provided by Qingdao Administration for Industry and Commerce. Data on international tourism are provided by Qingdao Tourism Bureau. The above data are prepared and compiled by the Division of Trade and External Economic Relations Statistics of Qingdao Municipal Bureau of Statistics.

16－1 限额以上住宿和餐饮业法人企业经营情况(2015 年)
BUSINESS CONDITIONS OF ENTERPRISES OF HOTELS AND CATERING SERVICES ABOVE DESIGNATED SIZE(2015)

单位:万元(10 000 yuan)

项目	Item	营业额 Turnover	#客房收入 Income from Guest Rooms	餐费收入 Catering Income	商品销售收入 Income from Commodity Sales	其他收入 Other Income
总　计	**Total**	**890 691**	**227 440**	**591 948**	**29 630**	**41 672**
一、住宿业	**Hotels**	**425 331**	**209 560**	**167 597**	**13 105**	**35 069**
国有企业	State-owned Enterprises	77 456	32 267	35 395	1 488	8 306
集体企业	Collective-owned Enterprises	519	244	268	2	6
其他企业	Other Enterprises	347 356	177 049	131 934	11 616	26 757
独立门店	Freestanding Stores	408 545	197 875	163 045	12 940	34 685
连锁总店	General Chain Stores	394	362	8	6	18
连锁门店	Chain Stores	6 230	5 684	441	39	67
其他门店	Other Stores	10 163	5 640	4 104	121	298
五星	Five Star Class	146 740	69 387	63 460	1 978	11 915
四星	Four Star Class	99 050	43 340	47 018	2 574	6 118
三星	Three Star Class	53 719	26 620	21 666	1 881	3 553
二星	Two Star Class	3 354	1 199	1 868	226	60
一星	One Star Class					
其他	Others	122 469	69 015	33 585	6 447	13 423
二、餐饮业	**Catering Services**	**465 360**	**17 880**	**424 351**	**16 524**	**6 604**
国有企业	State-owned Enterprises	3 184	1 323	1 773		87
集体企业	Collective-owned Enterprises	1 656	321	1 302	28	5
其他企业	Other Enterprises	460 520	16 236	421 277	16 497	6 511
独立门店	Freestanding Stores	164 714	16 631	133 971	10 961	3 151
连锁总店	General Chain Stores	264 549	646	262 624	1 279	
连锁门店	Chain Stores	1 036		1 036		
其他门店	Other Stores	35 061	603	26 721	4 285	3 453

16 -2 限额以上住宿业财务状况(2015 年)

FINANCIAL SITUATION OF HOTELS ABOVE DESIGNATED SIZE(2015)

单位:万元(10 000 yuan)

指标	Indicator	合 计 Total	国有经济 State-owned Enterprises	集体经济 Collective-owned Enterprises	外商及港澳台经济 Foreign Funded Enterprises and Enterprises with Funds from Hong Kong, Macao and Taiwan	其它 Other Enterprises
单位数	**Number of Enterprises**	**164**	**23**	**1**	**11**	**129**
年末资产负债	**Year-end Assets-Liability**					
资产合计	Total Assets	1 135 086	128 823	1 428	372 490	632 345
流动资产合计	Sub-total of Current Assets	405 499	49 472	628	69 350	286 049
负债合计	Total Liabilities	844 661	77 482	2 736	296 234	468 209
所有者权益合计	Total Owners' Equities	290 425	51 341	-1 308	76 256	164 136
损益及分配	**Loss Profits and Distribution**					
主营业务收入	Revenue from Principal Business	415 876	76 301	519	94 408	244 648
主营业务成本	Cost of Principal Business	133 303	20 873	133	29 035	83 262
主营业务税金及附加	Taxes and Extra Charges on Principal Business	22 935	4 030	29	5 371	13 505
营业利润	Profits from Principal Business	-13 754	-1 909	-160	-3 617	-8 068
其他业务利润	Profits from other Business	15 026	1 839		3 124	10 063
销售费用	Operating Costs	118 291	32 895	160	19 051	66 185
管理费用	Management Expenses	132 525	20 148	356	34 933	77 088
财务费用	Financial Expenses	22 892	1 029	3	7 108	14 752
利润总额	Total Profits	-11 840	266	-160	-5 891	-6 055
其他	**Others**					
应付职工薪酬	Total Wages Payable in This Year	101 068	23 764	190	21 524	55 590
主营业务利润率	Profitability of Principal Business	-2.85	0.35	-30.83	-6.24	-2.50

16-3 限额以上餐饮业财务状况(2015年)
FINANCIAL SITUATION OF CATERING SERVICES ABOVE DESIGNATED SIZE(2015)

单位:万元(10 000 yuan)

指标	Indicator	合计 Total	国有经济 State-owned Enterprises	集体经济 Collective-owned Enterprises	外商及港澳台经济 Foreign Funded Enterprises and Enterprises with Funds from Hong Kong, Macao and Taiwan	其它 Other Enterprises
单位数	**Number of Enterprises**	**170**	**4**	**2**	**18**	**146**
年末资产负债	**Year-end Assets-Liability**					
资产总计	Total Assets	486 069	7 693	537	149 301	328 538
流动资产合计	Sub-total of Current Assets	237 996	2 508	519	40 164	194 805
负债合计	Total Liabilities	415 605	4 080	533	119 642	291 350
所有者权益合计	Total Owners' Equities	70 464	3 614	4	29 659	37 187
损益及分配	**Loss Profits and Distribution**					
主营业务收入	Revenue from Principal Business	463 606	3 184	1 660	228 351	230 411
主营业务成本	Cost of Principal Business	231 829	1 671	1 171	110 071	118 916
主营业务税金及附加	Taxes and Extra Charges on Principal Business	23 973	142	93	12 329	11 409
营业利润	Profits from Principal Business	7 110	-216	49	7 142	135
其他业务利润	Profits from other Business	6 094	29		3 855	2 210
销售费用	Operating Costs	133 543	911	321	67 462	64 849
管理费用	Management Expenses	57 387	691	23	24 318	32 355
财务费用	Financial Expenses	9 521	14	3	5 113	4 391
利润总额	Total Profits	5 374	-220	49	7 299	-1 754
其他	**Others**					
应付职工薪酬	Total Wages Payable in This Year	68 994	1 039	251	14 649	53 055
主营业务利润率	Profitability of Principal Business	1.16	-6.91	2.95	3.20	-0.76

16－4 住宿和餐饮业企业网点数(2015 年底)

ENTERPRISES OUTLETS OF HOTELS AND CATERING SERVICES(END OF 2015)

单位:个(unit)

市、区名称	Region	合 计 Total	住宿业 Hotels	餐饮业 Catering Services
全市	**Whole Municipality**	**2 386**	**864**	**1 522**
市南区	Shinan District	670	311	359
市北区	Shibei District	367	156	211
李沧区	Licang District	199	57	142
崂山区	Laoshan District	181	72	109
青岛(西海岸)黄岛新区	Qingdao (West Coast) Huangdao New District	513	122	391
黄岛区	Huangdao District	513	122	391
青岛前湾港保税港区	Qingdao Free Trade Port Area of China			
城阳区	Chengyang District	188	51	137
即墨市	Jimo	119	43	76
胶州市	Jiaozhou	70	25	45
平度市	Pingdu	46	19	27
莱西市	Laixi	30	7	23
红岛经济区	Qingdao National High-tech Industrial Development Zone	3	1	2

16 –5 住宿和餐饮业企业从业人员(2015 年底)

ENTERPRISES EMPLOYMENT OF HOTELS AND CATERING SERVICES(END OF 2015)

单位：人(person)

市、区名称	Region	合 计 Total	住宿业 Hotels	餐饮业 Catering Services
全市	**Whole Municipality**	**22 127**	**8 744**	**13 383**
市南区	Shinan District	6 537	3 614	2 923
市北区	Shibei District	2 817	1 245	1 572
李沧区	Licang District	1 521	706	815
崂山区	Laoshan District	1 834	715	1 119
青岛(西海岸)黄岛新区	Qingdao (West Coast) Huangdao New District	4 753	1 095	3 658
黄岛区	Huangdao District	4 753	1 095	3 658
青岛前湾港保税港区	Qingdao Free Trade Port Area of China			
城阳区	Chengyang District	1 450	423	1 027
即墨市	Jimo	1 604	417	1 187
胶州市	Jiaozhou	888	289	599
平度市	Pingdu	424	150	274
莱西市	Laixi	253	74	179
红岛经济区	Qingdao National High-tech Industrial Development Zone	46	16	30

16－6 住宿和餐饮业个体网点数(2015 年底)

INDIVIDUAL OUTLETS OF HOTELS AND CATERING SERVICES(END OF 2015)

单位:个(unit)

市、区名称	Region	合计 Total	住宿业 Hotels	餐饮业 Catering Services
全市	**Whole Municipality**	**52 393**	**8 539**	**43 854**
市南区	Shinan District	4 538	933	3 605
市北区	Shibei District	6 239	1 396	4 843
李沧区	Licang District	2 897	404	2 493
崂山区	Laoshan District	2 760	358	2 402
青岛(西海岸)黄岛新区	Qingdao (West Coast) Huangdao New District	11 492	2 083	9 409
黄岛区	Huangdao District	11 480	2 082	9 398
青岛前湾港保税港区	Qingdao Free Trade Port Area of China	12	1	11
城阳区	Chengyang District	6 983	915	6 068
即墨市	Jimo	4 538	618	3 920
胶州市	Jiaozhou	6 774	1 074	5 700
平度市	Pingdu	3 655	559	3 096
莱西市	Laixi	2 231	159	2 072
红岛经济区	Qingdao National High-tech Industrial Development Zone	286	40	246

16－7 住宿和餐饮业个体从业人员(2015 年底)

INDIVIDUAL EMPLOYMENT OF HOTELS AND CATERING SERVICES(END OF 2015)

单位：人(person)

市、区名称	Region	合 计 Total	住宿业 Hotels	餐饮业 Catering Services
全市	**Whole Municipality**	**219 023**	**30 020**	**189 003**
市南区	Shinan District	23 175	3 557	19 618
市北区	Shibei District	22 646	4 053	18 593
李沧区	Licang District	16 242	1 155	15 087
崂山区	Laoshan District	10 755	933	9 822
青岛(西海岸)黄岛新区	Qingdao (West Coast) Huangdao New District	43 144	6 722	36 422
黄岛区	Huangdao District	43 117	6 719	36 398
青岛前湾港保税港区	Qingdao Free Trade Port Area of China	27	3	24
城阳区	Chengyang District	34 190	4 463	29 727
即墨市	Jimo	19 544	2 576	16 968
胶州市	Jiaozhou	27 236	4 249	22 987
平度市	Pingdu	12 691	1 711	10 980
莱西市	Laixi	8 538	513	8 025
红岛经济区	Qingdao National High-tech Industrial Development Zone	862	88	774

16－8 入境旅游人数(2000－2015年)

NUMBER OF OVERSEA VISITOR ARRIVALS (2000－2015)

项目	Item	2000	2005	2006	2007
总　计	**Total**	**260 592**	**684 407**	**854 462**	**1 081 476**
一、外国人	**Foreigner**	**177 098**	**596 177**	**751 403**	**925 384**
#韩国	Korea	69 878	295 111	373 712	509 369
日本	Japan	67 215	177 121	221 542	242 500
美国	United States	10 384	23 284	32 256	37 509
俄罗斯	Russia	4 820	12 062	17 457	10 949
德国	Germany	3 820	10 646	14 440	14 560
新加坡	Singapore	6 321	6 060	8 332	10 918
英国	United Kingdom	2 798	5 744	10 047	12 175
加拿大	Canada	1 865	4 397	5 727	7 095
法国	France	2 491	5 166	7 377	8 452
意大利	Italy	1 555	3 963	4 022	6 062
澳大利亚	Australia	1 817	4 257	7 106	8 505
菲律宾	Philippines	7 947	3 459	1 812	2 461
泰国	Thailand	780	3 261	2 464	2 682
印尼	Indonesia	1 241	2 349	2 301	3 127
新西兰	New Zealand	442	710	980	1 106
二、港澳和台湾同胞	**Chinese Compatriots from Hong Kong, Macao and Taiwan**	**60 367**	**88 230**	**103 059**	**156 092**

16－9 入境旅游收入(2000－2015年)

EARNINGS FROM INTERNATIONAL TOURISM (2000－2015)

项目	Item	2000	2005	2006	2007
总　计	**Total**	**118 164**	**340 899**	**434 100**	**502 926**
旅游购物	Shopping	20 742	67 047	78 882	95 705
住宿费	Accommodation	17 443	37 277	44 011	53 662
餐饮费	Dining	11 223	33 557	39 611	48 182
交通费	Transportation	35 252	128 112	140 831	183 425
邮电费	Postal and Telecommunication Services	5 502	18 394	21 654	26 111
文化娱乐费	Culture and Entertainment	6 894	20 240	23 900	29 180
游览	Sightseeing				26 502
其他	Other Services		36 272	85 210	40 158

单位:人次(person-time)

2008	2009	2010	2011	2012	2013	2014	2015
800 455	**1 000 670**	**1 080 511**	**1 156 391**	**1 270 113**	**1 282 814**	**1 280 526**	**1 338 098**
697 391	**801 424**	**826 628**	**809 043**	**877 593**	**905 415**	**951 732**	**996 191**
340 648	363 181	382 225	298 096	338 383	338 191	366 584	389 832
210 090	261 553	242 082	216 755	185 613	146 080	135 179	140 762
28 998	28 745	35 539	45 842	48 431	54 178	57 907	62 771
3 774	9 525	15 793	15 750	26 432	26 519	25 356	28 529
11 261	14 735	21 626	26 178	26 311	19 014	21 723	23 425
10 683	17 453	13 444	16 626	16 316	16 305	19 975	21 310
10 657	9 103	17 639	23 955	28 385	19 496	22 817	23 812
5 467	7 741	9 279	12 007	11 678	9 727	9 483	10 659
6 067	7 030	11 766	12 019	15 595	21 422	17 828	19 388
3 871	3 747	3 867	7 028	5 622	5 679	7 705	8 747
7 940	6 641	8 223	15 465	16 644	11 149	15 339	16 798
2 075	7 800	14 140	14 259	7 546	18 630	6 668	7 300
2 236	3 685	2 572	3 271	2 369	3 692	4 803	5 331
1 589	4 221	7 863	8 128	4 571	10 011	6 568	5 692
1 161	2 029	1 597	6 265	6 448	1 452	2 549	2 872
103 064	**199 246**	**253 883**	**347 348**	**392 520**	**377 399**	**328 794**	**342 511**

单位:万元(10 000 yuan)

2008	2009	2010	2011	2012	2013	2014	2015
347 645	**377 000**	**399 688**	**441 171**	**519 495**	**511 158**	**503 900**	**566 742**
66 053	70 763	74 104	80 823	93 872	94 055	109 246	122 473
37 198	41 093	43 933	59 823	59 378	58 577	62 232	69 879
33 374	36 569	38 747	40 191	51 378	51 065	44 041	49 589
9 039	9 877	145 551	134 425	170 238	180 945	160 492	180 791
17 382	18 812	19 081	16 720	23 014	22 950	19 400	21 593
20 163	22 394	24 032	36 132	32 832	32 103	33 409	36 271
18 773	21 037	22 978	51 705	32 832	32 152	44 192	49 930
145 663	29 745	31 262	21 353	55 951	39 311	30 888	36 216

16-10 国内旅游人数及收入(2015年)
NUMBER OF DOMESTIC TOURISM INCOME(2015)

指　标	Indicator	单位	Unit	2015
国内旅游人数	**Number of Domestic Tourists**	**万人次**	**10000 person-times**	**7 322**
1.过夜旅游者人数	Number of Overnight Tourists	万人次	10000 person-times	4 391
(1)旅游住宿设施国内旅游人数	Domestic Tourists Staying Overnight at Hotels	万人次	10000 person-times	2 826
(2)住亲友家去景点的国内旅游人数	Domestic Tourists Staying Overnight at Relatives and Friends's Home	万人次	10000 person-times	1 565
2.不过夜旅游者(一日游人数)	Number of Same-day (One-day Sightseeing) Tourists	万人次	10000 person-times	2 931
旅游景点接待一日游人数	One-day Sightseeing Tourists Received by Tour Scenes	万人次	10000 person-times	2 931
(1)本地一日游人数	Number of Local One-day Sightseeing Tourists	万人次	10000 person-times	1 901
(2)外地一日游人数	Number of One-day Sightseeing Tourists from Outside Areas	万人次	10000 person-times	1 030
国内旅游人均花费	**Per Capita Expenditure of Domestic Tourist**	**元**	**yuan**	**2 066**
国内旅游收入	**Earings from Domestic Tourism**	**亿元**	**100 million yuan**	**1 133**
1.接待过夜旅游者收入	Earings from Overnight Tourists	万元	10000 yuan	9 071 806
2.接待不过夜旅游者(一日游)收入	Earings from Same-day(One-day Sightseeing) Tourists	万元	10000 yuan	2 258 194

主要统计指标解释

住宿餐饮业营业额 指住宿和餐饮业法人企业、产业活动单位在经营活动中因提供服务或销售商品等取得的收入,包括客房收入、餐费收入、商品销售收入和其他收入。客房收入指住宿和餐饮业法人企业、产业活动单位在经营活动中因提供住宿服务取得的客房收入。餐费收入指住宿和餐饮业法人企业、产业活动单位因为顾客提供就餐服务取得的收入,包括经烹饪、调制加工后出售的各种食品,如主食、炒菜、凉拌菜等的收入。商品销售收入指住宿和餐饮业法人企业、产业活动单位伴随服务而出售商品所取得的收入。其他收入指营业收入中除客房收入、餐费收入、商品销售收入以外的其他收入,包括娱乐、健身和商务服务等。

国内旅游者 是指不以谋求职业、获取报酬为目的,离开惯常居住环境,到国内其它地方从事参观、游览、度假等旅游活动(包括外出探亲、疗养、考察、参加会议和从事商务、科技、文化、教育、宗教活动过程中的旅游活动),出行距离超过10公里,出游时间超过6小时,但不超过12个月的我国大陆居民。

入境旅游者 指来我国参观、访问、旅行、探亲、访友、休养、考察、参加会议和从事经济、科技、文化、教育、体育、宗教等活动的外国人、华侨、港澳和台湾同胞的人数。不包括外国在我国的常驻机构,如领事馆、通讯社、企业办事处的工作人员;来我国常住的外国专家、留学生以及在岸逗留不过夜人员。

Explanatory Notes on Main Statistical Indicators

Business Revenue of Hotels and Catering Services refer to revenue received from providing services or selling commodities by corporate enterprises and establishments engaged in hotel and catering services, including income from hotel rooms, from catering services, from selling of commodities and from other services. Income from hotel rooms refers to income of corporate enterprises and establishments by providing lodging services. Income from catering services refers to income of corporate enterprises and establishments by providing catering services, including selling of cooked or prepared foods such as stable food, cooked dishes or cold dishes. Income from selling of commodities refers to income of corporate enterprises and establishments by selling commodities that accompany the services they provide. Income from other activities refers to income received other than income from hotel rooms, catering services or selling of commodities, such as income from providing recreation, fitness or business services.

Domestic Tourists refers to residents in mainland China who are not for the purpose of seeking employment, remuneration, and leaving the usual living environment, elsewhere to engage in domestic visitors, sightseeing, vacation travel (including to go out to visit relatives, infirmary, observing, participate in the meeting and engage in business, science and technology, culture, education, religious activities in the course of tourism activities), trip distance of more than 10 km, trips longer than six hours, but not more than 12 months.

Entrance Tourists refers to foreigners, overseas Chinese, Chinese compatriots from Hong Kong, Macao and Taiwan coming to China for sight-seeing, visits, tours, family reunions, vacations, study tours, conferences and other activities of a business, scientific and technological, cultural, educational and religious nature. It does not include representatives and employees of resident institutions of foreign countries in China such as embassies, consulates, news agencies and offices of foreign companies and organizations, nor does it include long-term foreign experts or students residing in China, or persons in transition without spending a night in China.

17

教育、科技和文化

EDUCATION, SCIENCE & TECHNOLOGY AND CULTURE

简要说明

一、本篇资料的主要内容

本篇资料主要反映了全市教育、科技和文化事业基本情况。教育部分主要包括高等教育、中等教育、初等教育、成人教育、职业教育、幼儿园等方面的基本情况。科技部分主要包括科研机构、科学技术奖励、大中型工业企业技术开发情况。文化部分主要包括文化、文物、广播、电视、报纸杂志出版、图书出版等方面的发展状况。

二、本篇资料的来源

1、教育部分，技工学校的资料来源于市人力资源和社会保障局，其他资料来源于市教育局。

2、科技部分，科研机构及科技奖励资料来源于市科技局，大中型工业企业科技活动资料来源于市统计局统计调查年报。

3、文化部分，图书、杂志、报纸出版有关资料来源于青岛出版集团、海大出版社，其他资料来源于市文化广电新闻出版局。

本篇资料由市统计局人口和社会科技统计处整理提供。

Brief Introduction

I. Main Content

Data in this chapter show the basic conditions of education, science & technology and culture. Data on education show the development of higher education, secondary education, primary education, adult education, vocational education and kindergartens. Data on science & technology show the basic conditions of science research institutions, scientific and technological achievements and prizes, scientific & technological activities of large and medium-size industrial enterprises. Data on culture show the basic conditions of arts, cultural relics, broadcasting, television and publication of newspapers, magazines and books.

II. Source of Data

(1)In education component, data on the basic conditions of technical schools are provided by Qingdao Municipal Bureau of Human Resources and Social Security, and the other data on education are provided by Qingdao Municipal Bureau of Education.

(2)In science & technology component, data on science research institutions and scientific & technological achievements and prizes are provided by Qingdao Municipal Bureau of Science and Technology. Data on scientific and technological activities are from the annual report of scientific and technological activities, which is provided by Qingdao Municipal Bureau of Statistics.

(3)In culture component, data on publication of books, magazines and newspapers are provided by Qingdao Publishing Group and Ocean University Press. The other data are provided by Qingdao Municipal Bureau of Cluture, Broadcasting, Television, Press and Publication.

Data in this chapter are provided and compiled by the Division of Population and Science & Technology of Qingdao Municipal Bureau of Statistics.

17－1 各级各类学校基本情况(2015年)
BASIC STATISTICS ON SCHOOLS BY LEVEL AND TYPE OF SCHOOL(2015)

项目	Item	学校数(所) Schools (unit)	毕业生数(人) Graduates (person)	招生数(人) New Students Enrollment(person)	在校学生数(人) Students Enrollment(person)	教职工数(人) Teachers and Staff(person)	#专任教师 of which: Full-time Teachers
研究生	Postgraduates		9 451	10 739	30 565		
普通高等学校	Regular Institutions of Higher Education	24	79 784	92 251	322 260	29 620	19 213
中等专业学校	Specialized Secondary Schools	6	9 277	11 405	33 038	918	639
技工学校	Technical Schools	23	8 077	8 884	30 202	2 121	1 847
职业学校	Vocational Schools	47	22 758	19 276	48 590	7 233	5 732
普通中学	Regular Secondary Schools	293	117 648	111 210	355 401	38 042	32 940
初中	Junior Secondary Schools	231	76 505	73 176	238 715	24 579	22 278
高中	Senior Secondary Schools	62	41 143	38 034	116 686	13 463	10 662
小学	Primary Schools	772	73 773	91 748	536 492	34 725	33 330
特殊教育学校	Special Education Schools	12	361	345	2 325	623	508
幼儿园	Kindergartens	2 221	77 469	88 796	232 564	25 827	17 253
成人高等学校	Adult Institutions of Higher Education	1	36 202	38 794	109 970	104	56
成人中等学校	Adult Secondary Education Schools	4	3 521	1 534	7 298	128	106
成人初等学校	Adult Primary Education Schools						

注:1. 成人中等学校仅包括成人中学和成人中专。
Note:1. Adult secondary education schools refer to adult secondary schools and adult specialized secondary schools.

17－2 主要年份各级各类学校在校学生数

MAJOR YEAR'S STUDENTS ENROLLMENT OF SCHOOLS BY LEVEL AND TYPE OF SCHOOL

单位：人(person)

年份 Year	普通高等学校 Regular Institutions of Higher Education	中等学校 Secondary Schools	中等专业学校 Specialized Secondary Schools	普通中学 Regular Secondary Schools	职业中学 Vocational Schools	技工学校 Technical Schools	小学 Primary Schools
1949	1 007	13 804	1 600	12 204			213 470
1952	2 761	27 951	3 770	24 181			413 286
1957	3 133	56 689	4 985	51 604	100		482 397
1962	4 381	62 646	2 791	58 639	243	973	522 921
1965	2 987	99 605	9 405	88 187	1 490	523	788 485
1970	320	222 521	105	220 262	2 154		728 433
1975	1 151	350 309	3 144	346 403		762	928 153
1978	3 465	464 584	4 269	457 460	2 000	865	634 905
1980	6 783	325 935	5 195	318 193	1 344	1 203	816 970
1985	10 631	327 446	11 475	279 915	33 945	2 111	691 341
1988	14 408	352 576	11 819	306 943	28 933	4 881	629 212
1989	15 183	348 367	14 401	296 318	32 283	5 365	634 794
1990	15 433	351 365	15 118	296 163	34 568	5 516	632 314
1991	15 491	353 410	14 618	298 568	34 421	5 803	612 772
1992	16 470	367 480	14 763	307 903	38 242	6 572	585 381
1993	23 858	383 043	16 877	318 179	40 743	7 244	583 585
1994	25 018	420 077	20 582	347 667	43 734	8 094	593 419
1995	24 908	450 212	23 744	372 335	46 044	8 089	595 891
1996	26 076	468 561	26 951	382 760	50 131	8 719	607 284
1997	27 434	463 619	28 543	362 305	61 640	11 131	626 749
1998	29 507	442 525	28 757	336 918	65 989	10 861	625 308
1999	33 681	459 520	26 955	352 238	70 236	10 091	583 594
2000	46 131	497 391	25 192	398 458	63 894	9 847	534 922
2001	60 728	542 400	25 358	443 693	62 003	11 346	499 147
2002	82 539	575 599	27 421	467 628	67 085	13 465	478 634
2003	168 439	586 704	28 948	461 435	75 221	21 100	467 560
2004	201 739	598 804	30 881	436 117	101 553	30 253	476 897
2005	239 761	569 230	33 522	391 148	106 400	38 160	479 781
2006	260 339	554 308	32 051	365 192	116 487	40 578	483 892
2007	264 917	558 527	28 011	360 410	130 156	39 950	484 775
2008	269 314	582 932	25 330	373 884	143 126	40 592	477 230
2009	275 157	56 4476	22 739	377 427	127 792	36 518	465 031
2010	284 788	535 079	24 014	380 025	98 560	32 480	462 722
2011	291 453	505 051	25 905	373 226	74 892	31 028	479 513
2012	296 645	489 103	27 005	369 580	65 419	27 099	484 985
2013	300 246	484 025	28 389	365 110	61 594	28 932	496 343
2014	313 486	479 260	28 751	362 599	58 170	29 740	516 529
2015	322 260	467 231	33 038	355 401	48 590	30 202	536 492

17－3 主要年份普通高等学校基本情况
MAJOR YEAR'S BASIC STATISTICS ON REGULAR INSTITUTIONS OF HIGHER EDUCATION

单位：人(person)

年 份 Year	学校数(所) Schools (unit)	毕业生数 Graduates	招生数 New Students Enrollment	在校学生数 Students Enrollment	教职工数 Teachers and Staff	#专任教师 of which: Full-time Teachers
1949	1		250	1 007	779	226
1952	2	262	565	2 761	12 530	308
1957	2	356	755	3 133	1 308	622
1962	5	647	653	4 381	1 866	749
1965	3	741	529	2 987	1 539	623
1970	2	684		320	1 178	486
1975	2	460	473	1 151	1 353	582
1978	4	739	1 782	3 465	2 829	1 176
1980	6	431	1 717	6 783	4 182	1 606
1985	7	1 828	3 823	10 631	5 561	2 181
1988	7	3 496	4 687	14 408	6 875	2 499
1989	7	3 891	4 567	15 183	7 174	2 554
1990	7	4 495	4 745	15 433	7 305	2 624
1991	7	4 880	4 954	15 491	7 282	2 489
1992	7	4 458	5 428	16 470	7 344	2 523
1993	7	3 140	9 449	23 858	7 366	2 520
1994	4	7 059	8 042	25 018	7 466	2 650
1995	4	7 828	7 978	24 908	7 545	2 682
1996	4	6 691	7 956	26 076	7 606	2 745
1997	4	7 091	8 503	27 434	7 790	2 813
1998	4	6 912	8 849	29 507	7 662	2 907
1999	4	7 202	11 584	33 681	7 662	2 928
2000	6	7 128	18 427	46 131	8 030	3 278
2001	6	8 991	22 787	60 728	8 706	4 058
2002	7	13 053	29 731	82 539	9 517	4 723
2003	25	25 747	61 975	168 439	18 911	10 293
2004	25	34 860	70 022	201 739	21 437	12 347
2005	25	46 114	79 725	239 761	23 078	13 894
2006	25	55 931	79 094	260 339	24 881	15 195
2007	25	68 354	78 728	264 917	25 956	16 005
2008	25	75 198	86 878	269 314	26 654	16 805
2009	25	69 475	81 025	275 157	26 983	16 870
2010	25	70 450	82 220	284 788	28 145	16 996
2011	22	79 466	84 434	291 453	28 151	17 120
2012	22	79 791	87 981	296 645	29 445	18 183
2013	22	78 974	85 707	300 246	28 958	18 396
2014	22	77 503	90 127	313 486	28 944	18 587
2015	24	79 784	92 251	322 260	29 620	19 213

17 -4 各类成人教育基本情况(2015 年)
BASIC STATISTICS ON ADULT EDUCATION(2015)

单位:人(person)

各类学校	Schools by Type of School	学校数(所) Schools (unit)	毕业生数 Graduates	招生数 New Students Enrollment	在校学生数 Students Enrollment	教职工数 Teachers and Staff	#专任教师 of which: Full-time Teachers
总　计	**Total**	**5**	**35 216**	**39 303**	**114 085**	**232**	**162**
成人高等教育	Adult Higher Education	1	31 695	37 769	106 787	104	56
广播电视大学	Broadcasting and TV Universities	1	169	369	704	104	56
职工、农民大学	Universities of Vocational and Agricultural Education						
函授、夜大学	Correspondence and Evening College Education		31 526	37 400	106 083		
管理干部学校	Cadre Management Schools						
成人中等教育	Adult Secondary Education	4	3 521	1 534	7 298	128	106
成人中等专业学校	Adult Specialized Secondary Schools	4	3 521	1 534	7 298	128	106

注：本年度成人高等自学考试毕业 1 474 人；参加成人高等单科班、进修班、短训班、专业证书班学习毕业(结业)52 542 人。

Note: 1 474 persons have been graduated from adult higher tech-oneself tests in the year, 52 542 persons have been graduated from adult higher single subject courses, training courses, short-term training course and specialized diploma courses.

17-5 分市、区普通中学情况(2015 年)
BASIC STATISTICS ON REGULAR SECONDARY SCHOOLS BY REGION(2015)

单位:人(person)

市、区名称	Region	普通高中 Regular Senior Secondary Schools				普通初中 Regular Junior Secondary Schools			
		学校数(所) Schools (unit)	毕业生数 Graduates	招生数 New Students Enrollment	在校生数 Students Enrollment	学校数(所) Schools (unit)	毕业生数 Graduates	招生数 New Students Enrollment	在校生数 Students Enrollment
全　市	**Whole Municipality**	**62**	**41 143**	**38 034**	**116 686**	**231**	**76 505**	**73 176**	**238 715**
市　直	Municipal Level	17	7 591	7 582	22 673	3	2 716	2 535	7 920
市南区	Shinan District					10	3 201	2 376	8 551
市北区	Shibei District					23	6 462	5 872	18 962
李沧区	Licang District					11	3 383	3 182	10 424
崂山区	Laoshan District	7	1 783	1 782	5 308	9	2 036	1 931	6 480
黄岛区	Huangdao District	11	7 195	6 383	19 464	34	12 605	12 099	38 116
城阳区	Chengyang District	5	2 580	2 709	8 070	15	5 050	5 265	16 253
即墨市	Jimo	7	6 299	5 363	17 131	31	11 334	11 670	37 128
胶州市	Jiaozhou	7	5 004	4 202	13 667	22	8 922	8 873	27 243
平度市	Pingdu	5	6 890	6 970	20 844	43	13 822	11 654	38 196
莱西市	Laixi	3	3 801	3 043	9 529	28	6 296	7 087	27 335
红岛经济区	Qingdao National High-tech Industrial Development Zone					2	678	632	2 107

17－6 分市、区职业中学、小学情况(2015 年)
BASIC STATISTICS ON VOCATIONAL SECONDARY SCHOOLS AND PRIMARY SCHOOLS BY REGION(2015)

单位:人(person)

市、区名称	Region	职业中学 Vocational Secondary Schools				小学 Primary Schools			
		学校数(所) Schools (unit)	毕业生数 Graduates	招生数 New Students Enrollment	在校生数 Students Enrollment	学校数(所) Schools (unit)	毕业生数 Graduates	招生数 New Students Enrollment	在校生数 Students Enrollment
全　市	**Whole Municipality**	**47**	**22 758**	**19 276**	**48 590**	**772**	**73 773**	**91 748**	**536 492**
市　直	Municipal Level	18	5 043	3 212	8 335				
市南区	Shinan District					28	4 111	5 007	29 105
市北区	Shibei District					65	6 450	9 768	51 735
李沧区	Licang District					32	3 421	5 911	29 230
崂山区	Laoshan District	1	631	675	1 898	26	2 117	3 957	20 035
黄岛区	Huangdao District	18	8 896	5 453	14 648	90	12 171	16 053	93 417
城阳区	Chengyang District	3	402	1 205	1 626	46	5 305	9 421	48 090
即墨市	Jimo	3	1 821	3 063	6 861	175	11 729	13 463	84 169
胶州市	Jiaozhou	1	2 288	2 445	6 550	78	8 810	9 336	64 124
平度市	Pingdu	1	1 802	1 908	4 983	145	11 767	11 491	75 769
莱西市	Laixi	2	1 875	1 315	3 689	81	7 233	6 720	36 695
红岛经济区	Qingdao National High-tech Industrial Development Zone					6	659	621	4 123

17－7 分市、区中小学教职工情况(2015 年)

BASIC STATISTICS ON TEACHERS AND STAFF IN SECONDARY AND PRIMARY SCHOOLS BY REGION(2015)

单位:人(person)

市、区名称	Region	普通中学 Regular Secondary Schools		职业中学 Vocational Secondary Schools		小学 Primary Schools	
		教职工数 Teachers and Staff	#专任教师 of which: Full-time Teachers	教职工数 Teachers and Staff	#专任教师 of which: Full-time Teachers	教职工数 Teachers and Staff	#专任教师 of which: Full-time Teachers
全　市	**Whole Municipality**	**38 042**	**32 940**	**7 233**	**5 732**	**34 725**	**33 330**
市　直	Municipal Level	3 358	2 573	2 161	1 494		
市南区	Shinan District	1 008	817			1 959	1 904
市北区	Shibei District	2 102	1 677			3 412	3 233
李沧区	Licang District	1 096	897			1 752	1 676
崂山区	Laoshan District	1 541	1 215	229	149	1 350	1 285
黄岛区	Huangdao District	6 119	5 553	1 545	1 332	6 018	5 797
城阳区	Chengyang District	2 520	2 113	680	582	2 582	2 482
即墨市	Jimo	5 767	5 104	717	623	5 418	5 275
胶州市	Jiaozhou	4 046	3 557	669	482	3 997	3 885
平度市	Pingdu	6 463	5 843	684	623	5 171	4 900
莱西市	Laixi	3 790	3 366	548	447	2 783	2 613
红岛经济区	Qingdao National High-tech Industrial Development Zone	232	225			283	280

17 -8 分市、区幼儿园基本情况(2015 年)
BASIC STATISTICS ON KINDERGARTENS BY REGION(2015)

单位:人(person)

市、区名称	Region	幼儿园(所) Kindergartens(unit)	幼儿数 Children	教职工数 Teachers and Staff	#专任教师 of which: Full-time teachers
全　市	**Whole Municipality**	**2 221**	**232 564**	**25 827**	**17 253**
市南区	Shinan District	52	12 790	1 931	947
市北区	Shibei District	109	25 889	2 682	1 754
李沧区	Licang District	43	14 571	1 897	964
崂山区	Laoshan District	112	12 257	1 892	1 081
黄岛区	Huangdao District	384	40 169	5 173	3 547
城阳区	Chengyang District	131	21 379	2 932	1 917
即墨市	Jimo	378	32 655	2 904	2 146
胶州市	Jiaozhou	409	25 919	2 733	1 967
平度市	Pingdu	423	31 418	2 232	1 737
莱西市	Laixi	156	13 605	1 192	960
红岛经济区	Qingdao National High-tech Industrial Development Zone	24	1 912	259	233

17-9 科研机构基本情况(1978-2015年)
BASIC STATISTICS ON SCIENTIFIC RESEARCH INSTITUTIONS(1978-2015)

年份 Year	独立自然科研机构(个) Independent Institutions of Natural Scientific Research(unit)	独立自然科研机构中科技人员(人) Personnel of Independent Institutions of Natural Scientific Research(person)	完成科研项目(项) Number of Scientific Research Projects Completed(item)	取得科技成果(项) Number of Achievements in S&T(item)
1978	31	2701	306	306
1980			481	297
1982	41	2 345	451	451
1983	48	3 182	530	530
1984	53	3 312	507	507
1985	52	3 673	552	552
1986	63	3 998	577	577
1987	76	4 629	579	579
1988	101	5 199	544	510
1989	111	5 885	544	688
1990	141	6 046	414	931
1991	72	5 665	753	753
1992	71	5 726	659	659
1993	69	5 545	546	546
1994	69	5 540	467	467
1995	59	5 286	441	441
1996	58	4 738	613	613
1997	54	4 577	418	418
1998	52	4 142	517	517
1999	58	3 771	606	606
2000	54	3 637	621	621
2001	50	3 191	457	457
2002	52	3 248	406	406
2003	53	3 246	589	589
2004	50	3 226	506	506
2005	50	3 234	438	438
2006	50	3 291	548	548
2007	50	3 432	506	506
2008	42	3 709	416	416
2009	43	3 727	572	572
2010	44	4 088	472	472
2011	47	4 548	345	345
2012	48	4 967	304	304
2013	48	6 057	433	433
2014	50	5 438	415	415
2015	54	6 037	639	639

注:1991年以后不包括民办科研机构。

Note:Since 1991,private institutions of scientific research are not included.

17－10 独立科学研究机构情况(2015 年)
BASIC STATISTICS ON INDEPENDENT INSTITUTIONS OF SCIENTIFIC RESEARCH(2015)

项　目	Item	计量单位	Unit	总　计 Total	中央属 Central	地方属 Local
机构数	Number of Institutions	个	unit	54	19	35
职工人数	Staff and Workers	人	person	8 017	5 285	2 732
科技人员	Personnel Engaged in S&T	人	person	6 037	4 127	1 910
经费收入	Funding for S&T	万元	10 000 yuan	348 234.3	288 013.9	60 220.4
经费支出	Expenditures for S&T	万元	10 000 yuan	345 452.9	291 979.3	53 473.6

17－11 科学技术奖励情况(2015 年)
AWARD STATISTICS ON SCIENCE AND TECHNOLOGY(2015)

项　目	Item	单位	Unit	自然科学奖 Natural Science Prizes Awarded	技术发明奖 Invention Prizes Awarded	科技进步奖 Scientific And Technological Progress Prizes Awarded	科学技术功勋奖 Scientific And Technological Credit Prizes Awarded	国际科技合作奖 International S&T Cooperation Prizes Award	最高奖 Highest Prizes Award
国家级	**National Level**	**项**	**item**		**1**	**12**			
#特等	Special Grade	项	item			1			
一等	First Prize	项	item						
二等	Second Prize	项	item		1	11			
省级	**Provincial Level**	**项**	**item**	**1**	**8**	**22**			
#一等	First Prize	项	item		4	5			
二等	Second Prize	项	item	1	3	11			
三等	Third Prize	项	item		1	6			
市级	**Municipal Level**	**项**	**item**	**10**	**15**	**119**		**9**	**2**
#一等	First Prize	项	item	2		12			
二等	Second Prize	项	item	3	6	42			
三等	Third Prize	项	item	5	9	65			

注：国际科技合作奖、最高奖不分等级。

Note: There is no grade in international scientific and technological cooperation prizes award and highest prizes award.

17－12 大中型工业企业技术开发主要相对指标(1995－2015年)
MAJOR INDICATORS OF TECHNOLOGY DEVELOPMENT OF LARGE AND MEDIUM-SIZE INDUSTRIAL ENTERPRISES(1995－2015)

项　目	Item	单位	Unit	1995	2000	2005	2006	2007	2008	2009	2010	2011	2012	2013	2014	2015
企业技术开发人员占全部职工比重	Percentage of Technology Development Personnel to Staff and Workers	%	%	2.6	5.7	4.4	4.9	5.9	5.6	5.8	6.7	7.7	7.4	8.3	8.5	
科学家工程师占技术开发人员比重	Percentage of Scientists and Engineers to Technology Development Personnel	%	%	39.0	62.3	66.1	63.1	62.4	63.0							
设有开发机构的企业占企业总数比重	Percentage of Enterprises Having Development Institutions to Total Number of Enterprises	%	%	59.3	29.7	20.8	21.8	26.1	24.6	24.0	26.2	28.1	26.7	25.1	25.8	24.0
科学家工程师占开发机构人员比重	Percentage of Scientists and Engineers to Personnel of Development Institutions	%	%	48.1	77.6											
平均每个企业技术开发经费筹集额	Average Funding for Technology Development of Each Enterprise	万元	10 000 yuan	118.2	873.0	1 535.8	1 577.0	1 805.0	1 815.6							
平均每个企业技术开发经费支出额	Average Expenditures for Technology Development of Each Enterprise	万元	10 000 yuan	114.5	812.0	1 626.0	1 716.0	1 931.0	1 894.9							
开发新产品用款占经费支出比重	Percentage of Expenditures on New Product Development to Total Expenditures	%	%	50.8	52.6	55.9	58.4	63.3	66.2							
技术开发经费支出占产品销售收入比重	Percentage of Expenditures on Technology Development to Revenue from Product Sales	%	%	1.0	3.1	2.7	2.7	2.6	2.3							
新产品产值比重	Percentage of Output Value of New Products	%	%		35.5	31.3	32.7	28.4	26.8	27.4	28.4	28.8	26.0	25.3	28.1	27.6
新产品销售额比重	Percentage of Sales Volume of New Products	%	%	12.2	32.7	32.5	32.4	30.5	28.7	28.8	28.9	29.3	27.0	27.2	28.0	28.3
新产品利税额比重	Percentage of Profits and Taxes of New Products	%	%	18.7	30.6											

17－13 主要年份文化机构数
MAJOR YEAR'S INSTITUTIONS OF CULTURE

单位：个(unit)

年 份 Year	合计 Total	#影剧院 Cinemas	文化馆 Cultural Centers	艺术表演团体 Art Performance Troupes
1949	24	9	3	3
1952	50	11	15	8
1957	99	16	11	15
1962	103	17	12	13
1965	117	18	13	13
1970	121	20	12	13
1975	249	21	12	16
1978	402	24	13	15
1980	661	24	12	17
1985	1 290	81	12	11
1988	1 473	84	12	11
1989	1 308	106	12	11
1990	1 323	106	12	11
1991	1 185	108	12	11
1992	1 167	108	12	11
1993	1 079	103	12	11
1994	964	78	12	11
1995	767	61	13	11
1996	761	61	13	11
1997	634	61	12	11
1998	491	51	12	11
1999	638	43	12	11
2000	637	45	12	11
2001	614	44	12	11
2002	590	44	11	11
2003	492	50	11	11
2004	476	29	12	11
2005	478	39	12	12
2006	446	40	12	12
2007	451	40	12	12
2008	456	40	12	12
2009	459	40	12	12
2010	465	40	12	12
2011	470	40	12	10
2012	475	36	12	8
2013	480	40	12	8
2014	488	43	13	9
2015	485	47	12	9

17－14 文化事业机构、人员数(2015 年)
NUMBER OF INSTITUTIONS AND PERSONNEL IN CULTURE(2015)

项目	Item	文化机构数(个) Number of Cultural Institutions(unit)		文化人员数(人) Number of Cultural Personnel(person)	
		2015	2014	2015	2014
一、艺术事业	**Art**	**27**	**27**	**853**	**1 184**
1. 艺术表演团体	Art Performance Troupes	9	9	573	889
2. 艺术表演场所	Art Centers	10	10	210	226
3. 艺术创作机构	Art Creation Institutions	5	5	40	39
4. 艺术研究机构	Art Research Institutions				
5. 艺术展览机构	Art Exhibition Institutions				
6. 其他	Others	3	3	30	30
二、图书馆事业	**Libraries**	**12**	**13**	**258**	**276**
公共图书馆	Public Libraries	12	13	258	276
#县(区)级图书馆	County Libraries	11	12	106	167
三、群众文化事业	**Mass Culture**	**148**	**149**	**736**	**665**
1. 群众艺术馆	Mass Art Centers				
2. 文化馆	Cultural Palaces	12	13	208	204
3. 文化站	Cultural Centers	136	136	528	461
4. 其他	Others				

17－15 分市、区艺术表演、电影发行及放映机构数(2015 年)

NUMBER OF INSTITUTIONS OF ART PERFORMANCE, FILMS DISTRIBUTION AND PROJECTION BY REGION(2015)

单位:个(unit)

市、区名称	Region	合计 Total	影剧院 Cinemas	电影发行机构 Institutions of Films Distribution	流动放映单位 Travelling Projection Units
全　市	**Whole Municipality**	**318**	**47**	**1**	**270**
市南区	Shinan District	8	7	1	
市北区	Shibei District	10	10		
李沧区	Licang District	6	4		2
崂山区	Laoshan District	5	2		3
黄岛区	Huangdao District	78	6		72
城阳区	Chengyang District	16	4		12
即墨市	Jimo	43	6		37
胶州市	Jiaozhou	39	4		35
平度市	Pingdu	66	3		63
莱西市	Laixi	45	1		44
红岛经济区	Qingdao National High-tech Industrial Development Zone	2	0		2

17－16 艺术表演、电影放映情况(2015 年)

STATISTICS ON ART PERFORMANCE AND FILMS PROJECTION(2015)

项　目	Item	机构数(个) Number of Institutions (unit)	座位数(个) Number of Seats (unit)	演出场次(场) Number of Performances (show)	观众人数(万人次) Number of Spectators (10 000 person-times)	票款收入(万元) Income from Ticket Sales (10 000 yuan)
艺术表演总计	Art Performance	10	6 355	421	30.8	1 684.3
电影放映总计	Films Projection	317	43 437	601 050	1 877	39 900
#影剧院	Cinemas	47	43 437	530 000	1 177	39 900
流动放映单位	Travelling Projection Units	270		71 050	700	

17 -17 文化部门艺术剧团情况(2015 年)
STATISTICS ON ART TROUPES OF CULTURAL DEPARTMENT(2015)

项 目	Item	剧团数（个）Number of Troupes (unit)	职工人数（人）Staff and Workers (person)	演出场次（场）Number of Performances (show)	观众人数(万人次) Number of Spectators (10 000 person-times)	演出收入（万元）Income from Performance (10 000 yuan)	拨款经费（万元）Appropriation Funds (10 000 yuan)
总 计	**Total**	**9**	**573**	**1 680**	**120.4**	**666.0**	**5 851.1**
一、按隶属关系分	**Grouped by Administrative Relationship**						
国营剧团	State-run Troupes	9	573	1 680	120.4	666.0	5 851.1
集体经营剧团	Collective-owned Troupes						
二、按剧种分	**Grouped by Type of Drama**						
1. 话剧团	Drama Troupes	1	117	186	9.3	63.0	60.0
2. 歌舞团	Song and Dance Troupes	1					
3. 戏曲剧团	Local Opera Troupes	4	202	671	80.5	215.9	1 700.5
#京剧	of which:Beijing Opera	1	94	140	7.5	152.6	610.0
4. 曲艺团	Recitation and Ballad Troupes						
5. 文工团(艺术团)	Cultural and Performance Troupes	3	254	823	30.6	387.1	4 090.6

17 -18 图书馆、文化馆情况
STATISTICS ON LIBRARIES AND CULTURAL CENTERS

项 目	Item	单位	Unit	2015		2014	
				全市合计 Total	#市区 Urban Area	全市合计 Total	#市区 Urban Area
公共图书馆	**Public Libraries**	个	**unit**	**12**	**8**	**13**	**9**
工作人员	Staff and Workers	人	person	258	196	276	213
藏书册数	Collection Books	千册	1 000 copies	6 039	5 012	5 829	4 807
阅览席位	Seating Capacity of Reading Rooms	张	seat	5 816	4 678	5 261	4 363
读者人数	Readers	万人次	10 000 person-times	443.6	378.1	442.5	372.1
文化馆	**Cultural Centers**	个	**unit**	**12**	**8**	**13**	**9**

主要统计指标解释

普通高等学校 指按照国家规定的设置标准和审批程序批准举办，通过国家统一招生考试，招收高中毕业生为主要培养对象，实施高等教育的全日制大学、独立设置的学院和高等专科学校、短期职业大学。

成人高等学校 指按照国家有关规定审批，招收通过全国成人高教统一招生考试的具有高中毕业或同等学历的在职从业人员，利用脱产、半脱产、业余或函授等多种形式对其实施高等学历教育，培养高等教育专科或本科毕业水平的专门人才，修业年限、课程设置和总学时数均按高等学历教育要求付诸实施的学校。包括广播电视大学、职工高等学校、农民高等学校、管理干部学院；教育学院、独立设置的函授学院等。

科技活动人员 指直接从事科技活动、以及专门从事科技活动管理和为科技活动提供直接服务，累计的实际工作时间占全年制度工作时间 10% 及以上的人员。

文化事业机构 指从事专业文化工作和为专业文化工作服务的独立建制的单独核算的单位。不包括这些单位另外举办独立核算的其他机构和各部门的业余文化组织。

Explanatory Notes on Main Statistical Indicators

Regular Institutions of Higher Education refer to educational establishments set up according to the government evaluation and approval procedures, enrolling graduates from senior secondary schools and providing higher education courses and training for senior professionals. They include full-time universities, colleges, high professional schools, high professional vocational schools and others.

Adult Institutions of Higher Education refer to educational establishments, set up in line with relevant rules approved by the government, enrolling staff and workers with senior secondary school or equivalent education, and providing higher education courses in many forms of correspondence, spare time, or full time for adults. Professionals thus trained receive a qualification equivalent to graduates studying regular courses at regular universities, colleges and professional colleges. Institutions of higher learning for adults include schools of high education for staff and workers, schools of high education for peasants, colleges for management cadres, pedagogical colleges, independent correspondence colleges, Radio and TV universities and other educational establishments.

Personnel Engaged in S&T Activities refer to personnel directly engaged in S&T activities, in the management of S&T activities, and in providing direct service to S&T activities, who spend over 10% of the total working hours in a year in S&T activities.

Cultural Institutions refer to units, which have their own organizational system and independent accounting system and specialize in or serve cultural development. They exclude other establishments run by these cultural institutions and amateur cultural groups established by various departments.

18 体育、卫生和民政、司法

SPORTS,PUBLIC HEALTH AND CIVIL AFFAIRS,JUDICIAL AFFAIRS

简要说明

一、本篇资料的主要内容

本篇资料反映了全市体育、卫生、民政、司法等社会事业的基本情况。体育部分主要包括主要年份运动员、教练员、裁判员发展人数、体育运动破纪录、获奖情况。卫生部分主要包括各类卫生机构及其人员、床位数。民政部分主要包括婚姻登记、社会救济、社会福利事业基本情况、殡葬服务情况。司法部分主要包括律师、公证、调解、社会治安基本情况。

二、本篇资料的来源

1、体育部分来源于市体育局。

2、卫生部分来源于市卫生局。

3、民政部分来源于市民政局。

4、司法部分，社会治安资料来源于市公安局，其他资料来源于市司法局。

本篇资料由市统计局人口和社会科技统计处整理提供。

Brief Introduction

I. Main Content

Data in this chapter show the basic conditions of sports, public health, civil affairs and judicial affairs. Data on sports are mainly including the number of athletes, coaches and referees, conditions of record and awards. Data on public health are mainly including the number of health institutions, personnel and beds. Data on civil affairs are mainly including the conditions of marriage registration, social relief, social welfare and funeral services. Data on judicial affairs are mainly including the conditions of lawyers, notarization, mediation and social order.

II. Source of Data

(1)Data on sports are provided by Qingdao Municipal Bureau of Physical.

(2)Data on public health are provided by Qingdao Municipal Bureau of Health.

(3)Data on civil affairs are provided by Qingdao Municipal Bureau of Civil Affairs.

(4)In judicial affairs component, data on social order are provided by Qingdao Municipal Bureau of Public Security and the other data are provided by Qingdao Municipal Bureau of Justice.

Data in this chapter are provided and compiled by the Division of Population and Science & Technology of Qingdao Municipal Bureau of Statistics.

18－1 体育事业情况(2000－2015 年)

STATISTICS ON SPORTS(2000－2015)

单位:人(person)

项目	Item	2000	2005	2006	2007	2008	2009	2010	2011	2012	2013	2014	2015
体育部门职工人数	**Staff and Workers in Sports Commissions**	**849**	**834**	**848**	**772**	**1 210**	**910**	**1 015**					**795**
#运动员	Athletes	90	87	81	55	452	512	287					259
教练员	Coaches	174	235	221	211	173	106	170	136				
重点体校	Key Sports Schools	126	117	166	249	109	97	115	129				
业余体校	Sparetime Sports Schools	142	223	220	145		160						
体育专业队	Professional Sports Teams	135	132	154	121		144	192	87	84	42	38	17
优秀运动员	Excellent Athletes	90	87	81	55	71	72	146	57				
优秀运动队专职教练员	Full-time Coaches of Excellent Sports Teams	18	23	48	47	106	92	97	54				89
等级裁判员发展人数	**Certified Referees**	**1 114**	**275**	**1 068**	**781**	**205**	**292**	**212**	**510**	**558**	**512**	**514**	**490**
#二级	Second Grades	451	275	1 068	781	181	252	169	510	484	463	514	490
三级	Third Grades	616											
等级运动员发展人数	**Certified Athletes**	**343**	**260**	**267**	**108**	**310**	**512**	**229**	**436**	**362**	**362**	**283**	**259**
#二级	Second Grades	209	260	267	108	281	448	229	436	256	362	283	259
三级	Third Grades	46											
少年级	Juvenile	88											

18－1 续表
continued

项目	Item	单位	Unit	2000	2005	2006	2007	2008	2009	2010	2011	2012	2013	2014	2015
全年获得奖牌数	**Number of Medals Won in the Year**	**枚**	**unit**	**347.5**	**669**	**829**	**481**	**494**	**602**	**754**	**829**	**746**	**659**	**576.5**	**596**
#国家级金牌	Golden Medals at National Level	枚	unit	45	62	71	61	26	30	14	105	88	90	48	51
国家级银牌	Silver Medal at National Level	枚	unit	28	48	54	38	21	23	7	49	100	44	21	44
省级金牌	Golden Medals at Provincial Level	枚	unit	116.5	187	363	116	168	207	459	225	193	174.5	202.5	149
省级银牌	Silver Medals at Provincial Level	枚	unit	62	174	144	93	122	149	116	155	110	111.5	121.5	126
体育运动破全国记录	**Records Broken the National Records**														
项目	Number of Events	项	item		2		1		1	1	2	1			
人数	Number of Persons	人	person		2		1		1	1	2	1			
次数	Number of Times	人次	person-time		4		1		1	1	2	1			
体育运动破全省记录	**Records Broken the Provincial Records**														
项目	Number of Events	项	item	7	3	5		2		1					
人数	Number of Persons	人	person	7	1	3		2		1					
次数	Number of Times	人次	person-time	7	3	5		2		1					

18－2 主要年份卫生事业基本情况
MAJOR YEAR'S BASIC STATISTICS ON PUBLIC HEALTH

年份 Year	卫生机构数（个）Health Institutions (unit)	#医院 of which: Hospitals	医疗床位数（张）Beds in Health Institutions (bed)	#医院 of which: Hospitals	卫生技术人员（人）Medical and Technical Personnel (person)	#医生 of which: Doctors	每千人口拥有医生数（人）Number of Doctors per 1000 Population (person)	每千人口拥有床位数（张）Number of Hospital Beds per 1000 Population (bed)
1949	80	26	1 079	970	2 637	1 292	0.32	0.27
1952	260	34	2 943	1 691	3 748	1 559	0.37	0.70
1957	624	45	5 163	2 656	6 941	2 578	0.53	1.07
1962	849	149	7 167	4 526	8 279	2 972	0.64	1.55
1965	912	162	8 428	5 003	9 051	3 586	0.73	1.72
1970	712	170	8 613	6 603	9 591	3 761	0.70	1.60
1975	959	181	10 902	9 078	13 558	4 566	0.80	1.90
1978	1 192	212	13 084	10 709	16 921	5 893	1.01	2.24
1980	1 253	212	14 170	11 345	19 265	6 781	1.14	2.38
1985	1 517	219	18 469	13 214	23 413	9 694	1.55	2.95
1987	1 553	228	21 667	15 463	26 669	11 738	1.81	3.34
1989	1 566	232	22 668	15 670	27 195	13 555	2.06	3.46
1990	1 563	235	23 541	16 586	27 932	13 761	2.08	3.56
1991	1 579	235	23 727	16 796	27 772	13 227	1.98	3.54
1992	1 562	236	24 765	17 269	28 305	13 157	1.95	3.67
1993	1 540	237	24 885	17 469	28 705	13 312	1.97	3.68
1994	1 335	242	24 732	17 882	28 938	13 535	1.99	3.64
1995	1 347	228	25 282	18 126	29 816	13 840	2.02	3.69
1996	2 216	228	24 334	18 344	30 048	13 790	2.00	3.53
1997	2 193	239	25 201	19 046	31 121	14 400	2.07	3.62
1998	2 190	237	24 887	19 083	31 623	14 327	2.05	3.56
1999	2 185	235	25 481	19 798	31 965	14 453	2.06	3.62
2000	2 911	231	24 392	20 057	32 160	14 860	2.10	3.45
2001	3 199	217	24 755	20 313	32 765	15 772	2.22	3.48
2002	3 050	213	21 370	20 662	31 469	13 371	1.87	2.99
2003	3 111	213	23 980	21 605	32 337	13 452	1.87	3.33
2004	2 923	219	25 432	23 465	32 937	13 953	1.91	3.48
2005	2 609	235	30 627	28 564	33 942	15 008	2.03	4.13
2006	2 834	232	28 724	26 653	34 360	15 451	2.06	3.83
2007	2 116	251	30 062	28 107	33 807	15 018	1.98	3.97
2008	1 985	249	32 350	29 874	36 574	16 260	2.14	4.25
2009	2 017	252	32 803	30 527	40 217	16 734	2.19	4.30
2010	2 147	254	36 066	33 383	43 285	17 696	2.32	4.72
2011	2 549	280	39 980	35 600	4 7347	18 310	2.39	5.22
2012	2 607	288	47 254	41 186	54 488	21 593	2.81	6.14
2013	2 936	285	44 876	39 725	59 961	24 113	3.12	5.80
2014	3 126	297	47 081	42 961	62 738	24 946	3.20	6.03
2015	3 146	308	48 601	45 066	65 264	26 270	3.35	6.20

18－3 各类卫生机构、床位、人员数(2015 年底)
NUMBER OF HEALTH INSTITUTIONS,BEDS AND EMPLOYED PERSONS(END OF 2015)

项　　目	Item	机构数(个) Health Institutions (unit)	床位数(张) Beds in Health Institutions (bed)	人员数(人) Personnel (person)
总　　计		**3 146**	**48 601**	**77 027**
一、医院合计	**Sub-total of Hospitals**	**308**	**45 066**	**57 276**
1. 医院	Hospitals	201	37 342	49 440
#综合医院	General Hospitals	116	24 855	33 892
中医医院	Hospitals Specialized in Traditional Chinese Medicine	17	4 495	6 109
中西医结合医院	Hospitals of Combination of Chinese and Western Medicine	3	607	575
专科医院	Specialized Hospitals	64	7 335	8 846
#口腔医院	Stomatological Hospitals	3	16	282
眼科医院	Ophthalmology Hospitals	4	226	428
肿瘤医院	Tumor Hospitals	2	404	580
心血管病医院	Cardiovascular Diseases Hospitals	5	1 020	1 197
精神病医院	Mental Hospitals	8	1 755	968
传染病医院	Infectious Disease Hospitals	2	640	483
皮肤病医院	The Skin Disease Hospital	1	20	20
骨科医院	Orthopaedics Hospitals	5	301	215
2. 卫生院	Sanitation Stations	107	7 724	7 836
二、社区卫生服务中心	**Neighborhood Service Centers**	**62**	**655**	**2 439**
三、门诊部	**Outpatient Service Stations**	**104**	**22**	**1 679**
四、诊所	**Clinics**	**1 976**		**7 063**
五、卫生所、医务室、护理站	**Medical Houses Nursing Station**	**290**	**10**	**882**
六、社区卫生服务站	**Neighborhood Service Stations**	**210**	**559**	**2 750**
七、急救中心	**First Aid Centers**	**3**		**161**
八、采供血机构	**Institutions of Blood Collection and Supply**	**1**		**234**
九、妇幼保健院(所、站)	**Maternity and Child Care Centers**	**12**	**407**	**1 250**
十、专科疾病防治院(所、站)	**Specialized Disease Prevention & Treatment Institutions**	**9**	**554**	**426**
十一、疾病预防控制中心(防疫站)	**Centers for Disease Control and Prevention (Epidemic Prevention Stations)**	**27**		**951**
十二、卫生监督所	**Sanitation Control Stations**	**12**		**350**
十三、卫生监督检验所(站)	**Sanitation Control and Test Stations**			
十四、计划生育技术服务机构	**Family Planning Service Institutions**	**88**		**434**
十五、临床检验中心(所、站)	**Clinical Laboratory Center**	**1**		**121**
十六、健康教育所(站、中心)	**Health Education Stations**	**1**		**4**
十七、其它卫生机构	**Other Health Institutions**	**33**		**250**
十八、疗养院	**Sanatoriums**	**9**	**1 328**	**757**

#卫生技术人员 Medical and Technical Personnel	#医生 Doctors	注册护士 Registered Nurses	药剂人员 Pharmacists	检验人员 Laboratory Technicians
65 264	**26 270**	**28 301**	**3 290**	**2 175**
48 104	**17 343**	**22 594**	**2 651**	**1 608**
41 021	14 483	20 085	2 095	1 323
28 343	9 924	14 188	1 375	880
5 250	1 851	2 563	335	147
505	393	33	55	18
6 908	2 309	3 295	329	278
242	113	104	4	0
272	98	133	10	8
479	152	265	30	22
956	320	435	24	36
785	201	466	38	20
394	139	186	28	30
15	4	4	2	1
180	68	61	11	4
7 083	2 860	2 509	556	285
2 037	**839**	**686**	**190**	**77**
1 410	**693**	**511**	**68**	**67**
7 044	**4 460**	**2 475**	**69**	**10**
864	**540**	**295**	**8**	**3**
2 291	**1 075**	**847**	**203**	**61**
96	**36**	**57**	**1**	**1**
159	**50**	**53**	**1**	**55**
987	**377**	**376**	**40**	**70**
368	**137**	**130**	**27**	**21**
732	**330**	**60**	**10**	**145**
292				
236	**111**	**46**	**1**	**3**
54	**5**	**2**		**39**
4	**3**		**1**	
188	**117**	**31**	**2**	**2**
398	**154**	**138**	**18**	**13**

18 -4 分市、区各类卫生机构、床位、人员数(2015 年底)

NUMBER OF HEALTH INSTITUTIONS, BEDS AND EMPLOYED PERSONS BY REGION (END OF 2015)

市、区名称	Region	机构数(个) Institutions (unit)	医院小计 Sub-total of Hospitals	#医院 Hospitals	卫生院 Sanitation Stations	社区卫生服务中心 Neighborhood Service Centers
全　市	**Whole Municipality**	**3 146**	**308**	**201**	**107**	**62**
市南区	Shinan District	359	25	25		10
市北区	Shibei District	629	40	40		21
李沧区	Licang District	445	14	14		13
崂山区	Laoshan District	229	13	11	2	3
黄岛区	Huangdao District	492	43	24	19	5
城阳区	Chengyang District	195	18	13	5	4
即墨市	Jimo	249	43	21	22	
胶州市	Jiaozhou	221	34	20	14	4
平度市	Pingdu	220	47	18	29	
莱西市	Laixi	107	31	15	16	2

18 -4 续表 1

continued

市、区名称	Region	采供血机构 Institutions of Blood Collection and Supply	妇幼保健院(所、站) Maternity and Child Care Centers	专科疾病防治院(所、站) Specialized Disease Prevention & Treatment Institutions
全　市	**Whole Municipality**	**1**	**12**	**9**
市南区	Shinan District	1	1	1
市北区	Shibei District		2	
李沧区	Licang District		1	
崂山区	Laoshan District		1	
黄岛区	Huangdao District		2	2
城阳区	Chengyang District		1	
即墨市	Jimo		1	1
胶州市	Jiaozhou		1	
平度市	Pingdu		1	3
莱西市	Laixi		1	2

社区卫生服务站 Neighborhood Service Stations	门诊部 Outpatient Service Stations	诊所、卫生所、医务室 Clinics Medical Houses	急救中心 First Aid Centers
210	**104**	**2 266**	**3**
34	22	251	
51	0	510	1
44	12	359	
26	19	160	
4	22	379	1
	8	145	
40	5	110	
	4	173	1
	11	138	
11	1	41	

疾病预防控制中心(防疫站) Centers for Disease Control and Prevention (Epidemic Prevention Stations)	卫生监督所 Sanitation Control Stations	卫生监督检疫所(站) Sanitation Control and Test stations	计划生育技术服务机构 Family Planning Service Institutions
27	**12**		**88**
1	1		
2	2		
1	1		
1	1		4
8	2		24
9	1		9
1	1		22
1	1		
1	1		17
2	1		12

18－4 续表2
continued

市、区名称	Region	健康教育所（站、中心）Health Education Station	临床检验中心（所、站）Clinical Laboratory Center	其他卫生机构 Other Health Institutions	疗养院 Sanatoriums	床位数（张）Beds in Health Institutions（bed）
全　市	**Whole Municipality**	**1**	**1**	**33**	**9**	**48 601**
市南区	Shinan District			3	9	6 969
市北区	Shibei District					11 112
李沧区	Licang District					2 500
崂山区	Laoshan District		1			917
黄岛区	Huangdao District					5 915
城阳区	Chengyang District					2 649
即墨市	Jimo	1		24		4 829
胶州市	Jiaozhou			2		5 073
平度市	Pingdu			1		4 618
莱西市	Laixi			3		4 019

18－4 续表3
continued

市、区名称	Region	专科疾病防治院（所、站）Specialized Disease Centers	人员数（人）Personnel（person）	卫生技术人员 Medical and Technical Personnel
全　市	**Whole Municipality**	**554**	**84 976**	**65 264**
市南区	Shinan District		12 098	9 701
市北区	Shibei District		19 439	16 477
李沧区	Licang District		6 773	5 962
崂山区	Laoshan District		3 239	2 242
黄岛区	Huangdao District	178	10 684	8 186
城阳区	Chengyang District		5 507	4 000
即墨市	Jimo		7 836	5 265
胶州市	Jiaozhou		6 989	4 944
平度市	Pingdu	306	6 992	4 714
莱西市	Laixi	70	5 419	3 773

医院小计 Sub-total of Hospitals	#医院 Hospitals	卫生院 Sanitation Stations	门诊部 Outpatient Service Stations	妇幼保健院(所、站) Maternity and Child Care Centers
45 066	**37 342**	**7 724**	**22**	**407**
5 639	5 639		2	
10 500	10 500			
2 340	2 340			
823	787	36	10	
5 464	3 846	1 618	4	100
2 560	2 364	196		
4 723	3 098	1 625	6	100
4 925	3 933	992		68
4 213	2 295	1 918		99
3 879	2 540	1 339		40

执业(助理)医师 Certified(Assistant) Doctors	注册护士 Registered Nurses	药剂人员 Pharmacists	检验人员 Laboratory Technicians	其他人员 Other Personnel
26 270	**28 301**	**3 290**	**2 175**	**4 276**
4 074	4 153	445	372	527
6 754	7 404	830	564	707
2 678	2 560	280	156	222
961	868	140	113	129
3 162	3 717	375	240	577
1 475	1 663	215	149	418
1 978	2 158	318	149	583
1 833	2 261	231	149	380
1 948	1 952	254	166	315
1 407	1 565	202	117	418

18 –5 收养性社会福利单位情况(2015 年)
BASIC STATICTICS ON SOCIAL WELFARE INSTITUTIONS(2015)

市、区名称	Region	单位数(个) Number of Institutions (unit)	年末职工人数(人) Number of Staff and Workers at Year-end (person)	年末床位数(张) Number of Beds at Year-end (bed)
全　市	**Whole Municipality**	**209**	**4 509**	**34 463**
市本级	Municipal Level	34	2 058	9 066
市南区	Shinan District	13	336	2 312
市北区	Shibei District	63	1 206	8 899
李沧区	Licang District	25	316	3 108
崂山区	Laoshan District	3	15	1 100
黄岛区	Huangdao District	29	111	3 346
城阳区	Chengyang District	12	150	2 502
即墨市	Jimo	1	13	141
胶州市	Jiaozhou	7	53	1 016
平度市	Pingdu	14	94	1 443
莱西市	Laixi	8	157	1 530

注:年末在院人数仅包括老年人与残疾人服务机构。
Note: At the end of the year, the number of people in hospitals includes the elderly and disabled service organizations only.

18 –6 社会救济情况(2015 年)
BASIC STATISTICS ON SOCIAL RELIEF(2015)

市、区名称	Region	城镇居民最低生活保障人数(人) Number of Persons Receiving Minimum Living Allowance in Urban Area(person)	城镇居民最低生活保障家庭数(户) Number of Households Receiving Minimum Living Allowance in Urban Area(household)	城镇低保资金支出(万元) Planned Expense of Funds for Minimum Living Allowance in Urban Area (10 000 yuan)
全　市	**Whole Municipality**	**33 524**	**19 599**	**29 498.2**
市南区	Shinan District	5 829	3 523	5 067.0
市北区	Shibei District	16 884	9 955	14 635.7
李沧区	Licang District	5 450	2 739	5 554.5
崂山区	Laoshan District	376	222	391.2
黄岛区	Huangdao District	1 180	733	1 212.3
城阳区	Chengyang District	392	249	347.1
即墨市	Jimo	1 371	863	973.7
胶州市	Jiaozhou	940	607	567.9
平度市	Pingdu	684	446	449.4
莱西市	Laixi	418	262	299.4

年末在院人数(人) Residences at Year-end (person)	优抚对象 Disabled Military Servicemen and Family Members of War Heroes and Military Servicemen	"三无"对象 Senior Citizen,Disabled Persons,Minors Non-ability to Work,Non-source of income and Non-supports the human or the provider	自费人员 Self-supporting Persons
21 782	**804**	**1 028**	**13 157**
7 712		219	1 332
999		11	919
5 992	39		5 776
2 199			2 199
149	107	85	64
1 634	245	502	848
906	5	70	681
50			
680			549
782	408	135	140
679		6	649

农村居民最低生活保障人数(人) Number of Persons Receiving Minimum Living Allowance in Rural Area(person)	农村居民最低生活保障家庭数(户) Number of Households Receiving Minimum Living Allowance in Rural Area(household)	农村低保资金支出(万元) Planned Expense of Funds for Minimum Living Allowance in Rural Area(10 000 yuan)
97 251	**61 241**	**48 748.7**
3 322	1 664	2 306.7
17 321	10 748	10 398.2
5 446	3 056	3 018.9
22 315	14 063	11 753.5
16 231	9 940	7 536.7
19 739	12 904	8 745.4
12 877	8 866	4 989.3

18-7 分市、区婚姻登记情况(2015年)

BASIC STATISTICS ON MARRIAGE REGISTRATION BY REGION(2015)

市、区名称	Region	准予登记结婚 Registered Marriages		
		合计(对) Total(couple)	初婚(人) First Marriages (person)	恢复结婚(对) Resumed Marriages (couple)
全　市	**Whole Municipality**	**64 066**	**97 823**	**72**
市本级	Municipal Level	261	323	3
市南区	Shinan District	6 956	11 081	2
市北区	Shibei District	8 351	11 911	
李沧区	Licang District	2 991	4 335	
崂山区	Laoshan District	3 188	5 285	
黄岛区	Huangdao District	9 785	14 461	
城阳区	Chengyang District	4 211	6 809	
即墨市	Jimo	7 698	11 576	
胶州市	Jiaozhou	6 021	8 986	
平度市	Pingdu	9 477	14 186	67
莱西市	Laixi	5 127	8 870	

再婚(人) Remarriages(person)		准予登记离婚(对) Registered Divorces (couple)	涉外婚姻登记(对) Registered Marriages with Foreigner(couple)
男 Male	女 Female		
15 199	**15 110**	**20 073**	**261**
110	89	50	261
1 514	1 317	2 076	
2 520	2 271	3 353	
857	790	1 078	
576	515	605	
2 537	2 572	3 032	
820	793	930	
1 894	1 926	2 421	
1 533	1 523	2 190	
2 205	2 563	2 840	
633	751	1 498	

18－8 律师、公证、调解、社会治安基本情况(2000－2015 年)

BASIC STATISTICS ON LAWYERS, NOTARIZATION, MEDIATION AND SOCIAL ORDER (1995－2015)

项　目	Item	单位	Unit	2000	2005	2006	2007	2008	2009
一、律师工作	**Lawyers**								
律师事务所	Law Offices	个	unit	76	116	122	140	159	203
律师工作者	Lawyers	人	person	1 439	1 941	2 218	2 594	2 915	3 144
专职	Full-time Lawyers	人	person	971	1 542	1 616	1 738	1 855	1 934
兼职(含特邀)	Part-time Lawyers	人	person	150	73	75	79	90	86
聘请常年法律顾问单位	Units with Permanent Legal Advisors	个	unit	2 508	3 564	4 032	4 075	4 086	4 457
全年办理民事代理	Agent of Civil Cases	件	case	5 571	11 104	10 556	19 460	20 547	29 025
刑事辩护	Defender of Criminal Cases	件	case	1 755	3 003	2 917	3 311	3 655	3 758
非诉讼事件	Agent of Non-litigious Legal Affairs	件	case	5 251	6 501	10 049	7 710	5 467	5 897
解答法律询问	Agent of Legal Advisory Services	件	case	58 385	27 880	26 518	27 393	31 571	30 123
代写法律事务文书	Agent of Legal Documents Written on Behalf of Clients	件	case	9 335	8 595	8 171	8 012	9 077	6 015
二、公证工作	**Notarization**								
公证处	Notary Offices	个	unit	15	15	15	13	13	13
公证人员	Notarial Personnel	人	person	152	196	209	208	214	214
公证员	Notaries	人	person	106	112	117	116	117	118
办理公证文书	Notarized Documents	件	case	120 849	105 787	100 513	95 704	101 766	97 019
三、人民调解	**People's Mediation**								
人民调解委员会	People's Mediation Committees	个	unit	9 750	11 480	10 897	11 216	11 223	9 643
调解人员	Mediators	人	person	34 714	46 735	34 487	35 553	33 875	32 675
调解民间纠纷	Civil Disputes Mediated	件	case	18 501	13 658	14 094	16 586	12 803	14 660
四、社会治安	**Social Order**								
交通事故发生次数	Traffic Accidents	次	time	15 601	7 051	5 559	4 465	3 025	2 570
死亡人数	Deaths	人	person	1 371	776	689	556	489	402
受伤人数	Injuries	人	person	8 620	6 639	5 685	4 603	3 273	2 943
经济损失	Losses	万元	10 000 yuan	4 815.70	2 208.20	1 514.00	1 291.40	991.50	854.80
火灾发生次数	Fire Accidents	次	time	3 088	1 948	1 400	962	840	773
死亡人数	Deaths	人	person	10	3	8	9	16	5
受伤人数	Injuries	人	person	43	3	5		13	
经济损失	Losses	万元	10 000 yuan	1 531.06	550.40	544.00	929.60	979.70	865.50

2010	2011	2012	2013	2014	2015
222	247	266	285	322	337
2 487	2 801	3 130	3 143	3 637	3 896
2 377	2 643	2 944	2 980	3 443	3 728
94	105	107	93	110	112
4 779	5 180	5 228	5 374	5 647	6 101
26 935	27 702	30 586	31 147	36 317	39 640
3 964	4 535	4 935	4 858	5 370	5 107
4 274	3 576	4 251	4 133	4 833	4 900
21 102	42 428	45 388	53 775	33 717	34 003
6 210	6 762	6 388	7 376	5 961	6 272
13	13	13	13	13	12
214	221	225	244	249	242
117	119	118	113	119	129
94 077	88 506	87 703	99 852	100 553	96 085
8 014	8 486	8 426	8 448	8 027	7 708
27 820	28 094	27 421	27 035	25 646	25 222
20 550	22 882	23 999	19 525	23 737	23 552
2 313	2 164	1 951	1 896	1 857	1 814
393	374	343	333	321	313
2 504	2 240	1 913	1 840	1 796	1 785
811.27	861.05	652.10	609.80	561.80	509.1
683	369	366	742	1170	1001
9	1	6	7	12	10
4	2	2	11	9	3
5 566.11	598.20	601.90	2 348.10	1 725.50	1 491.0

18－9 分区、市殡葬服务情况(2015 年)
BASIC STATISTICS ON FUNERAL SERVICES(2015)

市、区名称	Region	单位数(个) Number of Institutions (unit)	年末职工人数(人) Number of Staff and Workers at Year-end (person)	火化炉数(台) Number of Cremators (unit)	处理遗体数(具) Number of Remains Cremated (body)
全　市	**Whole Municipality**	**10**	**215**	**48**	**60 808**
市本级	Municipal Level	1	47	12	12 706
市南区	Shinan District				
市北区	Shibei District				
李沧区	Licang District				
崂山区	Laoshan District				
黄岛区	Huangdao District	2	23	7	8 692
城阳区	Chengyang District	1	19	5	6 346
即墨市	Jimo	1	14	7	9 008
胶州市	Jiaozhou	1	10	4	6 562
平度市	Pingdu	2	34	7	11 206
莱西市	Laixi	2	68	6	6 288

18 –9 续表
continued

市、区名称	Region	穴位数(个) Number of Graves (unit)	本年销售穴位数 Number of Graves Saled in the Year	安葬数(具) Number of Remains Buried(body)	本年安葬数 Number of Remains Buried in the Year
全 市	**Whole Municipality**	**23 858**	**334**	**5 497**	**675**
市本级	Municipal Level	19 897	203	2 543	549
市南区	Shinan District				
市北区	Shibei District				
李沧区	Licang District				
崂山区	Laoshan District				
黄岛区	Huangdao District				
城阳区	Chengyang District				
即墨市	Jimo				
胶州市	Jiaozhou				
平度市	Pingdu	1 500	88	1 500	88
莱西市	Laixi	2 461	43	1 454	38

主要统计指标解释

卫生机构 包括医疗机构、疾病预防控制中心(防疫站)、采供血机构、卫生监督及监测(检验)机构、医学科研和在职培训机构、健康教育所等。

医疗机构 包括医院、社区卫生服务中心(站)、疗养院、卫生院、门诊部、诊所(卫生所、医务室)、妇幼保健院(所、站)、专科疾病防治院(所、站)、急救中心(站)和临床检验中心。医疗机构分为非赢利性医疗机构和赢利性医疗机构。

医院 包括综合医院、中医医院、中西医结合医院、民族医院、各类专科医院和护理院。

医生 指在医疗、预防保健机构工作且取得《执业医师证书》的执业医师和执业助理医师。

卫生技术人员 指卫生事业机构中现任职务为卫生技术工作的人员。包括中医师、西医师、中西医结合高级医师、护师、中药师、西药师、检验师、其他技师、中医士、西医士、护士、助产士、中药剂士、西药剂士、检验士、其他技士、其他中医、护理员、中药剂员、西药剂员、检验员、其他初级卫生技术人员。

社会福利事业单位 指集中收养社会孤老、残、幼的机构,包括由民政部门管理的社会福利院、儿童福利院、精神病人福利院和城镇集体举办的福利院及农村集体举办的敬老院以及优抚医院和具有收养能力的社区服务中心等。

Explanatory Notes on Main Statistical Indicators

Health Care Institutions include: medical institutions, disease prevention and control centers (epidemic prevention stations), blood gathering and supplying institutions, health supervision and inspection (check up) institutions, medicinal scientific research and on-job training institutions, health education and so on.

Medical Organizations include: hospitals, health service centers (stations) of communities, nursing homes, health centers, clinics, clinics (health stations and infirmaries), maternity and child care agencies (centers and stations), special disease prevention and curing agencies (centers and stations), first aid centers (stations) and clinical inspection centers. Medical organizations are grouped by two types: profit-making and non-profit-making medical organizations.

Hospitals include: polyclinics, traditional Chinese medical hospitals, hospitals integrated with traditional Chinese therapeutics and western therapeutics, ethical hospitals, various specialties hospitals and nursing hospitals.

Doctors refer to certified physicians and certified assistant physicians with certifications working in medical and health care and prevention agencies.

Medical Technical Personnel refers to those medical workers employed institutions, including doctors of Chinese and Western medicine, senior doctors of integrated Chinese-Western medicine, head nurses, pharmacists of Chinese and Western medicine, laboratory specialists, other specialists, junior doctors of Chinese and Western medicine, nurses, midwives, druggists of Chinese and Western medicine, laboratory technicians, other technicians, other practitioners of Chinese medicine, nursing attendants, pharmacological workers of Chinese and Western medicine, laboratory workers, and other primary medical personnel.

Social Welfare Institutions refer to institutions taking care of old people without children, handicapped people and orphans. They include social welfare institutions run by civil affairs departments, children welfare institutions, social welfare institutions for mental patients, collective-owned old people's homes in rural areas, convalescent homes and community service centers with the capacity of receiving those people.

附　录
APPENDIX

2015 年省内各市主要经济指标对比情况

MAJOR ECONOMIC INDICATORS ON CITIES OF THE PROVINCE(2015)

主要指标 Indicator	单位 Unit	全省	青岛市 Qingdao	济南市 Jinan	淄博市 Zibo	枣庄市 Zaozhuang	东营市 Dongying
生产总值	亿元 (100 million yuan)	63 002.3	9 300.1	6 100.2	4 130.2	2 031.0	3 450.6
比上年增长 YOY Growth	%	8.0	8.1	8.1	7.1	7.1	6.9
规模以上工业增加值比上年增长 YOY Growth of Industrial Added Value above Designated Size	%	7.50	7.50	7.46	6.81	6.81	6.68
固定资产投资额 Investmentin Fixed Assets	亿元 (100 million yuan)	47 381.5	6 555.7	3 498.4	2 731.6	1 625.9	3 084.7
比上年增长 YOY Growth	%	13.9	14.2	14.2	13.6	13.8	13.9
进出口总额 Imports and Exports	亿美元 (100 million USD)	2 417.5	702.0	99.1	76.3	15.9	129.1
比上年增长 YOY Growth	%	-12.7	-12.1	-5.5	-14.6	10.7	-2.3
#出口 #Exports	亿美元 (100 million USD)	1 440.6	453.3	60.0	57.9	14.0	49.7
比上年增长 YOY Growth	%	-0.4	-1.0	-1.0	3.4	21.6	-18.5
进口 Imports	亿美元 (100 million USD)	976.9	248.7	39.2	18.4	1.9	79.4
比上年增长 YOY Growth	%	-26.1	-27.1	-11.6	-44.8	-33.1	11.6
社会消费品零售总额 Total Retail Sales of Consumer Goods	亿元 (100 million yuan)	27 761.4	3 713.7	3 410.3	1 949.7	805.4	728.1
比上年增长 YOY Growth	%	10.6	10.5	10.5	10.6	10.8	9.0
一般公共预算收入 General Public Budget Revenue	亿元 (100 million yuan)	5 529.3	1 006.3	614.3	317.9	149.3	220.1
比上年增长 YOY Growth	%	10.0	12.4	13.1	8.7	8.3	6.7
全体居民人均可支配收入	元 (yuan)	22 703	32 885	31 270	27 203	19 075	29 758
比上年增长 YOY Growth	%	8.8	8.6	8.5	8.2	8.4	8.0
城镇居民人均可支配收入 Per Capita Disposable Income of Urban Households	元 (yuan)	31 545	40 370	39 889	33 793	25 792	38 735
比上年增长 YOY Growth	%	8.0	8.1	8.0	7.6	7.2	7.1
农村居民人均可支配收入 Per Capital Net Income of Rural Households	元 (yuan)	12 930	16 730	14 232	14 531	12 038	13 887
比上年增长 YOY Growth	%	8.8	8.4	8.5	8.7	9.0	8.7

烟台市 Yantai	潍坊市 Weifang	济宁市 Jining	泰安市 Taian	威海市 Weihai	日照市 Rizhao	莱芜市 Laiwu	临沂市 Linyi	德州市 Dezhou	聊城市 Liaocheng	滨州市 Binzhou	菏泽市 Heze
6 446.1	5 170.5	4 013.1	3 158.4	3 001.6	1 670.8	665.8	3 763.2	2 750.9	2 663.6	2 355.3	2 401.0
8.4	8.3	8.4	8.1	8.5	7.5	6.6	7.1	7.6	8.8	7.1	9.3
7.90	8.35	7.95	7.55	8.61	8.43	6.47	6.74	7.95	12.82	8.00	13.05
4 667.1	4 516.7	2 891.0	2 618.2	2 543.7	1 407.8	619.1	3 219.2	2 237.9	2 100.8	1 990.2	1 073.3
13.9	13.9	13.9	13.9	14.1	14.0	13.5	13.9	14.1	14.6	13.8	14.1
493.9	189.2	54.4	22.8	151.8	169.4	19.0	87.4	31.7	50.7	81.4	43.3
-6.3	6.4	3.9	-23.2	-56.3	2.2	-14.4	-19.0	-9.3	-11.3	13.1	22.7
280.4	129.8	34.3	17.5	41.3	126.2	9.8	60.6	22.1	25.4	36.3	22.0
-4.6	5.3	5.1	1.0	-13.7	11.1	6.9	6.4	-0.8	6.3	-3.9	1.8
213.4	59.4	20.0	5.3	110.5	43.2	9.1	26.9	9.7	25.4	45.1	21.3
-8.5	8.8	2.0	-57.0	-63.1	-17.2	-29.5	-47.3	-24.0	-23.9	32.0	55.7
2 679.5	2 277.5	1 911.0	1 331.6	1 311.7	603.9	320.9	2 235.0	1 257.4	1 060.2	813.6	1 352.1
10.9	10.6	10.5	10.8	11.0	10.3	10.5	10.7	10.7	10.5	9.0	11.3
542.6	484.5	368.6	205.3	249.7	121.7	50.2	283.9	182.8	175.9	204.1	177.7
10.7	12.6	10.3	9.6	13.1	9.5	1.1	13.1	6.7	12.6	9.1	9.7
27 437	23 405	20 120	21 377	28 491	19 547	22 924	19 912	16 020	15 249	20 846	14 276
8.5	9.3	9.1	8.9	9.0	9.1	7.8	8.6	9.5	8.9	8.4	9.6
35 907	31 060	27 887	28 132	36 336	26 217	30 219	28 627	21 039	21 570	28 388	20 370
7.8	8.3	7.8	8.0	8.6	8.2	6.8	7.5	8.4	7.9	7.5	8.5
15 540	14 890	12 570	13 322	16 313	12 319	13 714	10 828	11 269	10 512	12 727	9 802
8.9	9.2	9.1	9.5	8.8	9.3	8.9	8.9	9.6	8.9	8.8	9.8

2015年十五个副省级城市主要经济指标对比情况

MAJOR ECONOMIC INDICATORS ON CITIES UNDER PROVINCIAL LEVELS(2015)

指标名称 Indicator	单位 Unit	青岛 Qingdao	沈阳 Shenyang	大连 Dalian	长春 Changchun	哈尔滨 Harbin
全市生产总值(GDP)	亿元 (100 million yuan)	9 300.1	7 280.5	7 731.6	5 530.0	5 751.2
比上年增长 YOY Growth	%	8.1	3.5	4.2	6.5	7.1
第一产业 Primary Industry	亿元 (100 million yuan)	364.0	341.4	453.3	343.3	672.6
比上年增长 YOY Growth	%	3.2	3.5	3.0	5.0	7.2
第二产业 Secondary Industry	亿元 (100 million yuan)	4 026.5	3 499.0	3 580.8	2 770.9	1 862.8
比上年增长 YOY Growth	%	7.1	0.9	0.9	4.1	4.1
第三产业 Tertiary Industry	亿元 (100 million yuan)	4 909.6	3 440.1	3 697.5	2 415.8	3 215.8
比上年增长 YOY Growth	%	9.4	6.3	8.2	9.8	9.3
三产占比	%	52.8	47.3	47.8	43.7	55.9
规模以上工业增加值 YOY Growth of Industrial Added Value above Designated Size	%	7.5	-2.9	-4.5	3.3	2.9
固定资产投资额 Investment in Fixed Assets	亿元 (100 million yuan)	6 555.7	5 326.0	4 559.3	4 400.0	4 595.7
比上年增长 YOY Growth	%	14.2	-18.9	-32.7	15.0	10.1
社会消费品零售总额 Total Retail Sales of Consumer Goods	亿元 (100 million yuan)	3 713.7	3 883.2	3 084.3	2 409.3	3 394.5
比上年增长 YOY Growth	%	10.5	8.2	8.5	8.8	10.5
进出口总额 Imports and Exports	亿美元 (100 million USD)	702.0	140.8	560.3	139.9	47.8
比上年增长 YOY Growth	%	-12.1	-10.8	-14.8	-32.5	-29.8
#出口 Exports	亿美元 (100 million USD)	453.3	67.9	263.5	19.2	23.6
比上年增长 YOY Growth	%	-1.0	-5.0	-12.8	-22.2	-31.5
进口 Imports	亿美元 (100 million USD)	248.7	72.9	296.9	120.7	24.2
比上年增长 YOY Growth	%	-27.1	-15.7	-16.5	-33.9	-28.1
一般公共预算收入 General Public Budget Revenue	亿元 (100 million yuan)	1 006.3	606.2	579.9	388.2	407.7
比上年增长 YOY Growth	%	12.4	-22.8	-25.7	-2.2	-3.7
城镇居民人均可支配收入 Per Capita Disposable Income of Urban Households	元 (yuan)	40 370	36 664	35 889	—	309 77
比上年增长 YOY Growth	%	8.1	7.1	6.8	—	7.5
农村居民人均可支配收入 Per Capital Net Income of Rural Households	元 (yuan)	16 730	13 498	14 667	—	13 375
比上年增长 YOY Growth	%	8.4	7.8	8	—	10.3
居民消费价格指数 Consumer Price Index	上年同期=100 preceding year=100	101.2	101.2	101.6	101.3	101.4

注:居民收入因进行统计制度改革,部分城市数据尚未最终确定。

Note:Data of residents´ income from some cities have not been difined due to statistic reform.

南京 Nanjing	杭州 Hangzhou	宁波 Ningbo	厦门 Xiamen	济南 Jinan	武汉 Wuhan	广州 Guangzhou	深圳 Shenzhen	成都 Chengdu	西安 Xi'an
9 720.8	10 053.6	8 011.5	3 466.0	6 100.2	10 905.6	18 100.4	17 503.0	10 801.2	5 810.0
9.3	10.2	8.0	7.2	8.1	8.8	8.4	8.9	7.9	8.2
232.4	287.7	285.2	23.9	305.4	359.8	228.1	5.7	373.2	220.2
3.4	1.8	1.8	-0.5	4.1	4.8	2.5	-1.7	3.9	5.0
3 916.1	3 910.6	3 924.5	1 509.0	2 307.0	4 981.5	5 786.2	7 205.5	4 723.5	2 165.5
7.2	5.6	4.8	7.9	7.4	8.2	6.8	7.3	7.2	6.8
5 572.3	5 855.3	3 801.8	1 933.1	3 487.8	5 564.3	12 086.1	10 291.8	5 704.5	3 424.3
11.3	14.6	12.5	6.5	8.9	9.6	9.5	10.2	9.0	9.5
57.3	58.2	47.5	55.8	57.2	51.0	66.8	58.8	52.8	58.9
8.1	5.4	3.8	7.9	7.5	8.5	7.2	7.7	7.3	6.6
5 426.0	5 556.3	4 506.6	1 896.5	3 498.4	7 725.3	5 406.0	3 298.3	7 007.0	5 166.0
-0.1	12.2	13.0	20.6	14.2	10.3	10.6	21.4	5.8	-12.5
4 590.2	4 697.2	3 349.6	1 168.4	3 410.3	5 102.2	7 933.0	5 017.8	4 946.2	3 405.4
10.2	11.8	12.0	8.9	10.5	11.6	11.0	2.0	10.7	10.1
532.4	665.7	1004.7	832.9	99.1	280.7	1 338.7	4 425.6	395.9	283.7
-7.0	-2.1	-4.0	-0.2	-5.5	6.3	2.5	-9.3	-29.0	15.0
315.0	500.7	714.3	535.0	60.0	151.5	811.7	2 640.8	239.7	132.0
-3.4	1.8	-2.3	0.6	-1.0	9.9	11.6	-7.1	-29.1	11.6
217.4	165.0	290.4	297.9	39.2	129.2	527.0	1 784.8	156.2	151.7
-11.6	-12.3	-8.0	-1.8	-11.6	2.3	-8.9	-12.2	-29.0	18.1
1 020.0	1 233.9	1 006.4	606.1	614.3	1 245.6	1 349.1	2 727.1	1 154.4	650.9
9.3	9.8	8.2	11.5	13.1	12.0	8.5	30.9	12.6	16.3
46 104	48 316	47 852	42 607	39 889	36 436	—	—	33 476	33 188
8.3	8.3	8.4	7.5	8.0	9.5	—	—	8.0	8.1
19 483	25 719	26 469	17 558	14 232	17 722	—	—	17 690	14 072
10.3	9.2	9.0	8.2	8.5	9.7	—	—	9.6	9.1
102.0	101.8	101.8	101.7	101.9	101.4	101.7	102.2	101.1	100.7

2015 年副省级城市之外部分城市主要经济指标情况

THE MAIN ECONOMIC INDICATORS OF SOME OTHER CITIES THAN THE SUB-PROVINCIAL CITY FOR(2015)

主要指标 Indicator	单位 Unit	北京 Beijing	天津 Tianjin	上海 Shanghai	重庆 Chongqing	苏州 Suzhou	无锡 Wuxi
全市生产总值(GDP)	亿元 (100 million yuan)	22 968.59	16 538.19	24 964.99	15 719.72	14 504.07	8 518.26
比上年增长 YOY Growth	%	6.9	9.3	6.9	11	7.5	7.1
#第一产业 Primary Industry	亿元 (100 million yuan)	140.21	210.51	109.78	1 150.15	215.71	137.72
比上年增长 YOY Growth	%	-9.6	2.5	-13.2	4.7	3.3	-0.1
第二产业 Secondary Industry	亿元 (100 million yuan)	4 526.44	7 723.6	7 940.69	7 071.82	7 045.12	4 197.43
比上年增长 YOY Growth	%	3.3	9.2	1.2	11.3	4.8	5.0
第三产业 Tertiary Industry	亿元 (100 million yuan)	18 301.94	8 604.08	16 914.52	7 497.75	7 243.24	4 183.11
比上年增长 YOY Growth	%	8.1	9.6	10.6	11.5	9.2	9.6
第三产业增加值占 GDP 比重	%	79.7	52.0	67.8	47.7	49.9	49.1
规模以上工业增加值同比增长 YOY Growth of Industrial Added Value above Designated Size	%	1.0	9.3	0.2	-	4.3	4.4
固定资产投资额 Investmentin Fixed Assets	亿元 (100 million yuan)	7 990.94	13 065.86	6 352.7	15 480.33	6 124.43	4 901.19
比上年增长 YOY Growth	%	5.7	12.1	5.6	17.1	-1.7	7.0
社会消费品零售总额 Total Retail Sales of Consumer Goods	亿元 (100 million yuan)	10 338.01	5 245.69	10 055.76	6 424.02	4 424.82	2 847.61
比上年增长 YOY Growth	%	7.3	10.7	8.1	12.5	9.0	9.2
进出口总额 Imports and Exports	亿美元 (100 million USD)	3 195.91	1 143.47	4 517.33	749.37	3 053.5	684.67
比上年增长 YOY Growth	%	-23.1	-14.6	-3.2	-21.5	-1.9	-7.7
#出口总额 Exports	亿美元 (100 million USD)	546.72	511.83	1969.69	553.33	1 814.59	422.32
比上年增长 YOY Growth	%	-12.3	-2.7	-6.3	-12.7	0.2	-4.5
实际使用外资金额 Foreign Investment Actually Utilized	亿美元 (100 million USD)	129.96	211.34	184.59	37.72	70.19	32.02
比上年增长 YOY Growth	%	43.8	12.0	1.6	-10.9	-13.6	10.3
一般公共预算收入 General Public Budget Revenue	亿元 (100 million yuan)	4 723.86	2 666.99	5 519.5	2 155.1	1 560.76	830
比上年增长 YOY Growth	%	17.3	11.6	13.3	12.1	8.1	8.1
城镇居民人均可支配收入 Per Capita Disposable Income of Urban Households	元 (yuan)	52 859	26 230	36 946	27 239	50 390	45 129
比上年增长 YOY Growth	%	8.9	8.0	5.0	8.3	8.0	8.1
农村居民人均可支配收入 Per Capital Net Income of Rural Households	元 (yuan)	20 569	18 482	23 205	10 505	25 580	24 155
比上年增长 YOY Growth	%	9.0	8.6	9.5	10.7	8.6	8.5
居民消费价格指数 Consumer Price Index	%	101.8	101.7	102.4	101.3	101.6	101.8